Pro Cryptography and Cryptanalysis with C++23

Creating and Programming Advanced Algorithms

Second Edition

Marius Iulian Mihailescu
Stefania Loredana Nita

Apress®

Pro Cryptography and Cryptanalysis with C++23: Creating and Programming Advanced Algorithms

Marius Iulian Mihailescu
Bucharest, Romania

Stefania Loredana Nita
Bucharest, Romania

ISBN-13 (pbk): 978-1-4842-9449-9
https://doi.org/10.1007/978-1-4842-9450-5

ISBN-13 (electronic): 978-1-4842-9450-5

Managing Director, Apress Media LLC: Welmoed Spahr
Acquisitions Editor: Steve Anglin
Development Editor: James Markham
Coordinating Editor: Gryffin Winkler
Copyeditor: Kim Burton

Cover designed by eStudioCalamar

Cover image designed by Freepik (www.freepik.com)

Distributed to the book trade worldwide by Apress Media, LLC, 1 New York Plaza, New York, NY 10004, U.S.A. Phone 1-800-SPRINGER, fax (201) 348-4505, e-mail orders-ny@springer-sbm.com, or visit www.springeronline.com. Apress Media, LLC is a California LLC and the sole member (owner) is Springer Science + Business Media Finance Inc (SSBM Finance Inc). SSBM Finance Inc is a **Delaware** corporation.

For information on translations, please e-mail booktranslations@springernature.com; for reprint, paperback, or audio rights, please e-mail bookpermissions@springernature.com.

Apress titles may be purchased in bulk for academic, corporate, or promotional use. eBook versions and licenses are also available for most titles. For more information, reference our Print and eBook Bulk Sales web page at http://www.apress.com/bulk-sales.

Any source code or other supplementary material referenced by the author in this book is available to readers on GitHub (https://github.com/Apress). For more detailed information, please visit http://www.apress.com/source-code.

Printed on acid-free paper

Table of Contents

iii

About the Authors

Marius Iulian Mihailescu, PhD, is an associate professor at the Faculty of Engineering and Informatics, Spiru Haret University in Bucharest, Romania. He is also the CEO of Dapyx Solution Ltd., a company based in Bucharest specializing in information security and cryptography-related research projects. He is a lead guest editor for applied cryptography journals and a reviewer for multiple publications with information security and cryptography profiles. He authored and co-authored more articles in conference proceedings, 25 articles, and books. For more than six years, he has been a lecturer at well-known national and international universities (the University of Bucharest, Titu Maiorescu University, and Kadir Has University in Istanbul, Turkey). He has taught courses on programming languages (C#, Java, C++, Haskell) and object-oriented system analysis and design with UML, graphs, databases, cryptography, and information security. He served three years as an IT officer at Royal Caribbean Cruises Ltd., dealing with IT infrastructure, data security, and satellite communications systems. He received his PhD in 2014, and his thesis was on applied cryptography over biometrics data. He holds two MSc in information security and software engineering.

Stefania Loredana Nita, PhD, is a lecturer at the Ferdinand I Military Technical Academy in Bucharest, Romania, and a software developer at the Institute of for Computers in Bucharest. Her PhD thesis was on advanced cryptographic schemes using searchable encryption and homomorphic encryption. She has been an assistant lecturer at the University of Bucharest, teaching courses on advanced programming techniques, simulation methods, and operating systems. She has authored several whitepapers and journal articles, as well as books on the Haskell programming language. Stefania is a lead guest editor for information security and cryptography issues, such as advanced cryptography and its future: searchable and homomorphic encryption. She has a master's degree in software engineering and bachelor's degrees in computer science and mathematics.

About the Technical Reviewer

 **Massimo Nardone** has more than 25 years of experience in security, web/mobile development, cloud, and IT architecture. His true IT passions are security and Android. He has been programming and teaching how to program with Android, Perl, PHP, Java, VB, Python, C/C++, and MySQL for more than 20 years. He has a master's degree in computing science from the University of Salerno, Italy.

He has worked as a CISO, CSO, security executive, IoT executive, project manager, software engineer, research engineer, chief security architect, PCI/SCADA auditor, and senior lead IT security/cloud/SCADA architect for many years. His technical skills include security, Android, cloud, Java, MySQL, Drupal, Cobol, Perl, web and mobile development, MongoDB, D3, Joomla, Couchbase, C/C++, WebGL, Python, Pro Rails, Django CMS, Jekyll, Scratch, and more.

He worked as visiting lecturer and supervisor for exercises at the Networking Laboratory of the Helsinki University of Technology (Aalto University). He holds four international patents (PKI, SIP, SAML, and Proxy areas). He is currently working for Cognizant as head of cybersecurity and CISO to help internally and externally with clients in information and cyber security areas, like strategy, planning, processes, policies, procedures, governance, awareness, and so forth. In June 2017, he became a permanent member of the ISACA Finland Board. Massimo has reviewed more than 45 IT books for different publishing companies and is the co-author of *Pro Spring Security: Securing Spring Framework 5 and Boot 2-based Java Applications* (Apress, 2019), *Beginning EJB in Java EE 8* (Apress, 2018), *Pro JPA 2 in Java EE 8* (Apress, 2018), and *Pro Android Games* (Apress, 2015).

PART I

Foundations

CHAPTER 1

Getting Started in Cryptography and Cryptanalysis

Cryptography and cryptanalysis are two fascinating and highly technical disciplines that have played a critical role in modern communication and security. Cryptography is the practice of protecting data using encryption algorithms, while cryptanalysis is trying to break those algorithms. Whether you have just become interested in these topics or have been studying them for some time, this step-by-step guide helps you get started in the world of cryptography and cryptanalysis. From understanding the basics of cryptography to exploring advanced techniques, this guide provides you with all the necessary information to become an expert in the field. Along the way, you learn about the history of cryptography, common algorithms and techniques used in encryption, and the tools and resources available to help you grow your knowledge. Therefore, let's get started!

Cryptography is the practice of protecting data by using encryption algorithms. The word *cryptography* comes from the Greek words *kryptos*, which means *hidden*, and *graphein*, which means *written*. As such, it has been around for a very long time, but it wasn't until the invention of the telegraph that it started to play a larger role in society. The telegraph was a critical piece of infrastructure in the nineteenth and twentieth centuries, and it needed a way to secure messages. As a result, cryptography became more standardized and public knowledge. The first standardized cipher was the Vigenère cipher, invented in 1553 but not publicly known until 1863. The next major cipher was the one-time pad, invented in 1917 and the first known completely unbreakable cipher. The next major advancement in cryptography came with the

© Marius Iulian Mihailescu and Stefania Loredana Nita 2023
M. I. Mihailescu and S. L. Nita, *Pro Cryptography and Cryptanalysis with C++23*,
https://doi.org/10.1007/978-1-4842-9450-5_1

invention of the computer and the rise of digital communications. Since then, there have been many advances in cryptography, including the invention of the RSA algorithm, which is widely used today.

Knowledge is one of the most important aspects to consider when designing and implementing complex systems, such as companies, organizations, and military operations. Information falling into the wrong hands can be a tragedy and result in a huge loss of business or disastrous outcomes. To guarantee communication security, cryptography can encode information so that no one can decode it without legal rights. Many ciphers have been broken when a flaw or weakness has been found in their design or enough computing power has been applied to break an encoded message. Cryptology consists of *cryptography* and *cryptanalysis*, as you see later.

With the rapid evolution of electronic communication, the number of issues raised by information security is significantly increasing every day. Messages that are shared over publicly accessible computer networks around the world must be secured and preserved and have the proper security mechanisms to protect against abuse. The business requirements in electronic devices and their communication consist of having digital signatures that can be legally recognized. Modern cryptography provides solutions to all these problems.

The idea of this book started from an experience that has been achieved through three directions: (1) cryptography courses for students (graduate and undergraduate) in computer science at the University of Bucharest and Titu Maiorescu University; (2) industry experience achieved in national and international companies; (3) ethical hacking best practices; and (4) security audit.

This book aims to present the most advanced cryptography and cryptanalysis techniques and their implementations using C++20. Most implementations are in C++20, using the latest programming language features and improvements (see Chapter 5).

The book is an advanced and exhaustive work, comprehensively covering all the most important topics in information security, cryptography, and cryptanalysis. The content of the book can be used in a wide spectrum of areas by multiple professionals, such as *security experts* with their audits, *military experts* and personnel, *ethical hackers*, teachers in academia, *researchers*, *software developers*, and *software engineers* when security and cryptographic solutions need to be implemented in a real business software environment, *student* courses (undergraduate and graduate levels, master's degree, professional and academic doctoral degree), *business analysts* and many more.

Cryptography and Cryptanalysis

It is very important to understand the meanings of the main concepts involved in a secure communication process and to see their boundaries.

- **Cryptology** is the science or art of secret writing; the main goal is to protect and defend the secrecy and confidentiality of information with the help of cryptographic algorithms.

- **Cryptography** is the defensive side of cryptology; the main objective is to create and design cryptographic systems and their rules. When you look at cryptography, you can see a special kind of art: protecting the information by transforming it into an unreadable format called *ciphertext*.

- **Cryptanalysis** is the offensive side of cryptology; its main objective is to study cryptographic systems with the scope of providing the necessary characteristics in such a way as to fulfill the function for which they have been designed. Cryptanalysis can analyze the cryptographic systems of third parties through the cryptograms realized with them so that it breaks them to obtain useful information for their business purpose. Cryptanalysts, code breakers, and ethical hackers deal with cryptanalysis.

- **Cryptographic primitives** represent well-established or low-level cryptographic algorithms for building cryptographic protocols; examples include hash functions and encryption functions.

This book provides a deep examination of all three sides from the practical side of view with references to the theoretical background by illustrating how a theoretical algorithm should be analyzed for implementation.

There are many different algorithms and techniques in modern cryptography. Here are a few of the more common ones.

- **Symmetric-key algorithms** use both sides of a communication to generate a shared secret key and then use that key to encrypt and decrypt messages. The most prominent example is AES, which is used by the US government and many businesses worldwide.

5

- **Asymmetric-key algorithms** use two different keys to encrypt and decrypt messages. The most common example is RSA, which secures websites and applications like Gmail.

- **Hash algorithms** are commonly used to create digital signatures for data and are sometimes used for message authentication. The most well-known example is probably the SHA family of hash algorithms.

- **Trapdoor function algorithms** generate digital signatures and are sometimes used to implement public-key encryption. The most common example is probably the RSA function.

- **One-time pad algorithms** are the only unbreakable ciphers requiring truly random keys. The most widely used OTP algorithm is the Vernam cipher, which was the basis for the encryption used by the US military in World War II.

Book Structure

The book is divided into 23 chapters divided into three parts: Part I (Chapters 1–8) covers foundational topics, Part II (Chapters 9–17) covers cryptography, and Part III (Chapters 18–23) covers cryptanalysis.

Part I includes topics from beginner to advanced level and from theoretical to practice. Chapter 2 discusses the basic concepts of cryptography. Chapter 3 covers a collection of key elements regarding complexity theory, probability theory, information theory, number theory, abstract algebra, and finite fields and how they can be implemented using C++20, showing their interaction with cryptography and cryptanalysis algorithms.

Chapters 4 and 5 focus on integer arithmetic and floating-point arithmetic processing. The chapter is vital, and other chapters and algorithm implementations depend on these chapters' content. Number representations and working with them on the computer's memory can represent a difficult task.

Chapter 6 discusses the newest features and enhancements of C++23. It presents how the new features and enhancements are important in developing cryptography and cryptanalysis algorithms and methods. It goes through three-way comparison, lambdas in unevaluated contexts, string literals, atomic smart pointers, <version> headers, ranges, coroutines, modules, and so forth.

Chapter 7 presents the most important guidelines for securing the coding process, keeping an important balance between security and usability based on the most expected scenarios based on trusted code. Important topics include securing state data, security and user input, security-neutral code, and library codes that expose protected resources.

Chapter 8 covers the libraries and frameworks that are developed in C++/C++23.

Part II covers the most important modern cryptographic primitives. Chapters 9–16 discuss advanced cryptography topics by showing implementations and how to approach this kind of advanced topic from a mathematical background to a real-life environment.

Chapter 9 discusses the basics of one of the most important branches of cryptography: elliptic-curve cryptography.

Chapter 10 introduces the Lattice Cryptography Library and hot its works for implementation, pointing out the importance of postquantum cryptography. Implementations of key exchange protocols proposed by Alkim, Ducas, Poppelmann, and Schwabe [1] are discussed. The discussion continues by instantiating Chris Peikert's key exchange protocol [2]. The implementation is based on modern techniques for computing, known as the *number theoretic transform* (NTT). The implementations apply errorless fast convolution functions over successions of integer numbers.

Chapter 11 and Chapter 12 present two important cryptographic primitives, homomorphic and searchable encryption. For searchable encryption (SE), Chapter 11 presents a framework using C++23 for SE, showing the advantages and disadvantages of removing the most common patterns from encrypted data. Chapter 12 discuss how to use the SEAL library in practical examples. The SEAL library contains one of the most important homomorphic encryption schemes: BGV (Brakerski-Gentry-Vaikuntanathan) [3].

Chapter 13 identifies the issues generated during implementing (ring) learning with error cryptography mechanisms. It gives an example of implementing the lattice-based key exchange protocol, a library used only for experiments.

Chapter 14 is based on the new concepts behind chaos-based cryptography and how it can be translated into practice. The chapter generates some new outputs, and its contribution is important for advancing cryptography as it is a new topic that didn't get the proper attention until now.

Chapter 15 discusses new methods and their implementations for securing big data environments, big data analytics, access control methods (key management for access control), attributed-based access control, secure search, secure data processing, functional encryption, and multiparty computation.

Chapter 16 points out the security issues about the applications running in a cloud environment and how they can be resolved during the design and implementation phase.

Part III deals with advanced cryptanalysis topics and shows how to pass the barrier between theory and practice and how to think about cryptanalysis in terms of practice by eliminating the most vulnerable and critical points of a system or software application in a network or distributed environment.

Chapter 17 introduces you to cryptanalysis by presenting the most important characteristics of cryptanalysis. Chapter 18 starts by showing the important criteria and standards used in cryptanalysis, how the tests of cryptographic systems are made, the process of selecting the cryptographic modules, the cryptanalysis operations, and classifications of cryptanalysis attacks.

Chapter 19 and Chapter 20 show how to implement and design linear, differential, and integral cryptanalysis. These chapters focus on techniques and strategies, and their primary role is to show how to implement scripts for attacking linear and differential attacks.

Chapter 21 presents the most important attacks and how they can be designed and implemented using C++23. You study the behavior of the software applications when they are exposed to different attacks, and you see how to exploit the source code. This chapter also discusses software obfuscation and why it is a critical aspect that needs to be considered by the personnel involved in implementing the software process. Additionally, you learn how this analysis can be applied to machine learning and artificial intelligence algorithms that can be used to predict future attacks over software applications that are running in a distributed or cloud environment.

Chapter 22 goes through the text characterization method and its implementation. It discusses chi-squared statistics; identifying unknown ciphers; index of coincidence; monogram, bigram, and trigram frequency counts; quad ram statistics as a fitness measure; unicity distance; and word statistics as a fitness measure.

Chapter 23 presents the advantages and disadvantages of implementing cryptanalysis methods, why they should have a special place when applications are developed in distributed environments, and how the data should be protected against such cryptanalysis methods.

As you become more advanced in your study of cryptography, you want to explore analysis techniques like frequency analysis, letter analysis, and statistics that can help you break ciphers that are not completely unbreakable. Sometimes, it is even possible to find flaws in algorithms and protocols that can be exploited for malicious purposes. For instance, cryptography is used in WEP and WPA/WPA2 networks to encrypt data. It has been discovered that cracking the WEP takes less than 10 minutes and that WPA/WPA2 is relatively easy to crack.

Internet Resources

The Internet has many resources that are very useful in keeping up with progress in the field.

- **Bill's Security Site** (`https://asecuritysite.com/`). This website contains various implementations of cryptographic algorithms. Bill Buchanan, a professor at the School of Computing at Edinburgh Napier University, created and updated the website.

- Books by **William Stallings** [4] [Stallings, 2010 #1] – Cryptography and Network Security (`http://williamstallings.com/Cryptography/`). The site contains a significant set of tools and resources and provides regular updates, keeping up with the most important advances in cryptography.

- **Schneier on Security** (`www.schneier.com/`). The website contains sections with books, essays, accurate news, talks, and academic resources.

Forums and Newsgroups

Usenet newsgroups (deprecated but very useful information can still be found) is dedicated to some of the important aspects of cryptography and network security. The following are the most important.

- **sci.crypt.research** is among the best groups for finding information about research ideas. It is a moderated newsgroup whose main purpose is to address research topics; most topics are related to the technical aspects of cryptology.

- **sci.crypt** is a group where you can find general discussions about cryptology and related topics.

- **sci.crypt.random-numbers** discusses random number generators.

- **alt.security** discusses general security topics.

- **comp.security.misc** discusses general computer security topics.

- **comp.security.firewalls** features discussions on firewalls and other related products.

- **comp.security.announce** covers CERT news and announcements.

- **comp.risks** discusses public risks from computers and users.

- **comp.virus** features moderated discussions on computer viruses.

Additionally, several forums deal with cryptography topics and news that are available on the Internet. The following are the most important.

- **Reddit Cryptography News and Discussions** [5] is a forum group featuring general information and news about different topics related to cryptography and information security.

- **Security forums** [6] contain vast topics and discussions about computer security and cryptography.

- **TechnGenix – Security** [7] is one of the most updated forums featuring cryptography and information security news. The group is maintained by world-leading security professionals in the field.

- **Wilders Security Forums** [8] features discussions and news about the vulnerabilities of software applications due to bad implementations of cryptographic solutions.

- **Security Focus** [9] is a forum with a series of discussions about vulnerabilities raised by the implementations of cryptographic algorithms.

- **Security InfoWatch** [10] discusses data and information loss.

- **TechRepublic – Security** [11] discusses practical aspects and methodologies for designing and implementing software applications.

- **Information Security Forum** [12] is a world-leading information security and cryptography forum. It features conferences, hands-on and practical tutorials, solving solutions to security and cryptographic issues.

Security Protocols and Standards

The following are specific standards for cryptography. They specify which algorithms should be used and how they should be implemented. There are many different cryptography standards, but the following are the most important.

- **Suite B** is a set of algorithms and protocols used by the US government. It contains both symmetric and asymmetric algorithms.

- **ISO/IEC 17799** is an international standard for information security. It contains a set of guidelines for cryptography.

- **BSI TR-02102-1 - BSI – Technical Guideline. Cryptographic Mechanisms: Recommendations and Key Lengths[1] (Part 1)** evaluates the security of a few different cryptographic mechanisms, providing some longer-term guidance in choosing appropriate cryptographic algorithms. However, there is no guarantee of

---

[1] See https://www.bsi.bund.de/SharedDocs/Downloads/EN/BSI/Publications/TechGuidelines/TG02102/BSI-TR-02102-1.pdf?__blob=publicationFile&v=6

completeness, so the BSI may not necessarily consider schemes that are not included to be secure.

- **BSI TR-02102-2. Cryptographic Mechanisms: Recommendations and Key Lengths, Part 2 – Use of Transport Layer Security (TLS)**[2] is a technical guideline with recommendations for using the TLS encryption protocol. In particular, the confidentiality, integrity, and authenticity of the sent information can be secured by its use for secure information transfer in data networks.

- **BSI TR-02102-3. Cryptographic Mechanisms: Recommendations and Key Lengths, Part 3 – Use of Internet Protocol Security (IPsec) and Internet Key Exchange (IKEv2)**[3] is a technical guideline with recommendations for using IPsec and IKEv2. In particular, the confidentiality, integrity, and authenticity of the sent information can be secured by its use for secure information transfer in data networks.

- **BSI TR-02102-4. Cryptographic Mechanisms: Recommendations and Key Lengths Part 4 – Use of Secure Shell (SSH) NIST Special Publication 800-18**[4] is a technical guideline with recommendations for using the Secure Shell cryptographic technology (SSH). Within an insecure network, this protocol can be used to create a secure channel.

- **Federal Information Processing Standard 140-2** is a FIPS standard that specifies cryptographic algorithms and protocols.

Many cryptographic techniques and implementations described in this book follow the following standards. Standards have been developed and designed to cover the management practices and the entire architecture of the security mechanisms, strategies, and services.

The following are the most important standards covered in this book.

---

[2] See https://www.bsi.bund.de/SharedDocs/Downloads/EN/BSI/Publications/TechGuidelines/TG02102/BSI-TR-02102-2.pdf?__blob=publicationFile&v=5
[3] See https://www.bsi.bund.de/SharedDocs/Downloads/EN/BSI/Publications/TechGuidelines/TG02102/BSI-TR-02102-3.pdf?__blob=publicationFile&v=5
[4] See https://www.bsi.bund.de/SharedDocs/Downloads/EN/BSI/Publications/TechGuidelines/TG02102/BSI-TR-02102-4.pdf?__blob=publicationFile&v=5

- The **National Institute of Standards and Technology (NIST)** represents the US federal agency that deals with standards, science, and technologies related to the US government. Except for the national goal, NIST Federal Information Processing Standards (FIPS) and Special Publications (SP) have a very important worldwide impact.

- The **Internet Society (ISOC)** represents one of the most important professional membership societies with organizational and individual members worldwide. ISOC provides leadership in the issues that are addressed and that confront the future perspective of the Internet and applications developed using security and cryptographic mechanisms with respect to the responsible groups, such as the Internet Engineering Task Force (IETF) and the Internet Architecture Board (IAB).

- The **International Telecommunication Union (ITU)** represents one of the most powerful organizations within the United Nations System. It coordinates and administers global telecom networks and services with governments and the private sector. **ITU-T** represents one of the three sectors of ITU. The mission of ITU-T consists of the production of standards that cover all the fields of telecommunications. The standards proposed by ITU-T are known as *recommendations*.

- The **International Organization for Standardization (ISO)** represents a worldwide federation that contains national standards bodies from over 140 countries. ISO is a nongovernmental organization to promote the development of standardization and activities related to activities with a view that it facilitates the international exchange of services to develop cooperation with intellectual, scientific, and technological activity. The results of ISO are as international agreements published as international standards.

From securing communication and storage of information, cryptography algorithms and protocols can be seen as guidelines and protocols used to ensure the secure communication and storage of information. The following are some widely used cryptography algorithms and protocols.

- The **Advanced Encryption Standard (AES)** is a symmetric-key encryption algorithm for encrypting electronic data.

- **RSA** is an asymmetric-key encryption algorithm used for secure data transmission.

- **Elliptic-curve cryptography (ECC)** is an approach to public-key cryptography based on the mathematics of elliptic curves.

- **Secure Sockets Layer (SSL)** and **TLS** are protocols for securing network communications.

- **IPSec** is a protocol for securing Internet communications at the network layer.

- **Pretty Good Privacy (PGP)** is a data encryption and decryption program that provides cryptographic privacy and authentication for data communication.

These are just a few examples, and many other cryptography standards are used today.

Cryptography Tools and Resources

There are numerous tools and resources to help you learn more about cryptography. Here are a few worth checking out.

- **Cracking Crypto** challenges provide a fun way to test your skills and are great for beginners. There are challenges in both cryptography and cryptanalysis, so you can pick whichever interests you more.

- **Dark Reading** is a website that publishes news articles on all aspects of information security. Their cryptography section regularly publishes articles on the latest developments in cryptography.

- There are many great **cryptography books**. If you prefer reading to online tutorials, there are plenty of worthy books to choose from.

- **Coursera**, **Pluralsight**, and **Udemy** offer online cryptography courses. These courses vary in length and difficulty and can help advance your knowledge. The following are some of the most interesting courses.

  - Coursera

    - Cryptography I by Dan Boneh, Stanford University

      `www.coursera.org/learn/crypto`

    - Cryptography II by Dan Boneh

      Stanford University

      `www.coursera.org/learn/crypto2`

    - Introduction to Applied Cryptography Specialization by William Bahn

      `www.coursera.org/specializations/introduction-applied-cryptography`

  - Pluralsight

    - Cryptography: The Big Picture

      `https://app.pluralsight.com/library/courses/cryptography-big-picture/table-of-contents`

    - Cryptography: Executive Briefing

      `https://app.pluralsight.com/library/courses/cryptography-executive-briefing/table-of-contents`

    - Cryptography Application

      `https://app.pluralsight.com/library/courses/cryptography-application/table-of-contents`

    - Securing Data with Asymmetric Cryptography

```
https://app.pluralsight.com/library/courses/
asymmetric-cryptography-securing-data/table-
of-contents
```

- Practical Encryption and Cryptography Using Python

```
https://app.pluralsight.com/library/courses/
practical-encryption-and-cryptography-using-
python/table-of-contents
```

- Building Secure Applications with Cryptography in.NET

```
https://app.pluralsight.com/library/courses/
dotnet-cryptography-secure-applications/table-
of-contents
```

Conclusion

The era in which we are living has an unimaginable evolution and incredible technologies that enable the instant flow of information at any time and place. The secret consists of the convergence process of the computer with the networks, a key force that forces the evolution and development of these incredible technologies from behind.

Cryptography and cryptanalysis are fascinating disciplines that have played a critical role in modern communication and security. This step-by-step work help you get started in the world of cryptography and cryptanalysis by providing you with all the necessary information to become an expert in programming and how to approach cryptographic algorithms. From understanding the basics of programming cryptography algorithms to exploring advanced techniques, this work helps you explore the fascinating technical disciplines that have played a critical role in modern communication and security.

This first chapter discussed the objectives of the book and its benefits. It covered the mission of the book, addressing the practical aspects of cryptography and information security and its main intention in using the current work. The increasing process of using systems that build using advanced information technologies has been shown to deeply impact our lives every day. All technologies are proving to be pervasive and ubiquitous.

The book represents the first practical step of translating the most important theoretical cryptography algorithms and mechanisms to practice through one of the most powerful programming languages (C++20).

This chapter accomplished the following.

- Each concept was explained to eliminate the confusion between cryptography, cryptanalysis, and cryptology.

- It discussed the book's structure. A roadmap introduced the dependencies of each chapter. Each chapter has been presented in detail, pointing out the main objective.

- A list of newsgroups, websites, and USENETs resources provides sources covering the latest news in cryptography and information security.

- It introduced the most significant standards used in cryptography and information security.

References

[1].   Alkim, E., Ducas, L., Pöppelmann, T., and Schwabe, P. (2016). Postquantum key exchange—a new hope. In 25th {USENIX} Security Symposium ({USENIX} Security 16) (pp. 327–343).

[2].   Peikert, C. (2014, October). Lattice cryptography for the Internet. In international workshop on postquantum cryptography (pp. 197–219). Springer, Cham.

[3].   Brakerski, Z., Gentry, C., and Vaikuntanathan V. (2011). Fully Homomorphic Encryption without Bootstrapping Cryptology ePrint Archive, Paper 2011/277, https://eprint.iacr.org/2011/277.

[4].   Stallings, W., Cryptography and Network Security - Principles and Practice. 5 ed. 2010: Pearson. 744.

[5].   Reddit. Cryptography News and Discussions. Available from: https://www.reddit.com/r/crypto/.

[6].   Forums, Security.; Available from: http://www.security-forums.com/index.php?sid=acc302c71bb3ea3a7d631a357223e261.

[7].   TechGenix, Security. Available from: `http://techgenix.com/security/`.

[8].   Wilders Security Forums. Available from: `https://www.wilderssecurity.com/`.

[9].   Security Focus. Available from: `https://www.securityfocus.com/`.

[10].   Security InfoWatch. Available from: `https://forums.securityinfowatch.com/`.

[11].   TechRepublic – Security. Available from: `https://www.techrepublic.com/forums/security/`.

[12].   Information Security Forum. Available from: `https://www.securityforum.org/`.

CHAPTER 2

Cryptography Fundamentals

Cryptographic history is incredibly long and fascinating. *The Code Book: The Secrets Behind Codebreaking* [1] is a comprehensive reference that provides a nontechnical history of cryptography. In the book, the story of cryptography begins in approximately 2000 BC, when the Egyptians used it for the first (known) time. It presents the main aspects of cryptography and hiding information for each period that is covered and describes the great contribution that cryptography had in both world wars. The art of cryptography often correlates with diplomacy, military, and government because its purpose is to keep sensitive data, such as strategies or secrets regarding national security, safe.

A crucial development in modern cryptography is the working paper "New Directions in Cryptography" [2] proposed by Diffie and Hellman in 1976. The paper introduced a notion that changed how cryptography was seen until then, namely, public-key cryptography. Another important contribution of this paper is an innovative way of exchanging keys. The security of the presented technique is based on the hardness assumption (basically, through the hardness assumption, we refer to a problem that cannot be solved efficiently) of the discrete logarithm problem. Even though the authors did not propose a practical implementation for their public-key encryption scheme, the idea was presented very clearly and started to draw attention in the international cryptography community.

The first implementation of a public-key encryption scheme was made in 1978 by Rivest, Shamir, and Adleman, who proposed and implemented their encryption scheme, currently known as RSA [3]. The hardness assumption in the RSA is the factoring of large integers. By looking in parallel between integer factorization for RSA and Shor's algorithm, we can note that Shor's algorithm runs in polynomial time for quantum

M. I. Mihailescu and S. L. Nita, *Pro Cryptography and Cryptanalysis with C++23*,
https://doi.org/10.1007/978-1-4842-9450-5_2

computers. This represents a significant challenge for any cryptographer using the hardness assumption for factoring large integers. The increasing applications and interest in the factoring problem led to new techniques. Important advances in this area were made in 1980, but none of the proposed techniques improved the security of the RSA.

Another important class of practical public-key encryption schemes was designed by ElGamal [4] in 1985. These are based on the hardness assumption of the discrete logarithm problem.

Other crucial contributions to public-key cryptography are the digital signature, for which the international standard ISO/IEC 9796 was adopted in 1991 [5]. The basis of the standard is the RSA public-key encryption scheme. A powerful scheme for digital signatures based on the discrete logarithm hardness assumption is the Digital Signature Standard, adopted by the United States government in 1994.

Currently, the trends in cryptography include designing and developing new public key schemes, adding improvements to the existing cryptographic mechanisms, and elaborating security proofs.

The book's objective is to provide a view of the latest updates of the principles, techniques, algorithms, and implementations of the most important aspects of cryptography in practice. It focuses on the practical and applied aspects of cryptography. You are warned about the difficult subjects and those that present issues and are guided to a proper bibliography in which best practices and solutions are found. Most of the aspects presented in the book are followed by implementations. This objective also serves to not obscure the real nature of cryptography. The book represents strong material for both implementers and researchers. The book describes the algorithms and software systems with their interactions.

Information Security and Cryptography

This book refers to the term and concept of *information* as to *quantity*. To go through the introduction to cryptography and to show its applicability by presenting algorithms and implementation technologies (such as C++), first, we need to have a basis for the issues that occur often in information security. When a particular transaction occurs, all parties involved must be sure (or ensure) that specific objectives related to information security are met. A list of these security objectives is given in Table 2-1.

Several protocols and security mechanisms have been proposed to defy the issues regarding information security when the information is sent in physical format (for example, documents). The objectives regarding information security may be accomplished by applying mathematical algorithms or work protocols to information that needs to be protected and additionally following specific procedures and laws. An example of physical document protection is sealed envelopes (the mechanism of protection) that cover the letter (the information that needs to be protected) delivered by an authorized mail service (the trusted party). In this example, the protection mechanism has its limitations. But the technical framework has rigorous rules, through which any entity that opens the envelope and does not have this right needs to be punished. There are situations in which the physical paper contains the information that needs to be protected, and has special characteristics that certify the originality of the data/information. For example, to refrain from forging banknotes, paper currency has special ink and matter.

Table 2-1. *Security Objectives*

Security Objective	Description
privacy/confidentiality	The information is kept secret from unauthorized entities.
signature	A technique that binds a signature by an entity (for example, a document).
authorization	The action of authorizing an entity to do or be something to send the information between the sender and the receiver.
message authentication	The process/characteristic through which the origin of the data is authenticated; another meaning is corroboration of the information source.
data integrity	The information is kept unaltered through techniques that keep away unauthorized entities or unknown means.
entity authentication/ identification	The action of validating the identity of an entity, which may be a computer, person, credit card, and so on.
validation	The action of making available a (limited) quantity of time for authorization for using or manipulating the data or resources.

(continued)

21

Table 2-1. (*continued*)

Security Objective	Description
certification	The process of confirming the information by a trusted party. or Acknowledgment of information by a trusted certification.
access control	The action of restricting access to resources to authorized parties.
timestamping	Metadata stamps the time of creation or the existence of information.
witnessing	The action of validating the creation/existence of the information made by an entity that is not the creator of the data.
receipt	The action of confirming the receiving of the information.
ownership	The action of giving an entity the legal rights to use or transfer a particular information/resource.
confirmation	The action of validating the fact that certain services have been accomplished.
revocation	The action of withdrawing certification or authorization.
nonrepudiation	The process of restraining the negation of other previous commitments or actions.
anonymity	The action of making anonym an entity's identity involved in a particular action/process.

From a conceptual point of view, how the information is manipulated did not change substantially. We consider storing, registering, interpreting, and recording data. However, a manipulation that changed significantly is copying and modifying the information. An important concept in information security is the *signature,* which represents the foundation for more processes, such as nonrepudiation, data origin authentication, identification, and witnessing.

The requirements introduced by legal and technical skills should be followed to achieve the security of information in electronic communication. On the other hand, the preceding protection objectives are not guaranteed to be fulfilled accordingly. The technical part of information security is assured by *cryptography.*

Cryptography represents the field that studies the mathematical techniques and tools that are connected to information security, such as confidentiality, integrity (data), authentication (entity), and the origin of authentication. Cryptography not only provides information security but also provides a specific set of techniques.

Cryptography Goals

From the security objectives presented in Table 2-1, the following represent a basis from which the others can be derived.

- privacy/confidentiality (Definitions 2.5 and 2.8)

- data integrity (Definition 2.9)

- authentication (Definition 2.7)

- nonrepudiation (Definition 2.6)

The following explains each of the four objectives in detail.

- **Confidentiality** represents a service that protects information content from unauthorized entities and access. Confidentiality is assured through different techniques, from mathematical algorithms to physical protection, that scramble the data into an incomprehensible form.

- **Data integrity** represents a service that prevents unauthorized alteration of the information. Authorized entities should be able to discover and identify unauthorized manipulation of data.

- **Authentication** represents a service that has an important role when data or application is authenticated, and it implies identification. The authentication process is applied on both extremities that use the data (for example, the sender and the receiver). The rule is that each involved party should identify itself in the communication process. It is very important that both parties that are involved in the communication process declare to each other their identity (the parties could be represented by a person or a system). At the same time, some characteristics of the data should accompany the data itself; for example, its origin, content, or the time of creation/sending.

From this point of view, cryptography branches authentication into two categories: authentication of the entity and authentication of the data origin. Data origin authentication leads to data integrity.

- **Nonrepudiation** represents a service that prevents the denials of previous actions made by an entity. When a conflict occurs because an entity denies its previous actions, it is resolved by an existing sinew showing the actions made over data.

One of the main goals of cryptography is to fulfill the four objectives on both sides—theory and practice.

Cryptographic Primitives

The book presents several fundamental cryptographic tools called *primitives*. Examples of primitives are encryption schemes (Definitions 2.5 and 2.8), hash functions (Definition 2.9), and schemes for digital signatures (Definition 2.6). Figure 2-1 presents a schematic description of these primitives and their relationship. Many cryptographic primitives are used in the book, and practical implementations are provided every time. Before using them in real-life applications, the primitives should be evaluated to check if the following criteria are fulfilled.

- **Level of security**. It is slightly difficult to quantify the level of security. However, it can be quantified as the number of operations to accomplish the desired objective. The level of security is usually defined based on the superior bound given by the volume of work necessary to defeat the objective.

- **Functionality**. To accomplish security objectives, in many situations, primitives are combined. You need to be sure that they work properly.

- **Operation methods**. When primitives are used, they need different inputs and have different ways of working, resulting in different characteristics. In these situations, the primitives provide very different functionalities that depend on the mode of operation.

- **Performance**. This concept is related to the efficiency that a primitive can achieve in a specific mode of operation.

- **Ease of implementation**. This concept is merely a process rather than a criterion, which refers to the primitive being used in practice.

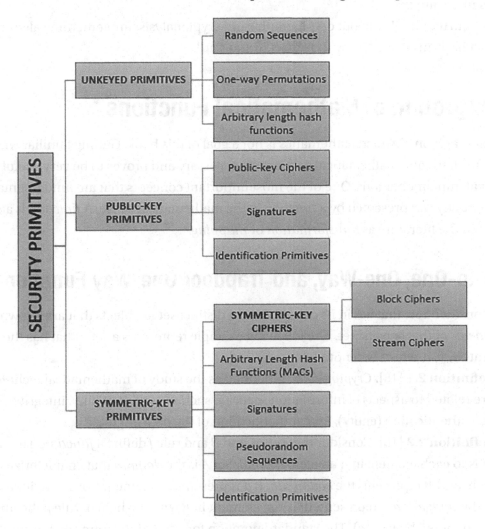

Figure 2-1. *Cryptographic primitive taxonomy*

The application and the available resources give importance to each of the criteria shown in Figure 2-1.

Cryptography may be seen as an art practiced by professionals and specialists who proposed and developed ad hoc techniques whose purpose was to fulfill important information security requirements. In the last few decades, cryptography has transitioned from an art to a science and discipline. There are dedicated conferences and events in many cryptography and information security fields. In addition, there are international professional associations, such as the International Association for Cryptologic Research (IACR), whose aim is to bring and promote the best research results in the area.

The current book is about cryptography and cryptanalysis: implementing algorithms and mechanisms using C++ with respect to standards.

Background of Mathematical Functions

A monograph on abstract mathematics is not a goal of this book. Getting familiar with some fundamental mathematical concepts is necessary and proves to be very useful in practical implementations. One of the most important concepts that are fundamental to cryptography is represented by a *function* in the mathematical sense. A *function* is also known in the literature as *transformation* or *mapping*.

One-to-One, One-Way, and Trapdoor One-Way Functions

Let's consider a *set* that has in its composition a distinct set of objects that are known as *elements* of that specific set. The following example represents a set A that has the elements a, b, c, which is denoted as $A = \{a, b, c\}$.

Definition 2.1 [18]. *Cryptography* is defined as the study of mathematical techniques that are related to aspects of information security, such as confidentiality, integrity (data), authentication (entity), and authentication of the data origin.

Definition 2.2 [18]. Consider that sets A and B and rule f define a *function*. The rule f assigns to each element in A an element in B. Set A is the *domain* that characterizes the function, and B represents the *codomain*. If a represents an element from A, written as $a \in A$, the *image* of a is represented by the element in B with the help of rule f; the image b of a is denoted by $b = f(a)$. The standard notation for a function f from set A to set B is represented as $f: A \rightarrow B$. If $b \in B$, then there is a preimage of b, which is an element $a \in A$ for which $f(a) = b$. The entire set of elements in B that have at least one preimage is known as the *image* of f, denoted as $Im(f)$.

Example 2.3. *(function)* Consider sets $A = \{a, b, c\}$ and $B = \{1, 2, 3, 4\}$, and the rule f from A to B as defined as $f(a) = 2$, $f(b) = 4$, $f(c) = 1$. Figure 2-2 represents sets A, B and function f. The preimage of the element 2 is a. The image of f is $\{1, 2, 4\}$.

Example 2.4. *(function)* Consider set $A = \{1, 2, 3, ..., 10\}$ and consider f to be the rule that for each $a \in A$, $f(a) = r_a$, where r_a represents the remainder when a^2 is divided by 11.

$$f(1) = 1 \quad f(6) = 3$$

$$f(2) = 3 \quad f(7) = 5$$

$$f(3) = 9 \quad f(8) = 9$$

$$f(4) = 5 \quad f(9) = 4$$

$$f(5) = 3 \quad f(10) = 1$$

function

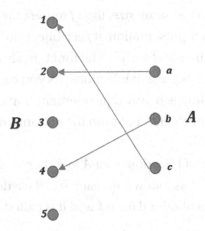

Figure 2-2. *Function f from a set A formed from three elements to a set B formed from five elements*

The image of f is represented by the set $Y = \{1, 3, 4, 5, 9\}$.

The scheme represents the main fundamental tool for thinking of a function (found in the literature known as the functional diagram), as depicted in Figure 2-2. Each element from the domain A has precisely one arrow originating from it. For each element from codomain B, you can have any number of arrows incident to it (including also zero lines).

Example 2.5. (function) Let's consider the following set defined as $A = \{1, 2, 3, ..., 10^{50}\}$ and consider f to be the rule $f(a) = r_a$, where r_a represents the remainder in the case when a^2 is divided by $10^{50} + 1$ for all $a \in A$. In this situation, it is not feasible to write down f explicitly, as in Example 2.4. The function is completely defined by the domain and the mathematical description that characterize the rule f.

One-to-One Functions

Definition 2.6 [18]. Consider a function or transformation $1 - 1$ (one-to-one) if each of the elements that can be found within the codomain B is represented as the image of at most one element in the domain A.

Definition 2.7 [18]. Let's consider that a function or transformation is onto if each of the elements found within the codomain B represents the image of at least one element that can be found in the domain. At the same time, a function $f: A \to B$ is known as being onto if $Im(f) = B$.

Definition 2.8 [18]. Function $f: A \to B$ is considered $1 - 1$ and $Im(f) = B$, and function f is called *bijection*.

Conclusion 2.9 [18]. If $f: A \to B$ is considered $1 - 1$, then $f: A \to Im(f)$ represents the bijection. In special cases, if $f: A \to B$ is represented as $1 - 1$ and A and B are represented as finite sets with the same size, then f represents a bijection.

Using the scheme and its representation, if f is a bijection, then each element from B has exactly one line that is incident with it. The function shown and described in Examples 2.3 and 2.4 does not represent bijections. As you can see in Example 2.3, element 3 does not have the image of any other element that can be found within the domain. In Example 2.4, each element from the codomain is identified with two preimages.

Definition 2.10 [18]. If f is a bijection from A to B then it is a quite simple matter to define a bijection g from B to A as follows: for each $b \in B$ we define $g(b) = a$ where $a \in A$ and $f(a) = b$. The function g is obtained from f, and it is called the inverse function of f and denoted as $g = f^{-1}$.

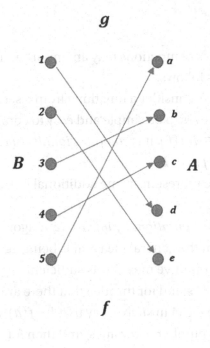

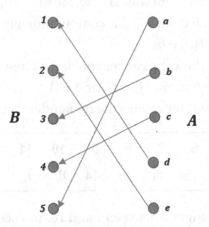

Figure 2-3. *Representation of a bijection f and its inverse g = f⁻¹*

Example 2.11. *(inverse function)* Consider sets $A = \{a, b, c, d, e\}$ and $Y = \{1, 2, 3, 4, 5\}$ and the rule f, which is given and represented by the lines in Figure 2-3. f represents a bijection, and its inverse g is formed by reversing the sense of the arrows. The domain of g is represented by B, and the codomain is A.

Note that if f is a bijection, then f^{-1} is also a bijection. The bijections in cryptography are tools used for message encryption. The inverse transformations are used for decryption. The main condition for decryption is for transformation to be a bijection.

One-Way Functions

In cryptography, certain types of functions play an important role. A definition for a one-way function is given as follows.

Definition 2.12 [18]. Let's consider a function f from a set A to a set B that is called a *one-way* function if $f(a)$ proves to be simple and *easy* to compute for all $a \in A$. But for "essentially all" elements $b \in Im\ (f)$, it is *computationally infeasible* to manage to find any $a \in A$ in such a way that $f(a) = b$.

Note 2.13 [18]. This note represents some additional notes and clarifications of the terms used in Definition 2.12.

For the terms *easy* and *computationally infeasible,* a rigorous definition is necessary, but it distracts attention from the general idea that is being agreed upon. Fur the goal of this chapter, the simple and intuitive meaning is sufficient.

The words "essentially all" stand for the idea that there are a couple of values $b \in B$ for which it is easy to find an $a \in A$ in such a way that $b = f(a)$. For example, one may compute $b = f(a)$ for a small number of a values, and then for these values, the inverse is known by a table look-up. A different way to describe this property of a one-way function is as follows: for any random $b \in Im\ (f)$, it is computationally feasible to have and find any $a \in A$ in such a way that $f(a) = b$.

The following examples show the concept behind a one-way function.

Example 2.14. *(one-way function)* Consider $A = \{1, 2, 3, ..., 16\}$ and define $f(a) = r_a$ for all the elements $a \in A$, where r_a represents the remainder when 3^x is divided by 17.

a	1	2	3	4	5	6	7	8	9	10	11	12	13	14	15	16
f(a)	3	9	10	13	5	15	11	16	14	8	7	4	12	2	6	1

Let's assume a number situated between 1 and 16. You see that it is very easy to find its image under f. Without having the table in front of you, for example, for 7, it is hard to find a given that $f(a) = 7$. If the number you are given is 3, then is quite easy that $a = 1$ is what you need.

Remember that this is an example focused on very small numbers. The key thing here is that the amount of effort to measure is different $f(a)$ and the amount of work in finding a given $f(a)$. Additionally, for large numbers, $f(a)$ can be efficiently computed using the square-and-multiply algorithm [20], where the process of finding a from $f(a)$ is harder to find.

Example 2.15 [18]. (one-way function) A prime number is defined as a positive integer. The integer is larger than 1, and its positive integer divisors are 1 and itself. Let's take into consideration the primes p = 50633 and q = 58411, compute $n = pq = 50633 \cdot 58411 = 2957524163$, and let's consider $A = \{1, 2, 3, ..., n - 1\}$. We define a function f on A by $f(a) = r_a$ for each $a \in A$, where r_a represents the remainder when x^3 is divided by n. For example, let's consider $f(2489991 = 1981394214$ since $2489991^3 = 5881949859 \cdot n + 1981394214$. Computing $f(a)$ represents a simple task, but reversing the procedure is difficult.

Trapdoor One-Way Functions

Definition 2.16 [18]. A trapdoor one-way function is represented as a one-way function $f : A \rightarrow B$ with an extra property that has information (also known as the trapdoor information); it is much more feasible to have an identification for any given $b \in Im (f)$, with an $a \in A$ in such a way that $f(a) = b$.

Example 2.15 shows the concept of a trapdoor one-way function. With extra information about the factors of $n = 2957524163$, it becomes much easier to invert the function. The factors of 2957524163 are large enough that it would be difficult to identify them by hand calculation. You should be able to identify the factors very easily with the help of some computer program. For example, if you have very large, distinct prime numbers (each number has approximately 200 decimal digits), p and q, with the technology of today, finding p and q from n is very difficult even with the most powerful computers, such as quantum computers. This is the well-known factorization problem known as the *integer factorization problem*.

One-way and one-way trapdoor functions form the fundamental basis for public-key cryptography. These principles are very important and become much clearer later when the implementation of cryptographic techniques occurs. It is vital and important to understand these concepts from this section as the main methods and the primary foundation for the cryptography algorithms to implement later in this chapter.

Permutations

Permutation represents functions that are in cryptographic constructs.

Definition 2.17 [18]. Consider S to be a finite set formed of elements. A *permutation* p on S represents a bijection, as defined in Definition 2.8. The bijection is represented from S to itself, $p : S \rightarrow S$.

Example 2.18 [18]. This example represents a permutation example. Let's consider the following permutation $S = \{1, 2, 3, 4, 5\}$. The permutation $p : S \to S$ is defined as follows.

$$p(1) = 2, p(2) = 5, p(3) = 4, p(4) = 2, p(5) = 1$$

A permutation can be described in different ways. It can also be written as an array, as follows, in which the top row in the array is represented by the domain and the bottom row is represented by the image under p as mapping.

$$p = \begin{pmatrix} 1 & 2 & 3\,4\,5 \\ 3 & 5 & 4\,2\,1 \end{pmatrix},$$

As the permutations are bijections, they have inverses. If the permutation is written as an away (second form), its inverse is very easily found by interchanging the rows in the array and reordering the elements from the new top row, and the bottom row has to be reordered accordingly. In this case, the inverse of p is defined as follows.

$$p^{-1} = \begin{pmatrix} 1 & 2 & 3\,4\,5 \\ 5 & 4 & 1\,3\,2 \end{pmatrix}$$

Example 2.19 [18]. This example represents a permutation example. Let's consider A to be the set of integers $\{0, 1, 2, ..., p \cdot q - 1\}$, where p and q represent two distinct large primes. We also need to suppose that neither $p - 1$ nor $q - 1$ can be divisible by 3. The function $p(a) = r_a$, in which r_a represents the remainder when a^3 is divided by pq, can be demonstrated and shown as the inverse permutation. The inverse permutation is currently computationally infeasible by computers unless p and q are known.

Inclusion

Involutions are known as the functions having their own inverses.

Definition 2.20 [18]. Let's consider a finite set S and f defined as a bijection S to S, denoted as $f : S \to S$. In this case, the function f is noted as *involution* if $f = f^{-1}$. Another way of defining this is $f(f(a)) = a$ for any $a \in S$.

Example 2.21 [18]. This example represents an involution case. Figure 2-4 depicts an example of involution. Note that if j represents the image of i, then i represents the image of j.

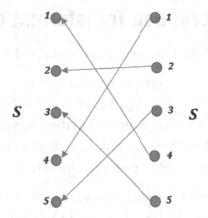

Figure 2-4. *Representation of an involution with a set S with five elements*

Concepts and Basic Terminology

It is very difficult to see and understand how cryptography was built using hard and abstract definitions when dealing with the scientific side of the field. The following lists the most important terms and key concepts that are used in this chapter.

Domains and Codomains Used for Encryption

- $\mathcal{A}$ is shown as a finite set known as the *alphabet of definition*. Consider as an example $\mathcal{A} = \{0,1\}$, which represents the binary alphabet, a frequently used alphabet as a definition.

- $\mathcal{M}$ is a set known as the *message space*. The message space has strings of symbols from an alphabet, $\mathcal{A}$. As an example, $\mathcal{M}$ may have binary strings, English text, French text, and so on.

- $\mathcal{C}$ is the ciphertext space. $\mathcal{C}$ has strings of symbols from an alphabet, $\mathcal{A}$, which is totally different from the alphabet defined for $\mathcal{M}$. An element from $\mathcal{C}$ is called *ciphertext*.

Encryption and Decryption Transformations

- The set $\mathcal{K}$ is called the *key space*. The elements of $\mathcal{K}$ are called *keys*.

- For each $e \in \mathcal{K}$, there is a unique transformation E_e, representing a bijection from $\mathcal{M}$ to $\mathcal{C}$ (i.e., $E_e : \mathcal{M} \rightarrow \mathcal{C}$). E_e is called the *encryption function* or *encryption transformation*. If the encryption process is reversed, then E_e should be a bijection, such that each unique plain message is recovered from one unique ciphertext.

   For each $d \in \mathcal{K}$, there is a transformation D_d, representing a bijection from $\mathcal{C}$ to $\mathcal{M}$ (i.e., $D_d : \mathcal{C} \rightarrow \mathcal{M}$). D_d is called a *decryption function* or *decryption transformation*.

- The process of *encrypting the message* $m \in \mathcal{M}$ or the *encryption of m* consists of applying the transformation E_e.

- The process of *decrypting the ciphertext* $c \in \mathcal{C}$ or the *decryption of c* consists of applying the transformation D_d over c.

- An encryption scheme has two important sets: $\{E_e : e \in \mathcal{K}\}$, which represents the set of encryption transformations, and $\{D_d : d \in \mathcal{K}\}$, which represents the set of decryption transformations. The relation between the elements of the two sets is the following: for each $e \in \mathcal{K}$, there exists a unique key $d \in \mathcal{K}$ such that $D_d = E_e^{-1}$; in other words, we have the relationship $D_d(E_e(m)) = m$ for all $m \in \mathcal{M}$. Another term for encryption schemes is *cipher*.

- In the preceding definition, the encryption key e and the decryption key d form a pair, usually denoted (e, d). In symmetric encryption schemes, *e* and *d* are the same, while in asymmetric (or public-key) encryption schemes, they are different.

- To *construct* an encryption scheme, the following components are needed: the message (or plain-text) space $\mathcal{M}$, the cipher-space $\mathcal{C}$, the key space $\mathcal{K}$, the set of encryption transformations $\{E_e : e \in \mathcal{K}\}$ and the set of decryption transformations $\{D_d : d \in \mathcal{K}\}$.

The Participants in the Communication Process

The following are components involved in the communication process.

- The *entity (party)* is that component that works with information: sending, receiving, manipulating it. The entities/parties in Figure 2-5 are *Alice*, *Bob*, and *Oscar*. However, in real applications, entities are not necessarily persons; they may be authorities or computers, for example.

- The *sender* is one of the entities of a two-party communication and initiates the transmission of the data. The sender in Figure 2-5 is *Alice*.

- The *receiver* is the other entity of a two-party communication and is the intended recipient of the information. The receiver in Figure 2-5 is *Bob*.

- The *communication channel* is the component through which the sender and the receiver communicate.

- The adversary is an unauthorized entity on a two-party communication, and it is different from the sender and the receiver. Its objective is to break the security on the communication channel to access the information. Other terms for the adversary[1] are *enemy*, *attacker*, *opponent*, *eavesdropper*, *intruder*, and *interloper*. It has different types (passive and active) and behaves differently according to aspects regarding the encryption scheme or its intentions. Often, the attacker clones and acts like the legitimate sender or the legitimate receiver.

---

[1] Alice and Bob. Available online: https://en.wikipedia.org/wiki/Alice_and_Bob

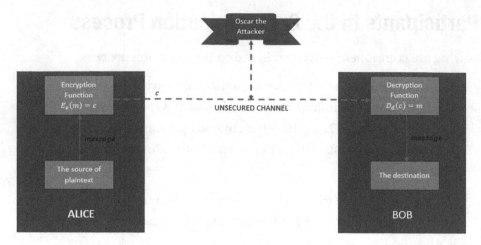

Figure 2-5. *Example of a two-party communication process applying encryption*

Digital Signatures

Digital signatures are very important in some processes, such as authentication, authorization, or nonrepudiation. The digital signature is used to map an individual's identity with a piece of information. When something is digitally signed, the message and the confidential information owned by an individual are converted into a tag called a signature.

The components of the signing process are as follows.

- $\mathcal{M}$ is the set of messages that can be signed.

- $\mathcal{S}$ is the set of *signatures*. These can have a form of binary strings with a predefined length.

- $\mathcal{S}_A$ represents the transformation between $\mathcal{M}$ and $\mathcal{S}$, called the *signing transformation,* and it is made by entity A. The entity keeps $\mathcal{S}_A$ secret and use it to sign messages from $\mathcal{M}$.

- V_A represents the transformation between $\mathcal{M} \times \mathcal{S}$ to the set {*true, false*}. The Cartesian product $\mathcal{M} \times \mathcal{S}$ contains the pair of elements (m, s) where $m \in \mathcal{M}$ and $s \in \mathcal{S}$. The transformation V_A is public, and it is used by different entities to check if the signatures were created by entity A.

CHAPTER 2   CRYPTOGRAPHY FUNDAMENTALS

Signing Process

The entity A called the signer creates a signature $s \in \mathcal{S}$ for a particular message $m \in \mathcal{M}$ using the following steps.

1. Compute $s = S_A(m)$.

2. Transmit the pair (m, s) to the desired receiver.

Verification Process

When the receiver entity B wants to check if the entity A created the signature s for the message m, it proceeds as follows.

1. Obtain the verification function V_A for entity A.

2. Compute $u = V_A(m, s)$.

3. If $u = true$, then the signature was created by entity A; if $u = false$, then the signature was not created by entity A.

Public-Key Cryptography

Public-key cryptography (PKC) has an important role in C++ when similar algorithms need to be incorporated. Many significant commercial libraries are implementing developer-specific public-key cryptography solutions, such as [21–30].

Next, let's look at how public-key cryptography works. For this, recall that $\mathcal{K}$ is the key space, and consider the set of encryption transformations $\{E_e : e \in \mathcal{K}\}$ and the set of decryption transformations $\{D_d : d \in \mathcal{K}\}$. Furthermore, consider the pair of encryption and decryption transformations (E_e, D_d), where E_e can be learned by anyone for every e. Since E_e, determining D_d must be computationally unrealizable (i.e., from a random ciphertext $c \in \mathcal{C}$), it must be impossible to determine the message $m \in \mathcal{M}$ such that $E_e(m) = c$. This property is strong, which means that the corresponding decryption key d (which must be secret/private) may not be computed/determined from either given e (which is public).

37

Look at Figure 2-6 and consider the communication channel between two parties, namely, Alice and Bob.

- Bob chooses a pair of keys (e, d).

- Bob makes the encryption key e publicly available, such that Alice can access it over any channel and keeps the decryption key secret and safe d. In the specialty literature, in PKC, the encryption key is called *the public key,* and the decryption key is called *the secret/private key.*

- When Alice wants to send a message $m \in \mathcal{M}$ to Bob, she uses Bob's public key e to determine the encryption transformation E_e, and then she applies it over m. Finally, Alice obtains the encryption $c = E_e(m) \in \mathcal{C}$ and sends it to Bob.

- When Bob wants to decrypt the encrypted message $c \in \mathcal{C}$ received from Alice, he uses his private key d to determine the transformation decryption D_d, and then he applies it over c. Finally, he obtains $m = D_d(c) \in \mathcal{M}$.

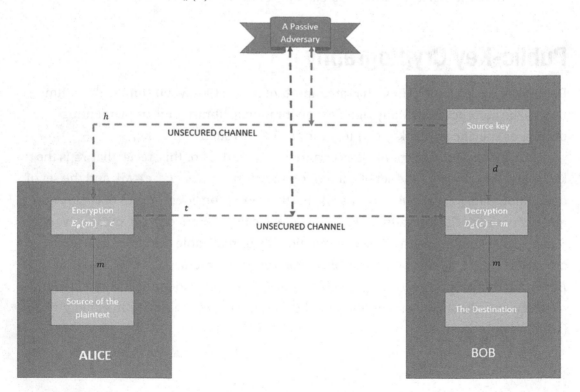

Figure 2-6. *The process of encryption using the public-key mechanism*

There is no need to keep the encryption key e secret, and it can be made public. Every individual can then send encrypted messages to Bob that can be decrypted only by Bob. Figure 2-7 illustrates the idea, where A_1, A_2, and A_3 represent different entities. Remember that if A_1 destroys message m_1 after encrypting it to c_1, then even A_1 is found in a position to not be able to recover m_1 from c_1.

Let's take the following analog as an example, to make it simple, by considering a metal with the cover secured by a lock with a particular combination. Bob is the only one who knows how to blend. If the lock stays open and made accessible to the public for different purposes, we find ourselves in a position where someone can let a message inside and lock the cover.

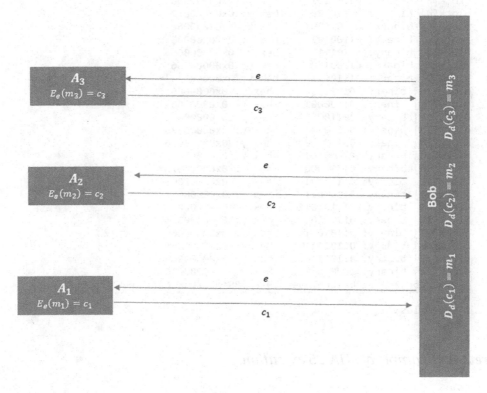

Figure 2-7. *How public-key encryption is used*

Hash Functions

Hash functions are one of the primary primitives in modern cryptography. Additionally, known as a one-way hash function is the hack function. A hash function represents a computationally efficient function that maps the binary string to binary strings with an arbitrary length with a fixed length known as hash values.

As an example of the implementation of a hash function (SHA-256, see Figure 2-8), let's examine the following implementation in C++ using C++2 new features (see Listing 2-1). The implementation is performed in accordance with the NIST.[2]

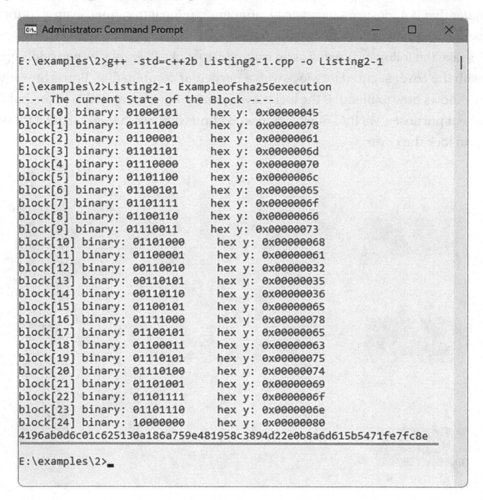

Figure 2-8. *Example of SHA-25 execution*

---

[2] NIST Hash Functions, https://csrc.nist.gov/projects/hash-functions

Listing 2-1. Source Code for Implementation of SHA256

```cpp
#include <iostream>        //** standard input/output library
#include <sstream>         //** templates and types for interoperation
                                    //** between flow buffers
and string objects
#include <bitset>          //** storing bits library
#include <vector>          //** for representing arrays as containers
#include <iomanip>         //** for manipulation of the parameters
#include <cstring>         //** for manipulation of the strings

using namespace std;       //** for avoiding writing "std::"

//** ASCII string will be converted into a binary representation
vector<unsigned long> binaryConversion(const string);

//** for adding padding to messages and ensuring that they are
//** multiple of 512 bits
vector<unsigned long> addPadOf512Bits(const vector<unsigned long>);

//** We will change the n 8 bit blocks to 32 bit words
vector<unsigned long> resizingTheBlock(vector<unsigned long>);

//** will contain the actual hash value
string computingTheHash(const vector<unsigned long>);

//** variables and constants used during debugging
string displayAsHex(unsigned long);
void outputTheBlockState(vector<unsigned long>);
string displayAsBinary(unsigned long);
const bool displayBlockStateAddOne = 0;
const bool displayDistanceFrom512Bit = 0;
const bool displayResultsOfPadding = false;
const bool displayWorkVariablesForT = 0;
const bool displayT1Computation = false;
const bool displayT2Computation = false;
const bool displayTheHashSegments = false;
const bool displayWt = false;
```

```
//** defined in accordance with the NIST standard
#define ROTRIGHT(word,bits) (((word) >> (bits)) | ((word) << (32-(bits))))
#define SSIG0(x) (ROTRIGHT(x,7) ^ ROTRIGHT(x,18) ^ ((x) >> 3))
#define SSIG1(x) (ROTRIGHT(x,17) ^ ROTRIGHT(x,19) ^ ((x) >> 10))
#define CH(x,y,z) (((x) & (y)) ^ (~(x) & (z)))
#define MAJ(x,y,z) (((x) & (y)) ^ ((x) & (z)) ^ ((y) & (z)))

//** in accordance with the latest updates of the NIST standard
//** we will replace BSIG0 with EP0 and BSIG1 with EP0 in our
//** implementation
#define BSIG0(x) (ROTRIGHT(x,7) ^ ROTRIGHT(x,18) ^ ((x) >> 3))
#define BSIG1(x) (ROTRIGHT(x,17) ^ ROTRIGHT(x,19) ^ ((x) >> 10))

#define EP0(x) (ROTRIGHT(x,2) ^ ROTRIGHT(x,13) ^ ROTRIGHT(x,22))
#define EP1(x) (ROTRIGHT(x,6) ^ ROTRIGHT(x,11) ^ ROTRIGHT(x,25))

//** we will verify if the process of checking (testing) is enabled
//** by the missed arguments in the command line.
//** The steps are as follows:
//** (1) Take the ascii string and convert it into n 8 bit segments by
//** represents the ascii value of each independent character
//** (2) add paddings to the message in order to get a 512 bit long
//** (3) Take each 8 bit ascii value separately and convert it to 32
//** bit words and create a combination of them.
//** (4) Calculate the hash and obtain the vallue
//** (5) if we are doing test, take the result and compare it with//**
    expected result
int main(int argc, char* argv[])
{
    string theMessage = "";
    bool testing = 0;

    switch (argc) {
        case 1:
            cout << "There is no input string found. The test will
be run using random first three letters abc.\n";
                theMessage = "abc";
```

```
                    testing = true;
                break;
            case 2:
                if (strlen(argv[1]) > 55)
                {
                        cout << "The string provided is biger than 55
characters in length. Enter a shorter string."
                                << " or message!\n";
                    return 0;
                }
                theMessage = argv[1];
                break;
            default:
            cout << "There are too many items in the command line. ";
                exit(-1);
                break;
        }
//** storing all the blocks
    vector<unsigned long> theBlocksArray;

    //** convert the message to a vector of strings by hiding it
//** represented it as an 8 bit variable
    theBlocksArray = binaryConversion(theMessage);

    //** add padd to it in order to get a full of 512 bits long
    theBlocksArray = addPadOf512Bits(theBlocksArray);

    //** create a separate combination of the 8 bit segments into
    //** single 32 bit sections
    theBlocksArray = resizingTheBlock(theBlocksArray);

    //** compute the hash using computingTheHash function
    string myHash = computingTheHash(theBlocksArray);

    //** if testing is found on true the software app will execute
//** a self-check by checking if the hash value computed for
//** "abc" is equal to the expected hash
```

```
        if (testing) {
                const string theCorrectHashForABC =
"ba7816bf8f01cfea414140de5dae2223b00361a3961
77a9cb410ff61f20015ad";
                    if (theCorrectHashForABC.compare(myHash)!= 0) {
                            cout << "\tThe test did not occur with success!\n";
                            return(1); }
                    else {
                            cout << "\tTest has been done with success!\n";
                            return(0); } }

    cout << myHash << endl;
    return 0;   }

//** the function purpose is to resize the blocks from 64 and 8 bit
//** to 16- and 32-bit sections. The function as input will take a
//** vector of individual 8 bit ascii values. As output, we will obtain a
//** vector with 32 bit words that are found within a combination of
//** ascii values.
vector<unsigned long> resizingTheBlock(vector<unsigned long>
inputOf8BitAsciiValues)
{
    vector<unsigned long>
outputOf32BitWordsCombinedAsAsciiValues(16);

    //** parse all 64 sections using a 4 step and mergem them
//** accordingly
    for(int i = 0; i < 64; i = i + 4) {
            //** create for beginning a big 32 bit section first
            bitset<32> temporary32BitSection(0);

            //** create a shifting of the blocks on their assigned
//** positions
            temporary32BitSection = (unsigned long)
inputOf8BitAsciiValues[i] << 24;
temporary32BitSection |= (unsigned long)
inputOf8BitAsciiValues[i + 1] << 16;
```

```
            temporary32BitSection |= (unsigned long)
inputOf8BitAsciiValues[i + 2] << 8;
            temporary32BitSection |= (unsigned long)
inputOf8BitAsciiValues[i + 3];
            //** set the new 32 bit word within the proper output of
//** the array location
            outputOf32BitWordsCombinedAsAsciiValues[i/4] =
temporary32BitSection.to_ulong(); }

    return outputOf32BitWordsCombinedAsAsciiValues; }


//** the function displays the contents of all the blocks as binary
//** format. The function is used only for debugging purposes.
void outputTheBlockState(vector<unsigned long>
vectorOfCurrentBlocks) {
    cout << "---- The current State of the Block ----\n";
    for (int i = 0; i < vectorOfCurrentBlocks.size(); i++) {
            cout << "block[" << i << "] binary: " <<
displayAsBinary(vectorOfCurrentBlocks[i])
                    << "       hex y: 0x" <<
displayAsHex(vectorOfCurrentBlocks[i]) << endl; }}

//** the function will display in hex format the content of the
//** blocks.
string displayAsHex(unsigned long input32BitBlock) {
    bitset<32> theBitSet(input32BitBlock);
    unsigned number = theBitSet.to_ulong();

    stringstream theStringStream;
    theStringStream << std::hex << std::setw(8) <<
std::setfill('0') << number;
    string temporary;
    theStringStream >> temporary;

    return temporary; }
```

//** the function will show the content of the blocks in hex. We are
//** using this function to avoid changing the stream from

```
//** hexa to dec and reversed as well.
string displayAsBinary(unsigned long input32OrLessBitBlock) {
      bitset<8> theBitSet(input32OrLessBitBlock);
      return theBitSet.to_string(); }
```

```
//** based on the string, it will take the entire set of the
//** characters and converts them into ascii binary.
vector<unsigned long> binaryConversion(const string
inputOfAnyLength) {
      //** the vector used to store all the ascii characters
vector<unsigned long> vectorBlockHoldingAsciiCharacters;

      //** take each character and convert the ascii character to
//** binary representation
      for (int i = 0; i < inputOfAnyLength.size(); ++i) {
            //** create a temporary variable. Use it to store the 8
//** bit template for ascii value
bitset<8> bitSetOf8Bits(inputOfAnyLength.c_str()[i]);

            //** template of 8 bit added into the block
vectorBlockHoldingAsciiCharacters.
push_back(bitSetOf8Bits.to_ulong());}

      return vectorBlockHoldingAsciiCharacters; }
```

```
//** get the ascii values stored as a vector in binary and add padding to
it to obtain a total of 512 bits.
vector<unsigned long> addPadOf512Bits(vector<unsigned long>
vectorBlockHoldingAsciiCharacters) {
      //** you can keep the variables names as given in the NIST
      //** for our implementation I have used my personal names for
//** variables to obtain a uniqueness of the code
```

```
//** the variable will store the length of the message in bits
int lengthOfMessageInBits =
vectorBlockHoldingAsciiCharacters.size() * 8;

      int zeroesToAdd = 447 - lengthOfMessageInBits;
```

```cpp
//** add another 8 bit block with the first bit being set to 1
    if(displayBlockStateAddOne)
            outputTheBlockState(vectorBlockHoldingAsciiCharacters);

    unsigned long t1Block = 0x80;
    vectorBlockHoldingAsciiCharacters.push_back(t1Block);

    if(displayBlockStateAddOne)
            outputTheBlockState(vectorBlockHoldingAsciiCharacters);
            outputTheBlockState(vectorBlockHoldingAsciiCharacters);

    //** we have 7 zeroes. We will need to subtract 7 from
//** zeroesToAdd
    zeroesToAdd = zeroesToAdd - 7;

    //** debug mode. Find how much we need to get close to 512 bit
    if (displayDistanceFrom512Bit) {
            cout << "lengthOfMessageInBits = " <<
lengthOfMessageInBits << endl;
            cout << "zeroesToAdd = " << zeroesToAdd + 7 << endl;//
Plus 7 so this follows the paper. }

    //** debug mode
    if (displayDistanceFrom512Bit)
            cout << "adding " <<
zeroesToAdd/8 << " empty eight bit blocks!\n";

//** add blocks of 8 bit length that will contain zeros
    for(int i = 0; i < zeroesToAdd/8; i++)
            vectorBlockHoldingAsciiCharacters.push_back(0x00000000);

    //** we are finding ourselves in 488 bits out 512 phase. Next
//** step is adding 1 in the binary representation to
//** form of eight bit blocks.
    bitset<64> theBig64BlobBit(lengthOfMessageInBits);
    if (displayDistanceFrom512Bit)
            cout << "1 in a 64 bit binary blob: \n\t" <<
theBig64BlobBit << endl;
```

```
        //** divide the 64 bit big into 8 bit segments
        string big_64bit_string = theBig64BlobBit.to_string();

        //** take the first block and push it to position 56
        bitset<8> temp_string_holder1(big_64bit_string.substr(0,8));
        vectorBlockHoldingAsciiCharacters.
push_back(temp_string_holder1.to_ulong());

        //** take the rest of the blocks with 8 bit length and push
        for(int i = 8; i < 63; i=i+8) {
                bitset<8>
temporaryStringHolder2(big_64bit_string.substr(i,8));

vectorBlockHoldingAsciiCharacters.
push_back(temporaryStringHolder2.to_ulong()); }

        //** just show in the console everything to know what
//** is happening in this freakin code
        if (displayResultsOfPadding) {
            cout << "Current 512 bit preprocessed hash in binary: \n";
                    for(int i = 0; i <
vectorBlockHoldingAsciiCharacters.size(); i=i+4)
                            cout << i << ": " << displayAsBinary(vector
                            BlockHoldingAsciiCharacters[i]) << "       "
                                << i + 1 << ": " << displayAsBinary(vector
                                BlockHoldingAsciiCharacters[i+1]) << "  "
                                << i + 2 << ": " << displayAsBinary(vector
                                BlockHoldingAsciiCharacters[i+2]) << "  "
                                << i + 3 << ": " << displayAsBinary(vector
                                BlockHoldingAsciiCharacters[i+3]) << endl;

        cout << "Current 512 bit preprocessed hash in hex: \n";
            for(int i = 0; i < vectorBlockHoldingAsciiCharacters.
            size(); i=i+4)
                    cout << i << ": " << "0x" + displayAsHex(vectorBlock
                    HoldingAsciiCharacters[i]) << "       "
                        << i + 1 << ": " << "0x" + displayAsHex(vector
                        BlockHoldingAsciiCharacters[i+1]) << "        "
```

```
                        << i + 2 << ": " << "0x" + displayAsHex(vectorBloc
kHoldingAsciiCharacters[i+2]) << "       "
                        << i + 3 << ": " << "0x" + displayAsHex(vectorBloc
kHoldingAsciiCharacters[i+3]) << endl; }
        return vectorBlockHoldingAsciiCharacters; }

//** the goal of the function is to compute the hash of the message
string computingTheHash(const vector<unsigned long>
blockOf512BitPaddedMessage)
{
        //** the following words are from the NIST standard.
        unsigned long constantOf32BitWords[64] = {
        0x428a2f98,0x71374491,0xb5c0fbcf,0xe9b5dba5,0x3956c25b,0x59f111f1,0
        x923f82a4,0xab1c5ed5,0xd807aa98,0x12835b01,0x243185be,0x550c7dc3,0
        x72be5d74,0x80deb1fe,0x9bdc06a7,0xc19bf174,0xe49b69c1,0xefbe4786,0x
        0fc19dc6,0x240ca1 cc,0x2de92c6f,0x4a7484aa,0x5cb0a9dc,0x76f988da,
        0x983e5152,0xa831c66d,0xb00327c8,0xbf597fc7,0xc6e00bf3,0xd5a79147,
        0x06ca6351,0x14292967,0x27b70a85,0x2e1b2138,0x4d2c6dfc,0x53380d13,0x
        650a7354,0x766a0abb,0x81c2c92e,0x92722c85,0xa2bfe8a1,0xa81a664b,0xc
        24b8b70,0xc76c51a3,0xd192e819,0xd6990624,0xf40e3585,0x106aa070,0x19
        a4c116,0x1e376c08,0x2748774c,0x34b0bcb5,0x391c0cb3,0x4ed8aa4a,0x5b9
        cca4f,0x682e6ff3,0x748f82ee,0x78a5636f,0x84c87814,0x8 cc70208,0x90be
        fffa,0xa4506ceb,0xbef9a3f7,0xc67178f2 };

        //** the initial hash values
        unsigned long static InitialHashValueFor32Bit_0 = 0x6a09e667;
        unsigned long static InitialHashValueFor32Bit_1 = 0xbb67ae85;
        unsigned long static InitialHashValueFor32Bit_2 = 0x3c6ef372;
        unsigned long static InitialHashValueFor32Bit_3 = 0xa54ff53a;
        unsigned long static InitialHashValueFor32Bit_4 = 0x510e527f;
        unsigned long static InitialHashValueFor32Bit_5 = 0x9b05688c;
        unsigned long static InitialHashValueFor32Bit_6 = 0x1f83d9ab;
        unsigned long static InitialHashValueFor32Bit_7 = 0x5be0cd19;

        unsigned long Word[64];
```

```
        for(int t = 0; t <= 15; t++) {
                Word[t] = blockOf512BitPaddedMessage[t] & 0xFFFFFFFF;

                if (displayWt)
                        cout << "Word[" << t << "]: 0x" <<
displayAsHex(Word[t]) << endl; }

        for(int t = 16; t <= 63; t++) {
                Word[t] = SSIG1(Word[t-2]) +
Word[t-7] + SSIG0(Word[t-15]) + Word[t-16];

                Word[t] = Word[t] & 0xFFFFFFFF;

                if (displayWt)
                        cout << "Word[" << t << "]: " << Word[t]; }

        unsigned long temporary_1;
        unsigned long temporary_2;
        unsigned long a = InitialHashValueFor32Bit_0;
        unsigned long b = InitialHashValueFor32Bit_1;
        unsigned long c = InitialHashValueFor32Bit_2;
        unsigned long d = InitialHashValueFor32Bit_3;
        unsigned long e = InitialHashValueFor32Bit_4;
        unsigned long f = InitialHashValueFor32Bit_5;
        unsigned long g = InitialHashValueFor32Bit_6;
        unsigned long h = InitialHashValueFor32Bit_7;

        if(displayWorkVariablesForT)
                cout << "             A        B        C        D          "
                        << "E        F        G        H     T1   T2\n";

        for( int t = 0; t < 64; t++) {
                //** according to the NIST Standard and Specification,
//** the BSIG1 is incorrect. We will replace it with EP1.
                temporary_1 = h + EP1(e) + CH(e,f,g) +
constantOf32BitWords[t] + Word[t];
                if ((t == 20) & displayT1Computation){
                cout << "h: 0x" << hex << h << "  dec:" << dec << h
                        << "  sign:" << dec << (int)h << endl;
                cout << "EP1(e): 0x" << hex << EP1(e) << "  dec:"
```

```
                  << dec << EP1(e) << "  sign:" << dec << (int)EP1(e)
                  << endl;
          cout << "CH(e,f,g): 0x" << hex << CH(e,f,g) << "  dec:"
                      << dec << CH(e,f,g) << "  sign:" << dec
                      << (int)CH(e,f,g) << endl;
          cout << "constantOf32BitWords[t]: 0x" << hex <<
constantOf32BitWords[t] << "  dec:" << dec
                          << constantOf32BitWords[t] << "  sign:" <<
    dec << (int)constantOf32BitWords[t] << endl;
          cout << "Word[t]: 0x" << hex << Word[t]
<< "  dec:" << dec << Word[t] << "  sign:" << dec
<< (int)Word[t] << endl;
          cout << "temporary_1 = 0x" << hex << temporary_1
<< "  dec:" << dec
                      << temporary_1 << "  sign:" << dec <<
(int)temporary_1 << endl; }

          //** according to the NIST Standard and Specification,
//** the BSIG0 is incorrect. We will replace it with EP0.
          temporary_2 = EP0(a) + MAJ(a,b,c);

          //** in order to get T2 we will display the variables
//** and operations
          if ((t == 20) & displayT2Computation) {
              cout << "a: 0x" << hex << a << "  dec:" << dec << a
                  << "  sign:" << dec << (int)a << endl;
              cout << "b: 0x" << hex << b << "  dec:" << dec << b
                  << "  sign:" << dec << (int)b << endl;
              cout << "c: 0x" << hex << c << "  dec:" << dec << c
                  << "  sign:" << dec << (int)c << endl;
              cout << "EP0(a): 0x" << hex << EP0(a) << "  dec:"
                << dec << EP0(a) << "  sign:" << dec << (int)EP0(a)
                << endl;
              cout << "MAJ(a,b,c): 0x" << hex
                << MAJ(a,b,c) << "  dec:"
                << dec << MAJ(a,b,c) << "  sign:" << dec
                << (int)MAJ(a,b,c) << endl;
```

```
cout << "temporary_2 = Ox" << hex << temporary_2 << "  dec:" << dec <<
temporary_2 << "  sign:" << dec << (int)temporary_2 << endl; }

            //** according to the NIST standard
            h = g;
            g = f;
            f = e;

//** Get the guarantee that we are still using 32 bits
            e = (d + temporary_1) & 0xFFFFFFFF;
            d = c;
            c = b;
            b = a;

//** Get the guarantee that we are still using 32 bits
            a = (temporary_1 + temporary_2) & 0xFFFFFFFF;

            //** display the content of each of the variables from
//** above according to the NIST standard.
    if (displayWorkVariablesForT) {
            cout << "t= " << t << " " ";
            cout << displayAsHex (a) << " " << displayAsHex (b)
 << " " << displayAsHex (c) << " " << displayAsHex
(d) << " "   << displayAsHex (e) << " " << displayAsHex (f) << " " <<
displayAsHex (g) << " " << displayAsHex (h) << " " << endl; } }

//** display the content of each of the hash segments
    if(displayTheHashSegments) {
            cout << "InitialHashValueFor32Bit_0 = " << displayAsHex
(InitialHashValueFor32Bit_0) << " + " << displayAsHex (a) << " " <<
displayAsHex (InitialHashValueFor32Bit_0 + a) << endl;
            cout << "InitialHashValueFor32Bit_1 = " << displayAsHex
(InitialHashValueFor32Bit_1) << " + " <<
displayAsHex (b) << " " << displayAsHex
(InitialHashValueFor32Bit_1 + b) << endl;
            cout << "InitialHashValueFor32Bit_2 = " << displayAsHex
                    (InitialHashValueFor32Bit_2) << " + " <<
 displayAsHex (c) << " " << displayAsHex
```

```
                   (InitialHashValueFor32Bit_2 + c) << endl;
                   cout << "InitialHashValueFor32Bit_3 = " << displayAsHex
                           (InitialHashValueFor32Bit_3) << " + " <<
                           displayAsHex (d) << " " << displayAsHex
                           (InitialHashValueFor32Bit_3 + d) << endl;
                   cout << "InitialHashValueFor32Bit_4 = " << displayAsHex
                           (InitialHashValueFor32Bit_4) << " + " <<
                           displayAsHex (e) << " " << displayAsHex
                           (InitialHashValueFor32Bit_4 + e) << endl;
                   cout << "InitialHashValueFor32Bit_5 = " << displayAsHex
                           (InitialHashValueFor32Bit_5) << " + " <<
                           displayAsHex (f) << " " << displayAsHex
                           (InitialHashValueFor32Bit_5 + f) << endl;
                   cout << "InitialHashValueFor32Bit_6 = " << displayAsHex
                           (InitialHashValueFor32Bit_6) << " + " <<
           displayAsHex (g) << " " << displayAsHex
           (InitialHashValueFor32Bit_6 + g) << endl;
cout << "InitialHashValueFor32Bit_7 = " << displayAsHex
   (InitialHashValueFor32Bit_7) << " + " << displayAsHex
   (h) << " " << displayAsHex (InitialHashValueFor32Bit_7
   + h) << endl;
           }

           //** for each hash add all the variables in order be sure that
//** we are still on the page with the 32 bit values
           InitialHashValueFor32Bit_0 = (InitialHashValueFor32Bit_0 + a)
& 0xFFFFFFFF;
           InitialHashValueFor32Bit_1 = (InitialHashValueFor32Bit_1 + b)
& 0xFFFFFFFF;
           InitialHashValueFor32Bit_2 = (InitialHashValueFor32Bit_2 + c)
& 0xFFFFFFFF;
           InitialHashValueFor32Bit_3 = (InitialHashValueFor32Bit_3 + d)
& 0xFFFFFFFF;
InitialHashValueFor32Bit_4 = (InitialHashValueFor32Bit_4 + e)
& 0xFFFFFFFF;
           InitialHashValueFor32Bit_5 = (InitialHashValueFor32Bit_5 + f)
& 0xFFFFFFFF;
```

```
        InitialHashValueFor32Bit_6 = (InitialHashValueFor32Bit_6 + g)
& 0xFFFFFFFF;
        InitialHashValueFor32Bit_7 = (InitialHashValueFor32Bit_7 + h)
& 0xFFFFFFFF;

        //** add the hash section in one piece one after the other in
//** order to obtain the 256 bit hash
        return displayAsHex(InitialHashValueFor32Bit_0) +
displayAsHex(InitialHashValueFor32Bit_1) + displayAsHex(InitialHashValue
For32Bit_2) +   displayAsHex(InitialHashValueFor32Bit_3) + displayAsHex(
InitialHashValueFor32Bit_4) + displayAsHex(InitialHashValueFor32Bit_5) +
                    displayAsHex(InitialHashValueFor32Bit_6) +
                    displayAsHex(InitialHashValueFor32Bit_7);
}
```

Hash functions are commonly used for digital signatures and in data integrity as well. A long message is generally hashed when dealing with digital signatures, and only the hash value is signed. The group that receives the message then hash the message received and check that the signature received is right for this hash value. Table 2-2 is a classification of keyed cryptographic hash functions. Table 2-3 is a classification of unkeyed cryptographic hash functions. Most functions are already implemented in C++ within the NIST or other trusted resources, such as CrypTool[3].

Table 2-2. *Keyed Cryptographic Hash Functions*

Name	Length of the tag	Type	References
BLAKE2	Arbitrary	Keyed hash function with prefix-MAC	[31][42]
BLAKE3	Arbitrary	Keyed hash function with supplied initializing vector (IV)	[32]
HMAC	-	-	[33]
KMAC	Arbitrary	Based on Keccak	[34][35]
MD6	512 bits	Merkle tree with NLFSR	[37]
PMAC	-	-	[38]
UMAC	-	-	[39]

---

[3] CrypTool, https://www.cryptool.org/en/

Table 2-3. *Unkeyed Cryptographic Hash Functions*

Name	Length	Type	References
BLAKE-256	256 bits	HAIFA structure [41]	[40]
BLAKE-512	512 bits	HAIFA structure [41]	[40]
GOST	256 bits	Hash	[43]
MD2	128 bits	Hash	
MD4	128 bits	Hash	[44]
MD5	128 bits	Merkle-Damgard construction [36]	[45]
MD6	Up to 512 bits	Merkle-tree NLFSR	[37]
RIPEMD	128 bits	Hash	[46]
RIPEMD-128	128 bits	Hash	[46][47][48]
RIPEMD-256	-	Hash	
RIPEMD-160	160 bits	Hash	
RIPEMD-320	320 bits	Hash	
SHA-1	160 bits	Merkle-Damgard construction [36]	[61]
SHA-256	256 bits	Merkle-Damgard construction	[50][51][54]
SHA-384	384 bits		[52][54]
SHA-512	512 bits		[53][54]
SHA-224	224 bits	Merkle-Damgard construction	[55]
SHA-3 (Keccak)	Arbitrary	Sponge function [50]	[56][57]
Whirlpool	512 bits	Hash	[58][59][60]

Case Studies

Caesar Cipher Implementation in C++23

This section gives the Caesar cipher implementation in C++23. The aim of this section is to explain how the aforementioned mathematical foundations can be useful during the implementation process and the advantages of understanding the basic mathematical mechanisms behind the algorithms behind them. This book does not dwell on the algorithm's mathematical history. If you want to go deep into the mathematical history, references [6–18] are recommended.

The encryption process used by the Caesar cipher can be represented as modular arithmetic by first transforming the letters into numbers. For this, follow *alphabet* $\mathcal{A} = \{A,\ldots,Z\} = 25$ in such a way that $A = 0$, $B = 1$, ..., $Z = 25$. The encryption of a letter x is done by a shift n and mathematically can be described as follows.

$$E_n(x) = (x + n)\, mod\, 26$$

The decryption is done similarly.

$$D_n(x) = (x - n)\, mod\, 26$$

Let's start the implementation of the algorithm (see Figure 2-9 and Listing 2-2).

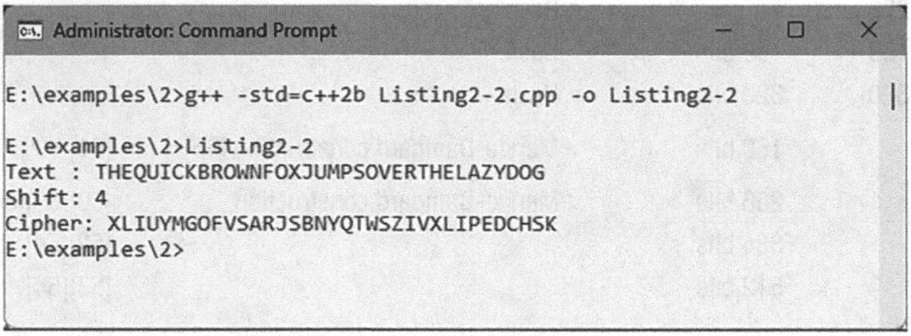
Administrator: Command Prompt
E:\examples\2>g++ -std=c++2b Listing2-2.cpp -o Listing2-2
E:\examples\2>Listing2-2
Text : THEQUICKBROWNFOXJUMPSOVERTHELAZYDOG
Shift: 4
Cipher: XLIUYMGOFVSARJSBNYQTWSZIVXLIPEDCHSK
E:\examples\2>

Figure 2-9. *Execution of Caesar cipher*

The application is very simple and easy to interact with.

Listing 2-2. Source Code for Caesar Cipher Implementation

```
#include <iostream>
using namespace std;

// This function receives text and shift and
// returns the encrypted text
string encrypt(string text, int s)
{
    string result = "";
```

```
    // traverse text
    for (int i=0;i<text.length();i++)
    {
        // apply transformation to each character
        // Encrypt Uppercase letters
        if (isupper(text[i]))
            result += char(int(text[i]+s-65)%26 +65);

    // Encrypt Lowercase letters
    else
        result += char(int(text[i]+s-97)%26 +97);
    }

    // Return the resulting string
    return result;
}

// Driver program to test the above function
int main()
{
    string text="THEQUICKBROWNFOXJUMPSOVERTHELAZYDOG";
    int s = 4;
    cout << "Text : " << text;
    cout << "\nShift: " << s;
    cout << "\nCipher: " << encrypt(text, s);
    return 0;
}
```

Vigenére Cipher Implementation in C++23

The Vigenére cipher (see Figure 2-10 and Listing 2-3) is one of the classic methods of encrypting alphabetic text using a sequence of different Caesar ciphers based on keyword keys. You can see it in some of the documentations as a type of polyalphabetic substitution.

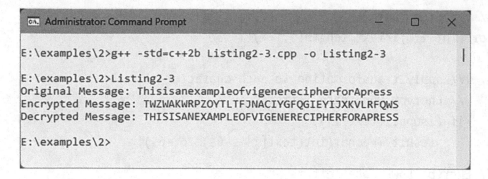

```
E:\examples\2>g++ -std=c++2b Listing2-3.cpp -o Listing2-3

E:\examples\2>Listing2-3
Original Message: Thisisanexampleofvigenerecipherfor Apress
Encrypted Message: TWZWAKWRPZOYTLTFJNACIYGFQGIEYIJXKVLRFQWS
Decrypted Message: THISISANEXAMPLEOFVIGENERECIPHERFORAPRESS

E:\examples\2>
```

Figure 2-10. *Vigenére cipher*

A short algebraic description of the cipher can be given as follows. The numbers are taken as numbers ($A = 0, B = 1$, etc.), and the addition operation is performed as *modulo* 26. The Vigenére encryption E using K as the key can be written as follows.

$$C_i = E_K(M_i) = (M_i + K_i) \bmod 26$$

Decryption D using the key K can be written as follows.

$$M_i = D_K(C_i) = (C_i - K_i) \bmod 26$$

$M = M_1...M_n$ is the message, $C = C_1...C_n$ represents the ciphertext and $K = K_1...K_n$ represents the key obtained by repeating the keyword $[n/m]$ times, in which m represents the keyword length.

Listing 2-3. Vigenére Source Code

```cpp
#include <iostream>
#include <string>
using namespace std;
class Vigenere {
    public:
        //** represents the key
      string key;

        //** the constructor of the class
        //** the chosen key
        Vigenere(string chosenKey) {
        for (int i = 0; i < chosenKey.size(); ++i) {
```

```
        if (chosenKey[i] >= 'A' && chosenKey[i] <= 'Z')
            this->key += chosenKey[i];
        else if (chosenKey[i] >= 'a' && chosenKey[i] <= 'z')
            this->key += chosenKey[i] + 'A' - 'a';
    }
}
string encrypt(string t)
{
    string encryptedOutput;
    for (int i = 0, j = 0; i < t.length(); ++i) {
        char c = t[i];
        if (c >= 'a' && c <= 'z')
            c += 'A' - 'a';
        else if (c < 'A' || c > 'Z')
            continue;
            //** added 'A' to bring it in range
            //** of ASCII alphabet [ 65-90 | A-Z ]
        encryptedOutput += (c + key[j] - 2 * 'A') % 26 + 'A';
        j = (j + 1) % key.length();
    }
    return encryptedOutput;
}
string decrypt(string t) {
    string decryptedOutput;
    for (int i = 0, j = 0; i < t.length(); ++i) {
        char c = t[i];
        if (c >= 'a' && c <= 'z')
            c += 'A' - 'a';
        else if (c < 'A' || c > 'Z')
            continue;

            //** added 'A' to bring it in range of
            //** ASCII alphabet [65-90 | A-Z]
        decryptedOutput += (c - key[j] + 26) % 26 + 'A';
        j = (j + 1) % key.length();
    }
```

```
        return decryptedOutput;}};
int main() {
    Vigenere myVigenere("APRESS! WELCOME");
    string originalMessage
                    ="ThisisanexampleofvigenerecipherforApress";
    string enc = myVigenere.encrypt(originalMessage);
    string dec = myVigenere.decrypt(enc);
    cout << "Original Message: "<<originalMessage<< endl;
    cout << "Encrypted Message: " << enc << endl;
    cout << "Decrypted Message: " << dec << endl;
}
```

Conclusion

This chapter introduced the fundamentals of cryptographic primitives and mechanisms. It covered the following.

- Security and information security objectives

- The importance of one-to-one, one-way, and trapdoor one-way functions in designing and implementing cryptographic functions

- Digital signatures and how they are working

- Public-key cryptography and how it impacts developing applications

- Hash functions

- Case studies illustrating the basic notions that you need to know before advancing to high-level cryptographic concepts

Chapter 3 goes through the basics of probability theory, information theory, number theory and finite fields. It discusses their importance and how they are related during the implementation already existent in C++ and how they are useful.

References

[1].   Simon Singh. *The Code Book: The Secrets Behind Codebreaking*, 2003.

[2].   W. Diffie and M. Hellman. 2006, New directions in cryptography. IEEE Trans. Information Theory. 22, 6 (September 2006), 644–654. DOI: `https://doi.org/10.1109/TIT.1976.1055638`.

[3].   R. L. Rivest, A. Shamir, and L. Adleman, A method for obtaining digital signatures and public-key cryptosystems, Communications ACM, vol. 21, no. 2, pp. 120–126, 1978.

[4].   ElGamal T., A Public Key Cryptosystem and a Signature Scheme Based on Discrete Logarithms. In: Blakley G.R., Chaum D. (eds) Advances in Cryptology. CRYPTO 1984. Lecture Notes in Computer Science, vol. 196. Springer, Berlin, Heidelberg.

[5].   ISO/IEC 9796-2:2010 – Information Technology – Security Techniques – Digital Signature schemes giving message recovery. Available online: `https://www.iso.org/standard/54788.html`.

[6].   Bruce Schneier and Phil Sutherland. 1995. Applied Cryptography: Protocols, Algorithms, and Source Code in C (2nd. ed.), ISBN: 978-0-471-12845-8. John Wiley & Sons, Inc., USA.

[7].   Stallings, William, and William Stallings. Cryptography and Network Security: Principles and Practice. Upper Saddle River, N.J: Prentice Hall, 1999. Print.

[8].   Douglas R. Stinson. 1995. Cryptography: Theory and Practice (1st. ed.), ISBN: 978-0-8493-8521-6, CRC Press, Inc., USA.

[9].   Koblitz, Neal. A Course in Number Theory and Cryptography. New York: Springer-Verlag, 1994. Print.

[10]. Koblitz, Neal, and A J. Menezes. Algebraic Aspects of Cryptography, 1999. Print.

[11]. Goldreich, Oded. Foundations of Cryptography: Basic Tools. Cambridge: Cambridge University Press, 2001. Print.

[12]. Goldreich, Oded. Modern Cryptography, Probabilistic Proofs and Pseudorandomness. Berlin: Springer, 1999. Print.

[13]. Luby, Michael G. Pseudorandomness and Cryptographic Applications. Princeton, NJ: Princeton University Press, 1996. Print.

[14]. Schneier, Bruce. *Secrets and Lies: Digital Security in a Networked World*. New York: John Wiley, 2000.

[15].   Peter Thorsteinson and Arun Ganesh, .NET Security and Cryptography. Prentice Hall Professional Technical Reference, 2003.

[16].   Adrian Atanasiu, Criptografie (Cryptography) – Volume 1, Publisher House: InfoData, 2007, ISBN: 978-973-1803-29-6, 978-973-1803-16-6. Available in Romanian Language.

[17].   Adrian Atanasiu, Protocoale de Securitate (Security Protocols) – Volume 2, Publisher House: InfoData, 2007, ISBN: 978-973-1803-29-6, 978-973-1803-16-6. Available in Romanian Language.

[18].   Alfred J. Menezes, Scott A. Vanstone, and Paul C. Van Oorschot. 1996. Handbook of Applied Cryptography (1st. ed.). CRC Press, Inc., USA, ISBN: 978-0-8493-8523-0.

[19].   Namespace System.Security.Cryptography, `https://docs.microsoft.com/en-us/dotnet/api/system.security.cryptography?view=netframework-4.8`.

[20].   Henri Cohen, Gerhard Frey, Roberto Avanzi, Christophe Doche, Tanja Lange, Kim Nguyen, and Frederik Vercauteren. 2012. Handbook of Elliptic and Hyperelliptic Curve Cryptography, Second Edition (2nd. ed.). Chapman & Hall/CRC.

[21].   OpenPGP Library for .NET. Available online: `https://www.didisoft.com/net-openpgp/`

[22].   Bouncy Castle .NET. Available online: `http://www.bouncycastle.org/csharp/`.

[23].   Nethereum. Available online: `https://github.com/Nethereum`.

[24].   Botan. Available online: `https://botan.randombit.net/`.

[25].   Cryptlib. Available online: `https://www.cs.auckland.ac.nz/~pgut001/cryptlib/`.

[26].   Crypto++. Available online: `https://www.cryptopp.com/`.

[27].   Libgcrypt. Available online: `https://gnupg.org/software/libgcrypt/`.

[28].   Libsodium. Available online: `https://nacl.cr.yp.to/`.

[29].   Nettle. Available online: `https://www.lysator.liu.se/~nisse/nettle/`.

[30].   OpenSSL. Available online: `https://www.openssl.org/`.

[31].   Guo J., Karpman P., Nikolić I., Wang L., Wu S. (2014) Analysis of BLAKE2. In: Benaloh J. (eds) Topics in Cryptology – CT-RSA 2014. CT-RSA 2014. Lecture Notes in Computer Science, vol. 8366. Springer, Cham.

[32].   Blake3. Available online: `https://github.com/BLAKE3-team/BLAKE3/`.

[33].   H. Krawczyk, M. Bellare, R. Canetti – HMAC: ekyed – Hashing for Message
         Authenticatio, RFC 2104, 1997.

[34].   API KMAC. Available online: `https://www.cryptosys.net/manapi/api_`
         `kmac.html`.

[35].   NIST Special Publication 800-185, *SHA-3 Derived Functions: cSHAKE, KMAC,*
         TupleHash and ParallelHash, John Kelsey, Shu-jen Chang, Ray Perlner,
         National Institute of Standards and Technology, December 2016.

[36].   I.B. Damgard, A design principle for hash functions, LNCS 435 (1990),
         pp. 516-527.

[37].   Ronal L. Rivest, The MD6 hash function. A proposal to NIST for
         SHA-3. Available online: `http://groups.csail.mit.edu/cis/md6/`
         `submitted-2008-10-27/Supporting_Documentation/md6_report.pdf`.

[38].   PMAC. Available online: `https://web.cs.ucdavis.edu/~rogaway/ocb/`
         `pmac.htm`.

[39].   UMAC. Available : `http://fastcrypto.org/umac/`.

[40].   BLAKE-256. Available : `https://docs.decred.org/research/blake-256-`
         `hash-function/`.

[41].   Biham, Eli; Dunkelman, Orr (24 August 2006). A Framework for Iterative
         Hash Functions - HAIFA. Second NIST Cryptographic Hash Workshop – via
         Cryptology ePrint Archive: Report 2007/278.

[42].   BLAKE2 Official Implementation. Available online: `https://github.com/`
         `BLAKE2/BLAKE2`.

[43].   GOST. Available online: `https://tools.ietf.org/html/rfc5830`.

[44].   Roland L. Rivest, The MD4 message digest algorithm, LNCS, 537, 1991,
         pp. 303-311.

[45].   Roland L. Rivest, The MD5 message digest algorithm, RFC 1321, 1992.

[46].   RIPEMD-128. Available online:

[47].   `https://homes.esat.kuleuven.be/~bosselae/ripemd/rmd128.txt`.

[48].   RIPEMD-160. Available online:

[49].   `https://homes.esat.kuleuven.be/~bosselae/ripemd160.html`.

[50].   RIPEMD-160. Available online: `https://ehash.iaik.tugraz.at/wiki/`
         `RIPEMD-160`.

[51].   Sponge and Duplex Construction.

[52].   Available online: `https://keccak.team/sponge_duplex.html`.

[53].   Henri Gilbert, Helena Handschuh: Security Analysis of SHA-256 and Sisters. Selected Areas in Cryptography 2003: pp175–193.

[54].   SHA256 .NET Class. Available online: `https://docs.microsoft.com/en-us/dotnet/api/system.security.cryptography.sha256?view=netframework-4.8`.

[55].   SHA384 .NET Class. Available online: `https://docs.microsoft.com/en-us/dotnet/api/system.security.cryptography.sha384?view=netframework-4.8`.

[56].   SHA512 .NET Class. Available online: `https://docs.microsoft.com/en-us/dotnet/api/system.security.cryptography.sha512?view=netframework-4.8`.

[57].   Descriptions of SHA-256, SHA-384, and SHA-512. Available online: `http://www.iwar.org.uk/comsec/resources/cipher/sha256-384-512.pdf`.

[58].   A 224-bit One-way Hash Function: SHA 224. Available online: `http://www.iwar.org.uk/comsec/resources/cipher/sha256-384-512.pdf`.

[59].   Hernandez, Paul (5 August 2015). "NIST Releases SHA-3 Cryptographic Hash Standard."

[60].   Dworkin, Morris J. (4 August 2015). "SHA-3 Standard: Permutation-Based Hash and Extendable-Output Functions." Federal Inf. Process. STDS. (NIST FIPS) – 202.

[61].   Paulo S. L. M. Barreto (2008-11-25). "The WHIRLPOOL Hash Function." Archived from the original on 2017-11-29. Retrieved 2018-08-09.

[62].   Whirlpool C# Implementation. Available online: `http://csharptest.net/browse/src/Library/Crypto/WhirlpoolManaged.cs`.

[63].   Xiaoyun Wang, Yiqun Lisa Yin, and Hongbo Yu, Finding Collisions in the Full SHA-1, Crypto 2005.

CHAPTER 3

Mathematical Background and Its Applicability

Mathematics is an important element of cryptography for many reasons. For example, many cryptographic algorithms produce unique and safe keys using mathematical concepts such as number theory, algebra, and probability theory. On the other hand, mathematics ensures that data remain encrypted and secure, as any attempt to break an algorithm must use math to identify weaknesses or vulnerabilities. Because its concepts are employed to build and apply algorithms, mathematics facilitates developing novel cryptographic protocols. For example, public key cryptography relies on mathematical problems that are thought difficult to solve, such as factorization and the discrete logarithm, making it difficult for an attacker to crack the encryption.

Similarly, symmetric key cryptography employs mathematical functions such as block ciphers and hash functions to ensure that only someone with the right key can decrypt the encrypted data.

Mathematics is the foundation for cryptography and its applications, making it a critical component of any encryption technique. This chapter discusses the importance of probability theory and its tools for modern cryptography. It shows how the elements and notions from probability theory can be implemented in real-life applications and programs and explains the most important steps that a professional cryptographer follows in implementing cryptographic algorithms.

The applications of probability theory to cryptography represent one of the challenging sides of cryptography and cryptanalysis. Between 1941 and 1942, Alain Turing (1912–1954) wrote the paper *The Applications of Probability to Cryptography*,[1] which was released by Government Communications Headquarters (GCHQ) to the

---

[1] The Applications of Probability to Cryptography, https://arxiv.org/abs/1505.04714.

© Marius Iulian Mihailescu and Stefania Loredana Nita 2023
M. I. Mihailescu and S. L. Nita, *Pro Cryptography and Cryptanalysis with C++23*,
https://doi.org/10.1007/978-1-4842-9450-5_3

National Archives, HW/25/37[2]. The paper written by Alan Turing describes some of the methods with application for probability theory for cracking the codes. He started his paper with the Vigenère cipher. Alan Turing brought proofs for the practical side by introducing and designing a unique method, its goal being to hide the entire complexity of mathematical apparatus in cryptography, reducing the process to a simple exercise using regular addition and trial and error. The tools introduced by him in the paper were *logarithms* and *probability*. It was necessary to understand how the cipher worked to fully understand how the tools were applied.

The concepts introduced in this chapter help practitioners understand basic mathematics to give a full appreciation to the solutions developed later.

Each mathematical concept has a quick presentation of the equations and mathematical expressions used during the implementation of the algorithms, providing examples of implementation in C++. The implementations are presented as case studies, counted from 1 to 10.

Probabilities

Probability theory is a key component in cryptography, as it helps to generate secure encryption keys by providing a greater sense of randomness. This is achieved by introducing a degree of uncertainty, which helps to make it difficult and time-consuming for a hacker to guess the correct encryption key. Probability theory is also used to assess the likelihood of a given encryption key being guessed or broken, enabling organizations to monitor and adjust their levels of security accordingly.

Overall, probability theory helps to strengthen cryptography by providing a greater sense of randomness and unpredictability. For example, in symmetric key cryptosystems, the system's security depends on the key's randomness. Probability theory could be utilized to evaluate the distribution of keys and the probability that an attacker can guess the correct key. Probability theory is used in public key cryptography to evaluate the security of mathematical problems that are the foundation of encryption, such as factoring big integers.

This section presents the main concepts, giving the most appropriate definitions of *experiment, probability distribution, event, complementary event,* and *mutually*

---

[2] Alan Turing Wartime Research Papers Released by GCHQ, `https://discovery.nationalarchives.gov.uk/details/r/C11510465`

exclusiveness. The definitions are given so that the professionals find the intersection between theory and practice in a very fashionable and easy way to follow. The concepts described in this chapter are helpful to having a clear understanding of the basics of cryptographic and cryptanalysis mechanisms and how they are projected using probabilities [1].

Definition 3.1 [1]. An *experiment* can be seen as a procedure producing one of the mentioned outcomes. Each of the outcomes is individual. The ones that are possible are called simple events. The whole set formed out of the possible outcomes is well known as the *sample space.*

The following discusses *discrete* sample spaces that have limited possible outcomes. The simple events of a sample space are written as S, labeled $s_1, s_2, ..., s_n$.

Definition 3.2 [1]. The probability distribution K over S is defined by a sequence of numbers $k_1, k_2, ..., k_n \geq 0$, and the sum of those numbers is equal to 1 ($k_1 + k_2 + ... + k_n = 1$). The number o_i can be interpreted as the *probability* of g_i. This is the outcome (result) of the processing experiment.

Definition 3.3 [1]. The *event E* represents a subset of the sample space S. In this situation, the *probability* that event E will occur denoted as $P(E)$, is defined as the sum of the probabilities o_i for all simple events g_i that belong to E. If $g_i \in S$, $P(\{s_i\})$ is simply denoted as $P(s_i)$.

Definition 3.4 [1]. Let's consider E as an event, and the *complementary event* is defined as being the set of simple events that do not belong to E, denoted as $\bar{E}$.

Demonstration 3.1 [1]. If $E \subseteq S$ represents an event, the following should be considered.

- $0 \leq P(E) \leq 1$. In addition, $P(S) = 1$ and $P(\phi) = 0$, where ϕ represents an empty set.

- $P(\bar{E}) = 1 - P(E)$.

- If the results in S are just as likely, we can consider $P(E) = \dfrac{|E|}{|S|}$.

Definition 3.5 [1]. Consider E_1 and E_2, two *mutually exclusive* events. They are mutually exclusive if $P(E_1 \cap E_2) = 0$. The showing nature of one or two events will have the chance to exclude the case that others have the possibility of taking place.

Definition 3.6 [1]. Take as an example the next two events, E_1 and E_2.

- $P(E_1) \leq P(E_2)$ if $E_1 \subseteq P(E_2)$.

- $P(E_1 \cup E_2) + P(E_1 \cap E_2) = P(E_1) + P(E_2)$. Accordingly, if E_1 and E_2 are considered mutually exclusive, then the following expression takes place $P(E_1 \cup E_2) = P(E_1) + P(E_2)$.

Conditional Probability

Definition 3.7 [1]. Let's consider E_1 and E_2 as two events, with $P(E_2) > 0$. The *conditional probability* for E_1 to give E_2 is written as $P(E_1|E_2)$ and is expressed as follows.

$$P(E_1|E_2) = \frac{P(E_1 \cap E_2)}{P(E_2)}$$

$P(E_1|E_2)$ measures the probability of how event E_1 takes place, given that E_2 has occurred.

Definition 3.8 [1]. Consider E_1 and E_2 as two events. Their relationship is one of *independency* if $P(E1 \cap E_2) = P(E_1)P(E_2)$.

Definition 3.9 (*Bayes' Theorem*) [1]. If we have two events E_1 and E_2 with $P(E_2) > 0$, then

$$P(E_1|E_2) = \frac{P(E_1)P(E_2|E_1)}{P(E_2)}$$

Random Variables

Let's consider a sample space S that has the distribution probability P.

Definition 3.10 [1]. Let X be a *random variable*. Declare a function that is applied on S for the set of real numbers. For each event $s_i \in S$, X there is a real number assigned $X(s_i)$.

Definition 3.11 [1]. Let X be the random variable on S. The *mean* or *expected value* of X is defined as follows.

$$E(X) = \sum_{s_i \in S} X(s_i)P(s_i)$$

For C++ implementation of the mean or expected value, refer to Case Study 3: Computing the Mean of Probability Distribution.

Definition 3.12 [1]. Consider X to be a random variable on S. In this case, the mean can be also expressed as follows:

$$E(X) = \sum_{x \in \mathbb{R}} x \cdot P(X = x)$$

Definition 3.13 [1]. Let's consider the following random variables on S: $X_1, X_2, ..., X_m$. The following are real numbers: $a_1, a_2, ..., a_m$, then the following expression needs to be satisfied.

$$E\left(\sum_{i=1}^{m} a_i X_i\right) = \sum_{i=1}^{m} a_i E(X_i)$$

Definition 3.14. Let's consider X the random variable. The *variance* of X of mean μ is defined by the nonnegative number that is expressed by

$$Var(X) = E\left((X - \mu)^2\right)$$

For C++ implementation of the mean or expected value, refer to Case Study 4: Computing the Variance.

The standard deviation of X is defined by the nonnegative square root of $Var(X)$.

For C++ implementation of the mean or expected value, refer to Case Study 5: Computing the Standard Deviation.

Birthday Problem

Definition 3.15 [1]. Consider two positive integers a, b with $a \geq b$, where the number $m^{(n)}$ is defined as follows.

$$m^{(n)} = m(m-1)(m-2)...(m-n+1)$$

Definition 3.15 [1]. Consider two nonnegative integers a, b with $a \geq b$. The *Stirling number of the second kind* is represented and noted as $\begin{Bmatrix} a \\ b \end{Bmatrix}$, is expressed as follows.

$$\begin{Bmatrix} a \\ b \end{Bmatrix} = \frac{1}{b!} \sum_{i=0}^{n} (-1)^{b-i} \binom{b}{i} i^{a}$$

The case of $\begin{Bmatrix} 0 \\ 0 \end{Bmatrix} = 1$ is considered an exception.

Demonstration 3.16 [1]. As an example, consider the classical occupancy problem by illustrating our example by showing the example with an urn that contains a balls. The balls are numbered (or labeled) with 1 to m. Let's imagine a scenario in which b balls are being extracted from the urn one at a time and being replaced at the same time, with their numbers being listed. The chance (probability) for l different balls to have been drawn is

$$P_1(a,b,l) = \begin{Bmatrix} b \\ l \end{Bmatrix} \frac{a^{(l)}}{a^{b}}, 1 \le l \le b$$

The birthday problem represents a special case of the occupancy problem.

Demonstration 3.17 [1]. Consider the birthday problem, where we have a jar with a balls numbered from 1 to a. Assume that a specific number of balls, h, are extracted from the urn one at a time, having them replaced, with their numbers listed.

Case 3.17.1 [1]. Consider the probability of at least one coincidence, such as a ball drawn at least twice from the urn, as follows.

$$P_2(a,h) = 1 - P_1(a,h,h) = 1 - \frac{a^{(h)}}{a^{h}}, 1 \le h \le m$$

Case 3.17.2 [1]. Let's consider h the number of balls extracted from the jar. If $h = O(\sqrt{a})$ and $a \to \infty$, then the following expression takes place.

$$P_2(a,h) \to 1 - \exp\left(-\frac{h(h-1)}{2a} + O\left(\frac{1}{\sqrt{a}} \right) \right) \approx 1 - \exp\left(-\frac{h^2}{2a} \right).$$

The demonstration explains why the probability distribution is known and the *birthday surprise* or *birthday paradox*. The probability that at least 2 people in a room with 23 people have the same birthday is $P_2(365, 23) \approx 0.507$, which is surprisingly large. The quantity $P_2(365, h)$ increases as h increases; for example, $P_2(365, 30) \approx 0.706$.

For C++ implementation of the *birthday paradox*, refer to Case Study 6: Birthday Paradox.

Information Theory

Because it provides a mathematical framework for quantifying information and assessing a system's entropy or randomness, information theory is fundamental for cryptography. Information theory is used in cryptography to calculate how much information an attacker may gain from an encrypted communication and how much randomness is necessary to ensure the security of a cryptographic system. For example, information theory may be used to evaluate the entropy of random number generators, which are utilized in many cryptographic systems for generating keys.

Therefore, the security of the system can be analyzed, and whether the keys are sufficiently random to prevent attackers from guessing the proper key by estimating the entropy of the generator can be checked. Information theory is also used to assess the security of encryption methods and calculate the minimum key length necessary to achieve a specific degree of security.

Furthermore, information theory provides a method for computing the quantity of information revealed by a cryptographic system. Information theory, for example, can be used to evaluate the information released by a ciphertext or side channel attacks such as timing attacks or power analysis. This information may be used to improve system security and uncover possible flaws.

Entropy

Let's denote with X a random variable that takes on a finite set of value $x_1, x_2, ..., x_n$, with the probability $P(X = x_i) = p_i$, where $0 \leq p_i \leq 1$ for each i, $1 \leq i \leq n$, in which the following sum expression takes place.

$$\sum_{i=1}^{n} p_i = 1$$

Additionally, let's declare Y and Z random variables that take a finite set of values [1].

The entropy of A is defined as a mathematical measure that is characterized as the amount of information that is provided by an observation o.

Definition 3.18 [1]. Let's denote A as a random variable. The *entropy* or uncertainty of A is defined by the following expression.

$$H(A) = -\sum_{j=1}^{m} p_j \lg p_j = \sum_{j=1}^{m} p_j \lg\left(\frac{1}{p_j}\right)$$

Through convention,

$$p_i \cdot \lg p_i = p_i \cdot \lg \left(\frac{1}{p_i} \right) = 0 \text{, if } p_i = 0$$

Definition 3.19 [1][5]. Let's consider A and B, two random variables. The *joint entropy* is defined by the following expression.

$$H(A,B) = \sum_{a,b} P(A=a,B=b) \lg \big(P(A=a,B=b) \big)$$

a and b go through all the values within the random variables, A and B.

Definition 3.20 [1]. Let's consider the following two random variables A and B, and suppose that the *conditional entropy* of A given $B = m$ is expressed as

$$H(A|B=v) = -\sum_{m} P(A=m|B=v) \lg \big(P(A=m|B=v) \big)$$

m goes through all over the values within the random variable A. In this case, the *conditional entropy* of A given B, also called the *equivocation* of B about A, is declared as

$$H(A|B) = \sum_{m} P(B=m) H(A|B=m)$$

m (an index) goes through all the values of B.

Number Theory

Number theory is very important in cryptography because many cryptographic techniques are based on mathematical problems addressed in number theory. Number theory also secures other cryptographic techniques, such as elliptic-curve cryptography. Additionally, techniques of number theory may be used to produce random prime numbers. Number theory also serves as a foundation for examining the security of cryptographic systems, such as by offering a method for studying key distribution and measuring the entropy of random number generators.

Integers

Starting from the idea that a set of integers $\{..., -3, -2, -1, 0, 1, 2, 3, ...\}$ is represented by the symbol Z, the following definitions occur.

Definition 3.21 [1]. Let's assume that we have two integers, x and y. Start from the idea that x *divides* y if there exists an integer d such that $y = x \cdot d$. If x is dividing y, then $x \mid y$.

Definition 3.22 (Division algorithm for integers) [1]. Consider two integers, x and y with $y \geq 1$; then, we have an ordinary long division of x by y that holds the integers *quot* (*quotient*) and *rem* (*remainder*) in such a way that

$$x = qout \cdot y + rem, \text{ where} 0 \leq rem < y$$

Definition 3.23 [1]. Consider d as an integer. Note that the *common divisor* of x and y exists if $d \mid x$ and $d \mid y$.

Definition 3.24 [1]. Assume that we have nonnegative integer e. The nonnegative integer e is known as the *greatest common divisor (gcd)* of the integers x and y. Note it as $e = \gcd(x, y)$ if

    a. e is a common divisor x and y

    b. $d \mid x$ and $d \mid y$, then $d \mid e$

Definition 3.25 [1]. Assume that we have nonnegative integer e. The nonnegative integer e is the *least common multiple (lcm)* of integers x and y. Note it as $e = lcm(x, y)$ if

    a. $x \mid e$ and $y \mid e$

    b. $x \mid d$ and $x \mid d$, then $e \mid d$

Algorithms in $\mathbb{Z}$

Let's consider two nonnegative integers, a and b, with $a \leq n$. Note that the number of bits from the binary representation of n is represented as $\lfloor lg\, n \rfloor + 1$. This value is approximated by $lg\, n$. The number of bit operations related to the four basic operations for integers is using the classical algorithms, as shown in Table 3-1.

Table 3-1. *The Bit Complexity of the Basic Operation in Z*

Operation	Bit complexity
Addition $a + b$	$O(lga + lgb) = O(lgn)$
Subtraction $a - b$	$O(lga + lgb) = O(lgn)$
Multiplication $a \cdot b$	$O((lga)(lgb)) = O((lgn)^2)$
Division $a = q \cdot b + r$	$O((lgq)(lgb)) = O((lgn)^2)$

Definition 3.26 [1]. The integers a and b are positive numbers with $a > b$, then we have $\gcd(a, b) = \gcd(b, a \bmod b)$.

Algorithm 3.27 *[1]. Euclidean algorithm for computing* **gcd** *for two integers*

INPUT :   *a and b, two non − negative integers with respect for $a \geq b$*

OUTPUT :   *the* gcd

1.   *while $b \neq 0$ then*

$$1.1. \ \ Set \ r \leftarrow a \bmod b, \ \ a \leftarrow b, b \leftarrow r$$

2.   *Return (a)*

The Euclidean algorithm can be extended so that it does not only yield the *gcd* of two integers *a* and *b* but also integers *x* and *y*, which satisfy $ax + by = d$.

Algorithm 3.28 *[1]. Pseudocode for extended Euclidean algorithm*

INPUT :   *x and y, non − negative numbers with the following condition $a \geq b$*

OUTPUT : *$h = \gcd(x,y)$ and integers w, z which satisfy $xw + yz = h$*

1.   *if $y = 0$ then*

    $h \leftarrow x$

    $w \leftarrow 1$

    $z \leftarrow 0$

    $return(h, w, z)$

2.   *declare and initialize $w_2 \leftarrow 1, w_1 \leftarrow 0, z_2 \leftarrow 0, z_1 \leftarrow 1$*

3.   *while y > 0 then*

3.1.   *quotient* $\leftarrow \dfrac{x}{y}$

remainder $\leftarrow x - quotient \cdot y$

$w \leftarrow w_2 - quotient \cdot w_1 ; z \leftarrow z_2 - quotient \cdot z_1$

3.2. $x \leftarrow y$
y $\leftarrow$ *remainder*

$w_2 \leftarrow w_1$

$w_1 \leftarrow w$

$z_2 \leftarrow z_1$

$z_1 \leftarrow z$

4.   *Set h* $\leftarrow x, w \leftarrow w_2, z \leftarrow z_2$

$return(h,w,z)$

Case Study 7: (Extended) Euclidean Algorithm provides an example of an implementation using C++ for both algorithms—Euclidean and the extended Euclidean.

Integers Modulo *n*

Let's consider *p* a positive integer.

Definition 2.30 [1]. Let *i* and *j* be two integers. We allege that g *is congruent to j modulo q*. The notation used is

$$i \equiv j \,(mod\, q), \text{ if } q \text{ will divide}(i - j)$$

q is called the *modulus* of congruence.

Definition 3.31 [1]. Be $n \in \mathbb{Z}_q$. The *multiplicative inverse* of *n* modulo *q* is represented by an integer $x \in \mathbb{Z}_q$ in such a way that $n\,x \equiv 1\,(mod\, q)$. If there is an *n* that exists, then *n* is unique, and we state that *n* is *invertible* or a *unit*. The inverse of *n* is noted asn^{-1}.

Case Study 8: Computing the multiplicative inverse under modulo q gives a C++ implementation of the multiplicative inverse under modulo q.

Definition 3.32. Chine Remainder Theorem (CRT) [1]. The integers n_1, n_2, ..., n_k represent a pairwise (occurring in pairs) that is relatively prim. Let's consider the following system formed out of simultaneous congruence.

$$j \equiv v_1 \ (mod \ g_1)$$

$$j \equiv v_2 \ (mod \ g_2)$$

$$\vdots$$

$$l \equiv v_n \ (mod \ g_k)$$

It is a system that has a unique solution modulo, $g = g_1 \, g_2 \cdots g_k$.

Case Study 9: Chinese Remainder Theorem provides a C++ implementation of the Chinese Remainder Theorem.

Definition 3.33. Gauss's Algorithm [1]. As you saw in the Chinese Remainder Theorem, the solution y for concurrent congruence may be calculated as $y = \sum_{h=1}^{l} b_h \cdot R_h \cdot L_h \ mod \ q$, where $R_i = q/q_h$ and $L_h = R_h^{-1} \ mod \ q_i$. The listed operations can be performed in $O((lgq)^2)$ bit operations.

Algorithms $\mathbb{Z}_m$

Be a positive integer m. As you have seen, the elements of Z_m is positive, then

$$(x+y) \, mod \, q = \begin{cases} x+y, & if \ x+y < q, \\ x+y-q, & if \ x+y \geq \end{cases}$$

Algorithm 3.34 [1]. Pseudocode for computing the multiplicative inverses inZm

$INPUT: \quad x \in \mathbb{Z}_m$

$OUTPUT: \quad x^{-1} \ mod \ m$

1. *Use Extended Euclidean algorithm and find the integers w and z such that xw + nz = h, where h = gcd (x, n)*

2. *If h > 1, we will have x^{-1} mod q which will not exist. Else, return (w).*

***Algorithm 3.35** [1]. Repeated square-and-multiply algorithm for exponentiation in Z_m*

INPUT : $x \in \mathbb{Z}_m$, and integer $0 \le t < m$ whose binary representation is $t = \sum_{j=0}^{o} t_j 2^j$.

OUTPUT : x^t mod m

1. *Set $y \leftarrow 1$. If t = 0 then return(y)*

2. *Set $C \leftarrow x$*

3. *If $t_0 = 1$ then set $y \leftarrow x$*

4. *For j from 1 to k do:*

   4.1. *Set $C \leftarrow C^2$ mod m*

   4.2. *If $t_j = 1$ then set $y \leftarrow C \cdot y$ mod m*

5. *return(y)*

The Legendre and Jacobi Symbols

The Legendre symbol represents the perfect tool for this purpose to check if an integer is a quadratic residue in a specific modulo.

Definition 3.36 [1]. Be q an odd prime and x an integer. The Legendre symbol, denoted as $\left(\dfrac{x}{q} \right)$, is defined as follows.

$$\left(\frac{x}{q} \right) = \begin{cases} 0, & if\ q\ |\ x \\ 1, & if\ x \in W_q\ . \\ -1, & if\ x \in \overline{W_q} \end{cases}$$

Property 3.37. Properties of the Legendre Symbol [1]. The following properties are considered. The following properties are known as the properties of the Legendre symbol. For the following properties, consider m to be an odd prime. Let's declare two integers $x, y \in Z$. The next properties specific to the Legendre symbol are listed as follows.

1. $\left(\dfrac{x}{m}\right) \equiv x^{\frac{m-1}{2}} \pmod{m}$. In particular, $\left(\dfrac{1}{m}\right) = 1$ and $\left(\dfrac{-1}{m}\right) = (-1)^{\frac{m-1}{2}}$.

    Since $-1 \in W_m$ if $m \equiv 1 \pmod{4}$ and $-1 \in \overline{W_m}$ if $m \equiv 3 \pmod{4}$.

2. $\left(\dfrac{xy}{m}\right) = \left(\dfrac{x}{m}\right)\left(\dfrac{y}{m}\right)$. Since if $x \in \mathbb{Z}_q^*$, then $\left(\dfrac{x^2}{m}\right) = 1$.

3. If $x \equiv y \pmod{m}$, then $\left(\dfrac{x}{m}\right) = \left(\dfrac{y}{m}\right)$.

4. $\left(\dfrac{2}{m}\right) = (-1)^{\frac{(m^2-1)}{8}}$. Since $\left(\dfrac{2}{m}\right) = 1$ if $m \equiv 1$ or $7 \pmod{8}$, and

    $\left(\dfrac{2}{m}\right) = -1$ if $m \equiv 3$ or $5 \pmod{8}$.

5. If m represents an odd prime distinct from p,

    $$\left(\dfrac{t}{m}\right) = \left(\dfrac{m}{t}\right)(-1)^{\frac{(t-1)(m-1)}{4}}.$$

The Jacobi symbol represents a generalization of the Legendre symbol for integers n, which are not odd and are not necessarily prime.

Definition 3.38. Jacobi Definition [1]. Let $m \geq 3$ represent an odd with a prime factorization as follows.

$$m = v_1^{h_1} v_2^{h_2} \ldots v_j^{h_j}$$

The Jacobi symbol $\left(\dfrac{x}{m}\right)$ has the following expression.

$$\left(\dfrac{x}{m}\right) = \left(\dfrac{x}{m_1}\right)^{h_1}\left(\dfrac{x}{m_2}\right)^{h_2}\ldots\left(\dfrac{x}{m_j}\right)^{h_j}$$

Consider that if n is prime, the Jacobi symbol is the Legendre symbol.

Property 3.39. Jacobi Symbol Properties [1]. Consider $x \geq 3$ and $y \geq 3$ as odd integers, and $i, j \in \mathbb{Z}$. The Jacobi symbol has the following properties.

1. $\left(\dfrac{i}{y}\right) = 0, 1, or -1$. Moreover, $\left(\dfrac{i}{y}\right) = 0$ if and only if $\gcd(i, y) \neq 1$.

2. $\left(\dfrac{ij}{y}\right) = \left(\dfrac{i}{y}\right)\left(\dfrac{j}{y}\right)$. Hence, if $i \in \mathbb{Z}_m^*$, then $\left(\dfrac{i}{y}\right) = 1$.

3. $\left(\dfrac{i}{yx}\right) = \left(\dfrac{i}{y}\right)\left(\dfrac{i}{x}\right)$.

4. If $i \equiv j \,(mod\, y)$, then $\left(\dfrac{i}{y}\right) = \left(\dfrac{j}{y}\right)$.

5. $\left(\dfrac{1}{y}\right) = 1$.

6. $\left(\dfrac{-1}{y}\right) = (-1)^{\frac{(y-1)}{2}}$. Hence, $\left(\dfrac{-1}{y}\right) = 1$ if $y \equiv 1 \,(mod\, 4)$, and $\left(\dfrac{-1}{y}\right) = -1$ if $y \equiv (3 \, mod\, 4)$.

7. $\left(\dfrac{2}{y}\right) = (-1)^{\frac{y^2-1}{8}}$. Hence, $\left(\dfrac{2}{y}\right) = 1$ if $y \equiv 1$ or $7 \,(mod\, 8)$, and $\left(\dfrac{2}{y}\right) = -1$ if $y \equiv 3$ or $5 \,(mod\, 8)$.

8. $\left(\dfrac{x}{y}\right) = \left(\dfrac{y}{x}\right)(-1)^{\frac{(x-1)(y-1)}{4}}$. In other words, $\left(\dfrac{x}{y}\right) = \left(\dfrac{y}{x}\right)$ unless both x and y are congruent to 3 modulo 4, in which case $\left(\dfrac{x}{y}\right) = -\left(\dfrac{y}{x}\right)$.

Algorithm 3.40. *Pseudocode of Jacobi Symbol. Pseudocode for Legendre symbol [1]*

$JACOBI\,(h,k)$

$INPUT:$ *odd integer $k \geq 3$ and an integer $h, 0 \leq h < k$*

$OUTPUT:$ *the Jacobi symbol* $\left(\dfrac{h}{k}\right)$

1. *If $h = 0$ then return 0.*

2. *If $h = 1$ then return 1.*

3. *Write $h = 2^t h_1$, where h_1 is odd.*

4. *If t is even then set $g \leftarrow 1$. Else set $g \leftarrow 1$ if $k \equiv 1$ or $7 \ (mod\ 8)$, or set $g \leftarrow -1$ if $k \equiv 3$ or $5 \ (mod\ 8)$.*

5. *If $k \equiv 3 \ (mod\ 4)$ and $h_1 \equiv 3 \ (mod\ 4)$ then set $g \leftarrow -g$.*

6. *Set $k_1 \leftarrow k \ mod \ h_1$.*

7. *If $h_1 = 1$ then return(g); else return $(g \cdot JACOBI(k_1, h_1))$.*

Finite Fields

Finite fields, also known as Galois fields, are used in cryptography because they provide a mathematical basis for specifying mathematical operations on a finite number of components. In cryptography, finite fields are mainly used to construct efficient algorithms for encryption and decryption, or they can be used to define mathematical problems, such as the discrete logarithm problem.

Basic Notions

Definition 3.41 [1]. Consider F to be a *finite field* that contains a finite number of elements. The *order of F* represents the number of elements in F.

Definition 3.42 [1]. The finite fields are characterized by a special uniqueness.

1. Let's assume that if P represents a finite field, then P contains h^j elements for a prime h and integer $j \geq 1$.

2. For each prime power order h^j, there is a unique finite field of order h^j. The field is noted as $\mathbb{G}_{h_j}$, or in some other literature references, we find $GF(h^j)$.

Definition 3.43 [1][5]. Let's say that if G_h represents a finite field of order $h = a^m$ and a is a prime, then the characteristic of $\mathbb{F}_h$ is p. Moreover, h has a copy of $\mathbb{Z}_a$ as a subfield. $\mathbb{F}_h$ can be viewed as an extension field of $\mathbb{Z}_a$ of degree m.

Polynomials and the Euclidean Algorithm

The following two algorithms represent the foundation for understanding how to compute and obtain *gcd* for two polynomials, $g(x)$ and $h(x)$, both of which are in $\mathbb{Z}_p[x]$.

Algorithm 3.43. *Euclidean Algorithm for* $\mathbb{Z}_p[x]$ *[1]*

$INPUT:$ *two polynomials* $g(x), h(x) \in \mathbb{Z}_p[x]$

$OUTPUT:$ gcd *of* $g(x)$ *and* $h(x)$

1. *while* $h(x) \neq 0$ *then*

    a. *set* $r(x) \leftarrow g(x)\ mod\ h(x)$, $g(x) \leftarrow h(x)$, $h(x) \leftarrow r(x)$

2. *return* $g(x)$

Algorithm 3.43. *Extended Euclidean Algorithm for* $\mathbb{Z}_p[x]$ *[1]*

$INPUT:$ *two polynomials* $g(x), h(x) \in \mathbb{Z}_p[x]$

$OUTPUT:$ $d(x) = \gcd\big(g(x), h(x)\big)$ *and polynomials* $s(x), t(x)$
         $\in \mathbb{Z}_p[x]$*which will satisfy* $s(x)g(x) + t(x)h(x) = d(x)$.

1. If $h(x) = 0$ *then set* $d(x) \leftarrow g(x)$, $s(x) \leftarrow 1$, $t(x) \leftarrow 0$

    a. *return* $(d(x), s(x), t(x))$

2. Set $s_2(x) \leftarrow 1$, $s_1(x) \leftarrow 0$, $t_2(x) \leftarrow 0$, $t_1(x) \leftarrow 1$.

3. while $h(x) \neq 0$ *then*

    a. $g(x) \leftarrow g(x)\ div\ h(x)$, $r(x) \leftarrow g(x) - h(x)q(x)$

    b. $s(x) \leftarrow s_2(x) - q(x)s_1(x)$, $t(x) \leftarrow t_2(x) - q(x)t_1(x)$

    c. $g(x) \leftarrow h(x)$, $h(x) \leftarrow r(x)$

    d. $s_{2(x)} \leftarrow s_1(x)$, $s_1(x) \leftarrow s(x)$, $t_2(x) \leftarrow t_1(x)$, *and* $t_1(x) \leftarrow t(x)$

4. Set $d(x) \leftarrow g(x)$, $s(x) \leftarrow s_2(x)$, $t(x) \leftarrow t_2(x)$.

5. return $d(x)$, $s(x)$, $t(x)$.

Case Study 1: Computing the Probability of an Event That Takes Place

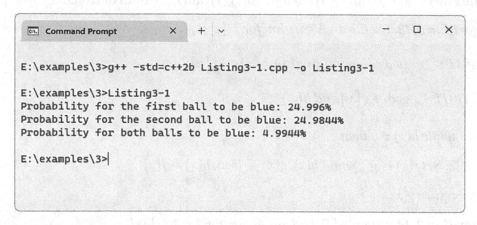

Figure 3-1. *Output for computing the probability*

Listing 3-1. Source Code

```
#include <iostream>
#include <vector>
#include <random>
#include <algorithm>

enum ColorTypes {
    Blue,
    NotBlue } ;

//** create a sequence container
typedef std::vector<ColorTypes> backpack;

backpack initializeBackpack(unsigned blue_balls, unsigned
                                            differentBalls)
{
    backpack backpackOfBalls ;

    for (unsigned i=0; i<blue_balls; ++i)
        backpackOfBalls.emplace_back(Blue);
```

```
    for (unsigned i=0; i<differentBalls; ++i)
        backpackOfBalls.emplace_back(NotBlue);

    return backpackOfBalls;        }

void randomize(backpack & backpackOfBalls) {
    //** Mersenne Twister - pseudo-random generator
    //** on 32-bit number using the state size of 19937 bits/
    //** std:random_device() will help us generate a
    //** nondeterministic random numbers
    static std::mt19937 engine((std::random_device()()));

    //** we will rearrange the elements in the
    //** following range [first, second] as follows fist =
    //** backpackOfBalls.begin() and second =
    //** backpackOfBalls.end()
    //** using "engine" declared above as a uniform random
    //** number generator
    std::shuffle(backpackOfBalls.begin(),
                        backpackOfBalls.end(), engine);
}

int main()
{
    //** constants initializations
    const unsigned theTotalOfSamples = 1000000;
    const unsigned blue_balls = 4;
    const unsigned differentBalls = 12;

    unsigned theFirstIsBlue = 0;
    unsigned bothAreBlue = 0;
    unsigned theSecondIsBlue = 0;

    auto backpackOfBalls = initializeBackpack(blue_balls,
                                        differentBalls);

    for (unsigned i=0; i<theTotalOfSamples; ++i)
    {
        randomize(backpackOfBalls);
```

```cpp
        if (backpackOfBalls[0] == Blue)
            ++theFirstIsBlue;

        if (backpackOfBalls[1] == Blue)
            ++theSecondIsBlue;

    if (backpackOfBalls[0]==Blue&&backpackOfBalls[1]==Blue)
            ++bothAreBlue;
}

float probabilityOfFirstBallToBeBlue =
                static_cast<float>(theFirstIsBlue) /
                                        theTotalOfSamples;

float probabilityForBothBallsToBeBlue =
                static_cast<float>(bothAreBlue) /
                                        theTotalOfSamples;

float probabilityForSecondBallToBeRed =
                static_cast<float>(theSecondIsBlue) /
                                        theTotalOfSamples;

std::cout << "Probability for the first ball to be blue: "
        << probabilityOfFirstBallToBeBlue * 100.0 << "%\n" ;

std::cout<< "Probability for the second ball to be blue: "
        << probabilityForSecondBallToBeRed * 100.0 << "%\n" ;

std::cout << "Probability for both balls to be blue: "
        << probabilityForBothBallsToBeBlue * 100.0 << "%\n" ;
}
```

Case Study 2: Computing the Probability Distribution

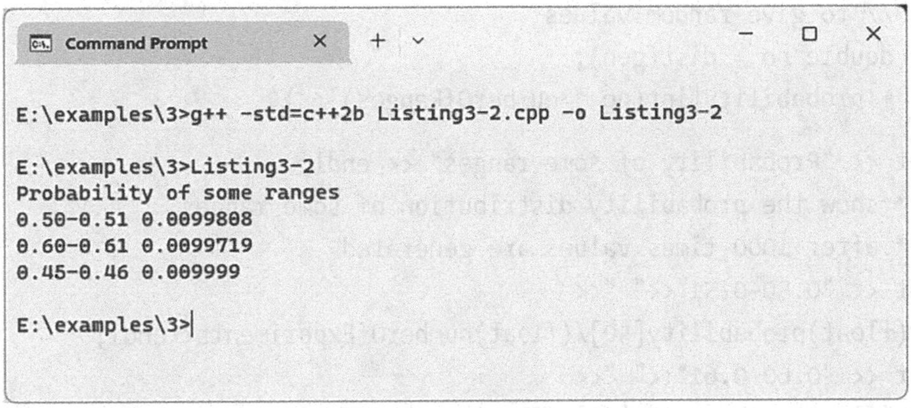

Figure 3-2. *Output of probability distribution*

Listing 3-2. Source Code

```cpp
//** this will be used for computing the distribution
#include <random>
#include <iostream>

using namespace std;

int main()  {
    //** declare default_random_engine object
    //** we will use it as a random number
    //** we will provide a seed for default_random_engine
    //** if a pseudo random is necessary
    default_random_engine gen;
    double x=0.0, y=1.0;

    //** initialization of the probability distribution
    uniform_real_distribution<double> dist(x, y);

    //** the number of experiments
    const int numberOfExperiments = 10000000;

    //** the number of ranges
    const int numberOfRanges = 100;
    int probability[numberOfRanges] = {};
```

```
for (int k = 0; k < numberOfExperiments; ++k) {
    // using operator() function
    // to give random values
    double no = dist(gen);
    ++probability[int(no * numberOfRanges)]; }

cout << "Probability of some ranges" << endl;
//** show the probability distribution of some ranges
//** after 1000 times values are generated
cout << "0.50-0.51"<<" "<<
    (float)probability[50]/(float)numberOfExperiments<<endl;
cout << "0.60-0.61"<<" "<<
    (float)probability[60]/(float)numberOfExperiments<<endl;
cout << "0.45-0.46"<<" "<<
    (float)probability[45]/(float)numberOfExperiments<<endl;

    return 0;
}
```

Case Study 3: Computing the Mean of the Probability Distribution

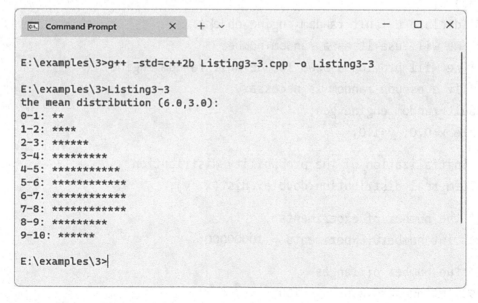

Figure 3-3. *Output for the mean of the probability distribution*

Listing 3-3. Source Code

```
#include <iostream>
#include <string>
#include <random>

int main()
{
  //** the constant represents the number of experiments
  const int numberOfExperiments=10000;
  //** the constant represents the
  //** maximum number of stars to distribute
  const int numberOfStarsToDistribute=100;

  std::default_random_engine g;
  std::normal_distribution<double> dist(6.0,3.0);

  int prob[10]={};

  for (int k=0; k<numberOfExperiments; ++k) {
    double no = dist(g);
    if ((no>=0.0)&&(no<10.0)) ++prob[int(no)];
  }

  std::cout << "the mean distribution (6.0,3.0):" << std::endl;

  for (int l=0; l<10; ++l) {
    std::cout << l << "-" << (l+1) << ": ";
    std::cout <<
            std::string(prob[l]*numberOfStarsToDistribute/
            numberOfExperiments,'*') << std::endl;
  }

  return 0;
}
```

Case Study 4: Computing the Variance

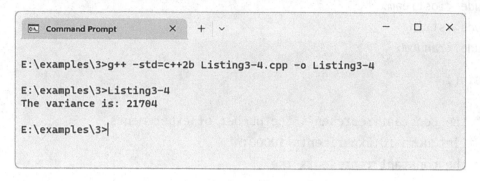

Figure 3-4. *Output of variance*

Listing 3-4. Source Code

```
#include<iostream>

using namespace std;

//** the below function is used
//** for computing the variance
int computingVariance(int n[], int h)        //**a=n, n=h
{
    //** computes the mean
    //** average of the elements
    int sum = 0;
    for (int k = 0; k < h; k++)
        sum += n[k];
    double theMean = (double)sum /
                     (double)h;

    //** calculate the sum squared
    //** differences with the mean
    double squared_differences = 0;
    for (int t=0; t<h; t++)
        squared_differences += (n[t] - theMean) *
                                    (n[t] - theMean);
```

```
    return squared_differences / h;
}

int main()
{
    int arr[] = {600, 470, 170, 430, 300};
    int n = sizeof(arr) / sizeof(arr[0]);
    cout << "The variance is: "
         << computingVariance(arr, n) << "\n";
    return 0;
}
```

Case Study 5: Computing the Standard Deviation

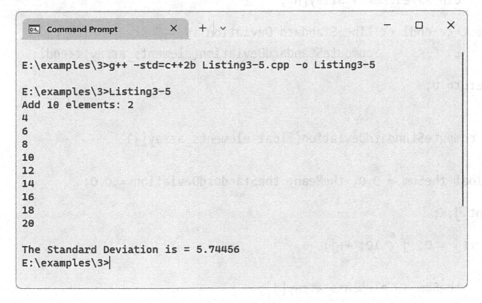

Figure 3-5. *Output of the standard deviation*

Listing 3-5. Source Code

```
#include <iostream>
#include <cmath>

using namespace std;

float computeStandardDeviation(float data[]);

int main()
{
    int n;
    float elements_array[10];

    cout << "Add 10 elements: ";
    for(n = 0; n < 10; ++n)
        cin >> elements_array[n];

    cout << endl << "The Standard Deviation is = " <<
                    computeStandardDeviation(elements_array)<<endl;

    return 0;
}

float computeStandardDeviation(float elements_array[])
{
    float theSum = 0.0, theMean, theStandardDeviation = 0.0;

    int j,k;

    for(j = 0; j < 10; ++j)
    {
        theSum += elements_array[j];
    }

    theMean = theSum/10;

    for(k = 0; k < 10; ++k)
```

```
theStandardDeviation += pow(elements_array[k] -
                           theMean, 2);

    return sqrt(theStandardDeviation/10);
}
```

Case Study 6: Birthday Paradox

Figure 3-6. *Output of birthday computation*

Listing 3-6. Source Code

```cpp
#include <ctime>
#include <cstdlib>
#include <iostream>

using namespace std;

int main(int argc, const char *argv[])
{
    const int processes = 15000;
    short int no_of_birthdays[365];
    int processesWithSuccess;
    bool IsSharedBirthday;

    //** we will time(NULL) as seed to be used for the
    //** pseudo-random number generator srand()
    srand(time(NULL));

    for (int no_of_people=2;no_of_people<45;
++no_of_people)
    {
        processesWithSuccess = 0;
        for (int i = 0; i < processes; ++i)
        {
            //** all birthdays will be set to 0
            for (int j=0;j<365;no_of_birthdays[j++] = 0);
            IsSharedBirthday = false;
            for (int j = 0; j < no_of_people; ++j)
            {
                //** if our given birthday is shared (this
 //** means that is assigned for more than one
 //** person) this will be a shared birthday
 //** and we will need to stop verifying.
                if (++no_of_birthdays[rand() % 365] > 1){
                    IsSharedBirthday = true;
                    break;
                }
```

```
    }
        if (IsSharedBirthday) ++processesWithSuccess;
    }

    cout << "The probability for " << no_of_people << "people from the
    same room to share the same birthday is \t"<<(float(processesWith
    Success)/ float(processes))<<endl;
  }
  return 0;
}
```

Case Study 7: (Extended) Euclidean Algorithm

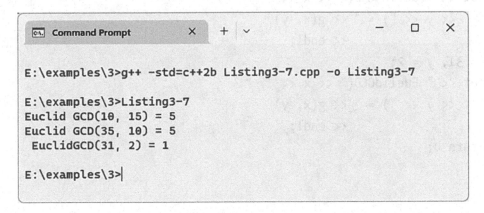

Figure 3-7. *Output of the Euclidean algorithm*

Listing 3-7. Source Code

```
//** NOTE: bits/stdc++ does not represent
//** a standard header file of the GNU C++ library.
//** If the code will be compiled with other
//** compilers than GCC it will fail
#include<stdio.h>

using namespace std;

//** the function will compute
//** GCD for two numbers
int g(int x, int y)  {
```

```cpp
    if (x == 0)
        return y;
    return g(y % x, x);
}

int main()
{
    int x = 10, y = 15;
    cout << "Euclid GCD(" << x << ", "
        << y << ") = " << g(x, y)
                        << endl;
    x = 35, y = 10;
    cout << "Euclid GCD(" << x << ", "
        << y << ") = " << g(x, y)
                        << endl;
    x = 31, y = 2;
    cout << " EuclidGCD(" << x << ", "
        << y << ") = " << g(x, y)
                        << endl;
    return 0;
}
```

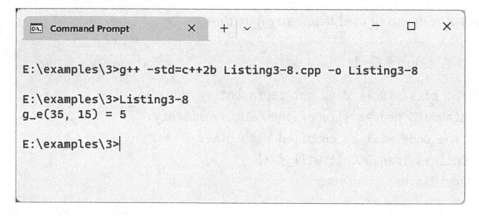

Figure 3-8. *Output of Extended Euclidean algorithm*

Listing 3-8. Source Code

```
#include <bits/stdc++.h>
using namespace std;

//** computing extended Euclidean algorithm
int g_e(int x, int y, int *w, int *z)
{
    //** this is the basic or ideal case
    if (x == 0)
    {
        *w = 0;
        *z = 1;
        return y;
    }

    //** variables for storing the results
    //** for the recursive call
    int a1, b1;
    int g = g_e(y%x, x, &a1, &b1);

    //** with help of the recursive call
    //** update a and b with the results
    *w = b1 - (y/x) * a1;
    *z = a1;

    return g;
}

// Driver Code
int main()
{
    int a, b, w = 35, y = 15;
    int g = g_e(w, y, &a, &b);
    cout << "g_e(" << w << ", " << y<< ") = " << g << endl;
    return 0;
}
```

Case Study 8: Computing the Multiplicative Inverse Under Modulo q

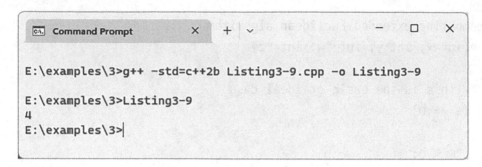

Figure 3-9. *Output of modular multiplicative inverse (basic and tricky form of the implementation)*

Listing 3-9. Code for Computing the Modular Multiplicative Inverse (Tricky Method)

```cpp
#include<iostream>
using namespace std;

//** this represents the basic method or tricky method
//** for finding the modulo multiplicative inverse of
//** x under modulo m
int modulo_inverse(int x, int m)
{
    x = x%m;
    for (int y=1; y<m; y++)
       if ((x*y) % m == 1)
           return y;
    return 1;
}

int main()
{
    int x = 3, m = 11;
    cout << modulo_inverse(x, m);
    return 0;
}
```

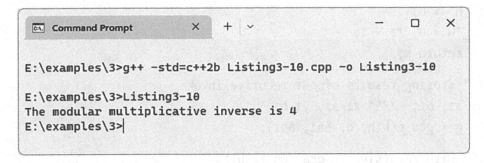

Figure 3-10. *Output of modular multiplicative inverse (when the number is coprime)*

Listing 3-10. Source Code

```cpp
#include<iostream>
using namespace std;

//** function for computing the extended Euclidean algorithm
int gcd_e(int x, int y, int *w, int *z);

void modulo_inverse(int h, int modulo)
{
    int i, j;
    int g = gcd_e(h, modulo, &i, &j);
    if (g != 1)
        cout << "There is no inverse.";
    else
    {
        //** we add the modulo in
        //** order to handle negative i
        int result = (i%modulo + modulo) % modulo;
        cout << "The modular multiplicative inverse is " <<
                                                result;
    }
}

//** we will compute the extended Euclidean algorithm
int gcd_e(int h, int k, int *w, int *z) {
    //** the "happy" case
```

```
    if (h == 0){
        *w = 0, *z = 1;
        return k; }

    //** storing results of our recurive invoke
    int a1, b1;   //** x1=a1, y1=b1
    int g = gcd_e(k%h, h, &a1, &b1);

    //** with recursive invocation results
    //** we will update x and y
    *w = b1 - (k/h) * a1;
    *z = a1;

    return g;
}

int main()
{
    int x = 3, modulo = 11;
    modulo_inverse(x, modulo);
    return 0;
}
```

Case Study 9: Chinese Remainder Theorem

Figure 3-11. *Output for Chinese remainder theorem*

Listing 3-11. Source Code

```cpp
#include<iostream>

using namespace std;

int inverse(int x, int modulo)
{
    int modulo0 = modulo, k, quotient;
    int a0 = 0, a1 = 1;

    if (modulo == 1)
       return 0;

    //** we will apply the extended Euclidean algorithm
    while (x > 1)
    {
        quotient = x / modulo;

        k = modulo;

        //** modulo represents the remainder
        //** continue with the same process as
        //** Euclid's algorithm
        modulo = x%modulo, x=k;

        k = a0;

        a0 = a1 - quotient * a0;

        a1 = k;
    }
    //** make a1 positive
    if (a1 < 0)
       a1 += modulo0;

    return a1;
}
```

```
int lookForMinX(int numbers[], int remainders[], int l)
{
    //** computing the product for all the numbers
    int product = 1;
    for (int j = 0; j < l; j++)
        product *= numbers[j];

    //** we initialize the result with 0
    int result = 0;

    //** apply the formula mentioned above
    for (int j = 0; j < l; j++)
    {
        int pp = product / numbers[j];
        result += remainders[j] * inverse(pp, numbers[j]) * pp;
    }

    return result % product;
}

int main(void) {
    int numbers[] = {3, 4, 5};
    int remainders[] = {2, 3, 1};
    int k = sizeof(numbers)/sizeof(numbers[0]);
    cout << "x is " << lookForMinX(numbers, remainders, k);
    return 0;
}
```

Case Study 10: The Legendre Symbol

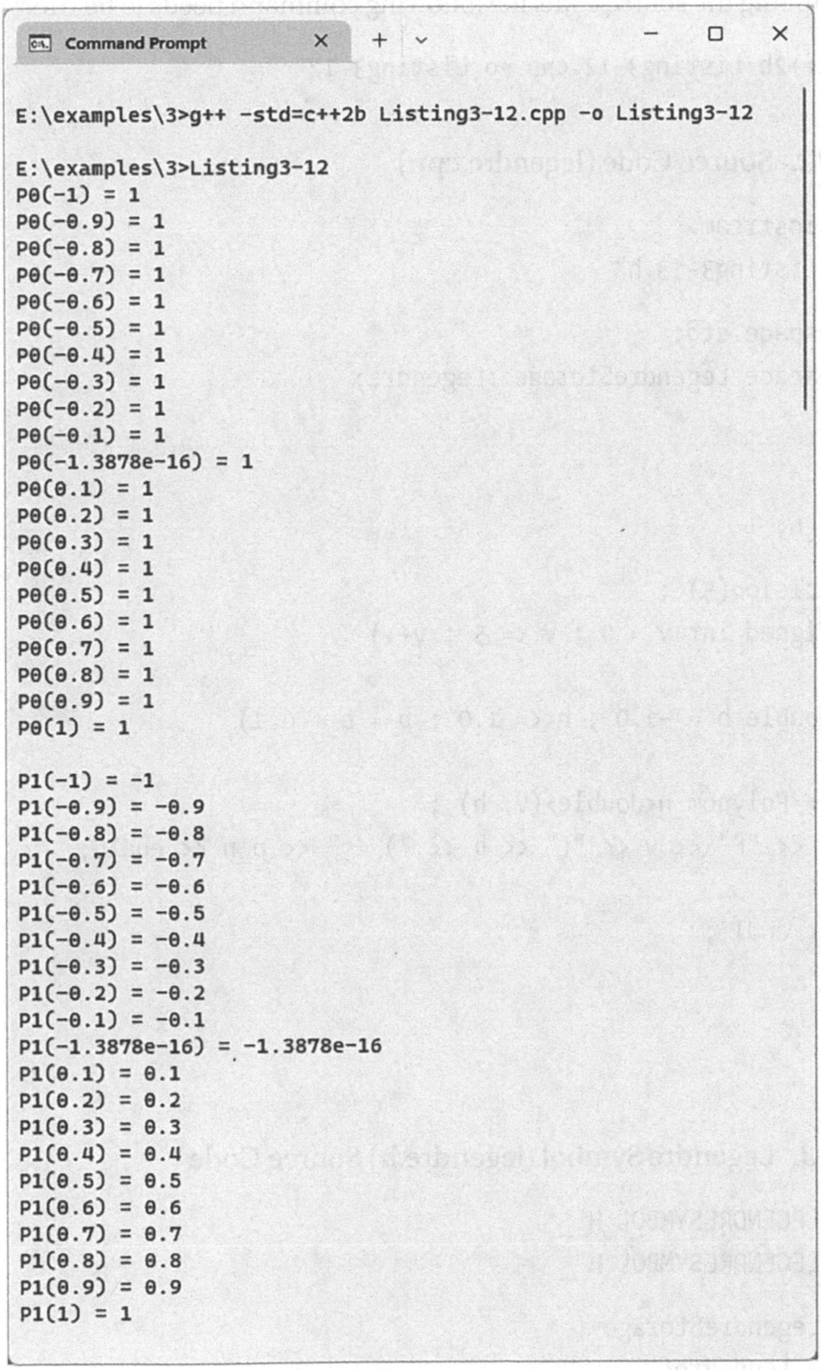

```
Command Prompt                    ×    + ∨              —    □    ×

E:\examples\3>g++ -std=c++2b Listing3-12.cpp -o Listing3-12

E:\examples\3>Listing3-12
P0(-1) = 1
P0(-0.9) = 1
P0(-0.8) = 1
P0(-0.7) = 1
P0(-0.6) = 1
P0(-0.5) = 1
P0(-0.4) = 1
P0(-0.3) = 1
P0(-0.2) = 1
P0(-0.1) = 1
P0(-1.3878e-16) = 1
P0(0.1) = 1
P0(0.2) = 1
P0(0.3) = 1
P0(0.4) = 1
P0(0.5) = 1
P0(0.6) = 1
P0(0.7) = 1
P0(0.8) = 1
P0(0.9) = 1
P0(1) = 1

P1(-1) = -1
P1(-0.9) = -0.9
P1(-0.8) = -0.8
P1(-0.7) = -0.7
P1(-0.6) = -0.6
P1(-0.5) = -0.5
P1(-0.4) = -0.4
P1(-0.3) = -0.3
P1(-0.2) = -0.2
P1(-0.1) = -0.1
P1(-1.3878e-16) = -1.3878e-16
P1(0.1) = 0.1
P1(0.2) = 0.2
P1(0.3) = 0.3
P1(0.4) = 0.4
P1(0.5) = 0.5
P1(0.6) = 0.6
P1(0.7) = 0.7
P1(0.8) = 0.8
P1(0.9) = 0.9
P1(1) = 1
```

Figure 3-12. *Output of Legendre symbol*

The source code for implementing the Legendre symbol is structured in two files: Listing3-12.cpp (see Listing 3-12), and Listing 3-13.h (see Listing 3-13).

For compiling the source code, the following command needs to be run.

```
g++ -std=c++2b Listing3-12.cpp -o Listing3-12
```

Listing 3-12. Source Code (legendre.cpp)

```cpp
#include <iostream>
#include "Listing3-13.h"

using namespace std;
using namespace LegendreStorage::Legendre;

int main()
{
  double p_n;

  cout.precision(5) ;
  for (unsigned int v = 0 ; v <= 5 ; v++)
  {
    for (double b = -1.0 ; b <= 1.0 ; b = b + 0.1)
    {
      p_n = Polynom_n<double>(v, b) ;
      cout << "P" << v << "(" << b << ") = " << p_n << endl ;
    }
    cout << endl ;
  }

  return 0 ;
}
```

Listing 3-13. Legendre Symbol (legendre.h) Source Code

```cpp
#ifndef __LEGENDRESYMBOL_H__
#define __LEGENDRESYMBOL_H__

namespace LegendreStorage {
  namespace Legendre{
```

```cpp
//** when n=0
template <class T> inline auto Polynom0(const T& x){
  return static_cast<T>(1);
}

//** when n=1
template <class T> inline auto Polynom1(const T& x){
  return x;
}

//** when n=2
template <class T> inline auto Polynom2(const T& x){
  return ((static_cast<T>(3)*x*x) -
    static_cast<T>(1)) / static_cast<T>(2);
}

//** polynom(x)
template <class T> inline auto Polynom_n(unsigned int h,
                                          const T& y)
{
  switch(h){
    case 0:
      return Polynom0<T>(y);

    case 1:
      return Polynom1<T>(y);

    case 2:
      return Polynom2<T>(y);

    default:
      break;}

  auto polynom_1(Polynom2<T>(y));
  auto polynom_2(Polynom1<T>(y));
  T polynom;

  for (auto a=3u; a<=h; ++a){
    polynom = ((static_cast<T>((2 * a) - 1)) * y *
```

```
                                                        polynom_1
        - (static_cast<T>(a - 1) * polynom_2)) /
                                            static_cast<T>(a);

    polynom_2 = polynom_1;
    polynom_1 = polynom;        }

   return polynom;    }}}
#endif
```

Conclusion

The current chapter discussed the importance of some mathematical tools used in most modern cryptography algorithms. It demonstrated how they can be implemented and explained the important steps of the algorithms. The chapter also covered the important aspects of the mathematical foundations, such as probability theory, information theory, number theory, and finite fields.

Each mathematical foundation presented the necessary equations and mathematical expressions used to implement the algorithms. Each equation or mathematical expression is demonstrated through an example of a software application implemented in C++ entitled a case study. Each case study has demonstrated the skills and knowledge needed to develop a secure and reliable code. The case studies were counted from 1 to 10.

Reaching the end of the chapter, you should now understand the important notions and terms, programming concepts, and algorithms used, both theoretical and practical, and how to quickly move from theory to practice.

References

[1].   *Menezes Alfred J.; Paul van Oorschot; Vanstone Scott A. (1996). Handbook of Applied Cryptography.* CRC Press. ISBN *0-8493-8523-7.*

[2].   *A. R. Meijer, Algebra for Cryptologists, 1st ed. New York, NY: Springer, 2016.*

[3].   *J. Hoffstein, J. Pipher, and J. H. Silverman, An Introduction to Mathematical Cryptography, 2nd ed. New York: Springer, 2014.*

[4].   *S. Rubinstein-Salzedo, Cryptography, 1st ed. New York, NY: Springer, 2018.*

[5].   *W. Stallings, Cryptography and Network Security: Principles and Practice, 6th ed. Prentice Hall Press, 2013.*

[6].   *K. Academy, Cryptography: Data and Application Security. Independently published, 2017.*

[7].   *C. T. Rivers, Cryptography: Decoding Cryptography! From Ancient to New Age Times. JR Kindle Publishing, 2014.*

[8].   *D. Stinson, Cryptography: Theory and Practice, Second Edition, 2nd ed. CRC/C&H, 2002.*

[9].   *H. Delfs and H. Knebl, Introduction to Cryptography: Principles and Applications, 3rd ed. New York, NY: Springer, 2015.*

[10].   *J. Katz and Y. Lindell, Introduction to Modern Cryptography, Second Edition, Boca Raton: Chapman and Hall/CRC, 2014.*

[11].   *X. Wang, G. Xu, M. Wang, and X. Meng, Mathematical Foundations of Public Key Cryptography. Boca Raton: CRC Press, 2015.*

[12].   *T. R. Shemanske, Modern Cryptography and Elliptic Curves. Providence, Rhode Island: American Mathematical Society, 2017.*

[13].   *S. Y. Yan, Primality Testing and Integer Factorization in Public-Key Cryptography. Springer, 2013.*

[14].   *L. M. Batten, Public Key Cryptography: Applications and Attacks. Hoboken, N.J: Wiley-Blackwell, 2013.*

[15].   *J. P. Aumasson, Serious Cryptography. San Francisco: No Starch Press, 2017.*

[16].   *S. Khare, The world of Cryptography: incl. cryptosystems, ciphers, public key encryption, data integration, message authentication, digital signatures.*

[17].   *A. Atanasiu, Securitatea informaţiei - Criptografie (Information Security - Cryptography). Infodata, 2007. [Romanian Language]*

[18].   *A. Atanasiu, Securitatea informaţiei - Protocoale de securitate (Information Security - Security Protocols). Infodata, 2009. [Romanian Language]*

[19].   *V. Preda, E. Simion, A. Popescu. Criptanaliza. Rezultate şi Tehnici Matematice (Cryptanalysis. Results and Mathematical Techniques). Universitatea Bucuresti Publisher, 2004 [Romanian Language]*

CHAPTER 4

Large Integer Arithmetic

The purpose of this chapter is to cover the main arithmetic operations and explain how to work with large integers. Some cryptographic algorithms require large integers that do not fit with the normal size of variables, such as `int`. It gives a quick overview of big integers and some libraries used to work with them.

The chapter offers a comprehensive guide on large integer arithmetic by providing a comprehensive overview of the basics, from understanding the fundamentals to exploring the various algorithms used to compute large numbers. It is very interesting to look at the past and get some chunks of history about large integer arithmetic, investigate different algorithms used to solve large-number problems and learn the basics of number theory. You'll also get an introduction to online tools to help students and professionals with large-number calculations. With this guide, you'll thoroughly understand the fundamentals of large integer arithmetic and the various algorithms and tools used to solve large-number problems.

A Bit of History

The concept of large integer arithmetic goes back to ancient civilizations. The Egyptians were known to have used large integers in their architectural designs, where the dimensions of temples, pyramids, and other architectural wonders were recorded in integers. Similarly, the Mayans used large integers in their astronomical calculations, using the numbers 1 to 13 to represent the 13 lunar cycles in a solar year. Traders in India and China were also known to use large integers in their monetary computations, where they used the numbers 1 to 99 to represent their monetary denominations. Large integer arithmetic was further developed in the tenth century by Persian mathematician Abu'l-Wafa, who introduced the Ghiya number system, which became the modern-day Bhulbhulaya number system. The Bhulbhulaya number system was an extension of the Ghiya number system, where Abu'l-Wafa introduced the Bhulbhulaya numbers

M. I. Mihailescu and S. L. Nita, *Pro Cryptography and Cryptanalysis with C++23*,
https://doi.org/10.1007/978-1-4842-9450-5_4

to represent very large numbers. The Bhulbhulaya numbers were used to describe astronomical measurements, distances, and monetary amounts, where the number system went off the limitations of the Ghiya number system.

What About Cryptography?

In implementing complex cryptography algorithms, operations with large integers can be very difficult. The limitations could be due to hardware equipment (e.g., processor, RAM) or programming languages.

In C++23, an integer is represented as 32 bits. Out of 32 bits, only 31 can be used for representing positive integer arithmetic. Cryptography is good when you are dealing with numbers that are up to two billion, or $2 \cdot 10^9$.

Some compilers have a long long type, such as GNU C++ or g++, that offer the possibility to represent integers of approximately nine quintillion, or $9 \cdot 10^{18}$.

Most simple cryptographic operations are good, but some cryptographic algorithms require more digits in their integer representation. Let's consider as an example the RSA (Rivest-Shamir-Adleman) public-key encryption cryptosystem, which requires approximately 300 digits. The computation often involves large numbers when dealing with specific real events and their probabilities. The output and achievement of the main result might be appropriate for C/C++. Compared with other complex computations, there are very large numbers.

Another interesting example is to find the chances of winning the jackpot from a lottery with one ticket. The combination number of 50 is taken six at a time, and "50 *choose* 6" is $\dfrac{50!}{\left(\left(50-6\right)! \cdot 6!\right)}$. The resulting number is 15.890.700, so the chances of winning are 1/15.890.700. Using the C++23 programming language, the number 15.890.700 can be easily represented. This could be tricky, and you can easily fall for naivety when implementing 50! (computed using a calculator in Windows), which is 3.041409320171e+64 or much more approximated

30,414,093,201,713,378,043,612,608,166,064,768,844,377,641,568,960,512,00 0,000,000,000

Using C++23 to represent that number is almost impossible, even using a 64-bit platform.

Algorithms Used for Large Integer Arithmetic

The addition modulo is the most basic algorithm used for solving problems with large numbers. In addition, modulo, you add two large numbers, but then you normalize the result to the closest number that fits into the precision of the addition operation. This means you discard the sum's fractional part and keep the rest as the final sum.

When implementing an addition algorithm for two large numbers, one of the most useful approaches is considering the numbers as *strings*[1]. In this case, the numbers provided as input can be very large, such examples can be numerous, and the numbers may not fit in a `long long int` variable. Based on the purpose of the algorithm, the mission of such an algorithm is to be able to compute the sum of the numbers provided as input.

Let's consider two large numbers: 2431989739 and 3947978705409241873. The example shown in Figure 4-1 uses CrypTool[2] to generate two large prime numbers by setting up an interval between a lower limit and an upper limit.

---

[1] See https://www.geeksforgeeks.org/sum-two-large-numbers/
[2] See https://www.cryptool.org/en/

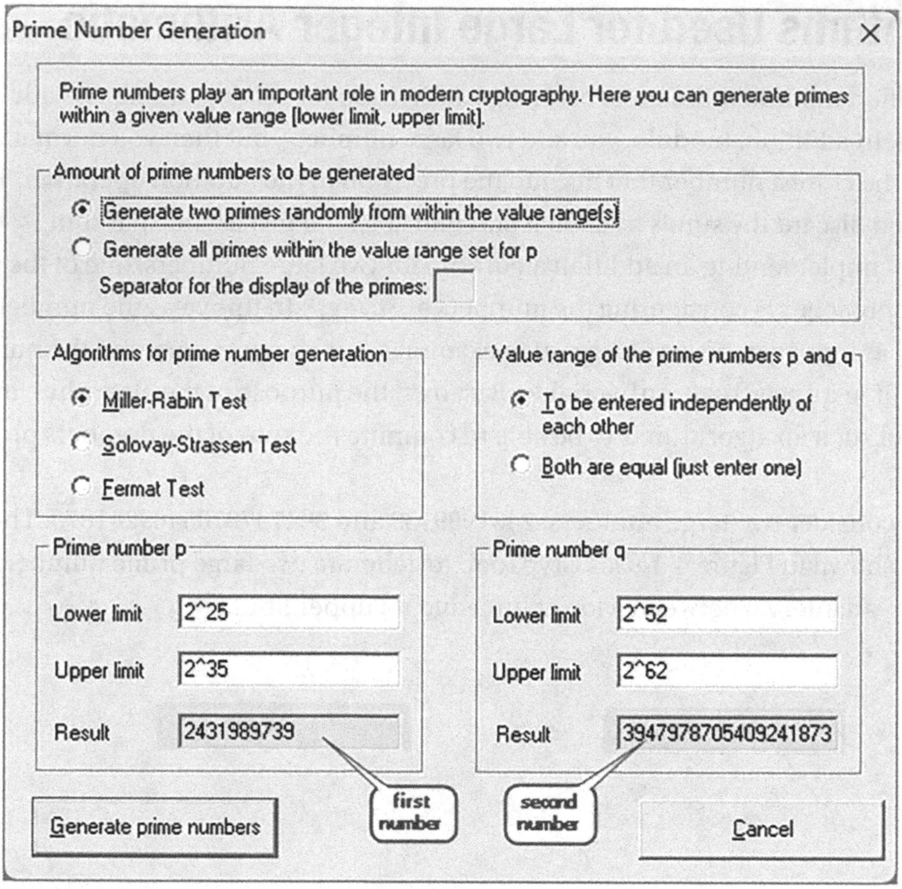

Figure 4-1. *Generating two large numbers for addition*

Let's consider the first basic/standard implementation (let's call it the elementary implementation) of the addition operation using integer variables (see Listing 4-1).

Listing 4-1. Elementary Implementation of Addition

```
#include <iostream>
using namespace std;

int main()
{
    int first_number;
    int second_number;

    int addition = 0;
```

110

```
    cout << "Enter first number = ";
    cin >> first_number;
    cout << "Enter second number = ";
    cin >> second_number;

    addition = first_number + second_number;

    cout<<"The addition is: " << addition << endl;

    return 0;
}
```

Let's run the example and examine the program's behavior. After entering the first number, the program exits because the number is larger than the size of the int variable (see Figure 4-2).

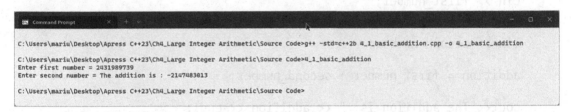

Figure 4-2. *A large number with an* int *variable*

The same situation applies to the long int. To run this example, open a command prompt window and run it using the following command.

```
g++ -std=gnu++2b 4_1_basic_addition.cpp -o 4_1_basic_addition
```

In the command, gnu++2b represents the new experimental version of C++23[3]. To allow C++23 support, add the command-line parameter -std=c++2b to your g++ command line. To enable GNU extensions in addition to the C++23 features, add -std=gnu++2b.

_____

[3] See https://gcc.gnu.org/projects/cxx-status.html

Listing 4-2 has the same situation as Listing 4-1 and Figure 4-2.

Listing 4-2. Case of long int Variable

```cpp
#include <iostream>
using namespace std;

int main()
{
    long int first_number;
    long int second_number;

    long int addition = 0;

    cout << "Enter first number = ";
    cin >> first_number;
    cout << "Enter second number = ";
    cin >> second_number;

    addition = first_number + second_number;

    cout<<"The addition is: " << addition << endl;

    return 0;
}
```

A success for adding large numbers can be obtained with long int (see Listing 4-3 and Figure 4-3) and unsigned long int (see Listing 4-4 and Figure 4-3, the same output as for Listing 4-3).

Listing 4-3. Case of long long int Variable

```cpp
#include <iostream>
using namespace std;

int main()
{
    long int first_number;
    long int second_number;

    long int addition = 0;
```

```
    cout << "Enter first number = ";
    cin >> first_number;
    cout << "Enter second number = ";
    cin >> second_number;

    addition = first_number + second_number;

    cout<<"The addition is: " << addition << endl;

    return 0;
}
```

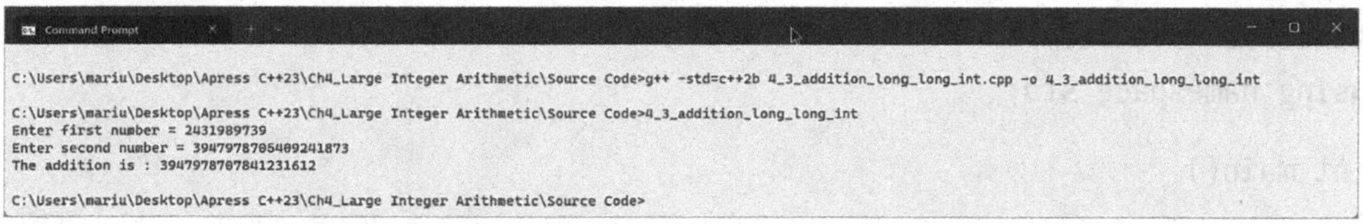

```
C:\Users\mariu\Desktop\Apress C++23\Ch4_Large Integer Arithmetic\Source Code>g++ -std=c++2b 4_3_addition_long_long_int.cpp -o 4_3_addition_long_long_int

C:\Users\mariu\Desktop\Apress C++23\Ch4_Large Integer Arithmetic\Source Code>4_3_addition_long_long_int
Enter first number = 2431989739
Enter second number = 3947979785409241873
The addition is : 3947979787841231612

C:\Users\mariu\Desktop\Apress C++23\Ch4_Large Integer Arithmetic\Source Code>
```

Figure 4-3. *A successful addition operation using a* `long long int` *variable*

Listing 4-4. Case of unsigned `long long int` Variable

```
#include <iostream>
using namespace std;

#include <iostream>
using namespace std;

int main()
{
    unsigned long long int first_number;
    unsigned long long int second_number;

    unsigned long long int addition = 0;

    cout << "Enter first number = ";
    cin >> first_number;
    cout << "Enter second number = ";
    cin >> second_number;
```

```
        addition = first_number + second_number;

        cout<<"The addition is: " << addition << endl;

        return 0;
}
```

To understand much better what types of variables for integers should be used, the following example (see Listing 4-5 and Figure 4-4) shows exactly the size (in bytes) that can be used within different variables for integers.

Listing 4-5. Variable Sizes

```cpp
#include <iostream>
using namespace std;

int main()
{
        cout << "Size of int : " << sizeof(int) << " bytes" << endl;
        cout << "Size of unsigned int : " << sizeof(unsigned int) << " bytes"
        << endl;
        cout << "Size of signed int : " << sizeof(signed int) << " bytes"
        << endl;
        cout << "Size of short int : " << sizeof(short int) << " bytes"
        << endl;
        cout << "Size of unsigned short int : " << sizeof(unsigned short int)
        << " bytes" << endl;
        cout << "Size of signed short int : " << sizeof(signed short int) <<
        " bytes" << endl;
        cout << "Size of long int : " << sizeof(long int) << " bytes"
        << endl;
        cout << "Size of signed long int : " << sizeof(signed long int) << "
        bytes" << endl;
        cout << "Size of unsigned long int : " << sizeof(unsigned long int)
        << " bytes" << endl;
        cout << "Size of long long int : " << sizeof(long long int) << "
        bytes" << endl;
```

CHAPTER 4   LARGE INTEGER ARITHMETIC

```
cout << "Size of unsigned long long int : " << sizeof(unsigned long
long int) << " bytes" << endl;

return 0;
}
```

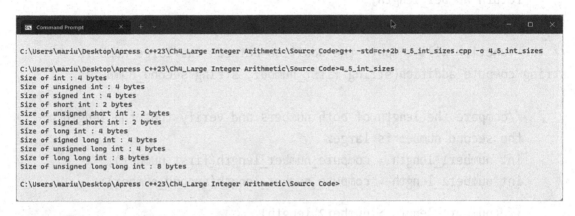

Figure 4-4. *Number of bytes for* `int` *variables*

Figure 4-4 shows that we cannot operate addition on large numbers. One of the most common solutions (see Listing 4-6 and Figure 4-5 for the output) is to consider the numbers as strings, reverse both strings, and keep adding the digits of the number one by one from the first index (using the reversed string) to the end for the smaller string (number), and append the addition % 10 (modulo operation) to the end of the result and keep track of the transporter by computing addition/10 (division operation). As a final step, take the result and reverse it.

Listing 4-6. Addition for Large Numbers Considering the Numbers As Strings

```
#include <iostream>
#include <algorithm>

using namespace std;

//compute the length of the number as string
int compute_number_length(string number)
{
    int number_length = 0;
    int i = 0;

    while(number[i])
```

```
        {
                number_length++;
                i++;
        }

        return number_length;
}
// the function will compute the addition between two large numbers
string compute_addition(string first_number, string second_number)
{
        //compare the length of both numbers and verify that the length of
        the second number is larger
        int number1_length = compute_number_length(first_number);
        int number2_length = compute_number_length(second_number);

        if (number1_length > number2_length)
                swap(first_number, second_number);

        //declare an empty string variable that will store the result
        in the end
        string result_of_addition = "";

        //compute for both strings the length
        int length_of_number1 = compute_number_length(first_number);
        int length_of_number2 = compute_number_length(second_number);

        reverse(first_number.begin(), first_number.end());
        reverse(second_number.begin(), second_number.end());

        int transporter = 0;
        for (int i=0; i<length_of_number1; i++)
        {
                //elementary addition computation of the digits and transporter
                or carrier
                int addition = ((first_number[i]-'0')+(second_number[i]-
                '0')+transporter);
                result_of_addition.push_back(addition%10 + '0');
```

```cpp
        //compute the transporter for the next step
        transporter = addition/10;
    }

    //push or add the remaining digits for a large number
    for (int i=length_of_number1; i<length_of_number2; i++)
    {
        int addition = ((second_number[i]-'0')+transporter);
        result_of_addition.push_back(addition%10 + '0');
        transporter = addition/10;
    }

    //push back or add the transporter
    if (transporter)
        result_of_addition.push_back(transporter+'0');

    //take the result and reverse it
    reverse(result_of_addition.begin(), result_of_addition.end());

    return result_of_addition;
}

//main function, read the numbers
int main()
{
    string first_number = "";
    string second_number = "";

    cout << "Enter first number = ";
    cin >> first_number;
    cout << "Enter second number = ";
    cin >> second_number;

    cout << "The addition is: " << compute_addition(first_number, second_number) << endl;

    return 0;
}
```

Let's run Listing 4-6 for the following numbers and examine the output of the addition. The first number is 2431989739243198973924319897392431989739243198 97392431989739243198973924319897392431989739. The second number is 3947978705439479787 05409241873394797870540924187339479787054092418733947978705409241873 09241873. The output is shown in Figure 4-5.

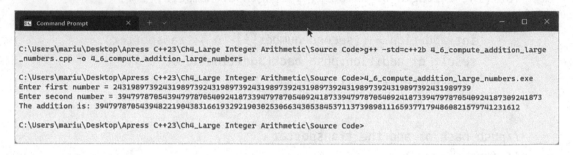

Figure 4-5. *Addition using large numbers*

Subtraction (Subtraction Modulo)

The process of subtraction is the same as the addition approach (see Listing 4-7 for the source code and Figure 4-6 for the output), except that you take the difference between the two numbers, and different implementations can be done or found with different references[4], where the algorithms and steps are quite similar.

Listing 4-7. Subtraction Approach

```
#include <iostream>
#include <algorithm>

using namespace std;

//reverse string (number)
void reverseNumber(string& number, int n, int i)
{
    while(n<i)
    {
        return;
    }
```

---

[4] See https://www.geeksforgeeks.org/difference-of-two-large-numbers/?ref=gcse

```
        swap(number[i], number[n]);
        reverseNumber(number, n-1, i+1);
}

//compute the length of the number as string
int compute_number_length(string number)
{
        int number_length = 0;
        int i = 0;

        while(number[i])
        {
                number_length++;
                i++;
        }

        return number_length;
}

//verify and return true if number 1 is smaller than number 2
bool check(string first_number, string second_number)
{
        // Calculate lengths of both strings
        int firstNumber = compute_number_length(first_number);
        int secondNumber = compute_number_length(second_number);

        int counter = 0;

        //return true if the first number is less than the second number
        while (firstNumber < secondNumber)
                return true;

        //return false if second number is less than first number
        while (secondNumber < firstNumber)
                return false;

        while(counter < firstNumber)
        {
                while (first_number[counter] < second_number[counter])
```

```
                    return true;
            while (first_number[counter] > second_number[counter])
                    return false;
        }

    return false;
}

//compute the difference between two numbers
string compute_difference(string first_number, string second_number)
{
    int transporter = 0;
    int counter = 0;
    int difference = 0;
    int startPoint = 0;

    //verify that number 1 is not smalle than number 2
    while (check(first_number, second_number))
        swap(first_number, second_number);

    //for storing the result
    string result = "";

    //compute the length of both strings
    int firstNumber = compute_number_length(first_number);
    int secondNumber = compute_number_length(second_number);

    startPoint = secondNumber;

    //reverse the strings
    reverseNumber(first_number, compute_number_length(first_
    number) - 1, 0);
    reverseNumber(second_number, compute_number_length(second_
    number) - 1, 0);

    //perform running the loop until the length of the small string
    (number)
    //add the digits of str1 to str2
```

```
while(counter < secondNumber)
{
      //compute the difference of the digits for the numbers
      int difference = ((first_number[counter] - '0') - (second_
      number[counter] - '0') - transporter);

      //in case that subtraction is less than zero, perform an
      addition of 10 into the subtraction and take the transporter as
      1 to compute the next step
      if (difference < 0)
      {
            difference += 10;
            transporter = 1;
      }
      else
            transporter = 0;

      result.push_back(difference + '0');

      counter++;
}

// subtract remaining digits of larger number
while(startPoint < firstNumber)
{
      int difference = ((first_number[startPoint] - '0') -
      transporter);

      // if the sub value is -ve, then make it positive
      if (difference < 0) {
            difference = difference + 10;
            transporter = 1;
      }
      else
            transporter = 0;

      result.push_back(difference + '0');
```

```cpp
            startPoint++;
        }

        // reverse resultant string
        reverse(result.begin(), result.end());

        return result;
}
// Driver code
int main()
{
        string first_number = "";
        string second_number = "";

        cout << "Enter first number = ";
        cin >> first_number;
        cout << "Enter second number = ";
        cin >> second_number;

        cout << "The addition is: " << compute_difference(first_number,
        second_number) << endl;

        return 0;
}
```

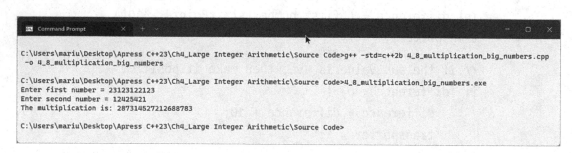

Figure 4-6. *The result of the difference*

Multiplication

Multiplication modulo is the same as addition modulo, except that you take the product of the two numbers. Examine Listing 4-8 and the output in Figure 4-7 for the proposed approach, which is similar to addition and subtraction.

Listing 4-8. Multiplication Operation

```cpp
#include <iostream>
#include <vector>
#include <algorithm>

using namespace std;

//compute the length of the number as string
int compute_number_length(string number)
{
    int number_length = 0;
    int i = 0;

    while(number[i])
    {
        number_length++;
        i++;
    }

    return number_length;
}

//the function will compute the multiplication operation between two
large numbers
string multiplicateTwoNumbers(string first_number, string second_number)
{
    int length_of_first_number = compute_number_length(first_number);
    int length_of_second_number = compute_number_length(second_number);

    while (length_of_first_number == 0 || length_of_second_number == 0)
        return "0";
```

```
//the result is stored in a vector in a reversed order
vector<int> result(length_of_first_number + length_of_second_
number, 0);

//we will use two indexes for both large numbers for identifying the
position within the result
int indexPosition_FirstNumber = 0;
int indexPosition_SecondNumber = 0;

int counter_1 = length_of_first_number-1;

//take from the right to the left within first number
while(counter_1>=0)
{
        int transporter = 0;
        int number1 = first_number[counter_1] - '0';

        //this is used for shifting the position to left once every
        multiplication with the digit is done within the second number
        indexPosition_SecondNumber = 0;

        int counter_2 = length_of_second_number-1;

        //take from right to left for the second number
        while(counter_2>=0)
        {
                //store the current digit of the second number
                int number2 = second_number[counter_2] - '0';

                //take the digit stored above and multiply the two large
                numbers with it, the result will be added to the previous
                result stored within the current position
                int additionCurrentDigitWithCurrentPosition =
                number1*number2 + result[indexPosition_FirstNumber +
                indexPosition_SecondNumber] + transporter;

                //take the carry or transporter for the next iteration
                transporter = additionCurrentDigitWithCurrentPosition/10;
```

```
                //save the result
                result[indexPosition_FirstNumber + indexPosition_
                SecondNumber] = additionCurrentDigitWithCurrentPosition % 10;

                indexPosition_SecondNumber++;
                counter_2--;
        }

        //save the transporter within next location
        while (transporter > 0)
                result[indexPosition_FirstNumber + indexPosition_
                SecondNumber] += transporter;

        //after each multiplication, shift and move the position to the
        left for the first digit within the first number
        indexPosition_FirstNumber++;

        counter_1--;
    }

    //don't take into consideration the 0 s from the right
    int zero_from_right = result.size() - 1;
    if (zero_from_right>=0 && result[zero_from_right] == 0)
        zero_from_right--;

    //if the case is 0 s - this means that both large numbers or at least
    one of the large numbers was 0
    while (zero_from_right == -1)
        return "0";

    //for storing the result as string
    string result_as_string = "";

    while (zero_from_right >= 0)
        result_as_string += std::to_string(result[zero_from_right--]);

    return result_as_string;
}

int main()
```

```
{
    string first_number = "";
    string second_number = "";

    cout << "Enter first number = ";
    cin >> first_number;
    cout << "Enter second number = ";
    cin >> second_number;

    cout << "The multiplication is: " << multiplicateTwoNumbers(first_
    number, second_number) << endl;

    return 0;
}
```

Figure 4-7. *The multiplication result*

Big Integers

This section examines other approaches that can be used for arithmetic operations using *big* integers. When working with cryptography algorithms and security mechanisms, the implementation process can be very tricky when providing an implementation that uses large numbers. Let's go through a step-by-step guide on how to work with large numbers.

One of the most interesting approaches is to transform a standard integer using different computations in a large integer. To achieve this task, let's write a function named transformIntToBigInt(A, 123). With the help of this function, initialize A as A[0]=3, A[1]=2, A[2]=1, and zeros for the remaining positions as A[3,...N-1]. Listing 4-9 examines how to accomplish the statement by using a simple implementation in C/C++. The BASE represents the bit sign.

Listing 4-9. Transforming a Standard Integer Using Different Computations into a Large Integer[5]

```
void transformIntToBigInt(int BigNo[], int number)
{
     int k;
     int bitSign;
     int BASE;

     //** start indexing with 0 position
     k = 0;

     //** if we still have something left
     //** within the number, continue
     while (number) {
           //** insert the digit that is least significant
           //** into BigNo[k] number
           BigNo[k++] = number % bitSign;

           //** we do not need the least significant bit
           number /= BASE;
     }

     //** complete the remainder of the array with zeroes
     while (k < N)
           BigNo[k++] = 0;
}
```

The algorithm in Listing 4-9 has $O(N)$ space and time.

Let's continue the adventure by looking at the possibility of adding one to a big int. This is a very helpful operation and is quite frequently used in cryptography. The advantage is that it is much easier than full addition.

---

[5] The code is meant to be a sketch of a function that transforms a simple integer to a big integer. The source code will not compile without a proper adjustment for a real cryptographic application.

Listing 4-10. Add One to a Big int[6]

```
void increment (int BigNo [])
{
        int i;
        int N;
        int BASE;

        //* start indexing with least significant digit

        i = 0;
        while (i < N)
        {
                //* increment the digit
                BigNo[i]++;

                //** if it overflows
                if (BigNo[i] == BASE)
                {
                        //** make it zero and move the index to next
                        BigNo[i] = 0;
                        i++;
                }
                else
                        //** else, we are done!
                        break;
        }
}
```

The algorithm shown in Listing 4-10 takes $O(n)$ for the worst case possible (just imagine something like 99999999999999999999....) and $\mathit{\Psi}(1)$ when you have the best case. The best case occurs when there is no overflow on the least significant digit.

---

[6] The code is meant to be a sketch of a function that transforms a simple integer to a big integer. The source code will not compile without a proper adjustment for a real cryptographic application.

Next, let's look at a method for adding two big integers. In this case, we want to add two large integers in two different arrays: BigNo1[0,..., N-1] and BigNo2[0,...,N-1]. The output result is saved in another array: BigNo3[0,...,N-1]. The algorithm is quite basic, and there is nothing fancy about it.

Listing 4-11. Addition Algorithm[7]

```
void addition(int BigNo1[], int BigNo2[], int BigNo3[])
{
    int j, overflowCarry, sum;
    int carry, N, BASE;

    //** There is no need to carry yet
    carry = 0;

    //** move from the least to the most significant digit
    for (j=0; j<N; j++)
    {
        //** the digit from j'th position of BigNo3[]
        //** represents the sum of j'th digits of
        //** BigNo1[] and BigNo2[] plus the overvflow carry
        sum = BigNo1[j] + BigNo2[j] + overflowCarry;

        //** if the sum will go out of the base then
        //** we will find ourselves in an overflow situation
        if (sum >= BASE)
        {
            carry = 1;

            //** adjust in such way that
            //** the sum will fit within a digit
            sum -= BASE;
        }
        else
            //** otherwise no carryOverflow
```

---

[7] The code is meant to be a sketch of a function that transforms a simple integer to a big integer. The source code will not compile without a proper adjustment for a real cryptographic application.

```
            carry = 0;

        //** add the result in the same sum variable
        BigNo3[j] = sum;
    }

    //** if we are getting to the
    //** end, we can expect an overflow
    if (carry)
        printf ("There is an overflow in the addition!\n");
}
```

Let's continue with multiplication by using a basic method to multiply two large numbers, X and Y, multiplying each X digit with each Y digit. The output is a partial product. The output result is shifted to the left for every new digit. Our `multiplying OneDigit` function multiplies an entire large integer using a single digit. The result is placed in a new large integer. We also present another function, `left_shifting`, which shifts the number to the left with a certain number of spaces. It is multiplied using b^i, where b is the base, and i represents the number of spaces. Let's take a quick look at the algorithm.

Listing 4-12. Multiplication[8]

```
void multiply (int BigInt1[], int BigInt2[], int BigInt3[])
{
    int length_of_integer;
    int x, y, P[length_of_integer];

    //** C stores the sum of
    //** partial products. It is initially 0.
    transformIntToBigInt (BigInt3, 0);

    //* for each digit in BigInt1
    for (x=0; x<length_of_integer; x++)
    {
```

---

[8] The code is meant to be a sketch of a function that transforms a simple integer to a big integer. The source code will not compile without a proper adjustment for a real cryptographic application.

```
        //** multiply BigInt2 by digit [x]
        multiplyUsingOneDigit (BigInt2, P, BigInt1[x]);

        //** left shifting the partial product with i bytes
        leftShifting(P, x);

        //** add the output result to the current sum
        addResult(BigInt3, P, BigInt3);
    }
}
```

Next, let's examine a function that uses a single digit to multiply.

Listing 4-13. Multiplying Using a Single Digit[9]

```
void multiplyUsingOneDigit (int BigOne1[], int BigOne2[],
                                          int number) {
    int      k, carryOverflow;
    int N, BASE;

    //** there is nothing related to
    //** extra overflow to be added at this moment
    carryOverflow = 0;

    //** for each digit, starting with least significant...

    for (k=0; k<N; k++){
        //** multiply the digit by number,
        //** putting the result in BigOne2
         BigOne2[k] = number * BigOne1[k];

        //** adding any extra overflow that is taking
        //** place starting with the last digit
        BigOne2[k] += carryOverflow;

        //** product is too big to fit in a digit
        if (BigOne2[k] >= BASE) {
```

---

[9] The code is meant to be a sketch of a function that transforms a simple integer to a big integer. The source code will not compile without a proper adjustment for a real cryptographic application.

```
            //** handle the overflow
            carryOverflow = BigOne2[k]/BASE;
            BigOne2[k] %= BASE;
        }
        else
            //** no overflow
            carryOverflow = 0;
    }
    if (carryOverflow)
        printf ("During the multiplication
                        we experienced an overflow!\n");
}
```

Let's continue with a function that shifts to leave a specific number of spaces.

Listing 4-14. Shift to Left of a Specific Number of Spaces[10]

```
void leftShifting (int BigInt1[], int number) {
    int i;

    //** moving from left to right,
    //** we will move anything with left n spaces
    for (i=N-1; i>= number; i--)
        BigInt1[i] = BigInt1[i- number];

    //** complete the last n digits with zeros
    while (i >= 0) BigInt1[i--] = 0;
}
```

Review of Large Integer Libraries

Several libraries and frameworks already implemented are dealing with high numbers. Their development process was suspended for some of them, but they are still used in cryptography applications.

---

[10] The code is meant to be a sketch of a function that transforms a simple integer to a big integer. The source code will not compile without a proper adjustment for a real cryptographic application.

The following libraries work with big integers.

- **Matt McCutchen**[11] proposes a very easy-to-use C++ library for calculations on big integers [1]. The code has very good explanations, and it is easy to follow. The results obtained in symmetric and asymmetric cryptography algorithms were promising. Most of the results were compared with other tools for reference and checking, such as CryptTool[12].

- **L3HARRIS Geospatial Solutions** is a library that is fast on computations is the Big Integer Class [2] from L3HARRIS Geospatial Solutions[13].

- **Boost Library**[14] is a strong library used to achieve tasks based on linear algebra, pseudorandom number generation, multithreading, image processing, regular expression, and unit testing. The library has an impressive set of independent libraries, approximately 160, and the documentation is well-structured and easy to follow and use [3].

- **GMP Library** is a free library that can be used for random precision arithmetic is GNU Multiple Precision Arithmetic Library (GMP)[15]. It offers large support for operations based on signed integers, rational numbers, and floating-point numbers (see Chapter 5 for more details). The library's only limitations are those that involve the available memory. The limits are $2^{32} - 1$ bits on 32-bit and $2^{37} - 1$ bits on 64-bit. The main interface is for C/C++, but there is also support for C#, .NET, and OCaml (easily can be ported for Haskell as well. For more information, take a look at [4], [5], and [11]). Additionally, there is important support for Ruby, PHP, Python, R, Perl, and Wolfram Language. The audience of the library includes cryptography software applications, security of the Internet, and algebra systems.

---

[11] Matt McCutchen's Web Site, `https://mattmccutchen.net/`

[12] CryptTool, `https://www.cryptool.org/en/`

[13] L3HARRIS Geospatial Solutions, `https://www.harrisgeospatial.com`

[14] Boost Library, `http://www.boost.org`

[15] GMP Library, `http://gmplib.org`

- **LibBF Library [8]** works with floating-point numbers represented in base 2. The library is based and implemented on the IEEE 754 standard [7]. The example provided on the library web page, TinyPI, is a very good example showing its power. This library is examined further in Chapter 5.

- **Bignum C++ Library [9]** (or TTMath is a larger library that includes Bignum C++ library) allows personal and commercial users to perform arithmetic operations. The types of integers supported are big unsigned integers, big signed integers, and big floating-point numbers. There is support for mathematical operations, such as adding, subtracting, dividing, and multiplying.

The current example, described in [10], creates an object characterized by two words each. On a 32-bit platform, the maximum value that can be held is $2^{32*2} - 1$. Note that the author shows that variables can be initialized with string or, if you are dealing with small values using a standard type such as unsigned int.

Listing 4-15. Using ttmath::UInt<>

```
#include <ttmath/ttmath.h>
#include <iostream>

int main()
{
    ttmath::UInt<2> firstA, secondB, thirdC;

        a = "8765";
        b = 3456;
        c = a*b;

        std::cout << thirdC << std::endl;
}
```

Conclusion

The chapter discussed the general representations of big integers and their operations. It analyzed the most important methods and approaches for computing addition, subtraction, and multiplication for large numbers. The chapter also discussed big integer libraries, providing the advantages that a professional needs when setting up an environment for developing cryptographic algorithms.

References

[1].   C++ Big Integer Library. Available online: `https://mattmccutchen.net/bigint/`. Last accessed: 12.12.2022.

[2].   BigInteger Class L3HARRIS Geospatial. Available online: `https://www.harrisgeospatial.com/docs/BIGINTEGER.html`. Last accessed: 12.12.2022

[3].   Boost Library Documentation. Available online: `https://www.boost.org/doc/libs/1_72_0/`. Last accessed: 12.12.2022

[4].   Nita, S. L. and Mihailescu, M. (2017). Practical Concurrent Haskell: With Big Data Applications. Apress.

[5].   Nita, S. L. and Mihailescu, M. (2019). Haskell Quick Syntax Reference. Apress.

[6].   Bellard. Available online: `https://bellard.org/libbf/`. Last accessed: 12.12.2022

[7].   IEEE 754-2019 – Standard for Floating-Point Arithmetic. Available online: `https://standards.ieee.org/content/ieee-standards/en/standard/754-2019.html`. Last accessed: 12.12.2022

[8].   LibBF Library. Available online: `https://bellard.org/libbf/`. Last accessed: 12.12.2022

[9].   Bignum Library. Available online: `https://www.ttmath.org/`. Last accessed: 12.12.2022

[10].   TTMath Samples. Available online: `https://www.ttmath.org/samples`. Last accessed: 12.12.2022

[11].   Mena, A. S. (2019). *Practical Haskell: A Real World Guide to Programming*. Apress.

CHAPTER 5

Floating-Point Arithmetic

Working with large numbers can be seen as abstract art, as covered in Chapter 4. If the encryption schemes are not implemented correctly, the entire cryptographic method might result in a serious fatality.

Floating-point mathematics and its significance for cryptography are the focus of this chapter.

Why Floating-Point Arithmetic?

Due to the representations and implementation techniques, floating-point arithmetic is an important subfield of mathematics that requires careful attention. In homomorphic encryption or chaos-based cryptography, this kind of arithmetic can be applied (covered in Chapter 14 and Chapter 12).

Systems that use both very small and very large real numbers can contain computations that use floating-point values. Their computations need a very quick procedure. A particular class of variables called *floating-point variables* may store real values, such as 5420.0, − 4.213,or 0.045634. The *floating* part of the name shows that the decimal point can "float."

Different floating-point data types, including the float, double, and long double types, are available in C++. The language does not define the size of these types, as you know from the case of C++ with integers. Most floating-point representations on current processors adhere to the IEEE 754 standard [1] for binary representation format. This standard specifies that a *float* type has four bytes, a *double* has eight, a *long double* has eight bytes (the same as the double), and both are 80 bits (by padding, there are 12 bytes or 16 bytes).

© Marius Iulian Mihailescu and Stefania Loredana Nita 2023
M. I. Mihailescu and S. L. Nita, *Pro Cryptography and Cryptanalysis with C++23*,
https://doi.org/10.1007/978-1-4842-9450-5_5

Always include at least one decimal when working with floating-point values. For the compiler to distinguish between a floating number and an integer, this is very useful. Cryptographers need to know this.

```
int a{5};          //** 5 represents an integer
double b{4.0};     //** 4.0 represents a floating point (with no
                   //** suffix - double type by default)
float c{2.0f};     //** 2.0 represents a floating point (f is the
                   //** suffix, which means a float type)
```

Displaying Floating-Point Numbers

Listing 5-1 shows how to display floating-point values.

Listing 5-1. Display Common Float Numbers

```
#include <iostream>

using namespace std;

int main()
{
    cout << 5.0 << endl;
    cout << 6.7f << endl;
    cout << 9876543.21 << endl;

    return 0;
}
```

The result shown in Figure 5-1 is achieved by running the example.

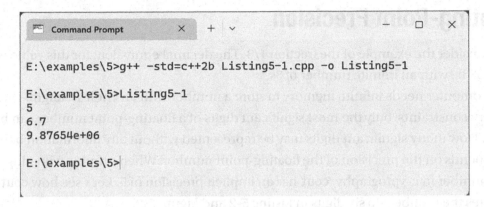

Figure 5-1. *The output of common float numbers*

By examining the program's output, you can see that, in the first instance, the output is 5 bytes, but the source code contains 5.0. This occurs as a result of the fractional part being equal to 0. The second instance prints the number exactly as it appears in the original code. In the third instance, scientific notation displays the number, which is beneficial for cryptography methods.

The Range of Floating Points

Table 5-1 gives the sizes, range, and precision according to the IEEE 754 standard.

Table 5-1. *IEEE 754 Standard Representation*

Size	Range	Precision
4 bytes	$\pm 1.18 \times 10^{-38}$ *to* $\pm 3.4 \times 10^{38}$	The most significant digits are 6–9; typically, 7 digits.
8 bytes	$\pm 2.23 \times 10^{-308}$ *to* $\pm 1.80 \times 10^{308}$	The most significant digits are 15–18; typically, 16 digits.
80-bits (typically 12 or 16 bytes)	$\pm 3.36 \times 10^{-4932}$ *to* $\pm 1.18 \times 10^{4932}$	The most significant digits are 18–21.
16 bytes	$\pm 3.36 \times 10^{-4932}$ *to* $\pm 1.18 \times 10^{4932}$	The most significant digits are 33–36.

On modern CPUs, the 80-bit floating-point is implemented using 12 or 16 bytes. It makes sense that the CPUs could manage data of this size.

Floating-Point Precision

Let's consider the example of the fraction 1/3. The decimal equivalent for this value is 0.3333333... with an infinite number of 3s.

A computer needs infinite memory to store a number with an endless length. Due to memory constraints, only the most significant digits of a floating-point number can be stored. How many significant digits may be represented without any information being lost depends on the precision of the floating-point number. When printing a floating-point number in cryptography, cout has an implicit precision of 6. Let's see how cout truncates the numbers to six digits in Listing 5-2 and Figure 5-2.

Listing 5-2. Representation of Floating-Point Precision

```
#include <iostream>

using namespace std;

int main()
{
    cout << 7.56756767f << endl;
    cout << 765.657667f << endl;
    cout << 345543.564f << endl;
    cout << 9976544.43f << endl;
    cout << 0.00043534345f << endl;

    return 0;
}
```

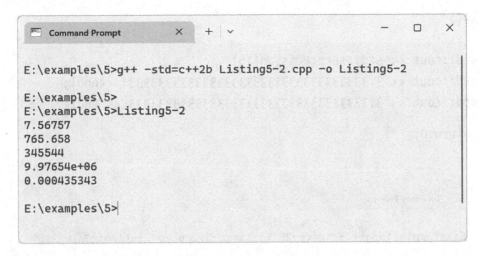

Figure 5-2. *Output of floating-point precision*

Keep in mind that there are only six important digits in each of the scenarios.

Observe that the output from cout in some situations is shown using scientific notations. Typically, the exponent is padded with a minimal number of digits, depending on the compiler that was used. The number of exponent digits displayed depends on the compiler; Visual Studio uses 3, whereas other compilers use 2 (that are implemented according to C99 instructions and standards).

Both sizes and the value stored affect how many digits and how precisely a floating-point number is represented. The precision of the *float* values is between 6 and 9, with the lowest number of important digits being 7. The precision of the *double* values is shown with 15 and 18 digits. Depending on how the bytes are used, *long double* numbers are represented with at least a precision of 15 or 33 significant digits.

The setprecision() method is used in Listing 5-3 to modify the default precision that cout or std::cout displays. The iomanip header contains the implementation for the setprecision() method. The result is shown in Figure 5-3.

Listing 5-3. Default Precision

```
#include <iostream>
#include <iomanip>

using namespace std;
```

```cpp
int main()
{
    std::cout << std::setprecision(16);
    std::cout << 3.3333333333333333333333333333333333f <<endl;
    std::cout << 3.3333333333333333333333333333333333 << endl;

    return 0;
}
```

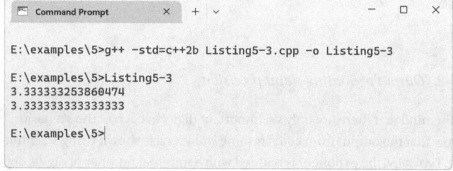

Figure 5-3. *Override the default precision*

The precision in Figure 5-3 has been set to 16 digits; therefore, each number is displayed with a 16-digit precision. The problems with precision do not only affect fractional numbers but also affect any number with multiple important digits.

Next Level for Floating-Point Arithmetic

Homomorphic encryption, a powerful form of encryption, is discussed in Chapter 12. A particular form of encryption called homomorphic encryption is employed as a professional technique for maintaining privacy, while storage and computations can be outsourced. Data can be encrypted using this sort of encryption and then outsourced to commercial (or public) environments for processing while still being encrypted. Ring learning with errors (see Chapter 13) is one of the sources of homomorphic encryption, which is connected to private set intersections [2].

Finding the correct approach to approximating a real number in such a way as to provide a compromise between range and precision is essential when dealing with complex cryptosystems, where floating-point representation constitutes the core of the encryption/decryption mechanisms.

The word *floating* refers to the ability of a number's decimal point to move, which indicates that it can be placed in any place connected to the important digits of the number. A floating-point number can be represented as four integers when dealing with complicated cryptosystems, such as homomorphic encryption.

$$a = \pm d \cdot n^{f-j}$$

n stands for the base, f for the exponent, j for precision, and d for the important digits, which must adhere to the following relationship.

$$0 \le d \le n^f - 1$$

For manipulating floating-point numbers, C++ provides the functions fmod, remainder, and remquo. These functions are all contained in the cmath header file. These fundamental functions, introduced in C++11, are used to handle straightforward mathematical operations involving floating-point values required for mainstream programming and encryption (low and simple concepts). The functions are relatively restrictive for advanced cryptography techniques and do not give cryptographers the necessary tools. Specialized libraries such as the Boost Multiprecision Library, TTMath, LibBF, GNU Multiple Precision Library perform difficult computations with large real numbers. These are the ones that enable experts to complete their difficult assignments using complex cryptosystems.

Conclusion

The chapter covered floating-point number general representations and how complex cryptosystems employ them. It examined the key ideas that a professional needs when setting up a workspace to create sophisticated cryptosystems that imply floating-point numbers.

The chapter also highlighted the significance of floating-point arithmetic for complex cryptosystems such as homomorphic encryption, chaos-based cryptography, lattice-based cryptography, or ring learning with errors. Advanced cryptosystems cannot be implemented correctly without thoroughly understanding floating-point arithmetic. Poor implementation can result in a major catastrophe for big data or commercial cloud computing environments.

References

[1]. *D. Zuras, M. Cowlishaw, A. Aiken, M. Applegate, D. Bailey, S. Bass, S. Canon, S. IEEE standard for floating-point arithmetic. IEEE Std, 754(2008), 1-70, 2008.*

[2]. H. Chen, K. Laine, and P. Rindal, *Fast Private Set Intersection from Homomorphic Encryption.* 2018.

[3]. Ducas and D. Micciancio, "FHEW: bootstrapping homomorphic encryption in less than a second," in Advances in Cryptology–Eurocrypt 2015, pp. 617–640, Springer, 2015.

[4]. S. Halevi and V. Shoup, "Algorithms in HElib," in Crypto'14, vol. 8616, Springer, 2014.

[5]. J. Campos, P. Sharma, E. Jantunen, D. Baglee, and L. Fumagalli, "The Challenges of Cybersecurity Frameworks to Protect Data Required for the Development of Advanced Maintenance," *Procedia CIRP*, vol. 47, pp. 222–227, 2016.

[6]. C. Burnikel and J. Ziegler, "Fast recursive division," Research Report, MPI-I-98-1-022, Max–Planck–Institut fur Informatik, Saarbrucken, Germany, 1998.

[7]. N. Dowlin, R. Gilad-Bachrach, K. Laine, K. Lauter, M. Naehrig, and J. Wernsing, "Manual for using homomorphic encryption for bioinformatics," Proceedings of the IEEE, vol. 105, no. 3, 2017.

[8]. J. H. Cheon, A. Kim, M. Kim, and Y. Song, "Homomorphic encryption for arithmetic of approximate numbers," in Proceedings of the International Conference on the Theory and Application of Cryptology and Information Security (ASIA-CRYPT'17), pp. 409–437, Hong Kong, China, December 2017.

CHAPTER 6

New Features in C++23

C++23 is an informal name for the next version of the standard C++ programming language, known as ISO/IEC 14882[1] and issued by the working group ISO/IEC JTC1/SC22/WG21. Materials related to the progress of C++23 are at `https://github.com/cplusplus/draft`, `https://en.cppreference.com/w/`, and `https://cplusplus.com/`.

The toolchain, which comprises all the many applications and services that work together to deliver unique tools within C++23, is one essential component of the current application development life cycle. They include testing tools, continuous integration, and delivery (CI/CD) pipelines, IDEs, editors, and code generators that produce scaffolding and deploy application frameworks. It is simple to become accustomed to one set of tools and use them exclusively.

C++23 is planned to be finalized by the end of 2023, providing features such as the support for standard library modules and a much faster compilation process.

Note Because of the COVID-19 pandemic, the meetings[2] were postponed (see the meetings from Varna, June 2022; Kona, Hawaii, February 2021; and New York,[3,4] November 2020). New features were added to the C++23 draft, and others were inserted once the virtual WG21 meeting was held on November 9, 2020. Some features remain the same as those from the C++20 version.

Many of the ambitions and features for the new C++23 have been postponed due to restrictions and pandemic situations, such as pattern matching, contracts, and concurrency models. The features will be developed within C++26.

---

[1] See `https://www.iso.org/standard/79358.html`

[2] See `https://www.open-std.org/jtc1/sc22/wg21/docs/papers/2020/p2145r0.html`

[3] See `https://isocpp.org/std/meetings-and-participation/upcoming-meetings`

[4] See `https://www.open-std.org/jtc1/sc22/wg21/docs/papers/2020/n4862.pdf`

© Marius Iulian Mihailescu and Stefania Loredana Nita 2023
M. I. Mihailescu and S. L. Nita, *Pro Cryptography and Cryptanalysis with C++23*,
https://doi.org/10.1007/978-1-4842-9450-5_6

According to Bjarne Stroustrup, the language will have support for a standard library module called std and support for coroutines. C++23 is developed under the ISO, and some of the new improvements are minor, but they will not be minor improvements. From the beginning, C++23 was not supposed to be a major upgrade for C++. Instead, versions C++11 and C++20 represented major improvements. For example, with the help of a standard library module, the well-known, simple program "Hello World" becomes what's shown in Listing 6-1. It is compiled ten times faster than the previous version that uses #include <iostream>.

Listing 6-1. Classic Hello World Example with Standard Library Module

```
import std;:

int main()
{
    std::cout << "Hello, World!\n";
}
```

Next, let's discuss the following new features from C++23 concerning the proposed schedule by WG21[5].

- Headers
- Core language features
- Library features

Headers

The following headers represent the most important features added in C++23.

- <expected>[6]
- <generator>[7]
- <flat_map>[8]

---

[5] See https://www.open-std.org/jtc1/sc22/wg21/docs/papers/2020/p1000r4.pdf
[6] See https://en.cppreference.com/w/cpp/header/expected
[7] See https://en.cppreference.com/w/cpp/header/generator
[8] See https://en.cppreference.com/w/cpp/header/flat_map

- <mdspan>[9]
- <print>[10]
- <spanstream>[11]
- <stacktrace>[12]
- <stdfloat>[13]
- <stdatomic>[14]

Next, let's discuss the <expected>, <generator>, and <flat_map> headers, as they are vital for the implementation of cryptography algorithms and any other secure algorithms that might be implemented as solutions, giving general information about their structure and how they are designed within the new C++23.

The <expected> Header

What is the purpose of <expected> header? The <expected> header[15] can be seen as a wrapper containing an expected value or an error value. Unfortunately, at this moment, there is not much information and few examples available online, except for those available at cppreference.com[16] or sobyte.net[17].

The <expected> header provides an easy way to store two values. Once an object is declared (e.g., std::expected), it can hold an *expected* value with type T or an *unexpected* value of type E. A description of the two parameters, T and E, is shown in Table 6-1.

---

[9] See https://en.cppreference.com/w/cpp/header/mdspan

[10] See https://en.cppreference.com/w/cpp/header/print

[11] See https://en.cppreference.com/w/cpp/header/spanstream

[12] See https://en.cppreference.com/w/cpp/header/stacktrace

[13] See https://en.cppreference.com/w/cpp/header/stdfloat

[14] See https://en.cppreference.com/w/cpp/header/stdatomic.h and https://github.com/dotnet/runtime/issues/57618

[15] See https://en.cppreference.com/w/cpp/utility/expected

[16] See https://en.cppreference.com/w/cpp/header/expected

[17] See https://www.sobyte.net/post/2022-05/cpp-std-expected/

Table 6-1. *Parameter Descriptions*

Template Parameter	Description
T	Represents the type of the expected value. There are two possible types: void or must comply with the requirements that characterize Destructible.[18]
E	Represents the type of the unexpected value. This parameter has to comply with Destructible requirements, and it has to be a valid template argument for std::unexpected.

Note   The main advantage of std::expected object is that it cannot be without value. The value must be either *expected* or *unexpected*. The stored value is allocated straight within the storage that it has been assigned with the declaration of the expected object.

The new C++23 comes with four new classes (expected, unexpected, bad_excepted_access, unexpect_t). Listing 6-2 is a short synopsis of the std namespace for <expected>, as it is presented and described by cpprefrence.com.[19]

Listing 6-2. std namespace for <expected> header[10]

```
namespace std {
  // class template unexpected
  template<class E> class unexpected;

  // class template bad_expected_access
  template<class E> class bad_expected_access

  // specialization of bad_expected_access for void
  template<> class bad_expected_access<void>;
```

---

[18] See https://en.cppreference.com/w/cpp/named_req/Destructible
[19] See https://en.cppreference.com/w/cpp/header/expected

```
  // in-place construction of unexpected values
  struct unexpect_t {
    explicit unexpect_t() = default;
  };
  inline constexpr unexpect_t unexpect{};

  // class template expected
  template<class T, class E> class expected;

  // partial specialization of expected for void types
  template<class T, class E> requires is_void_v<T> class expected<T, E>;
}
```

The <generator> Header

The <generator> header is part of the range's library.[20] The header helps us to have access to random number generation methods by providing a combination between generators and distributions.

The new approach within C++23 clears the difference between generators and distributions, although several issues[21,22,23] have been raised related to the formatting std::generator and other versions from C++20 std::format. A simple example of these issues is listed in Listing 6-3. We cannot make std::generator formattable due to its *const-iterable* or *copyable*, and the std::format gets as an argument the const&. In C++20, this was not a problem that programmers experienced, but in C++23, according to the reports, this represents a major problem due to the range adapters.

---

[20] See https://en.cppreference.com/w/cpp/ranges
[21] See https://isocpp.org/files/papers/P2418R2.html
[22] See https://isocpp.org/files/papers/P2418R2.html#biblio-p2286
[23] See https://isocpp.org/files/papers/P2418R2.html#biblio-p2168

Listing 6-3. An Example of an Issue Between std::generator (C++23) and std::format (C++20)

```
auto ints (int number) -> std::generator<int> {
  for (int n = 0; n < n; ++i)
  {
    co_yield n;
  }
}
// an error
std::format("{}", ints_coro(10));
```

The <flat_map> Header

The <flat_map> header is contained within the containers[24] library. Its purpose is to adapt a specific container to provide a collection of key-value pairs sorted using the unique keys.

As far as the reports are published about the evolution of C++23, the header will contain six classes, two functions, and two constants, as shown in Table 6-2.

---

[24] See https://en.cppreference.com/w/cpp/container

Table 6-2. *Classes, Functions, and Constants in the <flat_map> Header*

Classes	`flat_map`
	`flat_multimap`
	`sorted_unique_t`
	`sorted_equivalent_t`
	`std::uses_allocator<std::flat_map>`
	`std::uses_allocator<std::flat_multimap>`
Functions	`erase_if(std::flat_map)`
	`erase_if(std::flat_multimap)`
Constants	`sorted_unique`
	`sorted_equivalent`

Conclusion

This chapter discussed the new features that the new C++23 will deliver to programmers and professionals. It gave a short overview of the main classes, functions, and constants for those headers that can be used within cryptography applications.

The chapter has focused only on three headers, `<expected>`, `<generator>`, and `<flat_map>`, which a programmer that wishes to implement cryptography algorithms should take into consideration.

Now that you've reached the end of this chapter, you should understand C++20 and C++23 features and be able to identify sources that can help programmers improve their work in cryptography.

References

[1].   R. Siddhartha. *Sams Teach Yourself C++: In One Hour a Day*. Ninth edition, SAMS, 2022.

[2].   G. Rainer. *C++ Core Guidelines Explained: Best Practices for Modern C++*. 1st edition, Addison-Wesley Professional, 2022.

[3].   Ś. Rafał. *Modern CMake for C++ Discover a Better Approach to Building, Testing, and Packaging Your Software*. Packt Publishing Limited, 2022.

[4].   B. U. Sufyan, editor. *Mastering C++ Programming Language: A Beginner's Guide*. First edition, CRC Press, Taylor & Francis Group, 2022.

[5].   G. S. Tselikis. *Introduction to C++*. CRC Press, 2023.

CHAPTER 7

Secure Coding Guidelines

The vulnerabilities of software applications typically have high costs. In 2022, the global average total data breach cost was $4.35 million [1]. The efforts to eliminate vulnerabilities from the software application should focus on secure coding, avoiding vulnerabilities being deployed in the production phase.

Secure coding rules for development are necessary because they facilitate the prevention of security flaws and maintain the confidentiality, integrity, and availability of sensitive data processed by the application. Security flaws in applications, such as buffer overflows, SQL injection, or cross-site scripting (XSS), can be readily exploited by attackers to obtain unauthorized access to sensitive data, steal confidential information, or disrupt program operations. Developers may build code that is less prone to these sorts of security flaws and more resistant to attacks by following secure coding principles. Furthermore, secure code rules aid in the promotion of good coding practices and the creation of code that is manageable, legible, and scalable. Developers may produce code that is simpler to maintain, debug, and test by adopting best practices, which can lead to more efficient development and higher code quality.

Writing a secure source code represents a difficult task to achieve. It is very important to understand the implications of the code being written and to have a checklist of the "things" that need to be checked. The checklist helps developers quickly verify their code for well-known security problems. Usually, it is normal for verification to be performed by a security team and not by software developers or engineers. Software developers cannot be objective with their own code.

The idea of a checklist should start from the following idea: verifying the source code that processes data outside of its domain and considering the user input, the network communication, the process of the binary files, receiving output from database management systems or servers, and so on.

© Marius Iulian Mihailescu and Stefania Loredana Nita 2023
M. I. Mihailescu and S. L. Nita, *Pro Cryptography and Cryptanalysis with C++23*,
https://doi.org/10.1007/978-1-4842-9450-5_7

When working with a software application (it doesn't matter that the application is a desktop, web, or mobile), the idea that the application is secure because a well-known company developed it is just a myth. Don't trust and go on this path because most companies spend a lot of the budget on security incidents, maintenance, consultancy, and audit sessions.

There are two environments in which a software application is working, and its behavior is different because of that environment. The software application that is under analysis and development process within the company represents its circle of trust (at least, most companies think in this way, and they enjoy considering their infrastructure very resistant to security attacks). The behavior of the software application in that circle of trust represents the most critical environment in which an application can be developed and tested. No developer, IT security officer, or software analyst should hack their own code. This environment is the comfort zone. Once the application leaves that comfort zone and enters the real environment, the issues begin. The trust boundary is hard and easy to draw at the same time and creates a delimitation between the comfort zone and the real zone. It is not an easy task to achieve, especially if those application applications are running in a virtualized infrastructure, cloud, or big data environment.

In the comfort zone, malicious end users represent a security threat. The malicious end users attack the software application's confidentiality and/or integrity. One of the interesting methods and concepts proposed was *software obfuscation*.

Secure Coding Checklist

This section discusses and proposes a secure coding checklist (it can also be seen as a procedure). This is an example of such a checklist (see Table 7-1), which can be developed as much as you want. The checklist contains minimal examples of items that can be checked when code is written in C++, regardless of which operating system the code runs on. One of the most frequent practices among developers is to suppress warnings that are not beneficial.

The "CERT Coding Standards" and "Rules" sections discuss the most important rules to apply to your process of developing cryptographic algorithms. Each rule is well explained within the guide.

Table 7-1. *Example of Secure Coding Checklist*

No. #	Item to be checked	Description	Yes/No	Notes
1	***Compiler warnings***			

Make sure that the compiler output and a flag are raised for receiving notifications for the potential errors listed for the following items.

✓ `-Wall`
✓ `-Wmissing-declarations`
✓ `-Wmissing-prototypes`
✓ `-Wredundant-decls`
✓ `-Wshadow`
✓ `-Wstrict-prototypes`
✓ `-Wformat=2`

For more flags with their definitions and actions, the GCC Options to Request or Suppress Warnings section should be followed [2]. This is very useful if complex cryptographic algorithms and security schemes are being implemented.

| 2 | ***Enough buffer memory when working with strings*** | | | |

Check the following functions if there is an upper limit for the destination buffer when a copy process is done until '\0\' (NULL) is met. To avoid this situation, the recommendation is to allocate enough memory space for the destination buffer before copying the data.

✓ `strcpy()`
✓ `strcat()`
✓ `sprint()`
✓ `scanf()`
✓ `gets()`

(continued)

Table 7-1. (*continued*)

No. #	Item to be checked	Description	Yes/No	Notes
3	**Direct breaks in system security**			

Checking for untrusted input leads to a directly breach of the application security. This step protects the application against malicious users and attackers exploiting your program using metachars.

✔ system()
✔ popen()
✔ fork(2)
✔ exec(2)
✔ s_popen()
✔ HXproc_* [3]

4	**Wrong parameter size and unexpected results**			

When complex programs are written, for example, the implementation of SHA-256 from Chapter 2, Listing 2-9, assigning a wrong size of one of the parameters, or doing a wrong arithmetic operation can cause a serious pitfall, and immediately a fix should be provided. Make sure that the same size allocated for the parameters is the same size on the destination side. As a best practice, especially in implementing cryptography algorithms, it is better to work with size_t type. Be type-safe, and don't create overflows.

✔ strncpy()
✔ strncat()
✔ snprintf()

(*continued*)

Table 7-1. (*continued*)

No. #	Item to be checked	Description	Yes/No	Notes
5	***Too much memory allocated***			

Allocating too much memory and external parameters represents a certain part of the size. Then you are dealing with a wrong memory allocation and experience *denial-of-service*. To avoid this, use the following criteria.

✓ malloc(), calloc(), alloca()

✓ No integer overflows

✓ Avoid arithmetical issues

✓ Verification for any possible operation with untrusted
   integer that could lead for an integer overlow.

| 6 | ***Wrong casts*** | | | |

Avoid the following code. The compiler thinks that malloc returns an incorrect int. It creates a bug that hackers can easily exploit.

```
char *a = malloc(10) - bad cast
class BaseClass {};
class DerivedClass: public BaseClass {};

BaseClass b; BaseClass* pb;
DerivedClass d; DerivedClass* pd;

//good cast
pb = dynamic_cast<BaseClass*>(&d);

//bad cast
pd = dynamic_cast<DerivedClass*>(&b);
```

(*continued*)

Table 7-1. (*continued*)

No. #	Item to be checked	Description	Yes/No	Notes
7	*Variable parameter lists*			

When implementing security schemes based on strings, you experience a new type of problem that security analysts or ethical hackers enjoy playing with it when performing tests. Ethical hackers commonly use a simple test to check untrusted data to check if a function allows a variable as a list of parameters or arguments, such as *printf()*. The untrusted data (created by an ethical hacker) is directly used as a string format and not as an argument. The following logic should be used for any similar situations.

✓ Wrong way: `snprintf(buffer, sizeof(buffer), the_input_of_the_user)`

✓ Right way: `snprintf(buffer, sizeof(buffer), "%s", the_input_of_the_user)`

| 8 | *Operations with files* | | | |

When handling files during cryptographic operations, try to use `mkstemp()`.

| 9 | *File permissions* | | | |

Not everyone should be able to read or write from or to a file. To create files having assigned the wrong permission, try to use *unmask()*.

✓ At the beginning of the file use *unmask(077)*.

CERT Coding Standards

The CERT Coding Standards are a collection of safe coding rules produced by Carnegie Mellon University's CERT Coordination Center. These standards give rules and best practices for building secure and trustworthy code. They are intended to assist software developers in avoiding typical security vulnerabilities and ensuring the confidentiality, integrity, and availability of sensitive data processed by their applications. The CERT C++ Coding Standard has been developed only for versions of the C++ programming language defined by the ISO/IEC 14882-2014 standard.

The coding standard is very well organized and follows the following structure: identifiers, noncompliant code examples, compliant solutions, exceptions, risk assessment, automated detection, related vulnerabilities, and related guidelines [8].

Next, let's examine each item of the structure and its main objective and purpose.

Identifiers

This section provides the rules every identifier should follow. Each identifier has three parts.

- A three-letter mnemonic that represents the section within the standard.
- A numeric value of two digits is situated in the range 00 to 99.
- The language that is associated with it is represented as a suffix (e.g., -CPP, -C, -J, -PL).
  - -CPP: SEI CERT C++ Coding Standard [8]
  - -C: SEI CERT C Coding Standard [9]
  - -J: SEI CERT Oracle Coding Standard for Java [10]
  - -PL: SEI CERT Perl Coding Standard [11]

The three-letter mnemonic is used to group related coding practices and points out which category a related coding belongs to.

Noncompliant Code Examples and Compliant Solutions

Noncompliant code examples and compliant solutions demonstrate how to write code correctly and incorrectly per a given coding standard. A noncompliant code example is a piece of code that violates one or more of the coding standard's requirements. It might, for example, have an unsafe function, have insufficient input validation, or have a buffer overflow vulnerability.

A compliant solution, on the other hand, is a piece of code that adheres to the coding standards and provides a secure and trustworthy solution to the same problem. It may, for example, employ a secure function, provide rigorous input validation, and prevent buffer overflow problems. Noncompliant code examples and compliant solutions are used to teach and instruct developers on secure coding standards and to assist them in avoiding common security risks in their code. Developers may obtain a deeper knowledge of the best practices and strategies for building safe and dependable code by comparing and contrasting the noncompliant code examples with the compliant solutions. Examples of noncompliant code show code that violates the guideline. It is very important to keep in mind that these are only examples. The removal process of all appearances of the example does not mean that the code being analyzed complies with the SEI CERT standard.

Exceptions

Exceptions have an informative character and are not required to be followed. Any rules can have a set of exceptions that provide details about the circumstances in which the guideline does not need to be followed to ensure the software's safety, security, or reliability.

As with any type of exception, the principle is the same, no matter the programming language. Pay extra attention to the exceptions, catch any possible ones, and learn from them. Do not ignore and do not think that a programming language is perfect and has no bugs or certain doors that can be exploited.

Risk Assessment

The process of analyzing and measuring the likelihood and effect of possible security risks to an organization's information systems, data, and assets is known as risk assessment. A risk assessment seeks to identify and prioritize an organization's hazards and design and implement strategies to minimize or manage those risks. A risk assessment section is assigned for each CERT C++ Coding Standard guideline. The risk assessment section aims to provide software developers with the potential consequences for not following or addressing a specific rule or recommendation. Risk assessment appears to be a metric and is the main purpose of helping the remediation process of software applications and complex projects.

For each rule and recommendation, there is a *priority*. To assign a priority, it is recommended to understand IEC 60812 [12]. The priority is evaluated and assigned using a metric characterized by three analysis types: failure mode, effects, and criticality. Each rule also has a value assigned on a scale between 1 and 3, such as severity, likelihood, and remediation cost (see Table 7-2).

Table 7-2. *Assigning Values for Each Rule [8]*

Severity What are the consequences if the rule is ignored?

Value	Meaning	Examples of vulnerabilities
1	Low	Denial-of-service attack, unexpected termination
2	Medium	Information disclosure without any intention lead to the violation of the data integrity
3	High	Running code randomly

Likelihood Statistically speaking, what is the probability that a flaw has been introduced in the code by avoiding and ignoring the rule specifications and leading to a vulnerability that a malicious user could exploit?

Value	Definition
1	Unlikely
2	Probable
3	Likely

Remediation Cost What are the costs to follow and comply with the rule?

Value	Definition	Detection	Correction
1	High	Manual	Manual
2	Medium	Automatic	Manual
3	Low	Automatic	Automatic

For each of the rules, the values are multiplied together. The following metric (see Table 7-3) gives you a measure that can be useful to prioritize the rules within the application. The values are from 1 to 27. From all 27 values, only ten different values occur and are available in most cases, 1, 2, 3, 4, 6, 8, 9, 12, 18, and 27. Table 7-3 highlights the interpretations and meanings of the priorities and levels.

Table 7-3. *Levels and Priorities [8]*

Level	Priorities	Possible Interpretation
L1	12, 18, 27	High severity, likely, inexpensive to fix
L2	6, 8, 9	Medium severity, portable, medium cost to fix
L3	1, 2, 3, 4	Low severity, unlikely, expensive to repair

Automated Detection

Most rules and recommendations have automated detection processes and tools that help automatically diagnose violations. The Secure Coding Validation Suite [13] can be used to perform tests on the ability of analyzers to diagnose violations of the rules specified with ISO/IEC TS 17961:2013 [15], which is related to the rules of the SEI CERT C Coding Standard [14].

Related Guidelines

This section has a special slot when software applications are developed. According to the standard, it contains links, technical specifications, and guideline collections such as *Information Technology: Programming Languages, Their Environments, and System Software Interfaces: C Secure Coding Rules* [15]; *Information Technology: Programming Languages: Guidance to Avoiding Vulnerabilities in Programming Languages through Language Selection and Use* [16]; *MISRA C++ 2008: Guidelines for the Use of the C++ Language in Critical Systems* [17]; and CWE IDs in MITRE's Common Weakness Enumeration (CWE) [18]. [19]

Rules

Let's overview the main rules that strongly apply to implementing cryptographic algorithms and security schemes using C++23, especially with the new version. It is better to have in mind the following rules. Note that this chapter examines only six out of ten rules. All the explanations and examples are provided within the guide [20].

Some rules include rules from the C programming language that it applies to C++. The following rules can also be used within the procedure presented in Table 7-1.

Any information security officer, security analyst, or ethical hacker should design such a checklist. Developers can also use the checklist as a guide when developing critical cryptographic algorithms. Additionally, it is recommended to do a code review of the sections of the algorithms that are quite vulnerable and to make sure that the rules (Rule 01, Rule 02, Rule 03, Rule 05, Rule 06, and Rule 07) are followed as much as possible.

Following those rules gives security analysts or ethical hackers a certain level of trust that the security mechanisms (cryptographic algorithms, security protocols, security schemes, and other cryptographic primitives) are implemented properly and common vulnerabilities have been eliminated.

Rule 01. Declarations and Initializations (DCL)

Table 7-4. *Rule 01: Declarations and Initializations [20]*

Rule	Title
DCL50-CPP	Do not define a C-style variadic function.
DCL51-CPP	Do not declare or define a reserved identifier.
DCL52-CPP	Never qualify a reference type with const or volatile.
DCL53-CPP	Do not write syntactically ambiguous declarations.
DCL54-CPP	Overload allocation and deallocation functions as a pair in the same scope.
DCL55-CPP	Avoid information leakage when passing a class object across a trust boundary.
DCL56-CPP	Avoid cycles during the initialization of static objects.
DCL57-CPP	Do not let exceptions escape from destructors or deallocation functions.
DCL58-CPP	Do not modify the standard namespaces.
DCL59-CPP	Do not define an unnamed namespace in a header file.
DCL60-CPP	Obey the one-definition rule.
DCL30-C	Declare objects with appropriate storage durations.
DCL39-C	Avoid information leakage when passing a structure across a trust boundary.
DCL40-C	Do not create incompatible declarations of the same function or object.

Rule 02. Expressions (EXP)

Table 7-5. *Rule 02: Expressions [20]*

Rule	Title
EXP50-CPP	Do not depend on the order of evaluation for side effects.
EXP51-CPP	Do not delete an array through a pointer of the incorrect type.
EXP52-CPP	Do not rely on side effects in unevaluated operands.
EXP53-CPP	Do not read uninitialized memory.
EXP54-CPP	Do not access an object outside of its lifetime.
EXP55-CPP	Do not access a cv-qualified object through a cv-unqualified type.
EXP56-CPP	Do not call a function with a mismatched language linkage.
EXP57-CPP	Do not cast or delete pointers to incomplete classes.
EXP58-CPP	Pass an object of the correct type to va_start.
EXP59-CPP	Use offset of () on valid types and members.
EXP60-CPP	Do not pass a nonstandard-layout type object across execution boundaries.
EXP61-CPP	A lambda object must not outlive any of its reference-captured objects.
EXP62-CPP	Do not access the bits of an object representation that are not part of the object's value representation.
EXP63-CPP	Do not rely on the value of a moved-from object.

Rule 03. Integers (INT)

Table 7-6. *Rule 03: Integers [20]*

Rule	Title
INT50-CPP	Do not cast to an out-of-range enumeration value.
INT30-C	Ensure that unsigned integer operations do not wrap.
INT31-C	Ensure that integer conversions do not result in lost or misinterpreted data.
INT32-C	Ensure that operations on signed integers do not result in overflow.
INT33-C	Ensure that division and remainder operations do not result in divide-by-zero errors.
INT34-C	Do not shift an expression by a negative number of bits or greater than or equal to the number of bits in the operand.
INT35-C	Do not call a function with a mismatched language linkage.
INT36-C	Converting a pointer to an integer or integer to a pointer.

Rule 05. Characters and Strings (STR)

Table 7-7. *Rule 05: Characters and Strings [20]*

Rule	Title
STR50-CPP	Guarantee that storage for strings has sufficient space for character data and the null terminator.
STR51-CPP	Do not attempt to create a std::string from a null pointer.
STR52-CPP	Use valid references, pointers, and iterators to reference elements of a basic string.
STR53-CPP	Range check element access.
STR30-C	Do not attempt to modify string literals.
STR31-C	Guarantee that storage for strings has sufficient space for character data and the null terminator.
STR32-C	Do not pass a nonnull-terminated character sequence to a library function that expects a string.
STR34-C	Cast characters to unsigned chars before converting to larger integer sizes.
STR37-C	Arguments to character-handling functions must be representable as an unsigned char.
STR38-C	Do not confuse narrow and wide character strings and functions.

Rule 06. Memory Management (MEM)

Table 7-8. *Rule 06: Memory Management [20]*

Rule	Title
MEM50-CPP	Do not access freed memory.
MEM51-CPP	Properly deallocate dynamically allocated resources.
MEM52-CPP	Detect and handle memory allocation errors.
MEM53-CPP	Explicitly construct and destruct objects when manually managing object lifetime.
MEM54-CPP	Provide placement new with properly aligned pointers to sufficient storage capacity.
MEM55-CPP	Honor replacement dynamic storage management requirements.
MEM56-CPP	Do not store an already-owned pointer value in an unrelated smart pointer.
MEM57-CPP	Avoid using the default operator new for over-aligned types.
MEM30-C	Do not access freed memory.
MEM31-C	Free dynamically allocated memory when no longer needed.
MEM34-C	Only free memory is allocated dynamically.
MEM35-C	Allocate sufficient memory for an object.
MEM36-C	Do not modify the alignment of objects by calling realloc( ).

Rule 07. Input/Output (FIO)

Table 7-9. *Rule 07: Input/Output [20]*

Rule	Title
FIO50-CPP	Do not alternately input and output from a file stream without an intervening positioning call.
FIO51-CPP	Close files when they are no longer needed.
FIO30-C	Exclude user input from format strings.
FIO32-C	Do not perform operations on devices that are only appropriate for files.
FIO34-C	Distinguish between characters read from a file and EOF or WEOF.
FIO37-C	Do not assume that fgets() or fgetws() returns a nonempty string when successful.
FIO38-C	Do not copy a FILE object.
FIO39-C	Do not alternately input and output from a stream without an intervening flush or positioning call.
FIO40-C	Reset strings on fgets() or fgetws() failure.
FIO41-C	Do not call getc(), putc(), getwc(), or putwc() with a stream argument that has side effects.
FIO42-C	Close files when they are no longer needed.
FIO44-C	Only use values for fsetpos() returned from fgetpos().
FIO45-C	Avoid TOCTOU race conditions while accessing files.
FIO46-C	Do not access a closed file.
FIO47-C	Use valid format strings.

Conclusion

This chapter explained *rules* and *recommendations*. You pursued a journey of the most important security aspects that must be considered in developing cryptographic algorithms and security schemes. Secure coding rules are important because they help developers create secure applications, ensuring that there are no vulnerabilities that adversaries can exploit. Examples of security issues that can be avoided by following these rules are buffer overflows, malicious input, and other attacks. Code may be checked and certified to be safe by adhering to secure coding rules, and developers can utilize secure coding functions and libraries to prevent possible risks. Furthermore, the rules aid in avoiding hard-coded values, the safe management of memory, the sanitization of input and output, the use of secure encryption and hashing methods, and the protection of sensitive data. Following secure coding rules reduces the likelihood of security breaches and keeps your code secure.

Understanding the difference between a rule and a recommendation is very important. The general idea that has to be concluded at this point is that a rule has to follow a specific number of criteria compared with the *recommendation,* which represents a suggestion for improving code quality.

You should have acquired a significant amount of knowledge by the end of this chapter and now be capable of performing a security analysis of the source code, creating a secure coding checklist, filtering those aspects that are vital for the application, and instructing the developers as well on how to proceed when they are implementing cryptographic algorithms and written related source code.

References

[1]. Cost of a Data Breach. Available online: `https://www.ibm.com/reports/data-breach`. Last accessed: 15.1.2023

[2]. GCC Options to Request or Suppress Warnings. Available online: `https://gcc.gnu.org/onlinedocs/gcc/Warning-Options.html#Warning-Options`. Last accessed: 15.1.2023

[3]. HXprox_*, libHX – Get Things Done. Available online: `http://libhx.sourceforge.net/`. Last accessed: 15.1.2023

[4]. I. Staff, *Information Technology. Programming Languages. Guidance to Avoiding Vulnerabilities in Programming Languages Through Language Selection and Use (ISO/IEC TR 24772:2013)*. 2013.

[5]. *Information Technology - Programming Languages, Their Environments and System Software Interfaces - C Secure Coding Rules (ISO/IEC TS 17961:2012)*. 2012.

[6]. *Programming Languages — C++, Fourth Edition*. 2014.

[7]. R. C. Seacord and Carnegie, *Secure coding in C and C++*. Upper Saddle River, Nj: Addison-Wesley, 2013.

[8].   SEI CERT C++ Coding Standard: Available online: `https://wiki.sei.cmu.edu/confluence/pages/viewpage.action?pageId=88046682`. Last accessed: 15.1.2023

[9].   SEI CERT C Coding Standard. Available online: `https://wiki.sei.cmu.edu/confluence/display/c`. Last accessed: 3.2.2023

[10].   SEI CERT Oracle Coding Standard for Java. Available online: `https://wiki.sei.cmu.edu/confluence/display/java`. Last accessed: 3.2.2023

[11].   SEI CERT Perl Coding Standard. Available online: `https://wiki.sei.cmu.edu/confluence/display/perl`. Last accessed: 3.2.2023

[12].   *Analysis Techniques for System Reliability—Procedure for Failure Mode and Effects Analysis (FMEA)*, 2nd ed. (IEC 60812). Geneva, Switzerland: IEC, 2006.

[13].   Secure Coding Validation Suite. Available online: `https://github.com/SEI-CERT/scvs`. Last accessed: 3.2.2023

[14].   R. C. Seacord, *The CERT C coding standard: 98 rules for developing safe, reliable, and secure systems.* Upper Saddle River, Nj: Addison-Wesley, 2014.

[15].   *Information Technology—Programming Languages, Their Environments and System Software Interfaces—C Secure Coding Rules (ISO/IEC TS 17961).* ISO, 2012.

[16].   *Information Technology—Programming Languages—Guidance to Avoiding Vulnerabilities in Programming Languages through Language Selection and Use (ISO/IEC TR 24772:2013).* ISO, 2013.

[17].   Motor Industry Software Reliability Association, *MISRA C++ 2008 Guidelines for the Use of the C++ Language in Critical Systems*, 2008.

[18].   MITRE. Common Weakness Enumeration, Version 1.8. February 2010. Available online: `http://cwe.mitre.org/`. Last accessed: 3.2.2023

[19].   How this Coding Standard is Organized. Available online: `https://wiki.sei.cmu.edu/confluence/display/cplusplus/How+this+Coding+Standard+Is+Organized`. Last accessed: 3.2.2023

[20].   Rules. Available online: `https://wiki.sei.cmu.edu/confluence/pages/viewpage.action?pageId=88046322`. Last accessed: 3.2.2023

CHAPTER 8

Cryptography Libraries in C/C++23

The purpose of this chapter is to give a thorough list of C++ libraries that are compatible with C++23's new features. When professionals need access to a certain implementation of a particular functionality, time need not be wasted searching through many Internet resources to see other source code; professionals may gain insight into how to enhance their own code.

Overview of Cryptography Libraries

Table 8-1 provides a list of the most important cryptography libraries. The selection was mostly based on two metrics—execution speed and flexibility—and access to their source code based on their open source license. Professionals benefit greatly from having access to their source code since it allows them to compare their work and algorithms with those of other implementations, allowing them to enhance their work.

Table 8-1. *Main C/C++ Libraries*

Library Title	Developer Person/Industry	Programming Language	Open Source	References
OpenSSL	OpenSSL Project	C	X	[1][2][3]
Crypto++	Crypto C++ Project	C++	X	[7][8]
Botan	Jack Lloyd	C++	X	[5]
Libcrypt	GnuPC Community	C	X	[9][10]
GnuTLS	Simon Josefsson Nikos Mavrogiannopoulos	C	X	[11][12]
Cryptlib	Peter Gutmann	C	X	[13]

© Marius Iulian Mihailescu and Stefania Loredana Nita 2023
M. I. Mihailescu and S. L. Nita, *Pro Cryptography and Cryptanalysis with C++23*,
https://doi.org/10.1007/978-1-4842-9450-5_8

For each library, the best implementations of the cryptographic primitives (such as key generation and exchange, elliptic curve cryptography, public-key cryptography, hash functions, MAC algorithms, block ciphers, etc.) are introduced.

Hash Functions

Table 8-2 shows each cryptography library's features with different hash functions.

Chapter 2 presented a simple and basic implementation of the SHA-256 hash function, and you saw what it means to implement a hash function from scratch.

Table 8-2. *Existence of Hash Functions Within Cryptography Libraries*

Library Title	MD5	SHA-1	SHA-2	SHA-3	Whirlpool	GOST	BLAKE2
OpenSSL	X	X	X	X	X	X	X
Crypto++	X	X	X	X	X	X	X
Botan	X	X	X	X	X	X	X
Libcrypt	X	X	X	X	X	X	X
GnuTLS	The library represents the implementation of TLS, SSL, and DTLS protocols.						
Cryptlib	X	X	X	X	X	-	-

This section randomly selects a hash function from a library (e.g., MD5 implementation from OpenSSL) and provides some comments on their implementation. It is very important to mention that the implementation provided for the MD5 hash function is already implemented in OpenSSL, and this is done with respect to the original implementation from [4]. First, you need to download the openssl-1.1.1g.tar. gz file from source [4] and extract the content to access the source code (see Figure 8-1). Once extracted, navigate to the crypto folder following the path openssl-1.1.1g\ crypto. In this way, you can access the source code files of all the cryptographic algorithms implemented within the library.

KBytes	Date	File
9650	2023-Feb-07 15:38:20	openssl-1.1.1t.tar.gz (SHA256) (PGP sign) (SHA1)
14796	2023-Feb-07 15:38:20	openssl-3.0.8.tar.gz (SHA256) (PGP sign) (SHA1)
15115	2022-Dec-21 10:56:21	openssl-3.1.0-beta1.tar.gz (SHA256) (PGP sign) (SHA1)

Figure 8-1. *Downloading openssl-1.1.1g.tar.gz file with source code*

MD5 Hash Function Overview

This example is a simple algorithm and easy to follow and understand.

The implementation of MD5 has in its structure three files, two C/C++ files and one header file, and an ASM folder with three files written in Perl language (see Figure 8-2). The Perl files are optimizations for four platforms, such as 586, x86, x64, and sparc.

Figure 8-2. *Example of MD5 hash in action for a file*

Public-Key Cryptography

Most libraries include well-tested implementations of Public-Key Cryptography Standards (PKCS) (see Table 8-3).

Table 8-3. *Existence of Public-Key Cryptography Protocols Within Cryptography Libraries*

Library Title	PKCS#1	PKCS#5	PKCS#8	PKCS#12	IEEE P1363	ASN.1
OpenSSL	X	X	X	X	-	X
Crypto++	X	X	X	-	X	X
Botan	X	X	X	-	X	X
Libcrypt	X	X	X	X	X	X
Cryptlib	X	X	X	X	-	-

Next, let's demonstrate how to use public-key cryptography using OpenSSL. The following example should give a clearer idea about the workflow. Assume that two users—Alice and Bob—are communicating. The communication workflow is as follows.

Step 1: Alice generates a private key, `alicePrivKey.pem`, with 2048 bits (see Figure 8-3).

```
openssl genrsa -out alicePrivKey.pem 2048
```

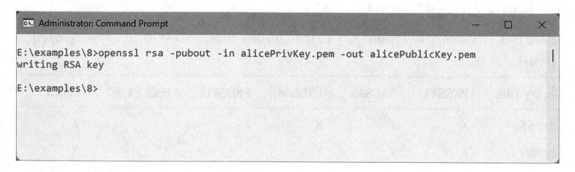

Figure 8-3. *Generating private key*

Step 2: Alice extracts the public key `alicePublicKey.pem` and sends it to Bob (see Figure 8-4).

```
openssl rsa -pubout -in alicePrivKey.pem -out alicePublicKey.pem
```

Administrator: Command Prompt   — ☐ ✕

```
E:\examples\8>openssl rsa -pubout -in alicePrivKey.pem -out alicePublicKey.pem
writing RSA key

E:\examples\8>
```

Figure 8-4. *Extracting public key*

Step 3: Bob encrypts the clear message (stored in the file *cleartext.txt*) and obtains the `encryptedWithAlicePubKey` file, which is sent to Alice (see Figure 8-5).

```
openssl rsautl -encrypt -in cleartext.txt -out encryptedWithAlicePubKey
-inkey alicePublicKey.pem -pubin
```

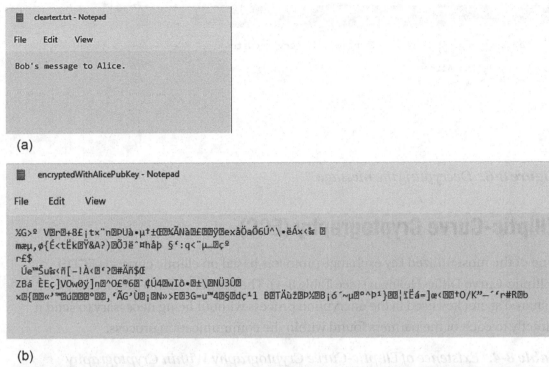

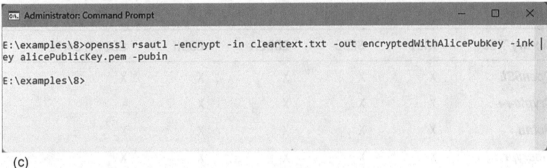

(c)

Figure 8-5. *Encrypting the clear message and obtaining the encrypted message (a) clear text (b) encrypted text (c) the process of encryption*

Step 4: Alice decrypts the message from Bob (see Figure 8-6).

```
openssl rsautl -decrypt -in encryptedWithAlicePubKey -inkey
alicePrivKey.pem
```

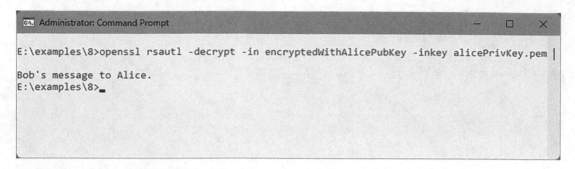

Figure 8-6. *Decrypting the message*

Elliptic-Curve Cryptography (ECC)

One of the most utilized key exchange protocols based on elliptic curves is ECDH (Elliptic-Curve Diffie-Hellman) (see Table 8-4). The purpose of this protocol is to set a shared secret key used in the encryption process without being necessary to send it directly to each of the partners found within the communication process.

Table 8-4. *Existence of Elliptic-Curve Cryptography Within Cryptography Libraries*

Library Title	NIST	SECG	ECDSA	ECDH	GOST R 34.10
OpenSSL	X	X	X	X	X
Crypto++	X	X	X	X	-
Botan	X	X	X	X	X
Libcrypt	X	X	X	X	X
Cryptlib	X	X	X	X	-

To avoid the mathematical apparatus behind the protocol, the workflow of the protocol is summarized as follows.

- Have a clear overview of the domain parameters exchanged between the communication partners (Alice and Bob).

- Alice generates a private key and a public key with the parameters of the domain.

- Bob also generates a private key and a public key with the domain parameters set.

- Both users exchange their public keys.

- Alice computes using the public key of Bob, and the shared function is characterized by a shared secret, known as the derived key of B.

- Bob does the same thing with the public key of Alice. The shared function and the shared secret are known as the derived key of A.

- Alice now uses the derived key of Bob for encrypting the message.

- Bob uses the derived key of Alice to encrypt the message.

- Both users can decrypt the message using their own private key.

Creating ECDH Keys

First, it is important to check what OpenSSL supports on your machine related to ECDH keys. To achieve these primary tasks, run the command `openssl ecparam -list_curves` (see Figure 8-7). The command lists a full list of curves that you can use. Most of them are implemented properly with respect to their standards. Their implementation in OpenSSL and the recent updates using C++23 new features made them easy to follow.

```
Administrator: Command Prompt                                                —    □    ×

E:\examples\8>openssl ecparam -list_curves                                              |
  secp112r1 : SECG/WTLS curve over a 112 bit prime field
  secp112r2 : SECG curve over a 112 bit prime field
  secp128r1 : SECG curve over a 128 bit prime field
  secp128r2 : SECG curve over a 128 bit prime field
  secp160k1 : SECG curve over a 160 bit prime field
  secp160r1 : SECG curve over a 160 bit prime field
  secp160r2 : SECG/WTLS curve over a 160 bit prime field
  secp192k1 : SECG curve over a 192 bit prime field
  secp224k1 : SECG curve over a 224 bit prime field
  secp224r1 : NIST/SECG curve over a 224 bit prime field
  secp256k1 : SECG curve over a 256 bit prime field
  secp384r1 : NIST/SECG curve over a 384 bit prime field
  secp521r1 : NIST/SECG curve over a 521 bit prime field
  prime192v1: NIST/X9.62/SECG curve over a 192 bit prime field
  prime192v2: X9.62 curve over a 192 bit prime field
  prime192v3: X9.62 curve over a 192 bit prime field
  prime239v1: X9.62 curve over a 239 bit prime field
  prime239v2: X9.62 curve over a 239 bit prime field
  prime239v3: X9.62 curve over a 239 bit prime field
  prime256v1: X9.62/SECG curve over a 256 bit prime field
  sect113r1 : SECG curve over a 113 bit binary field
  sect113r2 : SECG curve over a 113 bit binary field
  sect131r1 : SECG/WTLS curve over a 131 bit binary field
  sect131r2 : SECG curve over a 131 bit binary field
  sect163k1 : NIST/SECG/WTLS curve over a 163 bit binary field
  sect163r1 : SECG curve over a 163 bit binary field
  sect163r2 : NIST/SECG curve over a 163 bit binary field
  sect193r1 : SECG curve over a 193 bit binary field
  sect193r2 : SECG curve over a 193 bit binary field
  sect233k1 : NIST/SECG/WTLS curve over a 233 bit binary field
  sect233r1 : NIST/SECG/WTLS curve over a 233 bit binary field
  sect239k1 : SECG curve over a 239 bit binary field
  sect283k1 : NIST/SECG curve over a 283 bit binary field
```

Figure 8-7. *Obtaining a list of elliptic curves*

The fastest way to create the key pair is by using the following command (see Figure 8-8): `openssl ecparam -name prime256v1 -genkey -noout -out key.pem`.

```
Administrator: Command Prompt                                                —    □    ×

E:\examples\8>openssl ecparam -name prime256v1 -genkey -noout -out key.pem             |

E:\examples\8>
```

Figure 8-8. *Generating key pairs*

This output looks something like the following.

```
-----BEGIN EC PRIVATE KEY-----
MHcCAQEEIDqluredbEynt973tGCSuC156fxupbFfLMgwyUXCShSNoAoGCCqGSM49
AwEHoUQDQgAESBJihOUfo4fr+E4IB6uMwzqcAzqHDbFwCAWtGj9w94cWnFbeTbh1
BDcNwL9uKNICkrrCtM6h5EAgm9K2E3TGfw==
-----END EC PRIVATE KEY-----
```

If you want to see the details of the EC parameter, run the following command: openssl ec -in key.pem -text -noout. The command outputs something like what's shown in Figure 8-9.

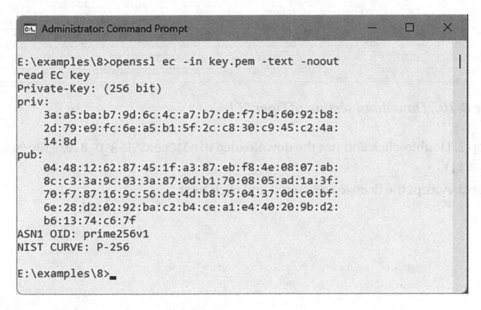

Figure 8-9. *Details of the EC parameter*

OpenSSL
Configuration and Installing OpenSSL

To properly configure and install OpenSSL, depending on the OS platform that is used, follow the steps in this section accordingly.

Installing OpenSSL on Windows 32/64

Step 1: Download the binaries for OpenSSL [3]. Download the latest version of the OpenSSL Windows installer by going to `https://slproweb.com/products/Win32OpenSSL.html`. Scroll down until you can download Win32/Win64 OpenSSL (see Figure 8-10).

File	Type	Description
Win64 OpenSSL v3.0.8 Light EXE | MSI	5MB Installer	Installs the most commonly used essentials of Win64 OpenSSL v3.0.8 (Recommended for users by the creators of OpenSSL). Only installs on 64-bit versions of Windows and targets Intel x64 chipsets. Note that this is a default build of OpenSSL and is subject to local and state laws. More information can be found in the legal agreement of the installation.
Win64 OpenSSL v3.0.8 EXE | MSI	140MB Installer	Installs Win64 OpenSSL v3.0.8 (Recommended for software developers by the creators of OpenSSL). Only installs on 64-bit versions of Windows and targets Intel x64 chipsets. Note that this is a default build of OpenSSL and is subject to local and state laws. More information can be found in the legal agreement of the installation.
Win32 OpenSSL v3.0.8 Light EXE | MSI	4MB Installer	Installs the most commonly used essentials of Win32 OpenSSL v3.0.8 (Only install this if you need 32-bit OpenSSL for Windows. Note that this is a default build of OpenSSL, and is subject to local and state laws. More information can be found in the legal agreement of the installation.
Win32 OpenSSL v3.0.8 EXE | MSI	116MB Installer	Installs Win32 OpenSSL v3.0.8 (Only install this if you need 32-bit OpenSSL for Windows. Note that this is a default build of OpenSSL and is subject to local and state laws. More information can be found in the legal agreement of the installation.
Win64 OpenSSL v3.0.8 Light for ARM (EXPERIMENTAL) EXE | MSI	5MB Installer	Installs the most commonly used essentials of Win64 OpenSSL v3.0.8 for ARM64 devices (Only install this VERY EXPERIMENTAL build if you want to try 64-bit OpenSSL for Windows on ARM processors. Note that this is a default build of OpenSSL and is subject to local and state laws. More information can be found in the legal agreement of the installation.
Win64 OpenSSL v3.0.8 for ARM (EXPERIMENTAL) EXE | MSI	113MB Installer	Installs Win64 OpenSSL v3.0.8 for ARM64 devices (Only install this VERY EXPERIMENTAL build if you want to try 64-bit OpenSSL for Windows on ARM processors. Note that this is a default build of OpenSSL and is subject to local and state laws. More information can be found in the legal agreement of the installation.
Win64 OpenSSL v1.1.1t Light EXE | MSI	3MB Installer	Installs the most commonly used essentials of Win64 OpenSSL v1.1.1t (Recommended for users by the creators of OpenSSL). Only installs on 64-bit versions of Windows. Note that this is a default build of OpenSSL.
Win64 OpenSSL v1.1.1t EXE | MSI	63MB Installer	Installs Win64 OpenSSL v1.1.1t (Recommended for software developers by the creators of OpenSSL). Only installs on 64-bit versions of Windows. Note that this is a default build of OpenSSL, and is subject to local and state laws. More information can be found in the legal agreement of the installation.
Win32 OpenSSL v1.1.1t Light EXE | MSI	3MB Installer	Installs the most commonly used essentials of Win32 OpenSSL v1.1.1t (Only install this if you need 32-bit OpenSSL for Windows. Note that this is a default build of OpenSSL and is subject to local and state laws. More information can be found in the legal agreement of the installation.
Win32 OpenSSL v1.1.1t EXE | MSI	54MB Installer	Installs Win32 OpenSSL v1.1.1t (Only install this if you need 32-bit OpenSSL for Windows. Note that this is a default build of OpenSSL and is subject to local and state laws. More information can be found in the legal agreement of the installation.

Figure 8-10. *Download section of OpenSLL*

Step 2: Double-click and run the downloaded `Win64OpenSSL-3_0_8.exe` file (see Figure 8-11).

Step 3: Accept the license agreement and click **Next**.

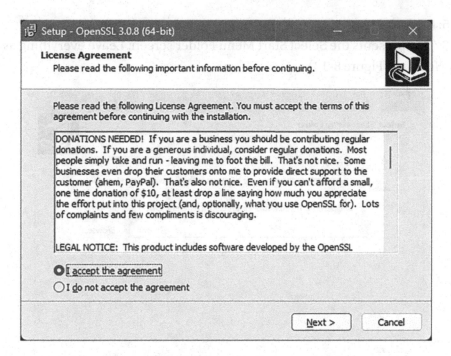

Figure 8-11. *OpenSSL license agreement*

Step 4: Specify the installation path and click **Next** (see Figure 8-12).

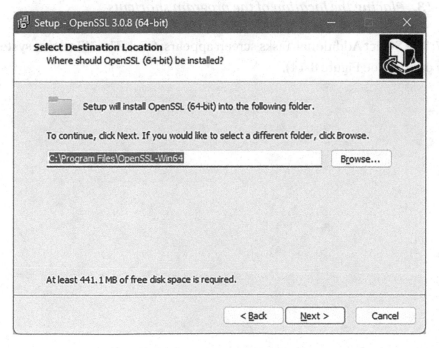

Figure 8-12. *Setting up the path to install OpenSSL*

Step 5: Click **Next**.

Step 6: This presents the Select Start Menu Folder screen. Leave everything as it is and click **Next** (see Figure 8-13).

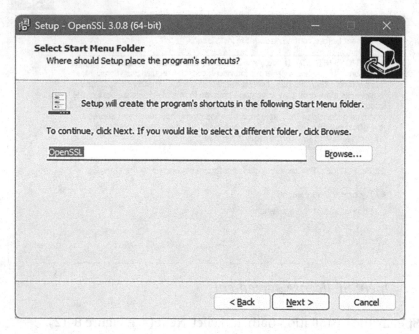

Figure 8-13. *Placing the location of the program shortcuts*

Step 7: The Select Additional Tasks screen appears. Click **The Windows system directory** option (see Figure 8-14).

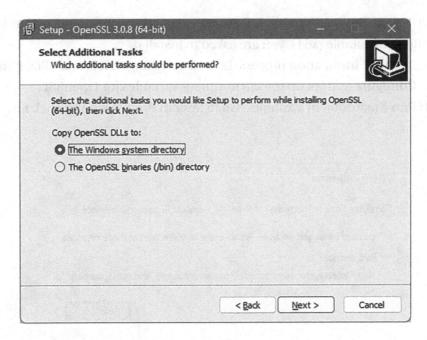

Figure 8-14. *Additional Tasks to perform*

Step 8: Click **Install** (see Figure 8-15).

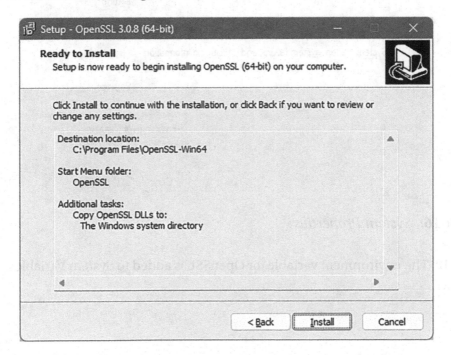

Figure 8-15. *Acknowledgment of the installation process and settings*

Step 8: The installation progresses. Remember that if you haven't installed Microsoft Visual C++ Redistributable (x64), you are asked to install it.

Step 9: Finish the installation process. Leave everything as it is and click **Finish**.

Step 10: Configure and set up the environment variables for OpenSSL.

Step 11: Run Environment Variables. Go to System Properties and click **Environment Variables**.

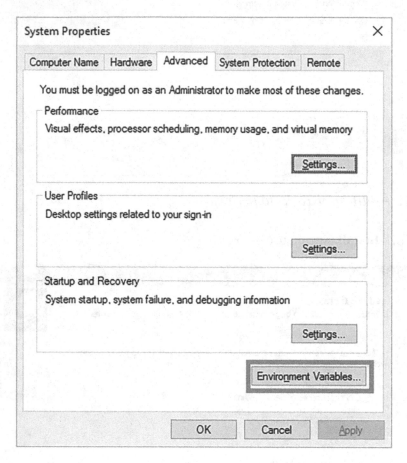

Figure 8-16. *System Properties*

Step 12: The environment variable for OpenSSL is added to System Variables. Click **New**.

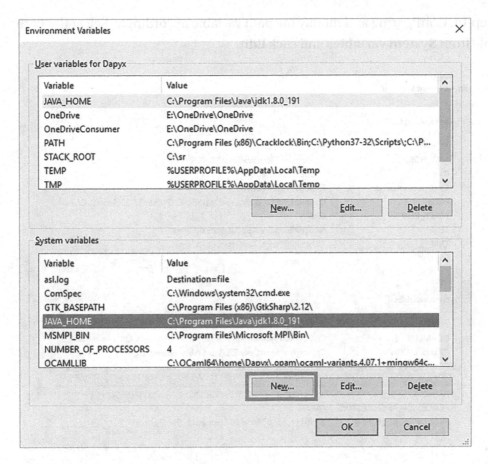

Figure 8-17. *Environment variables*

Step 13: Configuring the OPENSSL_CONF variable

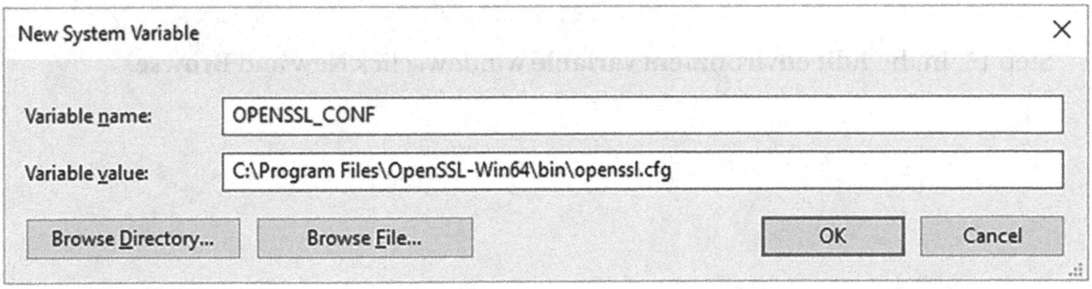

Figure 8-18. *New System Variable*

Step 14: Configuring and modify the path variable accordingly. Select the **Path** variable from **System variables** and click **Edit**.

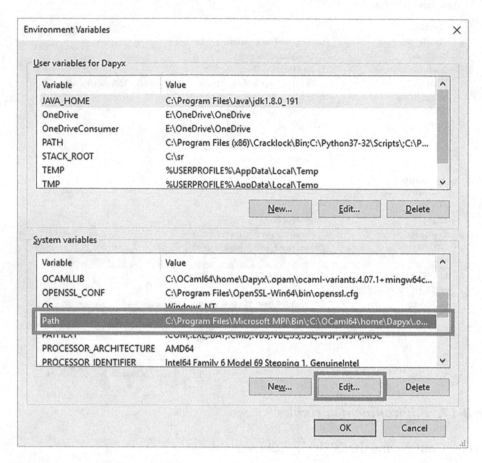

Figure 8-19. *Environment Variables: Path Variable*

Step 15: In the **Edit environment variable** window, click **New** and **Browse**.

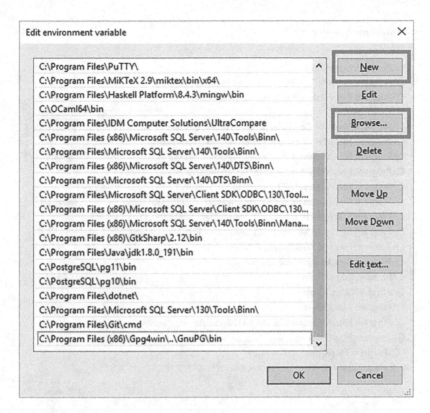

Figure 8-20. *Edit environment variable*

Step 16: Select the path to the OpenSSL bin folder and click **OK**. The new path should be added successfully. Close everything. If you have the command window open, close it and reopen it again for the update to be done correctly; otherwise, it does not work.

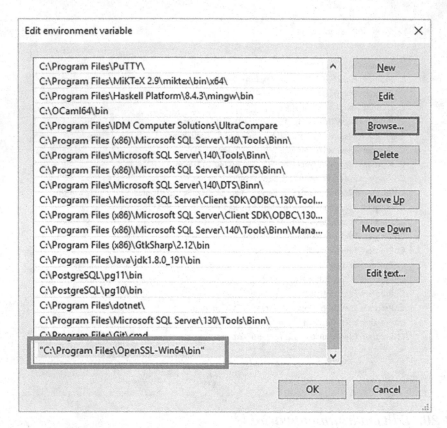

Figure 8-21.   *Verifying that the path for OpenSSL is added*

Step 17. Open Command (cmd.exe). Run the openssl command. If the OpenSSL> prompter appears in the window, it is the first sign of success.

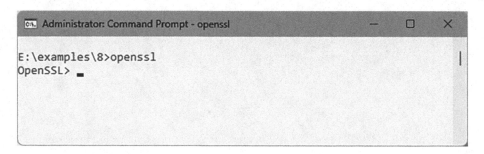

Figure 8-22.   *Checking OpenSSL, first step*

Step 18: Run the second command: version. Make sure that everything is set properly. You are successful if the version and date are returned, as shown in Figure 8-23.

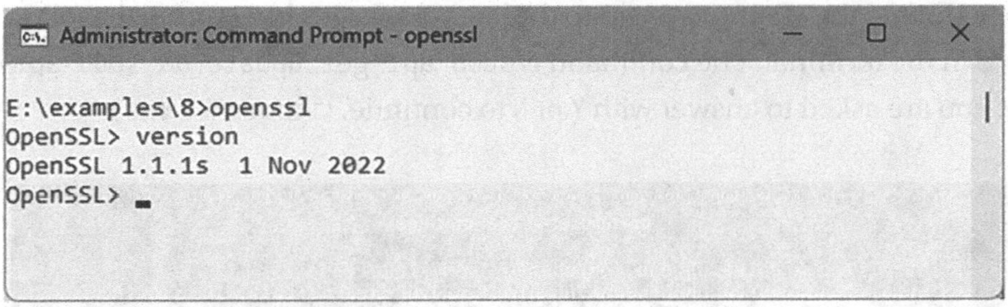

Figure 8-23. *Checking OpenSSL, second step*

Installing OpenSSL on Linux: Ubuntu Flavor

Usually, OpenSSL is already installed on Linux Ubuntu. This step-by-step guide uses the Ubuntu 22.04 LTS version.

Step 1: Check the OpenSSL version installed on your machine by running `openssl version -a` in the terminal.

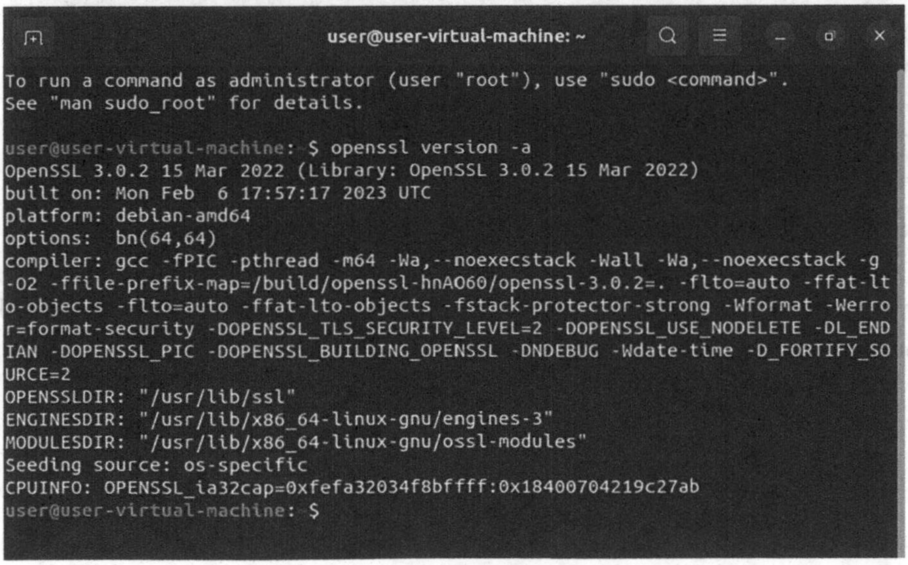

Figure 8-24. *Checking the OpenSSL version*

If you don't see it, the OpenSSL was not installed or configured properly. Let's proceed to install and configure OpenSSL.

Step 2: Update the Ubuntu system to the latest packages by running the following command in the terminal. The command is `sudo apt-get update && sudo apt-get upgrade`. You are asked to answer with Y or N to continue. Choose Y (Yes).

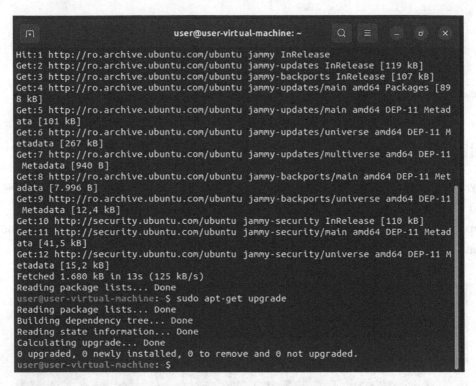

Figure 8-25. Updating the Ubuntu System with the latest packages

Step 3: Check the availability of OpenSSL packages to be installed from the official repository for Ubuntu using the command `apt show openssl`.

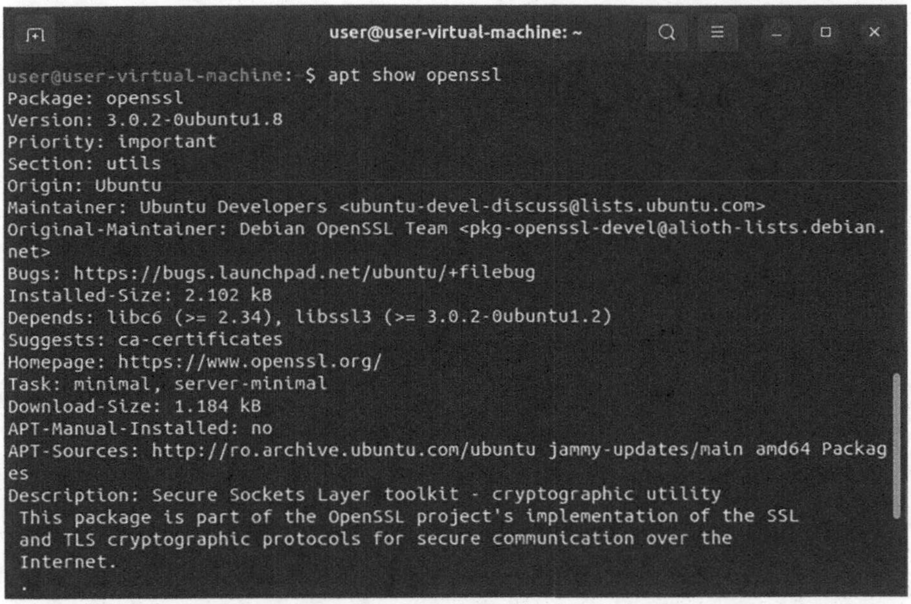

```
user@user-virtual-machine:~$ apt show openssl
Package: openssl
Version: 3.0.2-0ubuntu1.8
Priority: important
Section: utils
Origin: Ubuntu
Maintainer: Ubuntu Developers <ubuntu-devel-discuss@lists.ubuntu.com>
Original-Maintainer: Debian OpenSSL Team <pkg-openssl-devel@alioth-lists.debian.
net>
Bugs: https://bugs.launchpad.net/ubuntu/+filebug
Installed-Size: 2.102 kB
Depends: libc6 (>= 2.34), libssl3 (>= 3.0.2-0ubuntu1.2)
Suggests: ca-certificates
Homepage: https://www.openssl.org/
Task: minimal, server-minimal
Download-Size: 1.184 kB
APT-Manual-Installed: no
APT-Sources: http://ro.archive.ubuntu.com/ubuntu jammy-updates/main amd64 Packag
es
Description: Secure Sockets Layer toolkit - cryptographic utility
 This package is part of the OpenSSL project's implementation of the SSL
 and TLS cryptographic protocols for secure communication over the
 Internet.
 .
```

Figure 8-26.   *Checking for OpenSSL packages*

Step 4: The last step is to install the package using the command `sudo apt install openssl -y`.

```
user@user-virtual-machine:~$ sudo apt install openssl -y
Reading package lists... Done
Building dependency tree... Done
Reading state information... Done
```

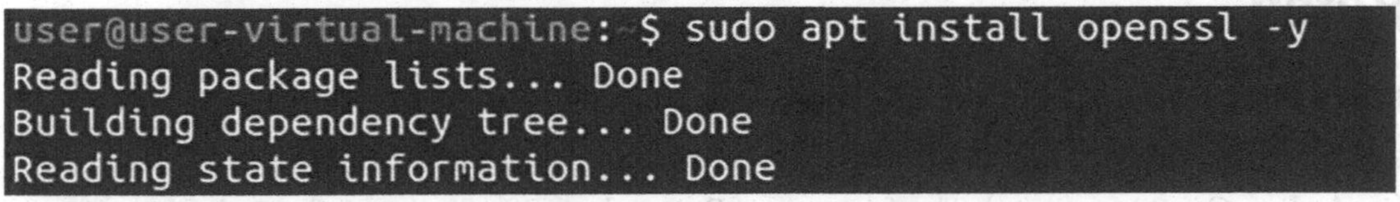

Figure 8-27.   *Installing OpenSSL packages*

OpenSSL is a robust and widely used open source cryptography library that supports many cryptographic functions and protocols, such as SSL/TLS, RSA, Diffie-Hellman, and elliptic curve cryptography (ECC). OpenSSL is regarded as a strong cryptography library for the following reasons.

- **Broad platform support**. OpenSSL is accessible on most operating systems, including Linux, macOS, Windows, and BSD. This makes it a popular option for cross-platform cryptography applications.

191

- **Wide range of cryptographic functions**. OpenSSL provides a broad selection of cryptographic functions and protocols, including symmetric and asymmetric encryption, hashing, digital signatures, and key exchange.

- **High performance**. OpenSSL is recognized for its high performance and efficiency. It has been designed for speed and supports hardware acceleration on a variety of devices.

- **Active development and community support**. A committed team of developers actively develops and maintains OpenSSL, and a large and active user community contributes to its development and testing.

- **FIPS 140-2 compliance**. OpenSSL is compatible with FIPS 140-2, a standard for cryptography modules used in federal systems in the United States. This indicates that OpenSSL has been rigorously tested and validated to guarantee that it meets stringent security requirements.

Botan

Botan [5] represents another powerful library that can be used in command lines as OpenSSL. The vast algorithms contain powerful and modern implementations (including C++23 features). The features of Botan that differentiate it from the rest of the libraries consist of the modules implemented for the Transport Layer Security (TLS) protocol. The features implemented with Botan make it a real candidate for inspiration and guidance among professionals, and its documentation represents a very important guide that is easy to follow.

The commands and instructions are the same as those for OpenSSL, with minor differences related to public-key algorithms.

CrypTool

A great software product for cryptography developed using C++ is CrypTool (CT) [6], version 1. The latest stable release for version CT1 is 1.4.42, and it can be downloaded from CrypTool's official website[1]. After downloading, launch the executable and follow the instructions to install it. When CT1 is opened, the main window looks as shown in Figure 8-28.

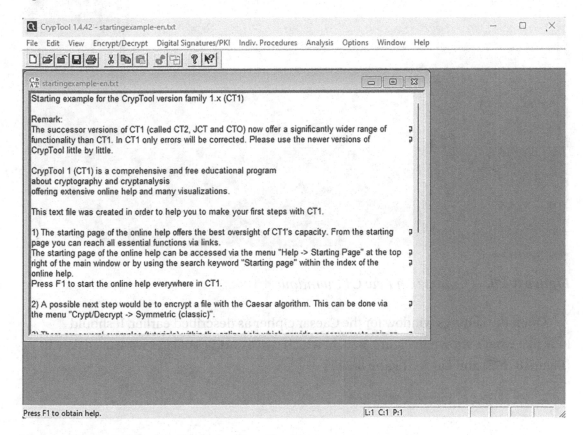

Figure 8-28. *Main windows in CrypTool 1*

The first example is the classical cipher, Caesar. It can be selected from **Encrypt/Decrypt ➤ Symmetric (classic) ➤ Caesar/Rot - 13...** Before selecting the Caesar cipher, close the `startingexample-en.txt` window and open a new window (**File ➤ New**). In the opened window type, the sentence **This is an example of Caesar cipher using CrypTool 1.** (see Figure 8-29).

---

[1] https://www.cryptool.org/en/ct1-downloads

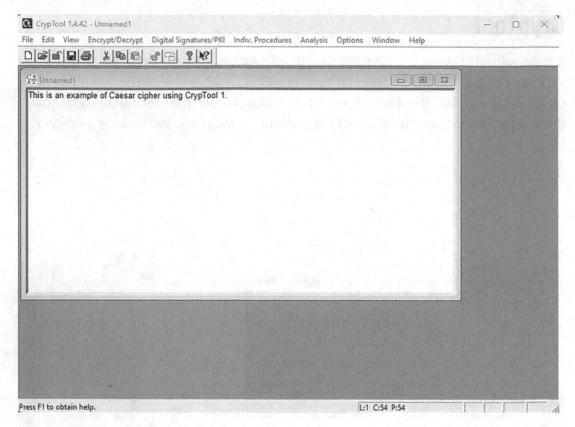

Figure 8-29. *The text in a new CT1 window*

Open the settings window for the Caesar cipher as described earlier. It should look like what's shown in Figure 8-30, in which two examples of keys were used: key B (Figure 8-30a) and key M (Figure 8-30b).

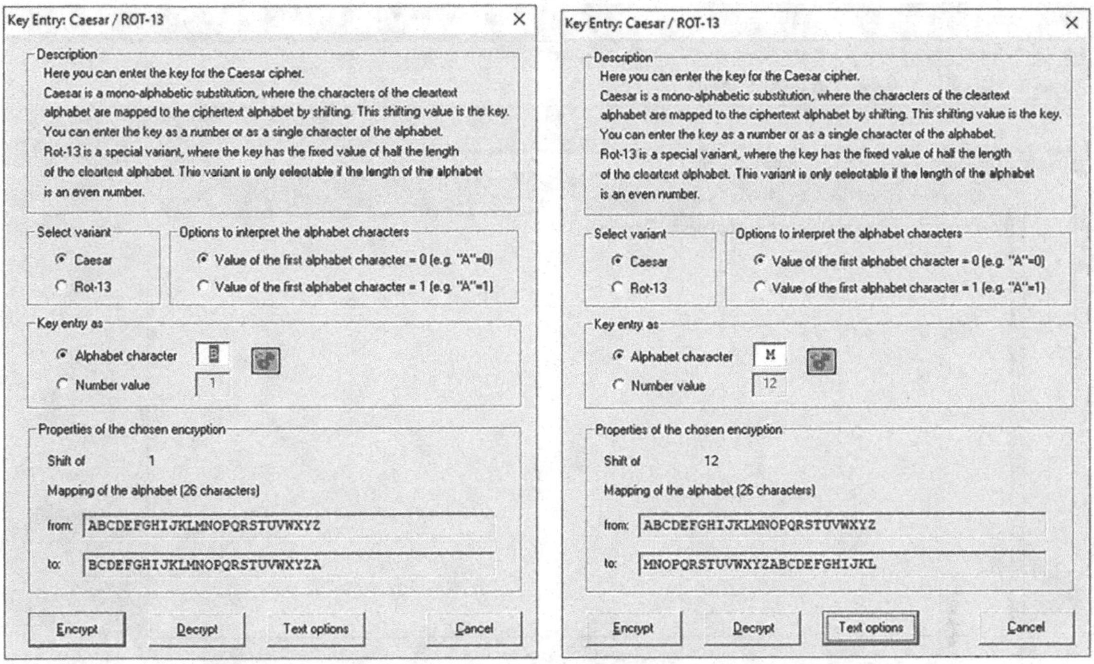

Figure 8-30. *(a) The default settings for the Caesar cipher (b) The chosen settings for the Caesar cipher*

The window contains a short description of the cipher. Note that Rot-13 is a particular case of the Caesar cipher, which shifts a particular letter with 13 positions (considering that the number of the letters in the English alphabet is 26, then its half is 13, from the name of the Rot-13). Keep the default variant, Caesar. On the right side, you can choose the index for the first letter of the alphabet, A, which can be either 0 or 1.

Furthermore, you should choose the key, which represents the number of positions with which a particular letter is shifted to the right in the alphabet. The key can be chosen as an alphabet letter or as a number. Keep the character option, and let's say the key is M. Figure 8-31b shows the changes from the chosen encryption's Properties settings; observe that A is mapped to M (0 is the position of A, which is shifted by 12 positions, i.e., 0+12=12; the twelfth letter of the English alphabet is M) and so on. Now press the **Encrypt** button. The result is shown in Figure 8-31.

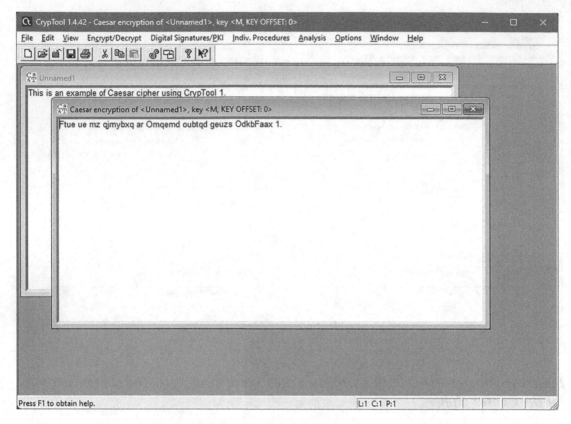

Figure 8-31. *Encryption using Caesar cipher*

Note that the cipher is not case-sensitive. Such additional settings can be accessed by selecting Text Option from the Key Entry: Caesar/ROT - 13 window (see Figure 8-32a). From this window, you can set to keep unchanged the characters that are not in the alphabet. Note the 1 and period (.) characters. The spaces are not encrypted. Furthermore, you can choose uppercase sensitivity, extend the alphabet, and set a reference for statistical use (see Figure 8-32b).

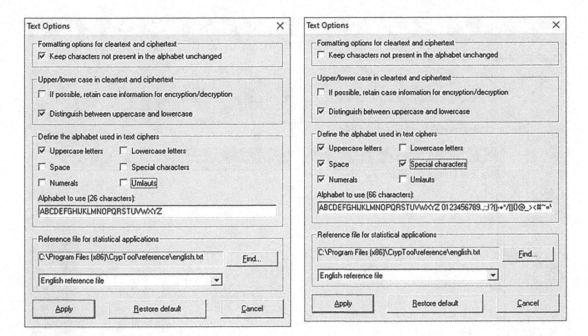

Figure 8-32. *(a) Choosing case sensitive option (b) More option for Text Option in Section Define the alphabet used in text ciphers*

Now let's return to our example. Close the Unnamed-1 window (or make sure that the emphasized window is *Caesar encryption of <Unnamed1>, key <M, KEY OFFSET: 0>*) and let's decrypt the result of the Caesar encryption obtained in Figure 8-31. For this, choose the Caesar cipher from the menu again and make the same setting as in the encryption. Note that Caesar is a symmetric cipher, which means that the same key is used for both encryption and decryption; therefore, set the key entry as an alphabet character and choose **M** and click the **Decrypt** button. The result is seen in Figure 8-33.

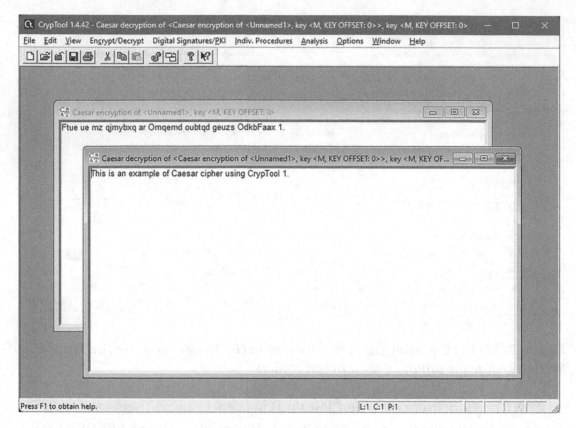

Figure 8-33. *The decryption using the Caesar cipher*

The next encryption system is RSA.

Next, select **Encrypt/Decrypt ➤ Asymmetric ➤ RSA Demonstrator**. The RSA *Demonstration* window should look like what's shown in Figure 8-34a.

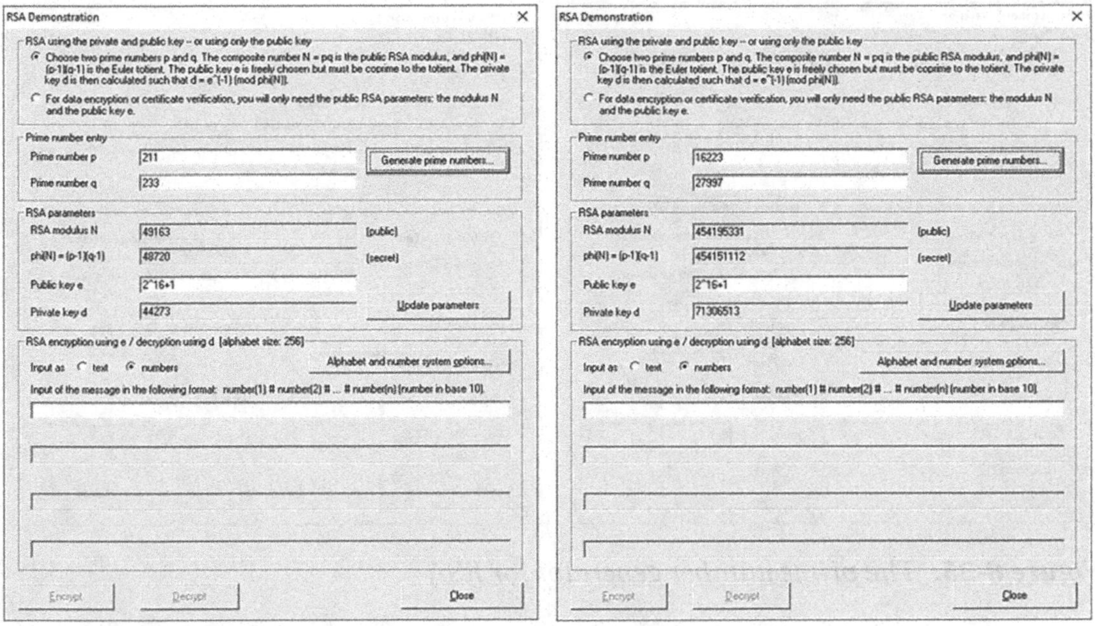

Figure 8-34. *(a) RSA Demonstrator window (b) RSA Demonstrator window after generating prime numbers*

Keep the default option of computing both the public key and the private key. Furthermore, you need to choose the parameters for the scheme. You can provide two prime numbers yourself, or you can generate two prime numbers using the generator. Click the **Generate prime numbers…** button. The window should look like what's shown in Figure 8-35a.

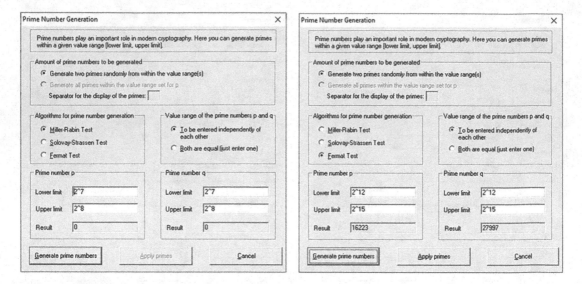

Figure 8-35. *The prime number generator for RSA*

Here, you can choose between three prime generators. Choose the Fermat test, set the lower limit to 2^{12} and the upper limit to 2^{15} for both p and q, opt for independent primes, and click the **Generate prime numbers** button (see Figure 8-35b).

To use these prime numbers, click the **Apply primes** button. After generating the prime number, note that the public and secret values were computed (see Figure 8-35b). Keep the default public key as $2^{16} + 1$, check **text** in the **Input as** the field, type: **This text is encrypted using RSA.**, and click the **Encrypt** button. The result should look like what is shown in Figure 8-36.

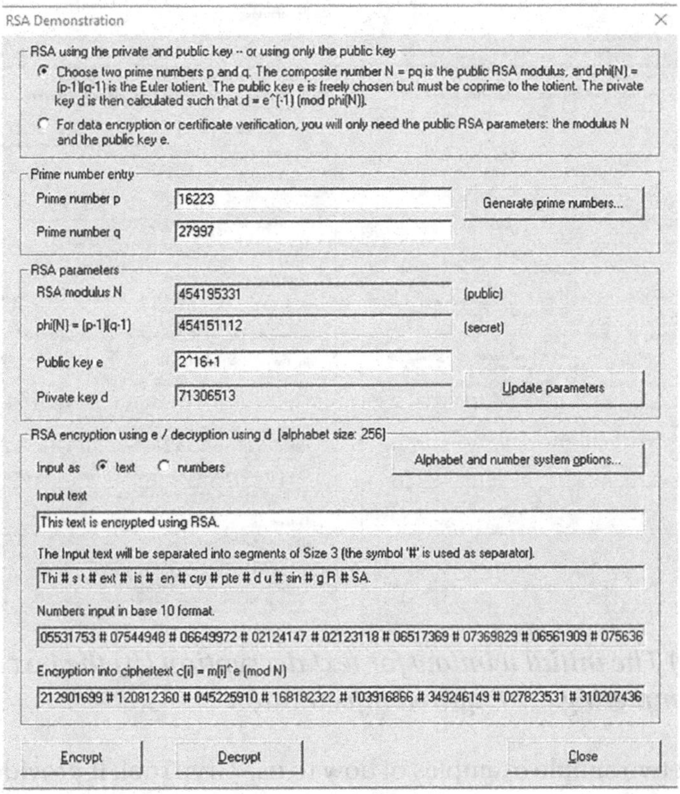

Figure 8-36. *Encrypted text using RSA*

To decrypt, you should not close the window, and you need to be a little careful. For decryption, copying the text resulted in the **Encryption into ciphertext c[i]=m[i]^e (mod N)** field. Our encrypted text would look as follows (and see Figure 8-37a).

212901699 # 120812360 # 045225910 # 168182322 # 103916866 # 349246149 # 027823531 # 310207436 # 009232756 # 131763739 # 089946941

Furthermore, select **numbers** for **Input as** and paste them. Then, press the **Decrypt** button. The decryption works correctly (see Figure 8-37b) because of the same plain text that was encrypted previously.

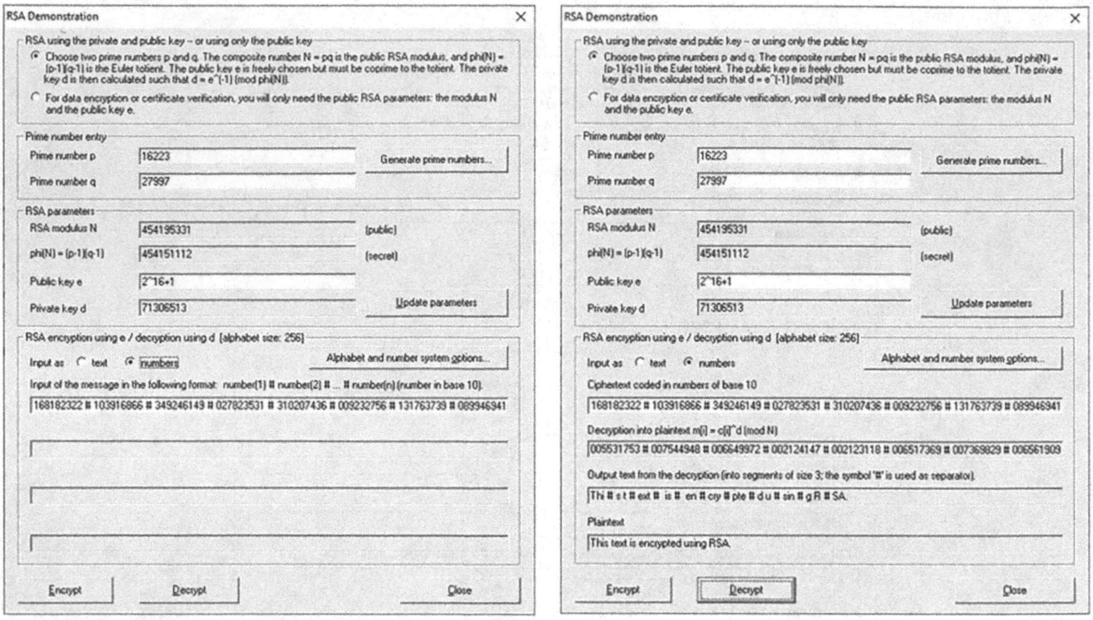

Figure 8-37. *(a) The initial window for text decryption (b) the text decryption window after completing the required information*

These are just two simple examples of how to use CrypTool. It provides many more encryption schemes and examples and can be used for attack simulations or to collect different statistical information.

Conclusion

This chapter provided a brief list of C++ libraries and showed how to install them on the Windows operating system or Ubuntu. One of the most useful libraries developed in C++ are OpenSSL, Botan, and CrypTool.

In this chapter, you learned about the following.

- Access to the most important open source cryptography libraries and frameworks

- The main cryptographic operations and how to interact with the libraries and frameworks

- Access to cryptography source code to compare the implementations of the algorithms

- How to learn from other professional developers (e.g., OpenSSL, Botan, etc.) best practices for developing cryptographic algorithms

References

[1].   OpenSSL: Cryptography and SSL/TLS Toolkit. Available online: `https://www.openssl.org/`. Last accessed: 21.2.2023

[2].   OpenSSL TLS/SSL and Crypto Library. Available online: `https://github.com/openssl/openssl`. Last accessed: 21.2.2023

[3].   Win32/Win 64 OpenSSL Installer for Windows. Available online: `https://slproweb.com/products/Win32OpenSSL.html`. Last accessed: 21.2.2023

[4].   OpenSSL Sources. Available online: `https://www.openssl.org/source/`. Last accessed: 21.2.2023

[5].   Botan: Crypto and TLS for Modern C++. Available online: `https://botan.randombit.net/`. Last accessed: 21.2.2023

[6].   CrypTool Portal. Available online: `https://www.cryptool.org/en/`. Last accessed: 21.2.2023

[7].   Crypto++. Available online: `https://cryptopp.com/`. Last accessed: 21.2.2023

[8].   Crypto++ Manual. Available online: `https://cryptopp.com/docs/ref/`. Last accessed: 21.2.2023

[9].   Libcrypt. Available online: `https://www.gnupg.org/related_software/libgcrypt/`. Last accessed: 21.2.2023

[10].   Libcrypt. Available online: `https://www.gnupg.org/documentation/manuals.html`. Last accessed: 21.2.2023

[11].   GnuTLS. Available online: `https://gnutls.org/`. Last accessed: 21.2.2023

[12].   GnuTLS Documentation. Available online: `https://gnutls.org/documentation.html`. Last accessed: 21.2.2023

[13].   Cryptlib. Available online: `https://www.cryptlib.com/`. Last accessed: 21.2.2023

PART II

Pro Cryptography

CHAPTER 9

Elliptic-Curve Cryptography

Elliptic-curve cryptography (ECC) represents a public-key cryptography approach based on the algebraic structure of elliptic curves over finite fields. ECC can be used in cryptography applications and primitives, such as *key agreements, digital signatures,* and *pseudorandom generators.* They can also be used for operations such as encryption, achieved through a combination of key agreement and a symmetric encryption scheme. Other interesting usages can be seen in several attempts at integer factorization algorithms that are based on elliptic curves (EC), with applications in cryptography, such as Lenstra Elliptic-Curve Factorization (L-ECC) [1]. Elliptic curves appeared for the first time in Diophantus [3], a subject that has remained close to Diophantine geometry [2].

Elliptic-curve cryptography (ECC) is the most secure type of encryption available today. It is used to protect data and communications from hackers, and it is becoming increasingly important to ensure the safety of sensitive information. ECC is a powerful tool that can protect a wide range of data, from emails and financial transactions to medical records and confidential documents.

This comprehensive chapter on ECC provides a deep dive into the technology and its applications. It covers the basics of ECC, how it works, and why it's so secure. It also discusses the pros and cons of different implementations and provides guidance on using ECC for secure data encryption. By the end of this guide, you'll have a thorough understanding of ECC and how to use it to protect your data.

ECC uses the properties of a special type of mathematical equation called an *elliptic curve* to generate keys and encrypt and decrypt data. To create a key, the sender's computer uses an algorithm to solve a complicated mathematical equation that generates a specific type of graph known as an elliptic curve. The graph is created on a two-dimensional coordinate system that looks like a donut when plotted on a graph.

© Marius Iulian Mihailescu and Stefania Loredana Nita 2023
M. I. Mihailescu and S. L. Nita, *Pro Cryptography and Cryptanalysis with C++23,*
https://doi.org/10.1007/978-1-4842-9450-5_9

For example, an elliptic curve could look like this: the curve is formed by plotting many points that form a continuous shape. The shape of the curve is determined by the values used to plot the points.

The advantages of elliptic curve cryptography can be summarized as follows.

- **Speed**. ECC is significantly faster than more complex encryption methods such as RSA.

- **Scalability**. ECC is more scalable than many other types of encryption because it does not require public key infrastructure (PKI).

- **Security**. ECC is one of the most secure types of encryption and has never been cracked in real-world scenarios.

- **Widely used**. ECC is widely used across many industries and is used by many governments and organizations around the world.

- **Low cost.** ECC is a relatively low-cost solution and can be implemented using open-source software.

Two main types of ECC are used for encryption: the *elliptic curve digital signature algorithm* (ECDSA) and the *elliptic curve integrated encryption scheme* (ECIES). Each has its own benefits and applications, and each can encrypt data in various ways.

ECDSA is a public-key cryptography used to authenticate and verify a sender's identity. It uses a similar process to generate keys as ECC but uses a different type of equation to create the graph. The graph produced by an ECD-DS signature is an elliptic curve.

ECIES is a type of encryption used to encrypt data. When implemented as an encryption scheme, ECIES uses two different elliptic curves: a public curve and a private curve. The public curve generates a shared secret to encrypt the original data. The secret is then decrypted using the private curve.

ECDSA and ECIES are secure and efficient encryption methods, but they are not the same. When choosing an implementation of ECC, it is important to consider the pros and cons of each method. ECDSA is more efficient than ECIES and requires less computing power. It is also useful for authentication, verification, and identification. However, it is less scalable than ECIES and requires a PKI. ECIES is less efficient than ECDSA and requires more computing power. It is less useful for authentication and verification but is more scalable than ECDSA and does not require a PKI.

The process of using ECC for secure data encryption comprises the following.

1. **Generate a key**. The first step in the process is to generate a key. The key is used to encrypt and decrypt data. The type of key generated depends on the type of encryption used.

2. **Encrypt data.** Once the data is encrypted, they cannot be decrypted without the key. It is recommended that data be encrypted in blocks (called a block cipher), which are portions of data that are processed all at once.

3. **Decrypt data.** Data is decrypted using the same process as encryption. The sender uses the key to decrypt the data and then transfers the information to the intended recipient.

4. **Store data securely**. Data should be securely stored after they are decrypted to remain private.

5. **Make** sure **data is authentic**. When data is sent over a network or the Internet, there is a chance that they could be intercepted and tampered with. To protect against this, authentication ensures that data come from the correct source and have not been tampered with or corrupted during transmission.

The potential risks associated with ECC are very important when implementing business software solutions, authentication protocols, and types of data that require security protection. There are a few potential risks that come along with using ECC for data encryption. One potential risk is that an organization may not understand how ECC works. If a company does not fully understand how ECC is implemented and how it works, it could put the integrity of its data at risk. Another potential risk is that a company does not have the expertise to manage its keys. It is important to have a good system in place for managing keys, especially if an organization is using ECC. It is also important to ensure that all keys are properly backed up and that there is a disaster-recovery plan in case something bad happens to the systems holding the keys.

The starting point of elliptic curve cryptography starts in public key cryptography (PKC). Using PKC in ECC, there is a special case for manipulating the elliptic curve points and how they are generated. The manipulation consists of two cases: multiplication and addition.

The main advantage of ECC is obtaining a certain level of security based on using shorter keys that are different from the "usual cryptography."

A second advantage is that elliptic curve cryptography is resistant to some attacks. Those attacks were designed and developed for integer factorization and discrete logarithms, which proved unsuccessful.

Before the practical implementation, some basic theoretical notions are presented to familiarize you with elliptic curve cryptography. The following section describes the required notions in Listing 9-1 and 9-2.

Theoretical Fundamentals

This section describes the main foundation that is necessary and must be understood before proceeding further with practical implementation. The graphical content and the representations of some of the equations are taken and cited from [4].

Let's start with the following example, in which a collection of balls is arranged to look like a regular pyramid so that there is only one ball on the top level. On the next level, there are four balls. On the next one, nine balls, and so on (see Figure 9-1).

Figure 9-1. Balls pyramid [4]

A logical question is raised: Is there a way of rearranging the balls into a squared matrix if the pyramid collapses? If the pyramid has only three levels, the rearranging process cannot be performed because there are $1 + 4 + 9 = 19$ balls, which is not a perfect square. When there is a single ball, the pyramid is organized with one level and a squared matrix with one line and one column.

If the pyramid has a height of x, then there are

$$1^2 + 2^2 + 3^2 + \ldots x^2 = \frac{x(x+1)(2x+1)}{6} \text{ balls.}$$

The intention is that the number is a perfect square number. To do this, you must resolve the following equation.

$$y^2 = \frac{x(x+1)(2x+1)}{6} \text{ in } N.$$

Such an equation represents the *elliptic curve equation* (see Figure 9-2).

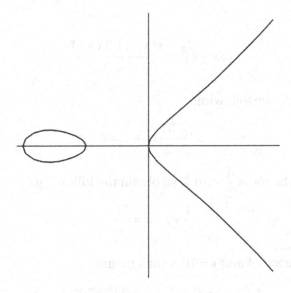

Figure 9-2. *Graphic for* $y^2 = \dfrac{x(x+1)(2x+1)}{6}$ *[4]*

The $y^2 = \dfrac{x(x+1)(2x+1)}{6}$ equation can be solved using the Diophantus method, using known points for finding other points. Using $(0,0)$ and $(1,1)$ points, obtain the following straight equation $y = x$. When you intersect the obtained curve with the equation of the line, you get the following relation.

$$x^2 = \frac{x(x+1)(2x+1)}{6} = \frac{1}{3}x^3 + \frac{1}{3}x^2 + \frac{1}{6}x$$

This is equivalent to the following.

$$x^3 - \frac{3}{2}x^2 + \frac{1}{2}x = 0$$

You already know two roots of this equation, $x = 0$ and $x = 1$, which are the coordinates on the Ox-axis of the intersection points between the equation of the line and curve. For three real numbers, a, b, c, you know the following.

$$(x-a)(x-b)(x-c) = x^3 + (a+b+c)x^2 + (ab+ac+bc)x - abc.$$

In our situation, for roots 0, 1, x we obtain $0 + 1 + x = \dfrac{3}{2}$, finding the coordinate point $\left(\dfrac{1}{2}, \dfrac{1}{2}\right)$. Because of the symmetry of the curve, there is also the coordinate point $\left(\dfrac{1}{2}, -\dfrac{1}{2}\right)$.

Continuing with the technique illustrated for points $\left(\dfrac{1}{2}, -\dfrac{1}{2}\right)$ and $(1, 1)$, obtain the equation of the line $y = 3x - 2$, which you intersect with the given curve, obtaining the following.

$$(3x-2)^2 = \frac{x(x+1)(2x+1)}{6}$$

This is equivalent to the following.

$$x^3 - \frac{51}{2}x^2 + \ldots = 0$$

We already know the roots $\dfrac{1}{2}$ and 1, so obtain the following.

$$\frac{1}{2} + 1 + x = \frac{51}{2},$$

From this, we have $x = 24$ and $y = 70$, which means

$$1^2 + 2^2 + 3^2 + \ldots + 24^2 = 70^2$$

If there are 4900 balls, they can be arranged as a pyramid with a height of 24 and arranged in a squared pyramid with 24 lines and 24 columns.

Weierstrass Equation

The "Practical Implementation" section in this chapter offers a practical solution using the Weierstrass equation.

Definition 9-1. Let's consider the following elliptic curve E as being the following set: $\{(x, y) | y^2 = x^3 + Ax + B\}$, in which the elements A, B, x, y are elements from the field K, defined as $K \in \{Q, R, C, Z_p, Z_q\}$, where p represents a prime number and $q = p^k$, $k \geq 1$ and A, B are constants.

Definition 9-2. An equation that is defined according to Definition 9-1 is called and known as the *Weierstrass equation.*

Definition 9-3. If K is a field and A, $B \in K$, then E is defined over the field K. For the points that have their coordinates in $L \subseteq K$, write $E(L)$. By definition, add a point to this set that does not belong to the affine plan, a point that is noted with ∞.

$$E(L) = \{\infty\} \cup \left\{ (x,y) \in L \times L, y^3 = x^3 + Ax + B \right\}$$

Intuitively, it is useful to think of the graph of the elliptic curve over the field of real numbers. This has two basic forms, as shown in Figure 9-3. Equation $y^2 = x^3 - x$ has three real roots and is distinct, and equation $y^2 = x^3 + x$ has one single real root. It is not allowed to have multiple roots; therefore, you must mention the condition, $4A^3 + 27B^2 \neq 0$.

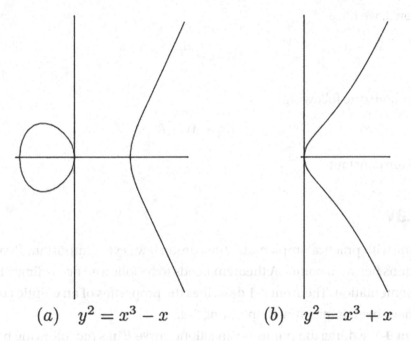

(a) $y^2 = x^3 - x$ (b) $y^2 = x^3 + x$

Figure 9-3. *The basic two forms of the elliptic curve over a real numbers field [4]*

If the roots are r_1, r_2, r_3, then

$$\left((r_1 - r_2)(r_1 - r_3)(r_2 - r_3) \right)^2 = -\left(4A^3 + 27B^2 \right).$$

Definition 9-4. The general form of an elliptic equation over a K field is called the *Weierstrass generalized equation* and has the following form.

$$y^2 + a_1 xy + a_3 y = x^3 + a_2 x^2 + a_4 x + a_6$$

$a_1...a_6$ are constants from K. This form is very useful, especially with the implementation later.

The generalized Weierstrass equation is useful for fields with two or three characteristics. For fields with different characteristics, we obtain the following.

$$\left(y + \frac{a_1 x}{2} + \frac{a_3}{2} \right)^2 = x^3 + \left(a_2 + \frac{a_1^2}{4} \right) x^2 + \left(a_4 + \frac{a_1 a_3}{2} \right) x + \left(\frac{a_3^2}{4} + a_6 \right)$$

This is equivalent to the following.

$$y_1^2 = x^3 + a_2' x^2 + a_4' x + a_6'$$

$y_1 = y + \dfrac{a_1}{2} x + \dfrac{a_3}{2}$ and a_2', a_4', a_6' are constants. For fields with characteristics that are different than 3, we have

$$x_1 = x + \frac{a_2'}{3}$$

And we obtain the following.

$$y_1^2 = x_1^3 + A x_1 + B$$

A and B are constants.

Group Law

When dealing with practical implementation, group law is very important for working with operations between points. A theorem needs to be followed accordingly to have a proper implementation. Theorem 9-1 describes the properties of an elliptic curve. The properties have been implemented in Listing 9-2.

Theorem 9-1. Adding the points on an elliptic curve E has the following properties.

- (commutativity) $P_1 + P_2 = P_2 + P_1, \forall\, P_1, P_2 \in E$

- (neutral element) $P + \infty = P, \forall\, P \in E$

- (inverse existance) $\forall P \in E, \exists\, P' \in E$ in such a way that $P + P' = \infty$ The P' point is noted usually with $-P$.

- (associativity) $(P_1 + P_2) + P_3 = P_1 + (P_2 + P_3), \forall P_1, P_2, P_3 \in E$

Practical Implementation

This section discusses the practical implementation of ECC using C++23 and provides a step-by-step basic implementation of ECC.

The example (see Figure 9-1, Listing 9-1, and Listing 9-2) represents the implementation of an elliptic curve over a finite field with order *P*. The following elliptic curve equation is used for our implementation.

$$y^2 \bmod P = x^3 + ax + b \bmod P$$

The implementation provided is structured in two parts.

- The implementation of the field finite element engine (`FFE_Engine.hpp`) in Listing 9-1. The file contains the signatures for the following operations and functions.

  - `int ExtendedGreatestCommongDivisor()` is the function that computes the extended greater common divisor.

  - `int InverseModular()` is the function that solves the linear congruence equation $x \times z = = 1 \; (mod \; n)$.

  - `FFE operator-() const` is the operator that represents the negation operation.

  - `FFE& operator=(int i)` is the operator that deals with the assignation with an integer.

  - `FFE<P>& operator=(const FFE<P>& rhs)` is the operator for assignation from the field element.

  - `FFE<P>& operator*=(const FFE<P>& rhs)` is an implementation for *= operator for assignation from field element.

  - `friend bool operator==(const FFE<P>& lhs, const FFE<P>& rhs)` is implementation of == operator for assignation from field element.

  - `friend FFE<P> operator/(const FFE<P>& lhs, const FFE<P>& rhs)` is an implementation for/operator for assignation from the field element as form (x,y).

- `friend FFE<P> operator+(const FFE<P>& lhs, const FFE<P>& rhs)` is an implementation for the + operator for assignation from the field element as form (x,y).

- `friend FFE<P> operator-(const FFE<P>& lhs, const FFE<P>& rhs)` is an implementation for the - operator for assignation from the field element as form (x,y).

- `friend FFE<P> operator+(const FFE<P>& lhs, int i)` is implementation for the *a + int* operator for assignation from the field element as form (x,y).

- `friend FFE<P> operator+(int i, const FFE<P>& rhs)` is an implementation for *int + a* operator for assignation from the field element as form (x,y).

- `friend FFE<P> operator*(int n, const FFE<P>& rhs)` is an implementation for *int * a* operator for assignation from the field element as form (x,y).

- `friend FFE<P> operator*(const FFE<P>& lhs, const FFE<P>& rhs)` is an implementation for *a * b* operator for assignation from the field element as form (x,y).

- `template<int T> friend ostream& operator<<(ostream& os, const FFE<T>& g)` is the `ostream` operator for showing and displaying in a readable format.

- The main program in Listing 9-2. The file contains the main implementation for elliptic curve cryptography. In the main program, a special focus must be on implementing the operators listed earlier. Another important aspect of this implementation is that at the beginning of the program, we can observe that our curve is defined over a finite field (Galois field) and that any point within the elliptic curve is formed from two elements that are within the Galois fields. Those points are created once there is a declaration instance of the elliptic curve. To implement the elliptic curve, the following

two declarations are needed: type EllipticCurve<OrderFFE_
EC> this_t and type EllipticCurve<OrderFFE_
EC>::EllipticCurvePoint point_t. Once we have the declaration,
we can proceed further with the representation of the Weierstrass
equation as $y^2 = x^3 + ax + b$, as represented in the following through
the constructor of the EllipticCurve class.

```
//** the Weierstrass equation as y^2 = x^3 + ax + b
Elliptic Curve (int CoefA, int CoefB)
     : ECParameterA(CoefA),
     ECParameterB(CoefB),
     tableOfPoints(),
     tableFilledComputated(false)
{}
```

The next step is to compute the points and to set true for the
tableFilledComputated Boolean variable, which is used to indicate if the table with
points has been filled or not for further computation (see Figure 9-4). The rest of the
functions are straightforward and represent basic cryptographic operations between
Alice, Bob, and Oscar, the malicious third party trying to decrypt the message.

```
C:\Users\mariu\OneDrive\Desktop\Apress C++23\09. Elliptic-Curve Cryptography\source code>g++ -std=c++2b ecc.cpp -o ecc.exe

C:\Users\mariu\OneDrive\Desktop\Apress C++23\09. Elliptic-Curve Cryptography\source code>ecc.exe
Basic Example of using Elliptic Curve Cryptography using C++20. Apress, 2020

Equation of the elliptic curve: y^2 mod 163 = (x^3+1x+1) mod 163

List of the points (x,Y) for the curve (i.e. the group elements):
(0, 1) (0, 162) (4, 45) (4, 118) (5, 72) (5, 91)
(6, 68) (6, 95) (7, 5) (7, 158) (9, 24) (9, 139)
(10, 14) (10, 149) (11, 56) (11, 107) (12, 33) (12, 130)
(14, 71) (14, 92) (15, 72) (15, 91) (16, 53) (16, 110)
(17, 81) (17, 82) (18, 31) (18, 132) (19, 14) (19, 149)
(20, 69) (20, 94) (21, 36) (21, 127) (27, 71) (27, 92)
(29, 28) (29, 135) (30, 25) (30, 138) (32, 53) (32, 110)
(33, 33) (33, 130) (34, 43) (34, 120) (37, 18) (37, 145)
(38, 44) (38, 119) (40, 54) (40, 109) (41, 60) (41, 103)
(44, 44) (44, 119) (45, 39) (45, 124) (47, 23) (47, 140)
(51, 64) (51, 99) (52, 36) (52, 127) (54, 77) (54, 86)
(57, 75) (57, 88) (58, 68) (58, 95) (62, 30) (62, 133)
(63, 45) (63, 118) (65, 6) (65, 157) (67, 52) (67, 111)
(68, 20) (68, 143) (69, 42) (69, 121) (70, 49) (70, 114)
(71, 19) (71, 144) (72, 41) (72, 122) (73, 70) (73, 93)
(74, 9) (74, 154) (81, 44) (81, 119) (82, 48) (82, 115)
(84, 11) (84, 152) (87, 76) (87, 87) (88, 59) (88, 104)
(89, 35) (89, 128) (90, 36) (90, 127) (93, 32) (93, 131)
(95, 55) (95, 108) (96, 45) (96, 118) (97, 42) (97, 121)
(99, 68) (99, 95) (100, 52) (100, 111) (107, 80) (107, 83)
(109, 58) (109, 105) (110, 78) (110, 85) (111, 70) (111, 93)
(112, 12) (112, 151) (113, 61) (113, 102) (114, 57) (114, 106)
(115, 53) (115, 110) (117, 16) (117, 147) (118, 33) (118, 130)
(119, 48) (119, 115) (120, 22) (120, 141) (121, 6) (121, 157)
(122, 71) (122, 92) (125, 48) (125, 115) (126, 2) (126, 161)
(127, 47) (127, 116) (130, 39) (130, 124) (134, 14) (134, 149)
(135, 29) (135, 134) (136, 60) (136, 103) (140, 6) (140, 157)
(142, 70) (142, 93) (143, 72) (143, 91) (144, 28) (144, 135)
(148, 69) (148, 94) (149, 60) (149, 103) (151, 39) (151, 124)
(152, 17) (152, 146) (153, 28) (153, 135) (155, 40) (155, 123)
(156, 38) (156, 125) (158, 69) (158, 94) (159, 52) (159, 111)
(160, 42) (160, 121)

Randomly - Point P  = (4, 45), 2P = (32, 110)
Randomly - Point Q = (4, 118), P+Q = (0, 0)
P += Q = (0, 0)
P += P = 2P = (32, 110)

Encryption of the message using elliptic curve principles

G = (90, 127), order(G) is 31
Alice - Public key (Pa) = 32*(90, 127) = (52, 36)
Bob - Public key (Pb) = 131*(90, 127) = (62, 133)
Oscar - Public key (Po) = 95*(90, 127) = (155, 40)


The clear text message send by Alice to Bob: (19, 72)
The message encrypted from Alice for Bob is represented as {Pa,c1,c2} and its content is = {(52, 36), 26, 58}

        The message decrypted by Bob from Alice is = (19, 72)

Oscar decrypt the message from Alice = (154, 80)


C:\Users\mariu\OneDrive\Desktop\Apress C++23\09. Elliptic-Curve Cryptography\source code>
```

Figure 9-4. *The output of the example*

Listing 9-1. Implementation of the Field Finite Element Engine (FFE_Engine)

```
namespace EllipticCurveCryptography
{
    //** basic functions for
    //** Finite Field Elements (FFE)
    namespace HelperFunctionFFE
    {
        //** Computing Extended GCD gives g = a*u + b*v
        int ExtendedGreatestCommongDivisor(int a, int b,
                                           int& u, int &v)
        {
            u = 1;
            v = 0;
            int g = a;
            int u1 = 0;
            int v1 = 1;
            int g1 = b;
            while (g1 != 0)
            {
                //** division using integers
                int q = g/g1;
                int t1 = u - q*u1;
                int t2 = v - q*v1;
                int t3 = g - q*g1;
                u = u1; v = v1; g = g1;
                u1 = t1; v1 = t2; g1 = t3;
            }

            return g;
        }

        //** providing solution and solving
        //** the linear congruence equation
        //** x * z == 1 (mod n) for z
        int InvMod(int x, int n)
```

```
        {
            //** "%" represents the remainder
            //** function, 0 <= x % n < |n|
            x = x % n;
            int u,v,g,z;
            g = ExtendedGreatestCommongDivisor(x, n,
                                                u,v);

        if (g != 1)
        {
            //** x and n has to be primes
            //** in order to exist an x^-1 mod n
            z = 0;
        }
        else
            z = u % n;

        return z;
    }
}

//** represents the element from a Galois field
//** we will use a specific behavior for the
//** modular function in which (-n) mod m will
//** return a negative number.
//** The implementation is done in such a way that
//** it will offer support for the basic
//** arithmetic operations, such as:
//** + (addition), - (subtraction), / (division)
//** and scalar multiplication.
//** The P served as an argument represents the
//** order for the field.
template<int P>
class FFE
{
  int i_;
```

```
void assign(int i)
{
    i_ = i;
    if ( i<0 )
    {
        //** The correction behavior
        //** is important.
        //** Using (-i) mod p we will make sure
        //** that the behavior is the proper one.
        i_ = (i%P) + 2*P;
    }

    i_ %= P;
}

public:
    //** the constructor
    FFE()
     : i_(0)
    {}

    //** another constructor
    explicit FFE(int i)
    {
        assign(i);
    }

    //** copying the constructor
    FFE(const FFE<P>& rhs)
     : i_(rhs.i_)
    {
    }

    //** providing access to
    //** the raw integer
    int i() const { return i_; }
```

```cpp
    //** implementation for negation operator
    FFE  operator-() const
    {
        return FFE(-i_);
    }

    //** assignation  assign from integer
    FFE& operator=(int i)
    {
        assign(i);
        return *this;
    }

    //** assignation from from field element
    FFE<P>& operator=(const FFE<P>& rhs)
    {
        i_ = rhs.i_;
        return *this;
    }

    //** implementation of "*=" operator
    FFE<P>& operator*=(const FFE<P>& rhs)
    {
        i_ = (i_*rhs.i_) % P;
        return *this;
    }

    //** implementation of "==" operator
    friend bool operator==(const FFE<P>& lhs,
                           const FFE<P>& rhs)
    {
        return (lhs.i_ == rhs.i_);
    }

    //** implementation of "==" operator
    friend bool operator==(const FFE<P>& lhs,
                           int rhs)
```

```
{
    return (lhs.i_ == rhs);
}

//** implementation of "!=" operator
friend bool operator!=(const FFE<P>& lhs,
                       int rhs)
{
    return (lhs.i_ != rhs);
}

// implementation of "a/b" operator
friend FFE<P> operator/(const FFE<P>& lhs,
                        const FFE<P>& rhs)
{
    return FFE<P>( lhs.i_ *
      HelperFunctionFFE::InvMod(rhs.i_,P));
}

//** implementation of "a+b" operator
friend FFE<P> operator+(const FFE<P>& lhs,
                        const FFE<P>& rhs)
{
    return FFE<P>( lhs.i_ + rhs.i_);
}

//** implementation of "a-b" operator
friend FFE<P> operator-(const FFE<P>& lhs,
                        const FFE<P>& rhs)
{
    return FFE<P>(lhs.i_ - rhs.i_);
}

// implementation of "a + int" operator
friend FFE<P> operator+(const FFE<P>& lhs,
                        int i)
```

```cpp
    {
        return FFE<P>( lhs.i_+i);
    }

    //** implementation of "int + a" operator
    friend FFE<P> operator+(int i,
                            const FFE<P>& rhs)
    {
        return FFE<P>( rhs.i_+i);
    }

    //** implementation of "int * a" operator
    friend FFE<P> operator*(int n,
                            const FFE<P>& rhs)
    {
        return FFE<P>( n*rhs.i_);
    }

    //** implementation of "a * b"
    friend FFE<P> operator*(const FFE<P>& lhs,
                            const FFE<P>& rhs)
    {
        return FFE<P>( lhs.i_ * rhs.i_);
    }

    //** the operator ostream for
    //** showing and displaying in
    //** readable format
    template<int T>
    friend ostream& operator<<(ostream& os,
                               const FFE<T>& g)
    {
        return os << g.i_;
    }
};
}
```

Listing 9-2. Implementation of the Main Program

```
//** Leave everything as it is.
//** Do not change the order of the inputs or namespaces.

#include <cstdlib>
#include <iostream>
#include <vector>

using namespace std;

#include <math.h>
#include "FFE_Engine.hpp"

namespace EllipticCurveCryptography
{
        //** Elliptic Curve over a finite field of order P:
        //** y^2 mod P = x^3 + ax + b mod P
        template<int OrderFFE_EC> class EllipticCurve
        {
            public:
                //** this curve is defined over the finite
                //** field (Galois field) Fp, this is the
                //** typedef of elements in it
                typedef FFE<OrderFFE_EC> ffe_element;

                 //** any point on elliptic curve is formed
                 //** from two elements that are within Fp
                 //**field (Galois Field). The points are
                 //** created once we declare an instance of
                 //** Elliptic Curve itself.
                class EllipticCurvePoint
                {
                    friend class EllipticCurve<OrderFFE_EC>;
                    typedef FFE<OrderFFE_EC> ffe_element;
                    ffe_element xCoordValue_;
                    ffe_element yCoordValue_;
                    EllipticCurve *ellipticCurve_;
```

```
//** core of the doubling multiplier
//** algorithm (see below)
//** multiplies acc by m as a series of
//** "2*accumulatorContainer's"
void DoublingMultiplierAlgorithm(int
        multiplier, EllipticCurvePoint&
        accumulatorContainer)
{
    if (multiplier > 0)
    {
        EllipticCurvePoint doublingValue =
            accumulatorContainer;
        for (int counter=0; counter <
                multiplier; ++counter)
        {
            //** doubling step
            doublingValue += doublingValue;
        }
        accumulatorContainer =
                            doublingValue;
    }
}

//** Implementation of doubling
//** multiplier algorithm.
//** The process stands on multiplying
//** intermediateResultAccumulator for
//** storing the intermediate
//** results with inputScalar.
//** This is done through
//** expansion in multiple
//** by 2 between the first of the
//** binary representation of inputScalar.
EllipticCurvePoint MultiplyUsingScalar(int
    inputScalar, const EllipticCurvePoint&
    intermediateResultAccumulator)
```

```
{
    EllipticCurvePoint
        accumulatorContainer =
        intermediateResultAccumulator;
    EllipticCurvePoint outputResult =
        EllipticCurvePoint(0,0,
                        *ellipticCurve_);
    int i = 0, j = 0;
    int iS = inputScalar;

    while(iS)
    {
        if (iS&1)
        {
```
//** Setting up the bit.
//** The computation is done by following the formula:
//** accumulatorContainer = 2^(i-j)*accumulatorContainer
DoublingMultiplierAlgorithm(i-j,accumulatorContainer);

outputResult += accumulatorContainer;

//** last setting for the bit
j = i;
```
        }
        iS >>= 1;
        ++i;
    }
    return outputResult;
}
```
//** the function deals with
//** adding two points on the curve

//** xCoord1, yCoord1, xCoord2=x2,
//** yCoord2=y2

```
void ECTwoPointsAddition(ffe_element
    xCoord1, ffe_element yCoord1,
    ffe_element xCoord2, ffe_element
    yCoord2, ffe_element & xCoordR, ffe_element &
    yCoordR) const
{
    //** dealing with sensitives cases
    //** for implying addition identity
    if (xCoord1==0 && yCoord1==0)
    {
        xCoordR = xCoord2;
        yCoordR = yCoord2;
        return;
    }
    if (xCoord2==0 && yCoord2==0)
    {
        xCoordR = xCoord1;
        yCoordR = yCoord1;
        return;
    }
    if (yCoord1==-yCoord2)
    {
        xCoordR = yCoordR = 0;
        return;
    }

    //** deal with the additions
    ffe_element s;
    if (xCoord1 == xCoord2 && yCoord1 ==
                        yCoord2)
    {
        //** computing 2*P
        s = (3*(xCoord1.i()*xCoord1.i()) +
            ellipticCurve_->a()) /
            (2*yCoord1);
```

```
    xCoordR = ((s*s) - 2*xCoord1);
}
else
{
    //** computing P+Q
    s = (yCoord1 - yCoord2) / (xCoord1
                              - xCoord2);
    xCoordR = ((s*s) - xCoord1 -
                      xCoord2);
}

if (s!=0)
{
    yCoordR = (-yCoord1 + s*(xCoord1 -
                          xCoordR));
}
else
{
    xCoordR = yCoordR = 0;
}
}

EllipticCurvePoint(int xPoint, int yPoint)
: xCoordValue_(xPoint),
  yCoordValue_(yPoint),
  ellipticCurve_(0)
{}

EllipticCurvePoint(int xPoint, int yPoint,
      EllipticCurve<OrderFFE_EC> &
      EllipticCurve)
 : xCoordValue_(xPoint),
   yCoordValue_(yPoint),
   ellipticCurve_(&EllipticCurve)
{}
```

```
             EllipticCurvePoint(const ffe_element&
                xPoint, const ffe_element& yPoint,
                EllipticCurve<OrderFFE_EC> &
                EllipticCurve)
            : xCoordValue_(xPoint),
              yCoordValue_(yPoint),
              ellipticCurve_(&EllipticCurve)
        {}

    public:
        static EllipticCurvePoint ONE;

        //** constructor
        EllipticCurvePoint(const
                    EllipticCurvePoint& rhsPoint)
        {
            xCoordValue_ = rhsPoint.xCoordValue_;
            yCoordValue_ = rhsPoint.yCoordValue_;
            ellipticCurve_ =
                        rhsPoint.ellipticCurve_;
        }

        //** the assignment process
        EllipticCurvePoint& operator=(const
                    EllipticCurvePoint& rhsPoint)
        {
            xCoordValue_ = rhsPoint.xCoordValue_;
            yCoordValue_ = rhsPoint.yCoordValue_;
            ellipticCurve_ =
                        rhsPoint.ellipticCurve_;
            return *this;
        }

        //** access x component as element of Fp
        ffe_element GetX() const { return
                        xCoordValue_; }
```

```cpp
//** access y component as element of Fp
ffe_element GetY() const { return
                    yCoordValue_; }

//** calculate the order of this point by
//** brute-force additions
unsigned int
    ComputingOrderBruteForceAddition
    (unsigned int maximum_period = ~0) const
{
    EllipticCurvePoint ecPoint = *this;
    unsigned int order = 0;
    while(ecPoint.xCoordValue_ != 0 &&
        ecPoint.yCoordValue_ != 0)
    {
        ++order;
        ecPoint += *this;
        if (order > maximum_period) break;
    }
    return order;
}

//** negation operator (-) that
//** gives the inverse of a point
EllipticCurvePoint operator-()
{
    return
        EllipticCurvePoint(xCoordValue_,
            -yCoordValue_);
}

//** equal (==) operator
friend bool operator==(const
  EllipticCurvePoint& lhsPoint,
  const EllipticCurvePoint& rhsPoint)
```

```cpp
{
    return (lhsPoint.ec_ == rhsPoint.ec_)
  && (lhsPoint.x_ == rhsPoint.x_) &&
    (lhsPoint.y_ == rhsPoint.y_);
}

//** different (!=) operator
friend bool operator!=(const
        EllipticCurvePoint& lhsPoint, const
        EllipticCurvePoint& rhsPoint)
{
    return (lhsPoint.ec_ != rhsPoint.ec_)
        || (lhsPoint.x_ != rhsPoint.x_) ||
        (lhsPoint.y_ != rhsPoint.y_);
}

//** Implementation of a + b operator
friend EllipticCurvePoint operator+(const
        EllipticCurvePoint& lhsPoint,
        const EllipticCurvePoint& rhsPoint)
{
    ffe_element xResult, yResult;
    lhsPoint.ECTwoPointsAddition(
            lhsPoint.xCoordValue_,
            lhsPoint.yCoordValue_,
            rhsPoint.xCoordValue_,
            rhsPoint.yCoordValue_,
            xResult,yResult);
    return
            EllipticCurvePoint(xResult,
                yResult,
                *lhsPoint.ellipticCurve_);
}
```

```
//** multiplying with scalar * int
friend EllipticCurvePoint operator*(int
    scalar, const
        EllipticCurvePoint& rhsPoint)
{
    return
        EllipticCurvePoint(rhsPoint).
                    operator*=(scalar);
}

//** Implementation of += operator
EllipticCurvePoint& operator+=(const
        EllipticCurvePoint& rhsPoint)
{
    ECTwoPointsAddition(xCoordValue_,
    yCoordValue_,rhsPoint.xCoordValue_,
    rhsPoint.yCoordValue_,xCoordValue_,
    yCoordValue_);
    return *this;
}

//** Implementation of *= int operator
EllipticCurvePoint& operator*=(int scalar)
{
    return (*this =
        MultiplyUsingScalar(scalar,*this));
}

//** display and print the point
//** using ostream
friend ostream& operator <<(ostream& os,
    const EllipticCurvePoint& p)
{
    return (os << "(" << p.xCoordValue_ <<
        ", " << p.yCoordValue_ << ")");
}
};
```

```
            //** performing the elliptic
            //** curve implementation
            typedef EllipticCurve<OrderFFE_EC> this_t;
            typedef class
                EllipticCurve<OrderFFE_EC>::
                        EllipticCurvePoint point_t;

            //** the Weierstrass equation
            //** as y^2 = x^3 + ax + b
            EllipticCurve(int CoefA, int CoefB)
            : ECParameterA(CoefA),
              ECParameterB(CoefB),
              tableOfPoints(),
              tableFilledComputated(false)
            {
            }

                //** compute all the points
                //** (from the group of elements) for
                //** Weierstrass equation. Note the
//** fact that if we are
                //** having a high order for the curve,
//** the computation process
                //** will take some time
            void CalculatePoints()
            {
                int x_val[OrderFFE_EC];
                int y_val[OrderFFE_EC];
                for (int counter = 0; counter <
                              OrderFFE_EC; ++counter)
                {
                    int nsq = counter*counter;
                    x_val[counter] = ((counter*nsq) +
                        ECParameterA.i() * counter +
                        ECParameterB.i()) % OrderFFE_EC;
                    y_val[counter] = nsq % OrderFFE_EC;
                }
```

```
    for (int counter1 = 0; counter1 <
             OrderFFE_EC; ++counter1)
    {
        for (int counter2 = 0; counter2 <
                 OrderFFE_EC; ++counter2)
        {
            if (x_val[counter1] ==
                 y_val[counter2])
            {
                tableOfPoints.push_back(Ellip
                ticCurvePoint(counter1,
                counter2,*this));
            }
        }
    }

    tableFilledComputated = true;
}

//** obtain the point (from the group of
//** elements) for the curve
EllipticCurvePoint operator[](int n)
{
    if ( !tableFilledComputated )
    {
        CalculatePoints();
    }

    return tableOfPoints[n];
}

//** the number og the elements
//** in the group
size_t Size() const { return
        tableOfPoints.size(); }
```

```cpp
//** the degree of the point for
//** the elliptic curve
int Degree() const { return OrderFFE_EC; }

//** the "a" parameter, as an element of Fp
FFE<OrderFFE_EC> a() const { return
                                ECParameterA; }

//** the "b" paramter, as an element of Fp
FFE<OrderFFE_EC> b() const { return
                                ECParameterB; }

//** print and show the elliptic curve in a
//** readable format using ostream   human
//** readable form
template<int ECT>
friend ostream& operator <<(ostream& os, const
        EllipticCurve<ECT>& EllipticCurve);

//** print and display all the elements
//** of the elliptic curve group
ostream& PrintTable(ostream &os,
                        int columns=4);

private:
    typedef std::vector<EllipticCurvePoint>
                            TableWithPoints;

    //** table with the points
    TableWithPoints tableOfPoints;

    //** first parameter of the
    //** elliptic curve equation
    FFE<OrderFFE_EC> ECParameterA;

    //** second parameter of the
    //** elliptic curve equation
    FFE<OrderFFE_EC> ECParameterB;
```

```
            //** boolean value to show if the
            //** table has been computed
             bool tableFilledComputated;
};

template<int ECT>
    typename EllipticCurve<ECT>::EllipticCurvePoint
            EllipticCurve<ECT>::EllipticCurvePoint::
            ONE(0,0);

template<int ECT>
ostream& operator <<(ostream& os, const
            EllipticCurve<ECT>& EllipticCurve)
{
    os << "y^2 mod " << ECT << " = (x^3" << showpos;
    if ( EllipticCurve.ECParameterA != 0 )
    {
        os << EllipticCurve.ECParameterA << "x";
    }

    if ( EllipticCurve.ECParameterB.i() != 0 )
    {
        os << EllipticCurve.ECParameterB;
    }

    os << noshowpos << ") mod " << ECT;
    return os;
}

template<int P>
ostream& EllipticCurve<P>::PrintTable(ostream &os,
                                        int columns)
{
    if (tableFilledComputated)
    {
        int col = 0;
        typename
         EllipticCurve<P>::TableWithPoints::
```

```cpp
            iterator iter = tableOfPoints.begin();
            for ( ; iter!=tableOfPoints.end(); ++iter )
            {
                os << "(" << (*iter).xCoordValue_.i() <<
            ", " << (*iter).yCoordValue_.i() << ") ";
                if ( ++col > columns )
                {
                    os << "\n";
                    col = 0;
                }
            }
        }
        else
        {
            os << "EllipticCurve, F_" << P;
        }
        return os;
    }
}

namespace utils
{
    float   frand()
    {
        static float norm = 1.0f / (float)RAND_MAX;
        return (float)rand()*norm;
    }

    int irand(int min, int max)
    {
        return min+(int)(frand()*(float)(max-min));
    }
}

using namespace EllipticCurveCryptography;
using namespace utils;
```

```cpp
int main(int argc, char *argv[])
{
    typedef EllipticCurve<163> elliptic_curve;
    elliptic_curve myEllipticCurve(1,1);

    cout << "Basic Example of using Elliptic Curve
            Cryptography using C++20. Apress, 2020\n\n";

    //** display some information about the
    //** elliptic curve and display some of the properties
    cout << "Equation of the elliptic curve: " <<
                                    myEllipticCurve << "\n";

    //** compute the points for the elliptic
    //** curve for equation from the above
    myEllipticCurve.CalculatePoints();

    cout << "\nList of the points (x,Y) for the curve (i.e.
                                    the group elements):\n";
    myEllipticCurve.PrintTable(cout,5);
    cout << "\n\n";

    elliptic_curve::EllipticCurvePoint P = myEllipticCurve[2];
    cout << "Randomly - Point P  = " << P << ", 2P = " <<
                                    (P+P) << "\n";

    elliptic_curve::EllipticCurvePoint Q =
                                    myEllipticCurve[3];
    cout << "Randomly - Point Q = " << Q << ", P+Q = " <<
                                    (P+Q) << "\n";

    elliptic_curve::EllipticCurvePoint R = P;
    R += Q;
    cout << "P += Q = " << R << "\n";

    R = P;
    R += R;
    cout << "P += P = 2P = " << R << "\n";
```

```
cout << "\nEncryption of the message using
                    elliptic curve principles\n\n";

//** as an example we will use Menes-Vanstone
//** scheme that is based on elliptic
//** curve for message encryption
elliptic_curve::EllipticCurvePoint G = myEllipticCurve[0];
while((G.GetY() == 0 || G.GetX() == 0) ||
            (G.ComputingOrderBruteForceAddition()<2))
{
    int n = (int)(frand()*myEllipticCurve.Size());
    G = myEllipticCurve[n];
}

cout << "G = " << G << ", order(G) is " <<
            G.ComputingOrderBruteForceAddition() << "\n";

//** Suppose that Alice wish to communicate with Bob
//** Alice and its public key
int a = irand(1,myEllipticCurve.Degree()-1);

//** generating the public key
elliptic_curve::EllipticCurvePoint Pa = a*G;
cout << "Alice - Public key (Pa) = " << a << "*" << G << "
                                = " << Pa << endl;

//** Bob and is public key
int b = irand(1,myEllipticCurve.Degree()-1);

//** the public key
elliptic_curve::EllipticCurvePoint Pb = b*G;
cout << "Bob - Public key (Pb) = " << b << "*" << G << " =
                                    " << Pb << endl;

//** Oscar - the eavesdropper and attacker
int o = irand(1,myEllipticCurve.Degree()-1);;
elliptic_curve::EllipticCurvePoint Po = o*G;
cout << "Oscar - Public key (Po) = " << o << "*" << G << "
                            = " << Po << endl;
```

```
cout << "\n\n";

//** Alice proceeds with the encryption
//** for her message and send it to Bob.
//** To achieve this, the first step is
//** to split the message into multiple
//** parts that are encoded using Galois
//** field (Fp), which is also the domain
//** elliptic curve.
int m1 = 19;
int m2 = 72;

cout << "The clear text message send by Alice to Bob: ("
                    << m1 << ", " << m2 << ")\n";

//** proceed with encryption using the key of Bob
elliptic_curve::EllipticCurvePoint Pk = a*Pb;
elliptic_curve::ffe_element c1(m1*Pk.GetX());
elliptic_curve::ffe_element c2(m2*Pk.GetY());

//** the message that is encrypted is composed from:
//** Pa - Alice public key
//** c1,c2
cout << "The message encrypted from Alice for Bob is
            represented as {Pa,c1,c2} and its content is =
            {" << Pa << ", " << c1 << ", " << c2 <<
            "}\n\n";

//** Bob computes the decryption for the message
//** received from Alice, using her public key
//** and the session value (integer b)
Pk = b*Pa;
elliptic_curve::ffe_element m1d  = c1/Pk.GetX();
elliptic_curve::ffe_element m2d = c2/Pk.GetY();

cout << "\tThe message decrypted by Bob from Alice is = ("
                << m1d << ", " << m2d << ")" << endl;
```

```
//** Oscar will intercept the message and
//** and he/she will try to decrypt it
//** using his/her key
Pk = o*Pa;
m1d = c1/Pk.GetX();
m2d = c2/Pk.GetY();

cout << "\nOscar decrypt the message from Alice = (" <<
              m1d << ", " << m2d << ")" << endl;

cout << endl;
}
```

Conclusion

Cryptography is a critical component of security and privacy for data stored in the cloud and across networks. ECC is the most secure type of encryption available today and is used to protect data and communications from hackers. ECC is a powerful tool that can protect a wide range of data, from emails and financial transactions to medical records and confidential documents. This comprehensive chapter on ECC provided a deep dive into the technology and its applications, and discussed elliptic curve cryptography and how it can be implemented.

In this chapter, you learned the following.

- The theoretical fundamentals for implementing elliptic curve cryptography

- How to apply theoretical mechanisms and theorems for operations with group law in practice

- How to implement the basic operations and transpose into practice elliptic curve cryptography

References

[1].   Lenstra Elliptic-Curve Cryptography. Available online: `https://en.wikipedia.org/wiki/Lenstra_elliptic-curve_factorization`. Last accessed: 25.2.2023

[2].   Diophantine Geometry. Available online: `https://en.wikipedia.org/wiki/Diophantine_geometry`. Last accessed: 25.2.2023

[3].   Diophantus. Available online: `https://en.wikipedia.org/wiki/Diophantus`. Last accessed: 25.2.2023

[4].   L. Washington, *Elliptic Curves: Number Theory and Cryptography*. Chapman & Hall/CRC, 2008.

CHAPTER 10

Lattice-based Cryptography

This chapter has an overview of lattice-based cryptography. You learn why lattices are important in cryptography and their challenges. Furthermore, you see how to develop a practical implementation that uses lattices, namely, the GGH (Goldreich–Goldwasser–Halevi) encryption scheme [1].

Lattice-based cryptography has emerged as a powerful tool for modern cybersecurity, providing a secure and reliable data encryption and authentication method. It is a type of cryptography based on mathematical lattices and is considered one of the most robust and secure forms of encryption. Lattice-based cryptography is a versatile and efficient tool that implements various cryptographic techniques and protocols. It is used in a wide range of applications, from secure communication in the military to online payments and digital signatures. With its unique properties, lattice-based cryptography has become an indispensable tool in the fight against cybercrime and protecting sensitive data. This chapter provides an overview of lattice-based cryptography, its advantages and disadvantages, and its importance in modern cybersecurity.

Lattice-based cryptography is a type of cryptography based on mathematical lattices. Lattices are an abstract mathematical structure used to represent the relationship between numbers. The word "lattice" refers to a grid-like pattern formed by points and axes. In cryptography, this lattice pattern defines a set of operations and transformations that can be applied to data. In essence, lattice-based cryptography is a particular set of algorithms that use this lattice pattern to create a ciphertext, which is then decrypted with the help of an inverse transformation. This is similar to how a wooden toy puzzle with a grid-like pattern is assembled: if you put the pieces together correctly, you return the original picture.

245

© Marius Iulian Mihailescu and Stefania Loredana Nita 2023
M. I. Mihailescu and S. L. Nita, *Pro Cryptography and Cryptanalysis with C++23*,
https://doi.org/10.1007/978-1-4842-9450-5_10

Lattices are important in cryptography because the hardness assumption based on them is considered quantum-resistant in the context where, in the last few years, the number of primitives in quantum cryptography has increased. While traditional encryption systems, such as RSA, Diffie-Hellman, and elliptic curve encryption systems, can be easily broken using quantum computers, encryption systems using lattices are among the few candidates that resist postquantum cryptography.

Advantages and Disadvantages of Lattice-based Cryptography

The *advantages* of lattice-based cryptography can be summarized as follows.

- **Wide applicability**. Lattice-based cryptography can be used in various applications, including authentication, data integrity, and confidentiality.

- **Versatility**. Lattice-based cryptography can implement many cryptographic techniques, such as public key cryptography, digital signatures, and authentication methods.

- **Ease of use**. Lattice-based cryptography is particularly suitable for software applications, where its simplicity and flexibility make it easier to use and integrate into existing systems.

- **Efficiency**. Compared to other cryptographic methods, such as finite fields, lattice-based cryptography is more efficient, performing better in speed and energy consumption.

- **Security**. Lattice-based cryptography has strong mathematical foundations, making it a secure and reliable system.

- **Robustness**. The security of lattice-based cryptography is ensured by mathematical proofs and rigorous mathematical analysis, making the system more robust against attacks.

The following are some of the *disadvantages*.

- **Complexity**. Although lattice-based cryptography is a powerful system with a wide range of applications, it is also a complex mathematical system requiring specific skills to understand and implement.

- **Data volume**. Lattice-based cryptography works best with large data sets but can be less efficient when dealing with smaller amounts of data.

- **Not quantum-resistant**. There is a concern that lattice-based cryptography is not quantum-resistant, making it vulnerable to quantum computing attacks. To address this issue, there are ongoing efforts to develop new lattice-based algorithms resistant to quantum computing.

- **Implementation complexity**. To use lattice-based cryptography, one must design and implement a cryptographic system that uses lattices as an underlying mathematical structure.

- **Poor inherent randomness**. Lattice-based cryptography is not a good choice for creating random numbers, so applications requiring a high level of randomness might warrant a different technique.

Applications of Lattice-based Cryptography

Lattice-based cryptography has an important number of applications, from research to industry applications, which are summarized as follows.

- **Cryptography**. Lattice-based cryptography is used in various cryptographic applications, such as data encryption, digital signatures, and authentication.

- **Quantum computing**. Lattice-based cryptography is also used to protect against quantum computing attacks.

- **Quantum key distribution**. Lattice-based cryptography is used for quantum key distribution (QKD), a technique for creating a secret key between two parties communicating over an insecure channel.

- **Factoring and discrete logarithm problems**: Lattice-based cryptography is also used to solve factoring and discrete logarithm problems.

- **Mathematical problems**. Lattice-based cryptography can also be used to solve a wide range of mathematical problems, such as integer factorization and the graph isomorphism problem.

Security of Lattice-based Cryptography

Lattice-based cryptography is a mathematically robust cryptographic method that uses a lattice structure to encrypt and decrypt data. It is based on the computational hardness of certain problems, such as integer factorization, graph isomorphism, and the halting problem. The system is secure because these problems are very difficult to solve and require a considerable amount of computing power, if not an impossible amount, making it practically impossible to crack the system unless you have more computing power than the entire world combined. Lattice-based cryptography is a key component in many technologies, including the Internet of Things, online payments, and secure communication. Due to its strong mathematical foundations, lattice-based cryptography is secure and reliable. Moreover, it is resistant to a wide range of attacks, including brute-force attacks, side-channel attacks, and known plaintext attacks.

Lattice-based Cryptography and Quantum Computing

Lattice-based cryptography is a powerful cryptographic technique that protects sensitive data against various threats, including quantum computing attacks. Quantum computing is an emerging technology that promises to solve certain problems exponentially faster than traditional computers, making conventional cryptographic techniques vulnerable to attack. Many modern cryptographic techniques rely on quantum-resistant algorithms to protect sensitive data against quantum computing threats. What makes an algorithm quantum-resistant?

In general, quantum-resistant algorithms have one or more of the following properties

- They do not depend on a problem being hard to solve.

- They do not have a problem with noise.

- They do not have a problem with decoherence.

However, using lattices in cryptography is not an easy task regarding the applicability and practical implementations because these are complex mathematical constructions that require a solid background in algebra and understanding abstract concepts.

Mathematical Background

This section briefly overviews the main elements and techniques required as minimum theoretical information about the lattices and the mathematical background that a professional should know.

Take into consideration the space R^n and a base in R^n of the form $b = (b_1, ..., b_n)$, with $b_1, ..., b_n \in R$. A lattice has the following form.

$$L(b) = \{\Sigma a_i b_i \mid a_i \in Z\}$$

In the preceding construction, a_i is an integer number, and b_i is the ith element of the basis b. Moreover, L is the set of all linear combinations with integer coefficients. An immediate example of a lattice is Z^n, generated by the standard basis in R^n. Figure 10-1 shows a lattice in the Euclidean plane.

Figure 10-1. *Lattice in Euclidean plane*[1]

---

[1] Source: https://en.wikipedia.org/wiki/Lattice_(group

Examples of lattice problems are the shortest vector problem (SVP), closest vector problem (CVP), shortest independent vector problem (SIVP), GapSVP, GapCVP, bounded distance decoding, covering radius problem, and shortest basis problem. In cryptography, SVP and CVP are mainly used as hardness assumptions in cryptosystems.

For SVP, the following elements are given: a vector space V, a basis b in the vector space, and a norm N. Knowing the lattice $L(b)$, it is required to compute the shortest vector $v \in V$ such that v's norm in V represents the minimum distance defined in L. In other words, the vector $v \in V$ should be found such that

$$\|v\| = \lambda\big(L(b)\big)$$

In the preceding relation, $\|.\|$ represents the norm in V, $L(b)$ is the lattice defined over the basis b and λ is the minimum distance defined in $L(b)$. The relation gives the search variant of the SVP. The following are the other two variants.

- **Calculation**. Find the minimum distance in lattice $\lambda(L(b))$ when given basis b and lattice $\lambda(L(b))$.

- **Decision**. Determine whether $\lambda(L(b)) \leq d$ or $\lambda(L(b)) > d$ when given basis b, lattice $\lambda(L(b))$ and real value $d > 0$.

A generalization of SVP is CVP, where informally speaking, given a vector $v \in V$, it is required to find the vector u in $L(b)$ that is nearest to v. Note that v is not necessarily in $L(b)$. In some cases, there is an additional condition: the distance between v and u should not exceed a given value.

For more information about the lattices used in cryptography, consult [2] and [3].

Example

This section presents the GGH encryption scheme [1] that uses lattices. GGH is an asymmetric encryption scheme; it uses the public key for encryption and the private key for decryption. The algorithms of the cryptosystem are well-known key generation, encryption, and decryption. The following presents them as proposed in [1].

- Key generation: Given a security parameter, generate a basis b in the lattice L defined over an n-dimensional space with good properties (such as containing nearly orthogonal vectors) and a unimodular matrix A. The basis and the matrix compose the private key. The public key is computed as $B = A \cdot b$.

- Encryption: Given the message $m = (m_1, ..., m_n)$ and the error $e = (e_1, ..., e_n)$, the encryption is $c = m \cdot B + e$.

- Decryption: Given the encryption $c = (c_1, ..., c_n)$, the message is computed in two steps.

  1. Compute $c \cdot b^{-1}$. This yields $c \cdot b^{-1} = (m \cdot B + e)b^{-1} = m \cdot A \cdot b \cdot b^{-1} + e \cdot b^{-1} = m \cdot A + e \cdot b^{-1}$.

  2. Remove $e \cdot b^{-1}$ using a technique such as Babai rounding, and compute $m = m \cdot A \cdot A^{-1}$.

Listing 10-1 provides the implementation of the encryption and decryption for GGH using the following values as keys.

$$b = (170019); A = (2335)$$

Listing 10-1. Encryption and Decryption Algorithm of the GGH Cryptosystem

```cpp
#include <iostream>
#include "math.h"

using namespace std;

void encrypt(double message[100], double public_B[100][100], double error_
vals[100], int dimension, double output_encrypted_text[100]);
void decrypt(int dimension, double encrypted_message[100], double private_
basis[100][100], double unimodular_matrix[100][100], double output_
message[100]);
double matrix_determinant(double square_matrix[100][100], int dimension);
void matrix_inverse(double matrix[100][100], int dimension, double output_
inverse[100][100]);
void matrix_multiplication(double matrix1[100][100], double matrix2[100]
[100], double output[100][100], int dimension) ;
void matrix_addition(double matrix1[100][100], double matrix2[100][100],
double output_sum[100][100], int dimension);
void get_cofactor(double matrix[100][100], double aux[100][100], int p,
int q, int n);
void adjoint_matrix(double matrix[100][100], double adjoint[100][100],
int dimension);
```

```
bool inverse_matrix(double matrix[100][100], double inv_matrix[100][100],
int dimension);
void vector_to_matrix(double v[100], int dimension, double output_
matrix[100][100]);
void matrix_to_vector(double matrix[100][100], double output_v[100], int
dimension);
void print_matrix(double matrix[100][100], int n, string message);
void print_vector(double vect[100], int n, string message);
void print_message(string message);

int main()
{
    int message_length = 2;

    double b[100][100] = {{17.0, 0.0}, {0.0, 19.0}}; // the private
    basis -> b
    double b_inverse[100][100];

    inverse_matrix(b, b_inverse, message_length);

    double A[100][100] = {{2.0, 3.0}, {3.0, 5.0}}; // the private
    unimodular matrix -> A
    double A_inverse[100][100];
    inverse_matrix(A, A_inverse, message_length);

    double B[100][100]; // the public key -> B
    matrix_multiplication(A, b, B, message_length);

    // Encryption
    double enc_message[100]; // stores the encryption of the message -> c
    double message[100] = {2, -5}; // the message -> m
    double error_vals[100] = {1, -1}; // the error values -> e

    print_vector(message, message_length, "message");
    encrypt(message, B, error_vals, message_length, enc_message);
    print_vector(enc_message, message_length, "encrypted message");

    // Decryption
    double recovered_message[100];
```

```
        decrypt(message_length, enc_message, b, A, recovered_message);
        print_vector(recovered_message, message_length, "recovered message");
}

// Auxiliary function that prints a matrix on the console
void print_matrix(double matrix[100][100], int n, string message)
{
        cout<<endl<<"***"<<message<<"***"<<endl;

        for(int i = 0; i < n; i++)
        {
            for(int j = 0; j < n; j++ )
                cout<<matrix[i][j]<<"      ";

            cout<<endl;
        }

        cout<<endl;
}

// Auxiliary function that prints a vector on the console
void print_vector(double vect[100], int n, string message)
{
        cout<<endl<<"***"<<message<<"***"<<endl;

        for(int i = 0; i < n; i++)
        {
            cout<<vect[i]<<"      ";
        }

        cout<<endl;
}

// Auxiliary function that prints a string message on the console
void print_message(string message)
{
        cout<<endl<<"***"<<message<<"***"<<endl;
}
```

```
void encrypt(double message[100], double public_B[100][100], double error_
vals[100], int dimension, double output_encrypted_text[100])
{
    // c=m·B+e
    double aux_message[100][100], aux_enc_message[100][100], aux_error_
    vals[100][100];
    vector_to_matrix(message, dimension, aux_message);

    // Compute m·B -> aux_enc_message
    matrix_multiplication(aux_message, public_B, aux_enc_message,
    dimension);
    vector_to_matrix(error_vals, dimension, aux_error_vals);

    // Compute m·B+e -> output_encrypted_text
    matrix_addition(aux_enc_message, aux_error_vals, aux_enc_message,
    dimension);
    matrix_to_vector(aux_enc_message, output_encrypted_text, dimension);
}

void decrypt(int dimension, double encrypted_message[100], double private_
basis[100][100], double unimodular_matrix[100][100], double output_
message[100])
{
    // (1) Compute c * (b^(-1))
    // (2) Remove e * (b^(-1))
    // (3) Compute m * A * (A^(-1))
    double aux_enc_message[100][100], aux_message[100][100];
    double recovered_message[100][100];

    // Compute the inverse of the basis -> b_inverse
    double b_inverse[100][100];
    inverse_matrix(private_basis, b_inverse, dimension);

    // Compute the inverse of the unimodular matrix -> A_inverse
    double A_inverse[100][100];
    inverse_matrix(unimodular_matrix, A_inverse, dimension);
```

```
    // (1) Compute c * (b^(-1)) -> aux_enc_message
    vector_to_matrix(encrypted_message, dimension, aux_enc_message);
    matrix_multiplication(aux_enc_message, b_inverse, aux_message,
    dimension);

    // (2) Remove e * (b^(-1)) from aux_enc_message
    // Basically, the value aux_message[i][j] is rounded to the
    neareast integer
    for (int i=0; i<2; i++)
    {
        for (int j=0; j<2; j++)
            aux_message[i][j] = round(aux_message[i][j]);
    }

    // (3) Compute m * A * (A^(-1))
    matrix_multiplication(aux_message, A_inverse, recovered_message,
    dimension);
    matrix_to_vector(recovered_message, output_message, dimension);
}

// Computes the matrix multiplication between two matrices
void matrix_multiplication(double matrix1[100][100], double matrix2[100]
[100], double output[100][100], int dimension)
{
    for (int i = 0; i < dimension; i++)
    {
        for (int j = 0; j < dimension; j++)
        {
            output[i][j] = 0;
            for (int k = 0; k < dimension; k++)
                output[i][j] += matrix1[i][k] *  matrix2[k][j];
        }
    }
}
```

```
// Computes the matrix sum between two matrices
void matrix_addition(double matrix1[100][100], double matrix2[100][100],
double output_sum[100][100], int dimension)
{
    for(int i = 0; i < dimension; ++i)
        for(int j = 0; j < dimension; ++j)
            output_sum[i][j] = matrix1[i][j] + matrix2[i][j];
}

// Computes the cofactor of the element matrix[p][q]
void get_cofactor(double matrix[100][100], double aux[100][100], int p,
int q, int n)
{
    int i = 0, j = 0;

    for (int row = 0; row < n; row++)
    {
        for (int col = 0; col < n; col++)
        {
            if (row != p && col != q)
            {
                aux[i][j++] = matrix[row][col];

                if (j == n - 1)
                {
                    j = 0;
                    i++;
                }
            }
        }
    }
}

// computes the determinant of a square matrix
double matrix_determinant(double square_matrix[100][100], int dimension)
{
    double matrix_det = 0.0;
    double aux_matrix[100][100];
```

```
  if (dimension == 1)
    return square_matrix[0][0];

  if (dimension == 2)
    return ((square_matrix[0][0] * square_matrix[1][1]) - (square_
    matrix[1][0] * square_matrix[0][1]));
  else
  {
    for (int k = 0; k < dimension; k++) {
        int aux_i = 0;
        for (int i = 1; i < dimension; i++) {
            int aux_j = 0;
            for (int j = 0; j < dimension; j++) {
                if (j == k)
                continue;
                aux_matrix[aux_i][aux_j] = square_matrix[i][j];
                aux_j++;
            }
            aux_i++;
        }
        matrix_det = matrix_det + (pow(-1.0, k) * square_matrix[0][k] *
        matrix_determinant(aux_matrix, dimension - 1));
    }
  }
  return matrix_det;
}

// Computes the adjoint of a matrix
void adjoint_matrix(double matrix[100][100], double adjoint[100][100], int
dimension)
{
    if (dimension == 1)
    {
        adjoint[0][0] = 1;
        return;
    }
```

```
    int sign = 1;
    double aux[100][100];

    for (int i=0; i<dimension; i++)
    {
        for (int j=0; j<dimension; j++)
        {
            get_cofactor(matrix, aux, i, j, dimension);
            sign = ((i + j) % 2 == 0)? 1: -1;
            adjoint[j][i] = (sign)*(matrix_determinant(aux,
            dimension - 1));
        }
    }
}

// Computes the inverse of a matrix
bool inverse_matrix(double matrix[100][100], double inv_matrix[100][100],
int dimension)
{
    double det = matrix_determinant(matrix, dimension);
    if (det == 0)
    {
        return false;
    }

    double adj[100][100];
    adjoint_matrix(matrix, adj, dimension);

    for (int i=0; i<dimension; i++)
        for (int j=0; j<dimension; j++)
        {
            if(adj[i][j] / det == -0)
                adj[i][j] = 0.0;

            inv_matrix[i][j] = adj[i][j] / det;
        }
```

```
    return true;
}

// This function "converts" a vector (seen as a matrix with 1 line and
*dimension* columns) into a matrix
// The obtained matrix has on the first line the elements of the vector
// The remaining lines (*dimension* - 1) contrast 0
// This "conversion" is useful in the operations with matrices (addition,
multiplication)
void vector_to_matrix(double v[100], int dimension, double output_
matrix[100][100])
{
    for(int i = 0; i < dimension; i++)
    {
        output_matrix[0][i] = v[i];
    }

    for(int i = 1; i < dimension; i++)
        for (int j = 0; j < dimension; j++)
        {
            output_matrix[i][j] = 0;
        }
}

// This function "converts" a matrix into a vector
// All lines of the matrix has values of 0, except for the first line
// The first line of the matrix becomes the vector
void matrix_to_vector(double matrix[100][100], double output_v[100], int
dimension)
{
    for(int i = 0; i < dimension; i++)
    {
        output_v[i] = matrix[0][i];
    }
}
```

The result is shown in the Figure 10-2.

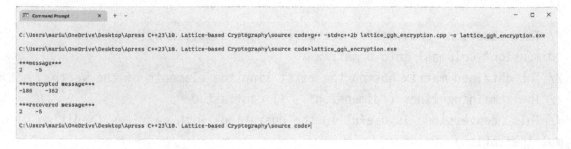

Figure 10-2. *The result of the Listing 10-1*

Conclusion

This chapter discussed lattice-based cryptography and its importance. You learned the following.

- The importance of lattice-based cryptography and its impact on the future of cryptography

- How to encrypt and decrypt using the GGH cryptosystem

- How to implement practical functions and methods related to lattices and matrices

You observed that lattice-based cryptography is a type of cryptography based on mathematical lattices and is considered one of the most robust and secure forms of encryption. It is a versatile and efficient tool, allowing for the implementation of various cryptographic techniques and protocols. Lattice-based cryptography is a particular set of algorithms that use this lattice pattern to create a ciphertext, which is then decrypted with the help of an inverse transformation. This is similar to how a toy wooden puzzle with a grid-like pattern is assembled: if you put the pieces together correctly, you see the original picture. Lattice-based cryptography is used in a wide range of applications, from secure communication in the military to online payments and digital signatures. With its unique properties, lattice-based cryptography has become an indispensable tool in the protection of sensitive data and the fight against cybercrime.

Lattice-based cryptography is a powerful tool for modern cybersecurity that provides a secure and reliable data encryption and authentication method. It is a type of cryptography based on mathematical lattices and is considered one of the most robust and secure forms of encryption. Lattice-based cryptography is a versatile and efficient tool, allowing for the implementation of a variety of cryptographic techniques and protocols. It is used in a wide range of applications, from secure communication in the military to online payments and digital signatures. With its unique properties, lattice-based cryptography has become an indispensable tool in the fight against cybercrime and the protection of sensitive data.

References

[1].   O. Goldreich, S. Goldwasser, and S. Halevi, "Public-key cryptosystems from lattice reduction problems", in Advances in Cryptology—CRYPTO'97: 17th Annual International Cryptology Conference Santa Barbara, California, USA August 17–21, 1997 Proceedings 17, Springer, 1997, pp. 112–131.

[2].   D. Micciancio and O. Regev, "Lattice-based cryptography", Post-quantum cryptography, pp. 147–191, 2009.

[3].   H. Knospe, *A course in cryptography*, vol. 40. American Mathematical Soc., 2019.

CHAPTER 11

Searchable Encryption

A method known as *searchable encryption* enables users to perform keyword searches on encrypted data without affecting the material's security. The fundamental idea is to encrypt the data so that the encryption keys are also stored in a searchable data structure, such as a search tree, so that the user may perform keyword searches without having to decode the entire set of data. This preserves the confidentiality of the data while enabling a secure and effective search of sensitive information. Searchable encryption is a particular case of fully homomorphic encryption which is studied.

Usually, searchable encryption is applied in cloud computing environments; for example, a company needs to store its clients' sensitive data in a cloud environment. For this, the company must keep the data secure, but it also wants to make search queries and retrieve data quickly and easily. Therefore, the company can implement a searchable encryption scheme that encrypts data and allows search queries *over* encrypted data. Authorized staff can then perform keyword searches on the encrypted data without having to decrypt the entire data set using a searchable data structure containing selected keywords. This enables the company to search for and retrieve data quickly and conveniently while protecting the confidentiality and privacy of the client data.

Consider the following example to better understand the searchable encryption method. A set of documents belong to data owner A and are kept on a cloud server. Data user B is permitted to view these documents. User A encrypts the documents before storing them on the server to keep them safe. In this instance, B is only permitted to look through documents (note that they are encrypted) or to read them (note that B can read a document only after it was retrieved from the server and decrypted).

If B wants to obtain documents from the server containing a certain keyword, such as *programming*, then B builds a value called the trapdoor using this search term, and the secret key B possesses then sends the trapdoor value to the server. The search algorithm is specified by the searchable encryption scheme used by the server, and the result is sent to B in an encrypted manner. Then, B can decrypt them only if it has a decryption key.

© Marius Iulian Mihailescu and Stefania Loredana Nita 2023
M. I. Mihailescu and S. L. Nita, *Pro Cryptography and Cryptanalysis with C++23*,
https://doi.org/10.1007/978-1-4842-9450-5_11

Another more applicable scenario is when a company creates software that eventually requires the clients' social security numbers (SSNs). The recommendations and best practices advise encrypting SSNs when dealing with them. This can be difficult because employees utilize SSNs, for instance, when looking for a user account. One solution is to allow staff members to search for a certain SSN using the encrypted SSNs (without decrypting them in any way). This would be achievable if the encryption method were searchable.

It is important to note that searchable encryption has great potential for allowing data users to search across encrypted data for a specific piece of content. In the healthcare industry, where patient medical records can be searched in encrypted form, searchable encryption is an immediate application. Other uses could be found in business, education, or any area where data searching is necessary.

Components

The entities and the algorithms are the components of a searchable encryption scheme. A full overview of these components is provided in this section.

Entities

The customers that use the software solution, the entity that maintains it, the kind of data, the roles supported by the solution, and other factors should be clarified before implementation. The following parties are involved in a system that employs a searchable encryption method.

- **Data owner**. The data owner, considered a reliable party, holds n documents with the identifiers $D = \{D_1, ..., D_n\}$ that are described by keywords (note that these are not metadata). The documents and the keywords are both outsourced. The data owner encrypts the documents using a searchable encryption scheme before outsourcing them to the server (along with the keywords, frequently grouped into an index structure).

- **Data user**. The search procedure may be started by the data user, who is an authorized user of the data. The data user creates a *trapdoor* value used to search through the encrypted data using the query keyword for which the search is done. Additionally, if the data user can access the private key, they can decrypt the documents found during the search process. Recall that a data user could also be the data owner.

- **Server**. Based on the trapdoor value from the data user, the server—regarded as semitrusted or honest-but-curious—stores the encrypted data and runs the search algorithm. It follows instructions for the search algorithms and can examine the provided data, which is why it is called semitrusted or honest-but-curious.

Types

The following cryptographic categories can be used to group searchable encryption schemes: *symmetric searchable encryption* (SSE) schemes and *public key searchable encryption* (PKSE) schemes. For SSE schemes, just one type of key is used for both encryption and decryption of the content. In other specific algorithms, PKSE schemes have two keys: a public key to encrypt the content and a private (or secret) key to decrypt the encrypted content.

The SSE schemes contain the following algorithms [1].

- `KeyGeneration`. The data owner runs this algorithm. A security parameter λ serves as the input, while the secret key SK is the output.

- `BuildIndex`. The data owner runs this algorithm, and its goal is to create an index structure containing the keywords that describe the documents. The server's secret key SK and the collection of documents D are the inputs, and the output is an index structure I. This approach starts with an empty index structure and adds keywords that characterize the current document to the index structure for every document in the set. Note that before being included in the index structure, the keywords are encrypted using the secret key SK in a specified manner that may differ from how the documents are encrypted. A hash table, a tree, or a similar data structure can be used as an index structure.

- **Trapdoor.** The data user runs this algorithm. The desired query keyword kw, for which the search process is activated, and the secret key SK are the inputs for the trapdoor algorithm, and the output is a value T_{kw} called the trapdoor. Note that the trapdoor algorithm encrypts more than just the search term kw. Instead, it manipulates something under control or adds a noise value.

- **Search.** The server handles the search algorithm. The index structure I obtained from the *BuildIndex* algorithm and the trapdoor value T_{kw} from the prior method are the inputs for the search algorithm. The search method should explain how the index structure is searched for the trapdoor value T_{kw} (keep in mind that T_{kw} is not just a plain keyword that has been simply encrypted).

The documents are given to the data user if the search algorithm finds one or more documents that include the search term; otherwise, the server delivers the appropriate message. The encrypting and decrypting algorithms are not listed because the data owner can select between two alternative encryption schemes, one to encrypt the documents and one for the searchable encryption technique. Because the searchable encryption system does not directly include the documents, this situation is feasible. Only the keywords and/or the index structure of encrypted keywords are used by all SSE scheme algorithms.

A little different from the SSE version, the following describes the PEKS scheme algorithms [2].

- **KeyGeneration.** This process, which the data owner also operates, is similar to the KeyGeneration from SSE. The result of key generation is a pair of keys this time, specifically the public and private keys, while the input is once again a security parameter (PK, SK).

- **Encryption.** This algorithm is run by the owner of the data and returns the encrypted value of the keyword KW under SK. Its inputs are a public key (PK) and a keyword (KW).

- **Trapdoor.** The data user executes this algorithm to produce the trapdoor value, similar to the trapdoor algorithm from SSE. The secret key SK and the search query term KW are the inputs and the trapdoor value T_{KW} corresponding to the keyword KW is the output.

- Test. The public key PK, an encrypted value C (representing the encryption of a keyword KW), and the trapdoor value T_{KW} are the inputs for the test procedure, which is run on the server. The test algorithm returns 1 when $KW' = KW$ and 0 when it does not.

The test algorithm does not only perform basic matching, and the trapdoor does not only perform encryption. However, the SSE schemes and PEKS schemes mentioned here are provided in accordance with how they were first used in this subject in the early publications [1] and [2]. Since then, the search process's supported choices and algorithmic changes have been made. Some works permit the use of multiple keywords.

In contrast, others enable fuzzy search based on keywords (which permits minor typos or format inconsistencies) [3], [4], or others enable semantic search (which returns documents that contain keywords from the query keyword's semantic field) [5].

Other efforts concentrate on the documents in that they can be changed directly on the server without being retrieved, decrypted, modified, and then stored again on the server. Other works concentrate on the index structure, which can also be updated immediately on the server [6]. The trapdoor and the search/test algorithm and encryption and decryption are the only algorithms in any searchable encryption system.

Security Characteristics

A *search pattern* and the *access pattern* are two examples of items that need to be secured in a searchable encryption system. The information that may be learned from the fact that two separate search results share the same query keywords is related to the search pattern. The collection of documents that emerged from a trapdoor corresponding to a specific keyword KW is related to the access pattern. Additionally, searchable encryption techniques must adhere to search query security criteria. Reference [7] states that searchable encryption schemes should include the following features: controlled searching (only authorized users may submit search queries), encrypted inquiries (the query search itself should be encrypted before being submitted to the server), encrypted queries (the query search itself should be encrypted before being submitted to the server), and query isolation (the server learns nothing from the queries that it receives).

The index structure should not be vulnerable; therefore, the SSE schemes should provide IND1-CKA and/or IND2-CKA (selected keyword attack for indexes) resistance. In IND1-CKA, all documents used to form the index structure are assigned the same number of keywords; however, in IND2-CKA, the number of keywords used to describe each document is flexible. However, the PEKS scheme should be resistant to the chosen keyword attack (that is, a challenge between an attacker and the structure that manages the PEKS scheme).

The *forward* and *backward privacy* for the dynamic searchable encryption schemes, which permits inserting, updating, or deleting to be applied over the set of documents or the keywords directly on the server, without the need to decrypt it, are security requirements that were recently added. Backward and forward privacies refer to the information found during the insertion, deletion, and updating processes. Forward privacy means that the current updating process is not connected to earlier operations. In contrast, backward privacy refers to the information found when a search is done for a term for which documents have been removed before the present search.

An Example

The example from [18] demonstrates the usage of searchable encryption, a complex encryption method that allows users to perform keyword searches inside encrypted documents. Remember that the participants in the system are the data user, who is authorized to submit search requests on the cloud server. The data owner, who owns a set of documents $S = \{D_1, ..., D_n\}$, who prepares the system by generating the keys, encrypts the documents and the keywords, and stores them on the cloud server, and the cloud server, which stores the documents in an encrypted format and executes the search algorithm.

The work [18] uses elliptic curves (see Chapter 9) in the searchable encryption scheme. Currently, elliptic curves are used in important areas such as blockchain ([14], [15]) and the Internet of Things ([16], [17]).

Figure 11-1 [18] shows an example of a searchable encryption scheme that uses elliptic curve cryptography and is designed for the big data environment (see Chapter 15). In [18], the Elliptic Curve Digital Signature Algorithm (ECDSA) is used to secure the content of the courses available for students on an e-learning platform. The security parameter (λ) for the key generation algorithm of the searchable encryption scheme is the private key from the ECDSA algorithm.

Due to the method's difficulty, attempts have been made, but there is no practical implementation of a searchable encryption system that can be utilized in a real context. However, an example of a demonstration can be found in [19], with the contributor's explicit warning: *This repository provides implementations of SSE as a proof of concept and cannot truly be used for real sensitive applications.* Before implementing a searchable encryption system, the following fundamental principles should be considered.

- The architecture of the software application (server, database, services, etc.)

- The hardware components and how they are managed for the current applications that include security and cryptographic techniques

- The architecture should be designed such that processes within the searchable encryption be represented as independent algorithms such that their deployment is made correctly between the end users and the existing network infrastructure

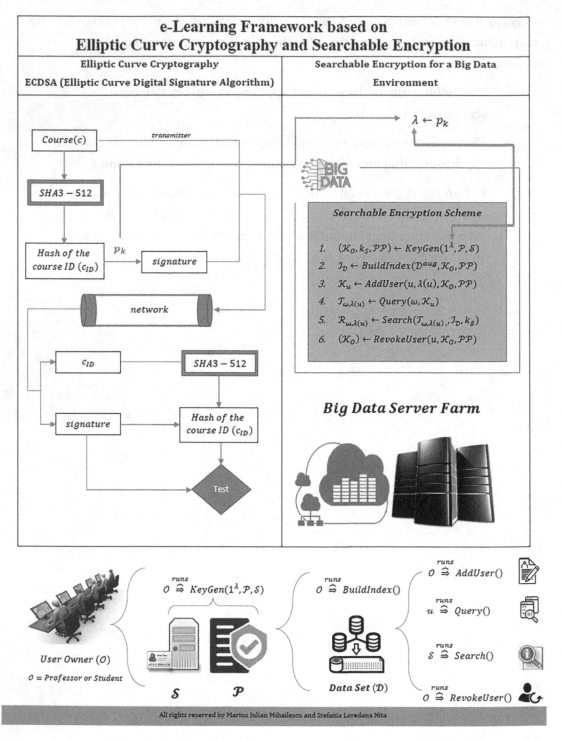

Figure 11-1. *An example of a practical searchable encryption scheme [18]*

Note that the searchable encryption scheme presented in Figure 11-1 is partitioned into more steps. Every step is an algorithm that can be considered a separate instance from the searchable encryption scheme. Furthermore, the instances can be implemented as software modules or services or IoT devices (for example, devices such as Intel NUC PC or a Raspberry PI). The distribution and deployment of the software modules or services among the users can be realized through a distributed network, for example, on a cloud computing network or a regular network for small and medium business architectures.

The algorithms in [18] show the steps in Figure 13-1, which presents a *searchable encryption for a big data environment*. Before implementing the steps, it is necessary to properly understand how the following steps are organized as independent algorithms.

1. $(K_O, K_s, PP) \leftarrow$ ***KeyGeneration***$(1^\lambda, P, S)$. The data owner O runs this probabilistic algorithm for which the input values are the security parameter λ, a policy P. The output is a tuple composed of the owner's secret key K_O, the server key K_s, and the public parameters PP.

2. $I_D \leftarrow$ ***BuildIndex***(D^{aug}, K_O, PP). The data owner O runs this probabilistic algorithm for which the input values are the description of the data set D^{aug} (namely, the keywords that describe each document) and the secret key of the owner (K_O), and the output is an index structure I_D.

3. $K_U \leftarrow (u, \lambda(u), K_O, PP)$. The data owner O runs this probabilistic algorithm to enroll a new user in the e-learning platform system. The input values for the algorithm are the identity of the new user, the level of access of the user (user's role), and the owner's O key. The output is the secret for the new user.

4. ***Trapdoor***$_{(\omega, \lambda(u))} \leftarrow$ ww ***Query***(ω, K_u). The data user that has the proper clearance $\lambda(u)$ for generating a search query runs this probabilistic algorithm. The input values are the keyword $\omega \in \Delta$ (where Δ is a dictionary of keywords) and the user's secret key. The output is the query token (trapdoor value) $Trapdoor_{(\omega, \lambda(u))}$.

5. $R_{(\omega, \lambda(u))} \leftarrow Searching(Trapdoor_{(\omega, \lambda(u))}, I_D, K_s)$. The server (S) runs this probabilistic algorithm that searches the index for the data items that contain the query keyword ω. The input values are the search query and the index, and the output is $R_{(\omega, \lambda(u))}$, which includes a set of identifiers of the data items $d_j \in D_{\omega, \lambda(u)}$ that contains the query keyword ω such that $\lambda(d_j) \leq \lambda(u)$, where $\lambda(u_i)$ is the access level of the user that triggered the search query or a failure symbol φ.

6. $(K_O) \leftarrow RevokeUser(u, K_O, PP)$. The data owner O runs this probabilistic algorithm for revoking a specific user from the system. The input values are the user's ID, the data owner's secret keys, and the server, while the output is new keys for the owner and server.

The searchable encryption scheme designed for this chapter can be correct if for all $k \in \mathbb{N}$, for all K_O, K_S output by $KeyGen(1^\lambda, P)$, for all D^{aug}, for all I_D that is output by $BuildIndex(D^{aug}, K_O)$, for all $\omega \in \Delta$, for all $u \in U$ for all K_u output by $AddUser(K_O, u, \lambda(u), PP)$, $Search(I_D, T_{\omega, \lambda(u)}) = D_{\omega, \lambda(u)}$.

Listing 11-1 presents the pseudocode, which is a sketch for the practical implementation of the searchable encryption scheme proposed in Figure 11-1. Note that the implementation is purely demonstrative, as the implementations (frameworks, libraries, etc.) for searchable encryption do not currently exist.

Listing 11-1. Guideline Implementation of the Searchable Encryption Scheme

```
#include <iostream>
#include <fstream>

class KeyGeneration
{
// Step 1
// The data owner runs the algorithm
// from KeyGeneration step (algorithm)

// global variables
public: string securityParameter;
        string ownerID;
```

```
        string policyContent;
        string serverIdentity;

// the function will return the policy,
// as a content or file
public: string GetPolicy(ifstream& policyContent)
{
string content = "";
if (policyContent.is_open())
{
    while (getline (policyContent, line))
    {
      content += line;
    }
    policyContent.close();
  }

  else policyContent = "Cannot read the policy file";
  return policyContent
}
// getting server identity can be tricky and it has
// different meanings, such as the name of computer,
// IP, active directory reference name etc...
// For the current example, we use the hardware ID
public: string GetServerIdentity()
{
string serverIdentity = "";

// Implementation for obtaining the server identity
// for this method, Windows WMI can be used
// this link provides more details:
// https://docs.microsoft.com/en-us/windows/win32/wmisdk/wmi-start-
page?redirectedfrom=MSDN

return serverIdentity
}
```

```
// class constructor
public: KeyGeneration(){}

// let's generate the secret key, server key
// and public parameters
// "#" represents the separator
public: string ReturnParameters(KeyGeneration kp)
{
string sbParameters = "";
sbParameters += kp.ownerSecretKey + "#" + kp.serverKey + "#" +
kp.publicParameters;
return sbParameters;
}
}

class BuildIndex
{
// Step 2
// the algorithm from BuildIndex step (algorithm)
// are run and invoked by the data owner

// constructor of the class
public: void BuildIndex(){}

// the function centralize the build index parameters
// after their initialization and processing
public: void UseBuildIndexParameters()
{
list<string> descriptionDataSet;
string ownerPrivateKey = "";
string outputIndex = "";
}

//simulation of getting the data set and their
//descriptions
public: list<string> GetDataSet()
{
list<string> ll;
```

```
for(int i = 0; i < dataSet.size(); i++)
{
ll.push_back(description[i]);
}
}

// getting the private of the owner
public: string ownerPrivateKey()
{
string privateKey = "";

// get the private key and work with it arround

return privateKey;
}

// get the index
public: string Index()
{
string index = "";

// implement the query for getting
// or generating the index

return index;
}
}

class AddUser
{
// Step 3
// the algorithm from AddUser step (algorithm)
// are run and invoked by the data owner
// constructor of the class AddUser
public: AddUser() {}

// property for getting the identity of the user
// see below the Class Student
public: string IdentityOfTheUser()
```

```
{
string identity = "";

// implement the way of getting
// the identity of the user

return identity;
}

// property for getting the owners key
public: string OwnerSecretKey()
{
string secretKey = "";

// implement the querying method
// for secret key

return secretKey;
}

public: void AssignSecretKeyToUser()
{
AddUser u = new AddUser();
Student stud = new Student(u. OwnerSecretKey);
}
}

Class query
{
// Step 4
// the algorithm from Query step (algorithm)
// are runned and invoked by the user

// constructor of the class Query
public: Query() {}

// function for getting the keywords
public: string Keyword()
{
string kw = "";
```

```
// query for the keywords;

return kw;
}
// function for getting the secret key of the users
public: string UserSecretKey()
{
string secretKey = "";

// implement the querying method
// for secret key

return secretKey;
}

// the generation of the output as query
// token for the trapdoor
public: string QueryToken()
{
string query_token = "";

// generate and build
// the query token for trapdoor

return query_token
}
}

Class Search
{
// Step 5
// the algorithm from Search step (algorithm)
// are run and invoked by the server

// the constructor of the Search class
public: Search() {}
```

```
public: string SearchQuery()
{
string query = "";

// take the search query

return query;
}

public: string Index()
{
string index = "";

// take the search query

return index;
}

public: string ReturnResult()
{
string result = "";
string setOfIdentifiers = "";

// based on the search query and index,
// get the set identifiers of the data items
setOfIdentifier = "query for identifiers";

// build the result. "#" is the separator for
// illustration purpose only
result = SearchQuery + "#" + Index;

return result;
}
}

class RevokeUser
{
// Step 6
// the algorithm from Search step (algorithm)
// are run and invoked by the data owner
```

```
// constructor of RevokeUser class
public: RevokeUser(){}

// second constructor of the class
// this can be implemented as a
// solution for revoking a user
public: RevokeUser(string userID, string secretKeyDataOwner, string
secretKeyServer)
{
// implement the revoking process

// output the new key for data owner

// output the new key for server
}
}

public class Course
{
// the db_panel represents an instance of the
// file which contains classes for each of tables
// from the database
public: Database db_panel;

// Class Courses it is a generated class and assigned
// to the table Courses from the database
public: Courses c;

// student ID
string demoStudentID = "435663";

// select the course ID based on the student
public: string GetCourse()
{
// select the courses for a
// specific user (student)
Course c = db_panel.GetCourse(student.Id);
```

```
return c;
}
}

Class Student
{
public: string secretKey {get; set;}
public: int StudentId {get; set;}
public: string CourseID {get; set;}
public: string StudentName {get; set;}
public: string StudentIdentity {get; set;}
public: string StudentPersonalCode {get; set;}

public: void Student(string secret_key)
{
      secretKey = secret_key;
}
}

string queryKeywod =
    SecureSearch. GetPrefix("123456789");

string resultStudent = SecureSearch.GetStudent. StartsWith(searchPrefix);
```

Conclusion

This chapter discussed searchable encryption methods and offered recommendations for potential use in practice that may benefit from searchable encryption.

Searchable encryption, which is a type of fully homomorphic encryption, has considerable potential. This chapter described the key elements of searchable encryption schemes. If you are interested in additional theoretical facets of searchable encryption, any of the references provide them with a more in-depth understanding of SE. You can refer to [11] or [12] for some contemporary pseudocode samples and [19] for an SSE implementation demonstration.

References

[1].   Goh, E. J. (2003). Secure indexes. IACR Cryptology ePrint Archive, 2003, 216.

[2].   Boneh, D., Di Crescenzo, G., Ostrovsky, R., and Persiano, G. (2004, May). Public key encryption with keyword search. In International conference on the theory and applications of cryptographic techniques (pp. 506–522). Springer, Berlin, Heidelberg.

[3].   Li, J., Wang, Q., Wang, C., Cao, N., Ren, K., and Lou, W. (2010, March). Fuzzy keyword search over encrypted data in cloud computing. In 2010 Proceedings IEEE INFOCOM (pp. 1–5). IEEE.

[4].   Bringer, J., Chabanne, H., and Kindarji, B. (2009, June). Error-tolerant searchable encryption. In 2009 IEEE International Conference on Communications (pp. 1–6). IEEE.

[5].   Lai, J., Zhou, X., Deng, R. H., Li, Y., and Chen, K. (2013, May). Expressive search on encrypted data. In Proceedings of the 8th ACM SIGSAC symposium on Information, computer and communications security (pp. 243–252).

[6].   Bost, R. (2016, October). $\sum$ οφος: Forward secure searchable encryption. In Proceedings of the 2016 ACM SIGSAC Conference on Computer and Communications Security (pp. 1143–1154).

[7].   Song, D. X., Wagner, D., and Perrig, A. (2000, May). Practical techniques for searches on encrypted data. In Proceeding 2000 IEEE Symposium on Security and Privacy. S&P 2000 (pp. 44–55). IEEE.

[8].   Ghareh Chamani, J., Papadopoulos, D., Papamanthou, C., and Jalili, R. (2018, January). New constructions for forward and backward private symmetric searchable encryption. In Proceedings of the 2018 ACM SIGSAC Conference on Computer and Communications Security (pp. 1038–1055).

[9].   Zuo, C., Sun, S. F., Liu, J. K., Shao, J., and Pieprzyk, J. (2019, September). Dynamic searchable symmetric encryption with forward and stronger backward privacy. In European Symposium on Research in Computer Security (pp. 283–303). Springer, Cham.

[10]. Crypteron Documentation, `https://www.crypteron.com/docs/`

[11]. Ma, C., Gu, Y., and Li, H. Practical Searchable Symmetric Encryption Supporting Conjunctive Queries without Keyword Pair Result Pattern Leakage.

[12]. Fu, S., Zhang, Q., Jia, N., and Xu, M. (2020). A Privacy-preserving Fuzzy Search Scheme Supporting Logic Query over Encrypted Cloud Data. Mobile Networks and Applications, 1–12.

[13].   Boneh, Dan, et al. Public key encryption with keyword search. International
         conference on the theory and applications of cryptographic techniques.
         Springer, Berlin, Heidelberg, 2004.

[14].   Bonnah, Ernest; Shiguang, Ju. Privacy Enhancement Scheme (PES) in a
         Blockchain-Edge Computing Environment (October 2019). IEEE Access 2020.

[15].   Rahman, Mohammad Shahriar, et al. Accountable cross-border data sharing
         using blockchain under relaxed trust assumption. IEEE Transactions on
         Engineering Management, 2020.

[16].   C. Bösch, P. Hartel, W. Jonker, and A. Peter, "A Survey of Provably Secure
         Searchable Encryption," *ACM Computing Surveys*, vol. 47, no. 2, pp. 1–51,
         Aug. 2014.

[17].   Panda, Prabhat Kumar, and Sudipta Chattopadhyay. A secure mutual
         authentication protocol for IoT environment. Journal of Reliable Intelligent
         Environments, 2020, pp. 1–16.

[18].   Mihailescu Marius Iulian, Nita Stefania Loredana, and Pau Valentin Corneliu.
         E-Learning System Framework using Elliptic Curve Cryptography and
         Searchable Encryption. In Proceedings of International Scientific Conference
         for e-Learning and Software for Education, vol. 1, pp. 545–552, 2020.

[19].   OpenSSE/opensse-schemes, Rafael Bost, `https://github.com/OpenSSE/
         opensse-schemes`

CHAPTER 12

Homomorphic Encryption

Homomorphic encryption is a form of encryption that enables computation on encrypted input without first decrypting it. This is significant because it enables calculations that protect the privacy of sensitive data, allowing sensitive data to be handled safely without the danger of exposure. This can be advantageous when privacy is an issue, such as cloud computing and big data analysis.

The most important condition in homomorphic encryption is that the value achieved by decrypting the result obtained by applying the calculations over the encrypted data must be the same as that achieved by applying the same calculations on the plain data. With these properties, homomorphic encryption schemes have great potential because they enable third-party entities to apply functions (therefore algorithms) to encrypted data without needing access to plain data. In this way, the data is protected and secured while being processed.

A real-life example is when you are on vacation in a foreign country, and you want to search on the Internet using your phone for local attractions, such as museums, exhibitions, or art galleries. Even this simple search on the Internet may reveal a lot of information about you: your exact location, your cultural interests, the time of the search query, and so on. If the search engine used a homomorphic approach, nothing would be revealed to anyone, including the search engine itself, because every piece of information and even the search query would be encrypted. Your result would also be encrypted; therefore, only you can decrypt it. Homomorphic encryption has applications in many areas, such as finance/business, healthcare, and any domain that works with sensitive data. Furthermore, some formal aspects of homomorphic encryption are given.

Considering two structures of the same type (groups, rings, or fields) and the corresponding operations $(A, *)$, $(B, \perp)$, the function $g : A \rightarrow B$ is called *homomorphism between A and B* if the following condition is satisfied.

$$g(x_1 * x_2) = g(x_1) \perp g(x_2), \forall x_1, x_2 \in A$$

© Marius Iulian Mihailescu and Stefania Loredana Nita 2023
M. I. Mihailescu and S. L. Nita, *Pro Cryptography and Cryptanalysis with C++23*,
https://doi.org/10.1007/978-1-4842-9450-5_12

Remember that a general encryption system consists of the following algorithms: key generation, encryption, and decryption. In addition to these three algorithms, homomorphic encryption schemes have an additional algorithm called evaluation and are usually denoted with `Eval`, which formally describes the most important rule mentioned. The `Eval` algorithm's input and output are in an encrypted format. In the `Eval` algorithm, the function g is applied over encrypted data c_1 and c_2, without accessing the plain data m_1 and m_2, and has the following property.

$$Dec\left(key_{priv}, Eval_g\left(key_{eval}, c_1, c_2\right)\right) = f\left(m_1, m_2\right)$$

In homomorphic encryption, only two operations must have homomorphic properties: addition and multiplication. This is because an arbitrary function can be represented as a circuit using just gates corresponding to the addition operation (OR gate) and multiplication operation (AND gate). The idea of homomorphic encryption started in the late 1970s; at that time, the concept was called *privacy homomorphism* [1]. Among the first encryption schemes with homomorphic properties is the unpadded RSA algorithm [2], in which the operation with homomorphic properties is multiplication.

$$Encryption\left(m_1\right) \cdot Encryption\left(m_2\right) = m_1^e m_2^e \bmod n$$

$$= \left(m_1 m_2\right)^e \bmod n$$

$$= Encryption\left(m_1 \cdot m_2\right)$$

In this computation, m_1, m_2 are two plain messages, and *Encryption* is the encryption function.

Homomorphic encryption schemes can be categorized into three classes, as follows.

- **Partial homomorphic encryption** (PHE) supports only one operation applied over encrypted data an unlimited number of times. Examples of PHE schemes are RSA [2], Goldwasser-Micali [3], and El-Gamal [4]. Most schemes from this category represent a basis for other homomorphic schemes.

- **Somewhat homomorphic encryption** (SWHE) supports both operations applied to the encrypted data but for a limited number of times. The encryption scheme from [5] is an example of SWHE.

- **Fully homomorphic encryption** (FHE) supports both operations over encrypted data an unlimited number of times. FHE is considered "cryptography's holy grail" or "the Swiss army knife of cryptography" [6] due to its capability to enable any computation over the encrypted data any number of times. In 2009, the first FHE scheme [7] was proposed, and the mathematical object used as the foundation is the ideal lattice. The scheme from [7] is very important in cryptography because it opened the way for the FHE schemes. Even though it is unpractical in the form in which it was proposed due to its complexity and abstraction, it represented a basis for subsequent schemes. In addition, in [7], a general framework for the FHE schemes was proposed.

Homomorphic encryption can be helpful in cloud computing and big data since it enables calculations on encrypted data while maintaining privacy and security. This can be valuable in applications requiring the processing and analysis of sensitive data where the danger of exposure is high.

However, it should be noted that homomorphic encryption is still a very recent and rapidly developing topic and that practical considerations now constrain its usage in large-scale cloud computing and big data contexts. They include high processing costs, poor performance, and restrictions on computations performed on encrypted data.

Full Homomorphic Encryption

This section explains fully homomorphic encryption (FHE) in more detail because it represents an important topic of cryptography that can resolve many security concerns and issues. A particular model of quantum computations, called *boson scattering*, enables quantum homomorphic encryption that provides theoretically limited security. This scheme makes wondering if quantum methods can generate theoretically secure FHE schemes. In [25], the authors prove that quantum techniques do not enable efficient theoretically secure FHE that completely hides the plaintext.

As mentioned in the previous section, the first FHE scheme was proposed by Craig Gentry in 2009, and the mathematical object that represents the foundation is the ideal lattices with the *hardness assumption* (problems regarding a topic that cannot be solved in an efficient time, i.e., in polynomial time), called the *ideal coset problem*. Following Gentry's scheme, many FHE schemes were proposed based on different mathematical techniques. A right-away subsequent work is [8], in which the FHE scheme uses integer arithmetic. However, the noise introduced in the schemes from [7] and [8] grows fast, representing a drawback because it greatly affects the applicability and security; thus, the homomorphic capabilities are restricted. Due to noise growth, decryption cannot be performed after some point.

In the second generation of the FHE schemes that include works such as [9] and [10], the noise is handled more efficiently, improving performance and powerful security under various hardness assumptions. The *leveled encryption schemes* and *bootstrappable encryption schemes* are the results of this generation. The first ones evaluate the circuits with a given polynomial depth, while the second ones can be modified to become FHE schemes. If an encryption scheme can evaluate its decryption circuit and one NAND gate, then it is a bootstrappable encryption scheme.

The third generation of FHE schemes is opened by the work [11], which uses a new technique to handle noise. The schemes of the third generation are less performant than those from the second generation, but their hardness assumptions can be weaker. The basis for many schemes in this generation is asymmetric multiplication. That is, considering two encrypted texts c_1, c_2, the product $c_1 \cdot c_2$ is different from the product $c_2 \cdot c_1$, although both products encrypt the same product $b_1 \cdot b_2$ of the plain texts b_1 and b_2.

FHE can be used in many areas of cryptography, including the following.

- **Outsourcing**. Private data can be kept safe if stored in third-party storage or analyzed by third-party entities. A classic example of this area is that of a company that stores its data on cloud storage. Before uploading the data to the cloud, the owner must encrypt it. FHE would be useful in such scenarios because the cloud provider can analyze the data from the company in an encrypted format without accessing the plain data. Moreover, the result of the computations is sent by the cloud provider in the encrypted format to the data owner, which is decrypted only by the decryption key's owner.

- **Private information retrieval (PIR) or private queries**. PIR and private queries are useful when a database is queried or an application uses a search engine. Another scenario is when a client wants to send a query to a database server, but the client wants the server to learn nothing about its query. The solution is as follows: the client encrypts the query and sends it to the server; then, the server applies the encrypted query over encrypted data and responds with the encrypted result.

- **General computations between two entities** (two-party
  computations). Consider two parties A and B, each of whom owns a
  secret input x and y, respectively, and a common function F known by
  both. To apply the function F over its private input x, party A computes
  $r = F(x, y)$. From here, A learns only the value of r and nothing about
  y. On the other hand, B learn nothing about x or r. This is the same
  as B computing $Fy(x)$ in the semihonest model, where A encrypts x
  and sends it to B because semantic security assures B learns nothing
  about the plain value corresponding to x. In such situations, using FHE
  would simplify the things because A would just apply F as $F(x,y)$ and
  achieve the result in an encrypted format. But it would need and learn
  nothing else because everything is encrypted, including F.

A Practical Example of Using FHE

The following are other well-known C++ libraries that implement FHE.

- HElib [12], developed at IBM, implements the schemes BFV
  (Brakerski/Fan-Vercauteren) [17] and CKKS (Cheon-Kim-Kim-Song)
  [18], and it can be used in Linux and MacOS distributions.

- TFHE [13] implements the scheme proposed in [15] and can be used
  with Linux distributions. In the same paper, the library is described.

- PALISADE [14] implements the BGV (Brakerski-Gentry-
  Vaikuntanathan) [16], BFV [17], CKKS [18], and FHEW schemes
  [19] and a more secure version of the TFHE scheme [13], including
  bootstrapping. It is supported on Linux, Windows, and macOS
  distributions.

- SEAL [20]–[23] implements the BFV [17] and CKKS [18] schemes and
  can be used with .NET or C++. In addition, the SEAL library can be
  used in Windows, Linux, or macOS environments.

These libraries provide robust tools for creating FHE in C++ programs. It should be
noted, however, that FHE is a computationally costly and complex procedure that may
not be ideal for many applications.

This section uses the SEAL library to demonstrate an FHE example. The SEAL library
implements BFV [12] and CKKS [13] encryption schemes.

In [12], the set of the polynomials with a maximum degree n and the coefficients computed modulo t is used in the definition of the encryption function. The formal representation of this set is $R_t = Z_t[x]/(x^n + 1)$. The encrypted text is from the R_q set, where the polynomials have coefficients modulo q. The addition and the multiplication are the homomorphic operations in this encryption scheme, preserving the ring structure of R_t. The value that needs to be encrypted using BFV schemes first needs to be brought to a polynomial form accepted by the structure R_t. In [12], the encryption scheme includes the following algorithms: SecretKeyGen (the security parameter is used to generate the secret key), PublicKeyGen (the secret key is used to generate the public key), EvaluationKeyGen (the secret key is used to generate the evaluation key), Encrypt (the plain value is encrypted using the public key), Decrypt (the encrypted value is decrypted using the secret key), Add (performs the addition between two encrypted values), and Multiply (performs the multiplication between two encrypted values). Keep in mind that the result of both operations, namely, addition and multiplication, have a form that is compatible with the structure R_q. For more information and a formal description of this encryption scheme, you can consult [12].

While [12] provides a way to apply modular arithmetic over integers, in [13], the authors provide ways to apply it over real numbers and complex numbers. In [13], the results are approximate, but the techniques are among the best for summing up real numbers in an encrypted format, applying machine learning algorithms on encrypted data, or computing the distance between encrypted locations.

Before using the SEAL library, some preparation steps are needed, which are described next.

First, install a version of Visual Studio 2022. The free community version can be found at https://visualstudio.microsoft.com/vs/community. Make sure that the C++ components (under *desktop development with C++*) are checked to be installed.

Then, download Git from https://git-scm.com/download/win and install it following the installation steps with the default values (needed to build and install the SEAL library). You also need to download and install CMake from https://cmake.org/download/. After everything is set, the SEAL library can be downloaded from the GitHub repository: https://github.com/microsoft/SEAL (when writing this book, the latest version of SEAL is 4.1.1).

After downloading the source code, extract the zip file. Use the default Seal-master and extract it at a desired path (in our example, E:\examples\seal). Make sure you have the following files in the folder, as shown in Figure 12-1. Pay attention to the entire path because it is important for building, installing, and using the library.

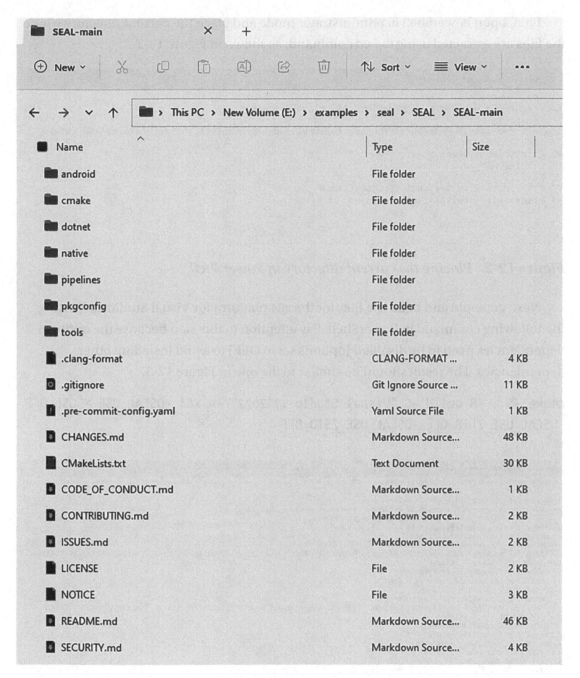

Figure 12-1. *Structure of the extracted files of the SEAL library*

The folder used for C++ development is the native folder from the solution. To use the SEAL library in your own C++ application, you first need to generate the seal.lib library. To do this requires several steps.

First, open PowerShell in administrator mode and place the current directory where the files are extracted using the cd command, as shown in Figure 12-2.

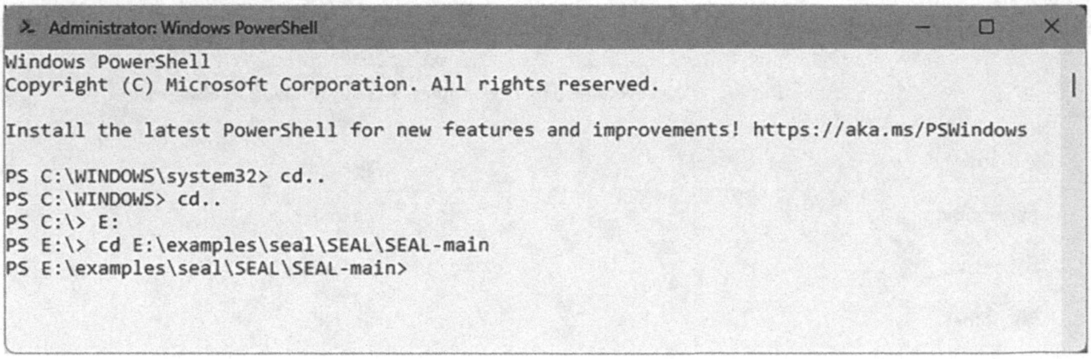

Figure 12-2. *Placing the current directory in PowerShell*

Next, generate and build the files for the x64 platform for Visual Studio 2022 using the following command in PowerShell. Pay attention to this step because the optional dependencies need to be disabled (options set to OFF) to avoid installing other dependencies. The result should be similar to the one in Figure 12-3.

```
cmake -S . -B build -G "Visual Studio 17 2022" -A x64 -DSEAL_USE_MSGSL=OFF
-DSEAL_USE_ZLIB=OFF -DSEAL_USE_ZSTD=OFF
```

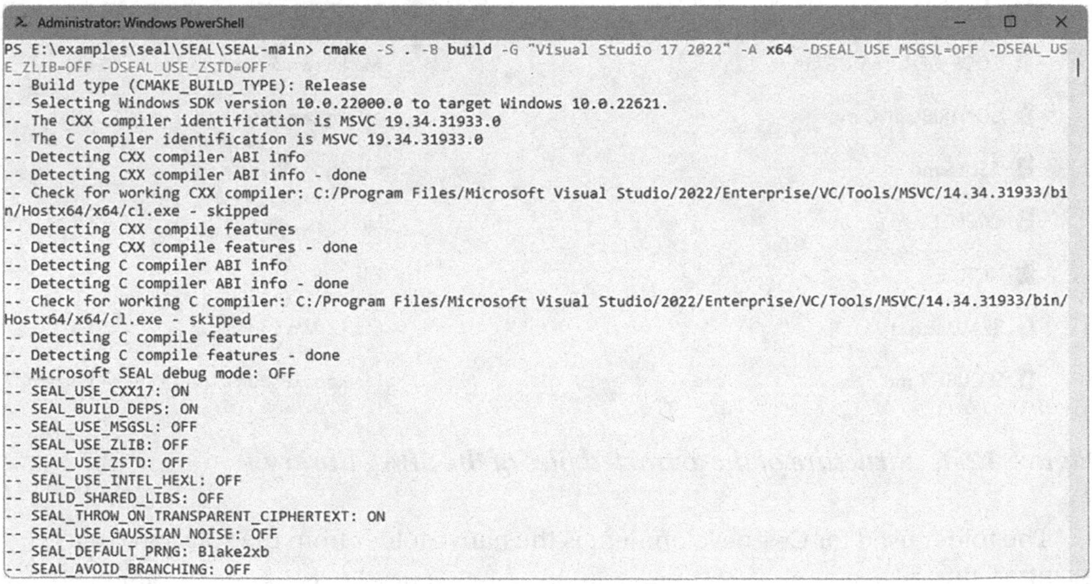

Figure 12-3. *Generate and build the files for the x64 platform*

If the desired platform is x86, then the following command should run.

```
cmake -S . -B build -G "Visual Studio 17 2022" -A Win32 -DSEAL_USE_
MSGSL=OFF -DSEAL_USE_ZLIB=OFF -DSEAL_USE_ZSTD=OFF
```

Next, generate and build the files for the Release configuration using the following command and as shown in Figure 12-4.

```
cmake --build build --config Release
```

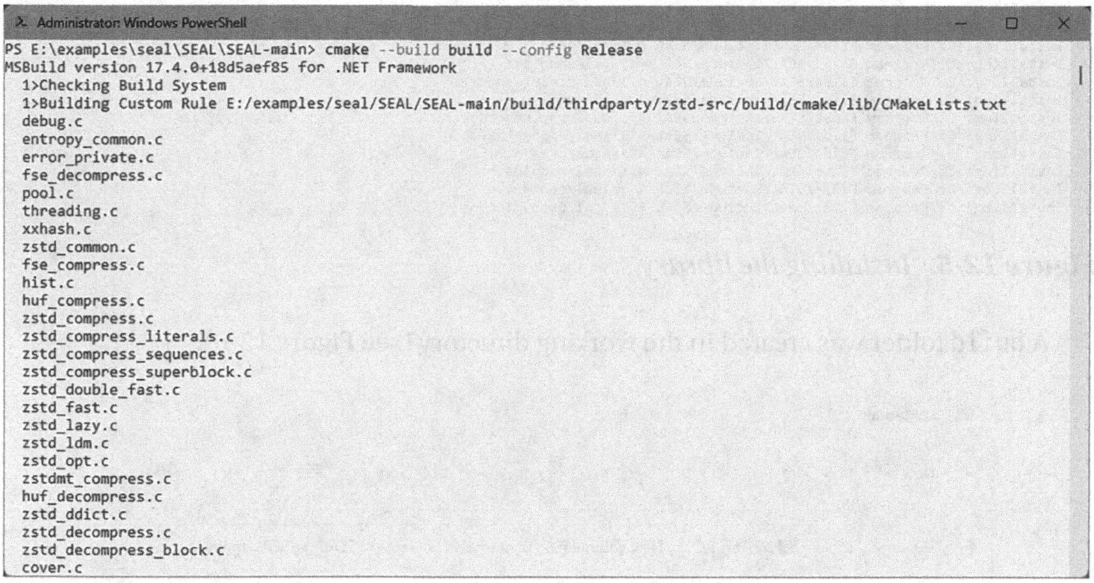
Administrator: Windows PowerShell
PS E:\examples\seal\SEAL\SEAL-main> cmake --build build --config Release
MSBuild version 17.4.0+18d5aef85 for .NET Framework
1>Checking Build System
1>Building Custom Rule E:/examples/seal/SEAL/SEAL-main/build/thirdparty/zstd-src/build/cmake/lib/CMakeLists.txt
debug.c
entropy_common.c
error_private.c
fse_decompress.c
pool.c
threading.c
xxhash.c
zstd_common.c
fse_compress.c
hist.c
huf_compress.c
zstd_compress.c
zstd_compress_literals.c
zstd_compress_sequences.c
zstd_compress_superblock.c
zstd_double_fast.c
zstd_fast.c
zstd_lazy.c
zstd_ldm.c
zstd_opt.c
zstdmt_compress.c
huf_decompress.c
zstd_ddict.c
zstd_decompress.c
zstd_decompress_block.c
cover.c

Figure 12-4. *Generate and build the files for the Release configuration*

Finally, an optional step is to install the library using the following command. The library is installed at path C:\Program Files (x86)\SEAL\ by default. The result should be similar to the one presented in Figure 12-5.

```
cmake --install build
```

```
>_  Administrator: Windows PowerShell                                              —    □    ×
PS E:\examples\seal\SEAL\SEAL-main> cmake --install build
-- Install configuration: "Release"
-- Installing: C:/Program Files/SEAL/include/SEAL-4.1/seal/util/config.h
-- Installing: C:/Program Files/SEAL/lib/seal-4.1.lib
-- Installing: C:/Program Files/SEAL/lib/cmake/SEAL-4.1/SEALTargets.cmake
-- Installing: C:/Program Files/SEAL/lib/cmake/SEAL-4.1/SEALTargets-release.cmake
-- Installing: C:/Program Files/SEAL/lib/cmake/SEAL-4.1/SEALConfig.cmake
-- Installing: C:/Program Files/SEAL/lib/cmake/SEAL-4.1/SEALConfigVersion.cmake
-- Installing: C:/Program Files/SEAL/include/SEAL-4.1/gsl
-- Installing: C:/Program Files/SEAL/include/SEAL-4.1/gsl/algorithm
-- Installing: C:/Program Files/SEAL/include/SEAL-4.1/gsl/assert
-- Installing: C:/Program Files/SEAL/include/SEAL-4.1/gsl/byte
-- Installing: C:/Program Files/SEAL/include/SEAL-4.1/gsl/gsl
-- Installing: C:/Program Files/SEAL/include/SEAL-4.1/gsl/gsl_algorithm
-- Installing: C:/Program Files/SEAL/include/SEAL-4.1/gsl/gsl_assert
-- Installing: C:/Program Files/SEAL/include/SEAL-4.1/gsl/gsl_byte
-- Installing: C:/Program Files/SEAL/include/SEAL-4.1/gsl/gsl_narrow
-- Installing: C:/Program Files/SEAL/include/SEAL-4.1/gsl/gsl_util
-- Installing: C:/Program Files/SEAL/include/SEAL-4.1/gsl/narrow
-- Installing: C:/Program Files/SEAL/include/SEAL-4.1/gsl/pointers
-- Installing: C:/Program Files/SEAL/include/SEAL-4.1/gsl/span
-- Installing: C:/Program Files/SEAL/include/SEAL-4.1/gsl/span_ext
-- Installing: C:/Program Files/SEAL/include/SEAL-4.1/gsl/string_span
-- Installing: C:/Program Files/SEAL/include/SEAL-4.1/gsl/util
-- Installing: C:/Program Files/SEAL/include/SEAL-4.1/seal/batchencoder.h
-- Installing: C:/Program Files/SEAL/include/SEAL-4.1/seal/ciphertext.h
-- Installing: C:/Program Files/SEAL/include/SEAL-4.1/seal/ckks.h
-- Installing: C:/Program Files/SEAL/include/SEAL-4.1/seal/modulus.h
-- Installing: C:/Program Files/SEAL/include/SEAL-4.1/seal/context.h
-- Installing: C:/Program Files/SEAL/include/SEAL-4.1/seal/decryptor.h
```

Figure 12-5. *Installing the library*

A build folder was created in the working directory (see Figure 12-6).

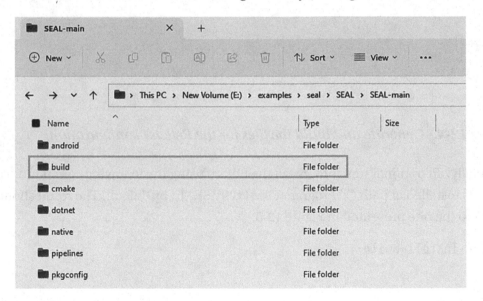

Figure 12-6. *The build folder*

With all these settings, the SEAL library, called seal-4.1.lib, is found under build\
lib\Release. You can proceed to create your own C++ application that uses SEAL.

Now let's create an application that uses FHE. Create in Visual Studio a new project of type **Console App** with C++ called `Seal-example`. Under the Source Files folder within the solution, a `cpp` file called `Seal-example.cpp` should exist, such as the code in Listing 12-1 and some default comments. The following examples follow the guidelines from [23].

Listing 12-1. The Initial Main Function

```cpp
#include <iostream>

int main()
{
    std::cout << "Hello World!\n";
}
```

Furthermore, the application needs to be prepared using the SEAL library as described next. First, right-click the SEAL-example solution and go to **Properties**. Here, make sure **All Configurations** and **All Platforms** are selected (see Figure 12-7).

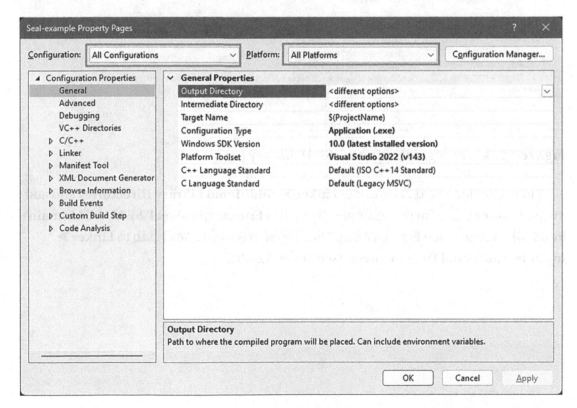

Figure 12-7. *Settings for using the SEAL library (1)*

Then, under **C/C++ ➤ General ➤ Additional Include Directories,** add the path where sources were generated (in our example, the path is **E:\examples\seal\SEAL\SEAL-main\native\src**, see Figure 12-8).

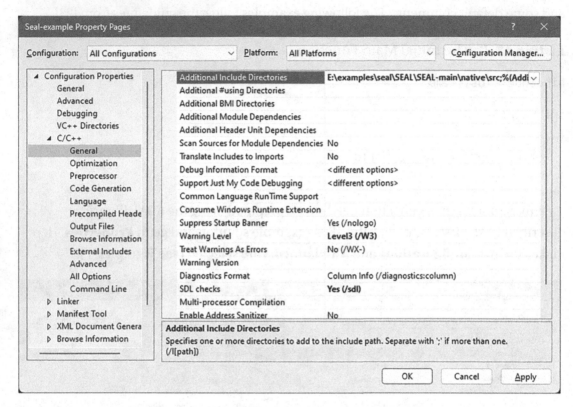

Figure 12-8. *Settings for using the SEAL library (2)*

Finally, include seal.lib: under **Linker ➤ Additional Library Directories** and add the path to seal.lib (in our example, the path is **E:\examples\seal\SEAL\SEAL-main\build\lib\Release**, see Figure 12-9a). The final step is to add seal.lib to **Linker ➤ Input ➤ Additional Dependencies** (see Figure 12-9b).

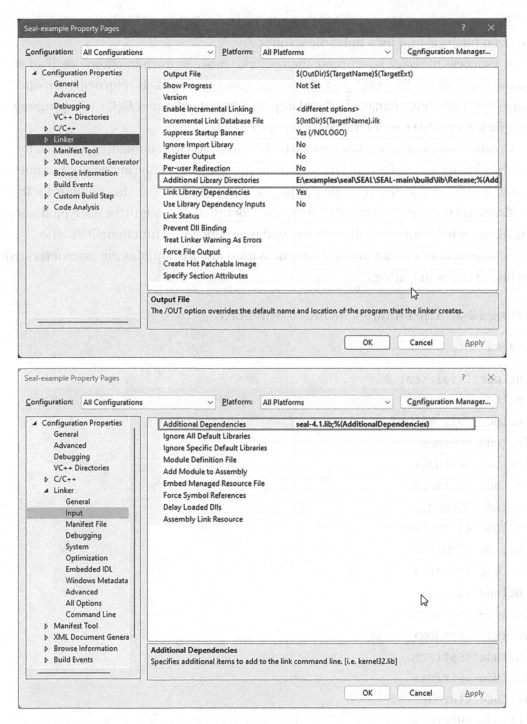

Figure 12-9. *(a) Settings for using the SEAL library for the main Linker options (b) Settings for using the SEAL library for Linker* ➤ *Input options*

To ensure that SEAL was added properly, just add the line in Listings 12-2 and 12-3 in the main function and then build the solution.

If a success message is returned, then you can proceed further; otherwise, if an error message similar to `'for_each_n': is not a member of'std'` is returned, then one more step is needed: change the **C++ Language Standard** under **C/C++ ➤ Language** from **Default** to **ISO C++17 Standard (/std:c++17)**.

Create a function called `seal_example_bfv`, in which functionalities provided by the SEAL library for the BFV encryption scheme are added. First, the encryption parameters should be added: the degree of the polynomials from the ring (n), the modulus for the coefficients of the plaintext (t), and the modulus for the coefficients of the encrypted text (q). The libraries in Listing 12-2 should be added to use the SEAL functionalities. The application is notified that the BFV scheme is used and instantiates the parameters using the line of codes in Listing 12-3.

Listing 12-2. The Libraries Included with SEAL

```
#pragma once

#include "seal/seal.h"
#include <iostream>
#include <algorithm>
#include <chrono>
#include <cstddef>
#include <fstream>
#include <iomanip>
#include <iostream>
#include <limits>
#include <memory>
#include <mutex>
#include <numeric>
#include <random>
#include <sstream>
#include <string>
#include <thread>
#include <vector>

using namespace std;
using namespace seal;
```

Listing 12-3. Instantiating the BFV Parameters

```
void seal_example_bfv()
{
    EncryptionParameters BFV_parameters(scheme_type:: bfv);}
```

After instantiating the BFV parameters, they should receive each value. *The degree of the polynomial modulus* is a power of 2 and represents the degree of a cyclotomic polynomial[1].

The recommended values are {1024, 2048, 4096, 8192, 16384, 32768}. With a higher value for the polynomial degree, more complex computations on the encrypted data can be made, but the drawback is that the performance decreases. A fair value is 4096, which allows an acceptable number of computations with good performance; therefore, this value is chosen for our application. The modulus for the coefficients of the plaintext is generally a positive integer. The value for this parameter is a power of two in our example.

Depending on the purpose of the application, the modulus can be a prime number. The modulus for the coefficient of the plaintext is used to provide the size in bits for the plain data and to establish limits for consumption in the multiplication operation. The last parameter is *the modulus for the coefficients of the encrypted text*, which represents a large integer value. The value for this modulus should be represented as a product of prime numbers. When a larger value is chosen, more computations over the encrypted data can be made. However, there is a relation between the degree of the polynomial modulus and the size in bits of the modulus for the coefficients of the encrypted text; therefore, a 4096 value corresponds to 109. Comprehensive explanations for the scheme's parameters can be found in [20] and [21].

Another functionality that needs a few words is *the noise budget*, representing the number of bits. In short, the initial noise budget is set depending on the encryption parameters and the rate with which the homomorphic operations (addition and multiplication) consume it. The parameter with the greatest influence in setting the noise budget is the coefficient modulus—when a higher value is picked. The budget is higher. When the noise budget for an encrypted text becomes 0, the decryption of the encrypted text cannot be performed because the noise it contains has a value that is too large.

---

[1] https://en.wikipedia.org/wiki/Cyclotomic_polynomial

With these brief descriptions, the parameters can be initialized using the lines of code in Listing 12-4, added in the function seal_example_bfv (keep the declaration in Listing 12-3).

Listing 12-4. Initialization of the BFV Parameters

```
size_t polynomial_degree = 4096;
BFV_parameters.set_poly_modulus_degree(polynomial_degree);
    BFV_parameters.set_coeff_modulus(CoeffModulus::BFVDefault(
    polynomial_degree));
BFV_parameters.set_plain_modulus(1024);
```

The SEAL context checks the correctness of the parameters (code added in function seal_example_bfv).

```
SEALContext seal_context(BFV_parameters);
```

Furthermore, the BFV encryption scheme classes need to be instantiated, as in Listing 12-5 (code added in function seal_example_bfv).

Listing 12-5. Instantiating the Classes for the BFV Encryption Scheme

```
KeyGenerator keygen(seal_context);
PublicKey encryption_key;
keygen.create_public_key(encryption_key);
SecretKey decryption_key = keygen.secret_key();
Encryptor bfv_encrypt(seal_context, encryption_key);
Evaluator bfv_evaluate(seal_context);
Decryptor bfv_decrypt(seal_context, decryption_key);
```

In the following, for our example, the polynomial $p(x) = 3x^4 + 6x^3 + 9x^2 + 12x + 6$ is evaluated for $x = 3$. For a quick check, use the value $x = 3$ to encrypt and then decrypt it. Listing 12-6 shows this process and some metrics (code added in seal_example_bfv function).

Listing 12-6. Encrypting and Decrypting x=3

```
int value_x = 3;
Plaintext x_plaintext(to_string(value_x));
cout << "The value x = " + to_string(value_x)
```

```
            + " is expressed as a plaintext polynomial 0x"
            + x_plaintext.to_string() + "." << endl;

Ciphertext x_ciphertext;
cout << "Encrypting x_plaintext to x_ciphertext..." << endl;
bfv_encrypt.encrypt(x_plaintext, x_ciphertext);

cout << "    - the size of the x_ciphertext (freshly
        encrypted) is : "
      << x_ciphertext.size() << endl;
cout << "    - the noise budget for x_ciphertext is : "
      << bfv_decrypt.invariant_noise_budget(x_ciphertext)
      << " bits" << endl;
Plaintext value_x_decrypted;
cout << "    - decryption of x_encrypted: ";
bfv_decrypt.decrypt(x_ciphertext, value_x_decrypted);
cout << "0x" << value_x_decrypted.to_string() << endl;
```

Next, call seal_example_bfv in the main function as follows.

```
int main()
{
    seal_example_bfv();
    return 0;
}
```

To run the application, do not forget to choose Release configuration and x64 platform, then press Ctrl+F5. The result should be similar to that in Listing 12-7 and Figure 12-10.

Listing 12-7. The Output for the Encryption, Decryption, and Metrics

```
The value x = 3 is expressed as a plaintext polynomial 0x3.
Encrypting x_plaintext to x_ciphertext...
    - the size of the x_ciphertext (freshly encrypted) is : 2
    - the noise budget for x_ciphertext is : 55 bits
    - decryption of x_encrypted: 0x3
```

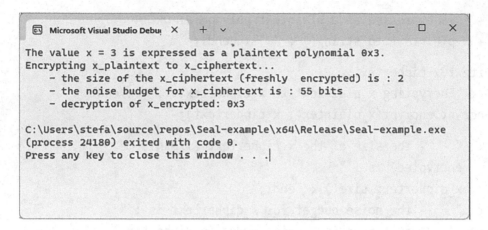

Figure 12-10. *The output for the encryption, decryption, and metrics*

The `plaintext` constructor converts the plain values to polynomials that have a degree lower than the modulus polynomial, for which the coefficients are represented as hexadecimal values. In SEAL, the encrypted text is represented as two or more polynomials with coefficients in the form of inter-values modulo the result of multiplying the prime numbers from `CoeffModulus` representation.

The object `x_ciphertext` instantiates the `Ciphertext` class and receives the value of the encryption of `x_plaintext` by calling the `encryption` method of the object `bfv_encrypt`. This method takes two parameters: the object that needs to be encrypted (`x_plaintext`) and the object in which the encryption of the first parameter should be put (`x_ciphertext`). The number of polynomials gives the size of the encrypted text; a fresh encrypted text has a size of 2, which is returned by the `size()` method of the object `x_ciphertext`.

The noise budget is computed by the `invariant_noise_budget()` method of the `bfv_encrypt` object, which takes the object `x_ciphertext as the parameter`. The `invariant_noise_budget()` is implemented in the `decryptor` class because it shows if the decryption works at some point in our computations. To decrypt the encrypted value obtained, use the `decrypt` method called the `bfv_decrypt` object. The decryption works because the value `0x3` in hexadecimal representation means 3.

For optimizations, the recommendation is that the polynomials be brought to a form that includes as few multiplication operations as possible because this is a costly operation that decreases the noise budget quickly. Therefore, $p(x)$ may be factorized as $p(x) = 3(x^2 + 2)(x + 1)^2$, which means first evaluate $(x^2 + 2)$, then $(x + 1)^2$ and then multiply the result between them by 3. To compute $(x^2 + 2)$, proceed as presented in Listing 12-8 (code added in `seal_example_bfv` function).

Listing 12-8. Computing $(x^2 + 2)$

```
cout << "Computing (x^2+2)..." << endl;
Ciphertext square_x_plus_two;
bfv_evaluate.square(x_ciphertext, square_x_plus_two);
Plaintext plain_value_two("2");
bfv_evaluate.add_plain_inplace(square_x_plus_two,
            plain_value_two);

cout << "    - the size of the square_x_plus_two is: "
    << square_x_plus_two.size() << endl;
cout << "    - the noise budget for square_x_plus_two is: "
    << bfv_decrypt.invariant_noise_budget(square_x_plus_two)
    << " bits" << endl;

Plaintext decrypted_result;
cout << "    - decryption of square_x_plus_two: ";
bfv_decrypt.decrypt(square_x_plus_two, decrypted_result);
cout << "0x" << decrypted_result.to_string() << endl;
```

After running the application, you get the result in Listing 12-9 and Figure 12-11.

Listing 12-9. The Result of Computing $(x^2 + 2)$

```
The value x = 3 is expressed as a plaintext polynomial 0x3.
Encrypting x_plaintext to x_ciphertext...
    - the size of the x_ciphertext (freshly encrypted) is : 2
    - the noise budget for x_ciphertext is : 55 bits
    - decryption of x_encrypted: 0x3
Computing (x^2+2)...
    - the size of the square_x_plus_two is: 3
    - the noise budget for square_x_plus_two is: 33 bits
    - decryption of square_x_plus_two: 0xB
```

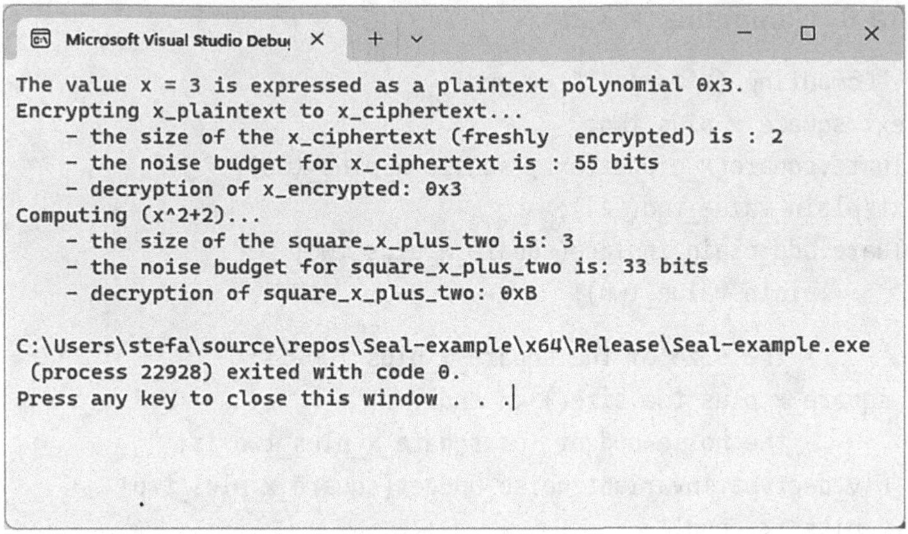

```
The value x = 3 is expressed as a plaintext polynomial 0x3.
Encrypting x_plaintext to x_ciphertext...
      - the size of the x_ciphertext (freshly  encrypted) is : 2
      - the noise budget for x_ciphertext is : 55 bits
      - decryption of x_encrypted: 0x3
Computing (x^2+2)...
      - the size of the square_x_plus_two is: 3
      - the noise budget for square_x_plus_two is: 33 bits
      - decryption of square_x_plus_two: 0xB

C:\Users\stefa\source\repos\Seal-example\x64\Release\Seal-example.exe
 (process 22928) exited with code 0.
Press any key to close this window . . .|
```

Figure 12-11. *The result of computing ($x^2 + 2$)*

Let's check. If you calculate $3^2 + 2$, you get 11, whose hexadecimal representation is 0xB; the noise budget is greater than 0, which means the decryption can be made. Observe that the bfv_evaluate object allows applying operations directly over the encrypted data. The collector variable for this example is square_x_plus_two. First, this variable keeps the encrypted value raised at power 2, i.e., x^2, using the method square(). Furthermore, add plain value 2 through the method add_plain_inplace(), which gives $x^2 + 1$. Remember that in our example, $x = 3$. The square() and add_plain_inplace() methods have two parameters: a source and a destination.

Similarly, compute $(x + 1)^2$, using x_plus_one_square as the collector variable (see Listing 12-10).

Listing 12-10. Computing $(x + 1)^2$

```
cout << "Computing (x+1)^2..." << endl;
Ciphertext x_plus_one_square;
Plaintext plain_value_one("1");
bfv_evaluate.add_plain(x_ciphertext, plain_value_one,
           x_plus_one_square);
bfv_evaluate.square_inplace(x_plus_one_square);
cout << "    - the size of x_plus_one_square is: "
     << x_plus_one_square.size() << endl;
```

```
cout << "    - the noise budget in x_plus_one_square is: "
    << bfv_decrypt.invariant_noise_budget(x_plus_one_square)
    << " bits" << endl;
cout << "    - decryption of x_plus_one_square: ";
bfv_decrypt.decrypt(x_plus_one_square, decrypted_result);
cout << "0x" << decrypted_result.to_string() << endl;
```

After running the application, you get Listing 12-11 and Figure 12-12.

Listing 12-11. The Result of Computing $(x + 1)^2$

```
The value x = 3 is expressed as a plaintext polynomial 0x3.
Encrypting x_plaintext to x_ciphertext...
    - the size of the x_ciphertext (freshly encrypted) is : 2
    - the noise budget for x_ciphertext is : 55 bits
    - decryption of x_encrypted: 0x3
Computing (x^2+2)...
    - the size of the square_x_plus_two is: 3
    - the noise budget for square_x_plus_two is: 33 bits
    - decryption of square_x_plus_two: 0xB
Computing (x+1)^2...
    - the size of x_plus_one_square is: 3
    - the noise budget in x_plus_one_square is: 33 bits
    - decryption of x_plus_one_square: 0x10
```

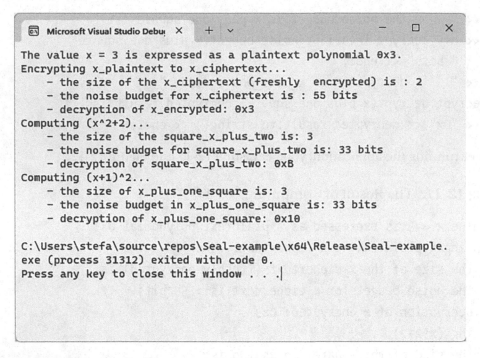

Figure 12-12. *The result of computing* $(x + 1)^2$

Indeed, if you compute $(3 + 1)^2$, you get 10, whose hexadecimal representation is 0×10; the noise budget is greater than 0, so the decryption still works.

The result of $3(x^2 + 2)(x + 1)^2$ is collected in the encryptedOutcome variable (see Listing 12-12).

Listing 12-12. *Computing* $3(x^2 + 2)(x + 1)^2$

```
cout << "Compute [3(x^2+2)(x+1)^2]." << endl;
Ciphertext enc_result;
Plaintext plain_value_three("3");
    bfv_evaluate.multiply_plain_inplace(square_x_plus_two,
        plain_value_three);
bfv_evaluate.multiply(square_x_plus_two, x_plus_one_square,
        enc_result);
cout << "    - the size of encrypted_result: "
    << enc_result.size() << endl;
```

```
cout << "    - the noise budget for encrypted_result: "
    << bfv_decrypt.invariant_noise_budget(enc_result)
    << " bits" << endl;
cout << "NOTE: If the noise budget is zero, the decryption can be
incorrect." << endl;
cout << "    - decryption of enc_result: ";
bfv_decrypt.decrypt(enc_result, decrypted_result);
    cout << "0x" << decrypted_result.to_string() << endl;
```

After running the application, you get what's shown in Listing 12-13 and Figure 12-13.

Listing 12-13. The Output of Computing $3(x^2 + 2)(x + 1)^2$

```
The value x = 3 is expressed as a plaintext polynomial 0x3.
Encrypting x_plaintext to x_ciphertext...
    - the size of the x_ciphertext (freshly encrypted) is : 2
    - the noise budget for x_ciphertext is : 55 bits
    - decryption of x_encrypted: 0x3
Computing (x^2+2)...
    - the size of the square_x_plus_two is: 3
    - the noise budget for square_x_plus_two is: 33 bits
    - decryption of square_x_plus_two: 0xB
Computing (x+1)^2...
    - the size of x_plus_one_square is: 3
    - the noise budget in x_plus_one_square is: 33 bits
    - decryption of x_plus_one_square: 0x10
Compute [3(x^2+2)(x+1)^2].
    - the size of encrypted_result: 5
    - the noise budget for encrypted_result: 4 bits
NOTE: If the noise budget is zero, the decryption can be incorrect.
    - decryption of enc_result: 0x210
```

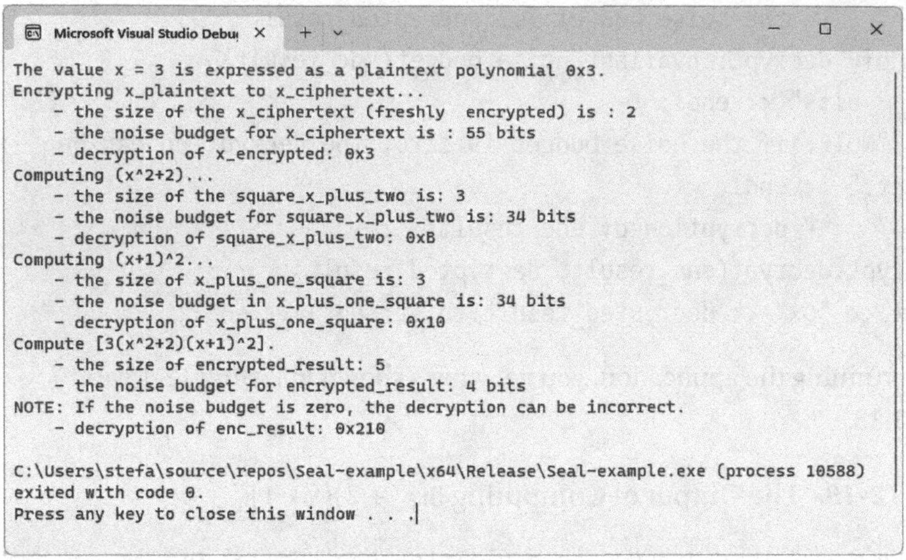

Figure 12-13. *The output of computing $3(x^2 + 2)(x + 1)^2$*

Indeed, if you compute $3(3^2 + 2)(3 + 1)^2$, you get 528. Note that the plaintext modulus is 1024, so 528 mod 1024 = 528, which has the 0x210 hexadecimal representation. The noise budget is greater than 0, which allowed us to decrypt the final encrypted result.

Listing 12-14 is in the Seal-example.cpp file.

Listing 12-14. The Entire Code

```
#pragma once

#include "seal/seal.h"
#include <iostream>
#include <algorithm>
#include <chrono>
#include <cstddef>
#include <fstream>
#include <iomanip>
#include <iostream>
#include <limits>
#include <memory>
#include <mutex>
#include <numeric>
```

```cpp
#include <random>
#include <sstream>
#include <string>
#include <thread>
#include <vector>

using namespace std;
using namespace seal;

void seal_example_bfv()
{
    EncryptionParameters BFV_parameters(scheme_type::BFV);

    size_t polynomial_degree = 4096;
    BFV_parameters.set_poly_modulus_degree(polynomial_degree);
    BFV_parameters.set_coeff_modulus(CoeffModulus::BFVDefault(
    polynomial_degree));
    BFV_parameters.set_plain_modulus(1024);

    auto seal_context = SEALContext::Create(BFV_parameters);

    KeyGenerator keygen(seal_context);
    PublicKey encryption_key = keygen.public_key();
    SecretKey decryption_key = keygen.secret_key();
    Encryptor bfv_encrypt(seal_context, encryption_key);
    Evaluator bfv_evaluate(seal_context);
    Decryptor bfv_decrypt(seal_context, decryption_key);

    int value_x = 3;
    Plaintext x_plaintext(to_string(value_x));
    cout << "The value x = " + to_string(value_x) + " is expressed as a
    plaintext polynomial 0x" + x_plaintext.to_string() + "." << endl;

    Ciphertext x_ciphertext;
    cout << "Encrypting x_plaintext to x_ciphertext..." << endl;
    bfv_encrypt.encrypt(x_plaintext, x_ciphertext);

    cout << "    - the size of the x_ciphertext (freshly encrypted) is : "
    << x_ciphertext.size() << endl;
```

```cpp
cout << "    - the noise budget for x_ciphertext is : " << bfv_decrypt.
invariant_noise_budget(x_ciphertext) << " bits"
    << endl;

Plaintext value_x_decrypted;
cout << "    - decryption of x_encrypted: ";
bfv_decrypt.decrypt(x_ciphertext, value_x_decrypted);
cout << "0x" << value_x_decrypted.to_string() << endl;

cout << "Computing (x^2+2)..." << endl;
Ciphertext square_x_plus_two;
bfv_evaluate.square(x_ciphertext, square_x_plus_two);
Plaintext plain_value_two("2");
bfv_evaluate.add_plain_inplace(square_x_plus_two, plain_value_two);

cout << "    - the size of the square_x_plus_two is: " << square_x_
plus_two.size() << endl;
cout << "    - the noise budget for square_x_plus_two is: " << bfv_
decrypt.invariant_noise_budget(square_x_plus_two) << " bits"
    << endl;

Plaintext decrypted_result;
cout << "    - decryption of square_x_plus_two: ";
bfv_decrypt.decrypt(square_x_plus_two, decrypted_result);
cout << "0x" << decrypted_result.to_string() << endl;

cout << "Computing (x+1)^2..." << endl;
Ciphertext x_plus_one_square;
Plaintext plain_value_one("1");
bfv_evaluate.add_plain(x_ciphertext, plain_value_one, x_plus_one_
square);
bfv_evaluate.square_inplace(x_plus_one_square);
cout << "    - the size of x_plus_one_square is: " << x_plus_one_
square.size() << endl;
cout << "    - the noise budget in x_plus_one_square is: " << bfv_
decrypt.invariant_noise_budget(x_plus_one_square) << " bits"
    << endl;
```

```
    cout << "     - decryption of x_plus_one_square: ";
    bfv_decrypt.decrypt(x_plus_one_square, decrypted_result);
    cout << "0x" << decrypted_result.to_string() << endl;

    cout << "Compute [3(x^2+2)(x+1)^2]." << endl;
    Ciphertext enc_result;
    Plaintext plain_value_three("3");
    bfv_evaluate.multiply_plain_inplace(square_x_plus_two, plain_
    value_three);
    bfv_evaluate.multiply(square_x_plus_two, x_plus_one_square, enc_
    result);
    cout << "     - the size of encrypted_result: " << enc_result.size()
    << endl;
    cout << "     - the noise budget for encrypted_result: " << bfv_decrypt.
    invariant_noise_budget(enc_result) << " bits"
        << endl;
    cout << "NOTE: If the noise budget is zero, the decryption can be
    incorrect." << endl;
    cout << "     - decryption of enc_result: ";
    bfv_decrypt.decrypt(enc_result, decrypted_result);
    cout << "0x" << decrypted_result.to_string() << endl;
}

int main()
{
    seal_example_bfv();
    return 0;
}
```

This section provides an easy example of how the SEAL library can be used with C++ on Windows distribution. However, real-life applications are much more complex, which raises the need to handle more complex functions and algorithms.

The SEAL library can be very useful, and its major advantage is that it does not depend on other external libraries. When applications work with the exact values of integers, the BFV encryption scheme implemented in the SEAL library is great. If the application needs to work with real or complex numbers, the CKKS encryption scheme is the best choice, which is also implemented in the SEAL library.

Conclusion

In this chapter, you learned the following.

- Homomorphic encryption

- Why FHE is so important

- Microsoft's SEAL library, which implements the BFV encryption scheme, on a simple example with a polynomial evaluation

References

[1].   R. L. Rivest, L. Adleman, and M. L. Dertouzos, "On data banks and privacy homomorphism", Foundations of secure computation, vol. 4, no. 11, pp. 169–180, 1978.

[2].   Rivest, Ronald L., Adi Shamir, and Leonard Adleman. "A method for obtaining digital signatures and public-key cryptosystems." Communications of the ACM 21.2 (1978): 120–126.

[3].   S. Goldwasser and S. Micali, "Probabilistic encryption & how to play mental poker keeping secret all partial information", in Providing sound foundations for cryptography: on the work of Shafi Goldwasser and Silvio Micali, 2019, pp. 173–201.

[4].   ElGamal, Taher. "A public key cryptosystem and a signature scheme based on discrete logarithms." IEEE transactions on information theory 31.4 (1985): 469–472.

[5].   D. Boneh, E.-J. Goh, and K. Nissim, "Evaluating 2-DNF Formulas on Ciphertexts.", in TCC, Springer, 2005, pp. 325–341.

[6].   B. Barak and Z. Brakerski. "The Swiss army knife of cryptography," http://windowsontheory.org/2012/05/01/the-swiss-army-knife-of-cryptography/, 2012. Last accessed: 28.2.2023

[7].   C. Gentry, "Fully homomorphic encryption using ideal lattices", in Proceedings of the forty-first annual ACM symposium on Theory of computing, 2009, pp. 169–178.

[8].   M. Van Dijk, C. Gentry, S. Halevi, and V. Vaikuntanathan, "Fully homomorphic encryption over the integers", in Advances in Cryptology–EUROCRYPT 2010: 29th Annual International Conference on the Theory and Applications of Cryptographic Techniques, French Riviera, May 30–June 3, 2010. Proceedings 29, Springer, 2010, pp. 24–43.

[9].   Z. Brakerski and V. Vaikuntanathan, "Efficient fully homomorphic encryption from (standard) LWE", SIAM Journal on computing, vol. 43, no. 2, pp. 831–871, 2014.

[10].   M. Yagisawa, "Fully homomorphic encryption without bootstrapping", Cryptology ePrint Archive, 2015.

[11].   C. Gentry, A. Sahai, and B. Waters, "Homomorphic encryption from learning with errors: Conceptually-simpler, asymptotically-faster, attribute-based", in Advances in Cryptology–CRYPTO 2013: 33rd Annual Cryptology Conference, Santa Barbara, CA, USA, August 18-22, 2013. Proceedings, Part I, Springer, 2013, pp. 75–92.

[12].   HElib, https://github.com/homenc/HElib. Last accessed: 1.3.2023

[13].   TFHE: Fast Fully Homomorphic Encryption over the Torus, Available online: https://tfhe.github.io/tfhe. Last accessed: 1.3.2023

[14].   PALISADE Homomorphic Encryption Software Library, Available online: https://palisade-crypto.org. Last accessed: 1.3.2023

[15].   I. Chillotti, N. Gama, M. Georgieva, and M. Izabachene, "Faster fully homomorphic encryption: Bootstrapping in less than 0.1 seconds", in Advances in Cryptology–ASIACRYPT 2016: 22nd International Conference on the Theory and Application of Cryptology and Information Security, Hanoi, Vietnam, December 4-8, 2016, Proceedings, Part I 22, Springer, 2016, pp. 3–33.

[16].   Z. Brakerski, C. Gentry, and V. Vaikuntanathan, "(Leveled) fully homomorphic encryption without bootstrapping", ACM Transactions on Computation Theory (TOCT), vol. 6, no. 3, pp. 1–36, 2014.

[17].   J. Fan and F. Vercauteren, "Somewhat practical fully homomorphic encryption", Cryptology ePrint Archive, 2012.

[18].   J. H. Cheon, A. Kim, M. Kim, and Y. Song, "Homomorphic encryption for arithmetic of approximate numbers", in Advances in Cryptology–ASIACRYPT 2017: 23rd International Conference on the Theory and Applications of Cryptology and Information Security, Hong Kong, China, December 3-7, 2017, Proceedings, Part I 23, Springer, 2017, pp. 409–437.

[19].   L. Ducas and D. Micciancio, "FHEW: bootstrapping homomorphic encryption in less than a second", in Advances in Cryptology–EUROCRYPT 2015: 34th Annual International Conference on the Theory and Applications of Cryptographic Techniques, Sofia, Bulgaria, April 26-30, 2015, Proceedings, Part I 34, Springer, 2015, pp. 617–640.

[20].   H. Chen, K. Laine, and R. Player, "Simple encrypted arithmetic library-SEAL v2. 1", in Financial Cryptography and Data Security: FC 2017 International Workshops, WAHC, BITCOIN, VOTING, WTSC, and TA, Sliema, Malta, April 7, 2017, Revised Selected Papers 21, Springer, 2017, pp. 3–18.

[21].   K. Laine, "Simple encrypted arithmetic library 2.3. 1", Microsoft Research `https://www.microsoft.com/en-us/research/uploads/prod/2017/11/sealmanual-2-3-1.pdf`, 2017.

[22].   Microsoft SEAL, Available online: `https://www.microsoft.com/en-us/research/project/microsoft-seal/`. Last accessed: 2.3.2023

[23].   Microsoft/SEAL, Available online: `https://github.com/Microsoft/SEAL`. Last accessed: 2.3.2023

[24].   M. R. Albrecht, "On dual lattice attacks against small-secret LWE and parameter choices in HElib and SEAL", in Advances in Cryptology–EUROCRYPT 2017: 36th Annual International Conference on the Theory and Applications of Cryptographic Techniques, Paris, France, April 30–May 4, 2017, Proceedings, Part II, Springer, 2017, pp. 103–129.

[25].   L. Yu, C. A. Pérez-Delgado, and J. F. Fitzsimons, "Limitations on information-theoretically-secure quantum homomorphic encryption", Physical Review A, vol. 90, no. 5, p. 050303, 2014.

CHAPTER 13

Ring Learning with Errors Cryptography

This chapter covers Ring Learning with Errors Cryptography (RLWE), one of the most important and challenging techniques for developing secure, complex applications and systems.

Cryptography has existed since ancient times, but it has become especially crucial in the digital age. It is a technique used to protect data, control access to sensitive information, and secure communications. Learning about error cryptography can help you understand this science's basic principles and applications. Errors cryptography is a branch of cryptography that detects, corrects, and prevents errors in digital communications. It is a vital tool for data security in today's digital environment. Error cryptography can protect data from corruption, tampering, or interception. Additionally, error cryptography can help ensure data accuracy and integrity and provide authentication of the sender and receiver. This article explores the basic principles and applications of error cryptography and how it can be used to protect data and communications.

Errors cryptography is the process of securing data against errors in transmission and storage. This process involves appropriate data formatting, encryption, and error correction methods. All these methods are used to secure data and ensure its authenticity, integrity, and accuracy. Errors cryptography is performed at three stages: transmission, storage, and processing. Transmission error cryptography is used for error detection and correction for transmitting data over a transmission channel. Storage error cryptography is used for error detection and correction for data stored on a storage medium. Processing error cryptography is used for error detection and correction for data that are in computer memory.

© Marius Iulian Mihailescu and Stefania Loredana Nita 2023
M. I. Mihailescu and S. L. Nita, *Pro Cryptography and Cryptanalysis with C++23*,
https://doi.org/10.1007/978-1-4842-9450-5_13

The learning with errors problem was introduced in 2005 by Oded Regev [4]. Since then, it has proven its potential to be a basis for future cryptography and its capability to generate complex cryptographic structures. LWE and related topics are widely used in lattice-based cryptography. You can find comprehensive studies, surveys, and deep formal aspects in the works [5, 6, 7].

LWE is a difficult computation problem (therefore, a hardness assumption in cryptography) that is the formal foundation for cryptographic algorithms and constructions. One such cryptographic construction is NewHope [8], an encapsulation method for postquantum keys. NewHope seeks to protect against cryptanalysis attacks launched on quantum computers. Another application of LWE is in homomorphic encryption, serving as a hardness assumption for many important (fully) homomorphic encryption schemes (see Chapter 12).

Errors cryptography uses the following principles: error detection, error correction, authentication, and data integrity. Let's go over the principles of error cryptography in detail.

- **Error detection** identifies when errors occur during the transmission of data. The most common method to detect errors is to use parity bits. Parity bits are used in many communication protocols to detect single-bit errors.

- **Error correction** corrects errors that were detected while data were being transmitted. Various techniques, such as Hamming and Reed-Solomon codes, are used to correct errors.

- **Authentication** validates who the sender and receiver are. It also validates that only authorized parties are part of the transmission. Authentication is important in the exchange of sensitive information.

- **Data integrity** ensures that the data is not corrupted while transmitted. Data can be corrupted in many ways, such as electromagnetic interference and noise.

There are many organizations and associations that standardize and regulate error cryptography, such as the International Organization for Standardization and the International Telecommunications Union.

RLWE is the LWE problem applied in rings of polynomials defined over finite fields. The RLWE problem represents a basis for future cryptography because it is resistant to known quantum algorithms such as Shor's algorithm; therefore, it remains a hardness assumption in the quantum ecosystem.

An advantage of the RLWE technique in front of LWE is the size of the keys. The size of the LWE keys is approximately the square of the size of the RLWE for the same number of bits of security. For example, for 128 bits of security, the keys of an LWE cryptosystem require 49.000.000 bits, while the keys of an RLWE cryptosystem require 7000 bits.

RLWE cryptographic algorithms can be divided into three categories, as follows.

- RLWE Key Exchange (RLWE-KE): In 2011, Jintai Ding, at the University of Cincinnati, used the associativity of matrix multiplication to propose a preliminary scheme for key exchange based on LWE and RLWE [9]. The study was published in 2012 after the idea was patented. Based on this work, Chris Peikert proposed a key transport scheme in 2014 [10].

- RLWE Signature (RLWE-S): The identification protocol proposed by Feige, Fiat, and Shamir in [11] represented the basis for the digital signature proposed in 2011 by Lyubashevsky. A further improvement of the digital signature [12] was proposed by GLP (Gunesyu, Lyubashevsky, and Popplemann) in [13].

- RLWE Homomorphic Encryption (RLWE-HE): You learned about homomorphic encryption in Chapter 12 and saw that homomorphic encryption enables computations to be applied directly over encrypted data. Among the first fully homomorphic encryption schemes that use RLWE is [14], which was proposed in 2011 by Brakersky and Vaikuntanathan.

The next section provides a minimum mathematical background for the LWE and RLWE.

Mathematical Background
Learning with Errors (LWE)

The quantum computer era is in an early stage; many of the current encryption systems with public keys are easy to break, which leads to the natural necessity of creating cryptosystems based on quantum-resistant hardness assumptions. LWE has this capability. The LWE problem's difficulty consists of computing the values that solve the following equation.

$$b = as + e$$

In an equation of this form, a and b can form the public key, s can be the secret key, and e can be an error value (or noise).

In cryptography, the LWE problem can be used in different topics. For example, based on LWE, secure public-key encryption schemes can be constructed against chosen plaintext or ciphertext attacks. Additionally, LWE can be a basis for oblivious transfer, fully homomorphic encryption, or identity-based encryption.

The preceding equality becomes $b = A \times s + e$ in [1] because it is applied to linear equations. Here, A becomes a matrix with two dimensions, and if s is a matrix with one dimension, then b and e are matrices with one dimension. Another possibility is that A and b are matrices with one dimension, and s is a scalar value.

The following presents a simple encryption scheme based on LWE [4]. Note that in the example, $p \in Z$ represents a prime number.

- Key generation: The following elements are chosen randomly: the vector $s \in Z_p^n$, the matrix A with m rows, which are m independent vectors of a uniform distribution, and the vector $e = (e_1, ..., e_m)$ of an error distribution defined over Z. Then, the value b is computed $b = As + e$. The secret key is the value s, and the public key is the pair (A, b).

- Encryption: Given the $m \in \{0, 1\}$ message to be encrypted, choose random samples from A and b, achieving $v_A = \sum a_i$ and $v_b = \sum b_j - \frac{p}{2} m$. The values a_i and b_i represent the samples from A and b, respectively. The encryption of m is the pair (u, v).

- Decryption: Compute $val = v_b - s v_A \ (mod\ p)$. If $val \leq \frac{p}{2}$, then the message is $m = 0$; otherwise, the message is $m = 1$.

The preceding example shows how LWE works. Examples of public key encryption schemes based on the LWE problem are [2] and Lindner-Peikert encryption schemes.

LWE problems are divided into two categories: LWE search and LWE decision.

LWE Search

Let m, n, $p \in Z$ be integer values, and let χ_s and χ_e be two distributions defined over the integer numbers set Z. Select the values $s \leftarrow \chi_s^n, e_i \leftarrow \chi_e$ and $a_i \leftarrow U\left(Z_p^n\right)$. Compute the value of $b_i := \langle a_i, s \rangle + e_i \bmod p$, where $i = 1, ..., m$. Given the tuple $(n, m, p, \chi_s, \chi_e)$, the *learning with errors search* variant problem consists of determining s knowing $\left(a_i, b_i\right)_{i=1}^m$.

In this definition, s represents a column-vector with n values, a_i represents a row-vector with n values from Z_p and b represents a column-vector with m elements from Z_p. The representation $x \leftarrow S$ shows that x is a random variable selected from the finite set S.

LWE Decision

Let n, $p \in Z$ be integer values, and let χ_s and χ_e be two distributions defined over the integer numbers set Z. Select the value $s \leftarrow \chi_s^n$, and pick two oracles as follows.

- $O: a \leftarrow U\left(Z_p^n\right), e \leftarrow \chi_e$; output$(a, \langle a, s \rangle + e \bmod p)$
- $U: a \leftarrow U\left(Z_p^n\right), u \leftarrow U\left(Z_p\right)$; output$(a, u)$

Given the tuple (n, p, χ_s, χ_e), the *learning with errors decision* variant means differentiating between O and U.

Ring Learning with Errors (RLWE)

The LWE problem applied in rings of polynomials with coefficients in a finite field is called the ring learning with errors (RLWE) problem. RLWE is used in different domains of cryptography, for example, in key exchange, homomorphic encryption, and signatures. The functionalities from RLWE are similar to the functionalities from simple LWE. For RLWE, the a, b, s, e variables from the first equality are polynomials. Let's examine how the two LWE variants' definitions adapt to RLWE.

RLWE Search

Let $n, p \in Z$ be integer values, with $n = 2^k$, let R be $R = \dfrac{Z[X]}{\langle X^n + 1 \rangle}$ and $R_p = \dfrac{R}{pR}$ and

let χ_s and χ_e be two distributions defined over the ring R_p. Select $s \leftarrow \chi_s$, $e \longleftarrow \chi_e$ and

$a \leftarrow U(R_p)$. Compute the value of $b := as + e$. Given the tuple (n, p, χ_s, χ_e), the *ring learning with errors search* variant problem consists of determining s knowing (a, b).

In this definition, R_p is actually $R_p = \dfrac{Z_p[X]}{\langle X^n + 1 \rangle}$.

RLWE Decision

Let $n, p \in Z_+$ be integer values and let χ_s and χ_e be two distributions defined over the ring R_p. Select the value $s \leftarrow \chi_s$, and pick two oracles as follows.

- $O : a \leftarrow U(R_p)$, $e \leftarrow \chi_e$; output$(a, as + e)$

- $U : a \leftarrow U(R_p)$, $u \leftarrow U(R_p)$; output(a, u)

Given the tuple (n, p, χ_s, χ_e), the *ring learning with errors decision* variant means differentiating between O and U.

An encryption scheme based on the hardness assumption of (R)LWE is secure if the advantage of any algorithm A (called attacker) with polynomial time in solving the (R) LWE problem is a negligible function.

Practical Implementation

Learning with errors (LWE) is a quantum-resistant technique in cryptography. On the practical side of the LWE, to implement a simple LWE example, you first need to generate a secret value and a random value. Furthermore, the implementation is intuitive, as you need to compute a value of the form $p[\ ] = t[\ ] \times secret_{key} + e$.

Listing 13-1 provides an implementation for a simple example of an encryption system based on the work of Oded Regev from [4]. The result of running the program is provided in Figure 13-1.

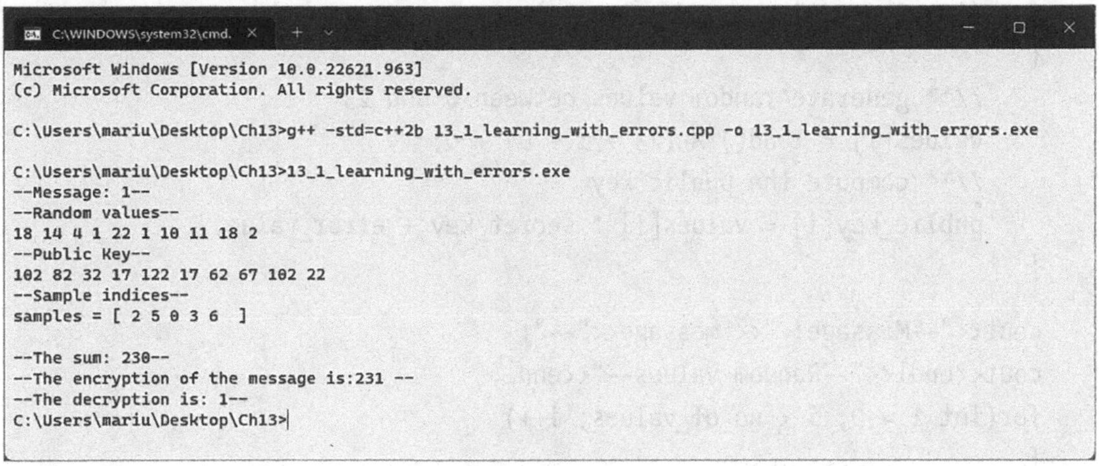

```
Microsoft Windows [Version 10.0.22621.963]
(c) Microsoft Corporation. All rights reserved.

C:\Users\mariu\Desktop\Ch13>g++ -std=c++2b 13_1_learning_with_errors.cpp -o 13_1_learning_with_errors.exe

C:\Users\mariu\Desktop\Ch13>13_1_learning_with_errors.exe
--Message: 1--
--Random values--
18 14 4 1 22 1 10 11 18 2
--Public Key--
102 82 32 17 122 17 62 67 102 22
--Sample indices--
samples = [ 2 5 0 3 6  ]

--The sum: 230--
--The encryption of the message is:231 --
--The decryption is: 1--
C:\Users\mariu\Desktop\Ch13>
```

Figure 13-1. *The result of running the program with a simple example of LWE encryption*

Listing 13-1. Implementation of a Simple LWE Example [4]

```cpp
#include <iostream>
#include <math.h>
#include <ctime>
using namespace std;

int main()
{
    srand(time(0));

    int no_of_values = 10;
    int public_key [no_of_values];
    int values [no_of_values];
    int secret_key = 5;
    int error_value = 12;
    int message = 1;

    int value = 0;
```

```cpp
for (int i = 0; i < no_of_values; i++)
{
    //** generate random values between 0 and 23
    values[i] = rand() % (23 + 1 - 0) + 0;
    //** compute the public key
    public_key[i] = values[i] * secret_key + error_value;
}

cout<<"--Message: "<< message<<"--";
cout<<endl<<"--Random values--"<<endl;
for(int i = 0; i < no_of_values; i++)
{
    cout<<values[i]<<" ";
}

cout<<endl<<"--Public Key--"<<endl;
for(int i = 0; i < no_of_values; i++)
{
    cout<<public_key[i]<<" ";
}

//** get half random samples from the public_key
int noOfSamples = floor(no_of_values / 2);
int samples [noOfSamples];
for(int i=0; i < noOfSamples; i++)
{
    //** generate a number of 5 random indices between 0 and 10
    samples[i] = rand() % ((no_of_values-1) + 1 - 0) + 0;
}
cout<<endl<<"--Sample indices--";
cout<<endl<<"samples = [ ";
for (int i=0; i < noOfSamples; i++)
{
    cout << samples[i] << " ";
}
cout<<" ]" << endl;
```

```
    int sum = 0;
    for (int i = 0; i < noOfSamples; i++)
    {
        sum += public_key[samples[i]];
    }

    cout<<endl<<"--The sum: " << sum << "--";

    if (message == 1)
        sum+=1;

    cout<<endl<<"--The encryption of the message is:" << sum <<" --";

    int decryption = sum % secret_key;

    if (decryption % 2 == 0)
        cout<<endl<<"--The decryption is: 0--";
    else
        cout<<endl<<"--The decryption is: 1--";

    return 0;
}
```

Listing 13-2 is a more complex example of public-key encryption that uses LWE, based on the work [5]. The result of running the program is shown in Figure 13-2.

Listing 13-2. Implementation of the LWE Encryption Method Proposed by Oded Regev in [5]

```
#include <iostream>
#include <math.h>
#include <ctime>
using namespace std;

int main()
{
    srand(time(0));

    int numberOfRandVals = 20;
    int values_A [20]; //** values_A is a set of random numbers; represents
    the public key
```

```
int secretValue = 5; //** represents the secret key
int values_error [numberOfRandVals]; //** represents the error values
int values_B [numberOfRandVals]; //** values_B is computed based on
values_A, secretValue, values_error; represents the public key

int q = 97; //** q is a prime number

//** generate random values
//** the number of random values is numberOfRandVals = 20
//** the range is 0 - q=97
for(int i=0; i < numberOfRandVals; i++)
{
    //** to generate a random value in a range MIN - MAX,
    //** we proceed as follows: val = rand() % (MAX + 1 - MIN) + MIN;

    //** generate random values between 0 - 97
    values_A[i] = rand() % (q + 1 - 0) + 0;
    //** generate small error values, between 1 - 4
    values_error[i] = rand() % (4 + 1 - 1) + 1;
    //** compute values_B using the formula B_i = A_i*s + e_i
    values_B[i] = values_A[i]*secretValue + values_error[i];
}

cout<<"--------- The parameters and the keys ---------" << endl;
cout<<"--Prime number (q)--" << endl;
cout<<"q = " << q << endl;
cout<<"--Public key (A, B)--" << endl;
cout<<"A = [ ";
for (int i=0; i < numberOfRandVals; i++)
{
    cout << values_A[i] << " ";
}
cout<<"]" << endl;

cout<<"B = [ ";
for (int i=0; i < numberOfRandVals; i++)
{
    cout << values_B[i] << " ";
}
```

```
cout<<"]" << endl;
cout<<"--Secret key (s)--" << endl;
cout<<"s = " << secretValue << endl;
cout<<"--Random error (e)--" << endl;
cout<<"e = [ ";
for (int i=0; i < numberOfRandVals; i++)
{
    cout << values_error[i] << " ";
}
cout<<"]" << endl;

cout<< endl << endl << "--------- Getting samples from the public
key... ---------";
int noOfSamples = floor(numberOfRandVals / 4); //** represents the
number of samples from the public key
int samples [noOfSamples];
for(int i=0; i < noOfSamples; i++)
{
    //** generate a number of 5 random indices between 0 and 19
    samples[i] = rand() % ((numberOfRandVals-1) + 1 - 0) + 0;
}
cout<<endl<<"--Sample indices--";
cout<<endl<<"samples = [ ";
for (int i=0; i < noOfSamples; i++)
{
    cout << samples[i] << " " " ";
}
cout<<" ]" << endl;
cout<<"--Sample pairs--";
for (int i=0; i < noOfSamples; i++)
{
    cout << endl <<"Sample " << i << ": ["
    << values_A[samples[i]] << " " << values_B[samples[i]] << "]";
}

cout<< endl << endl << "--------- Computing u and v... ---------";
```

```
int message = 0; //** the message to be encrypted can be a value
from {0, 1}
int u = 0, v = 0;
//** u = (sum (samples from values_A)) mod q
//** v = (sum (samples from values_B) + [q/2] * message) mod q
for (int i=0; i < noOfSamples; i++)
{
    u = u + values_A[samples[i]];
    v = v + values_B[samples[i]];
}

v = v + floor(q/2) * message;

u = u % q;
v = v % q;

cout<<endl<<"u = "<<u;
cout<<endl<<"v = "<<v;

cout<< endl << endl << "--------- Encrypting... ---------";

cout<<endl<<"--Message--";
cout<<endl<<"m = "<<message;
cout<<endl<<"--Encryption f the message--";
cout<<endl<<"Enc(m) = (" << u << ", " << v <<")";

cout<< endl << endl << "--------- Decrypting... ---------";
int result = (v - secretValue * u) % q;

int decryption;
if (result > q/2)
    decryption = 1;
else
    decryption  = 0;
cout<<endl<<"The message is: " << decryption;

return 0;
}
```

Listing 13-2 is an example of public key encryption based on LWE, which was proposed in [5]. secretValue represents the private key.

```
C:\WINDOWS\system32\cmd.  ×    +   ∨                                        —    □    ×

C:\Users\mariu\Desktop\Ch13>g++ -std=c++2b 13_2_oded_regev.cpp -o 13_2_learning_with_errors.exe

C:\Users\mariu\Desktop\Ch13>13_2_learning_with_errors.exe
--------- The parameters and the keys ---------
--Prime number (q)--
q = 97
--Public key (A, B)--
A = [ 51 56 51 9 30 71 22 64 10 39 10 77 4 84 87 21 66 96 39 74 ]
B = [ 256 283 259 46 154 359 113 324 52 196 51 386 23 421 436 108 332 483 198 374 ]
--Secret key (s)--
s = 5
--Random error (e)--
e = [ 1 3 4 1 4 4 3 4 2 1 1 1 3 1 1 3 2 3 3 4 ]


--------- Getting samples from the public key... ---------
--Sample indices--
samples = [ 16 11 8 8 3  ]
--Sample pairs--
Sample 0: [66 332]
Sample 1: [77 386]
Sample 2: [10 52]
Sample 3: [10 52]
Sample 4: [9 46]

--------- Computing u and v... ---------
u = 75
v = 92

--------- Encrypting... ---------
--Message--
m = 0
--Encryption f the message--
Enc(m) = (75, 92)

--------- Decrypting... ---------
The message is: 0
C:\Users\mariu\Desktop\Ch13>
```

Figure 13-2. *The result of running the program of the public-key LWE example*

The next step creates the public key. The public key is formed by the values from a set of random numbers (values_A) and a set of values (values_B), which are computed based on values_A, secretValue, and random errors (values_error). This example is implemented for a single bit.

To secure data over a computer network, data encryption is used. Data encryption is the process of converting data into a secret code so that only authorized people/devices can read it. There are many types of data encryption.

- **Symmetric encryption** uses a single key to both encrypt and decrypt data. The single key must be kept secret.

- **Asymmetric encryption** uses a public key to encrypt data and a private key to decrypt data.

- **Hashing** does not encrypt data but can be used to authenticate it.

The following is a simple workflow for this example.

- Between 0 and q (in the example, q=97), we selected a random set of 20 values in the stored in the array values_A that represents one of the components of the public key.

- Define the set values_B, where every element is computed as values_B[i]=values_A[i] x secretValue+values_error[i] mod q, where secretValue is the secret key and values_error represents a list of small random values, called *the error values*.

- The values_A and values_B sets form the public key, and secretValue represents the secret key. At this point, values_A and values_B can be shared with anyone who wants to proceed with the encryption of a message (with the condition of keeping secretValue secret). The encryption process uses samples from values_A and values_B. Based on those samples, take a bit message, and compute the following two values.

  - $u = \sum (values\_A_{samples})(mod\ q)$
  - $v = \sum (values\_B_{samples}) + \dfrac{q}{2} \times message(mod\ q)$

- At this point, the encrypted message is (u, v). To proceed with the decryption, compute the following.

  - $decryption = v - s \times u\ (mod\ q)$

- If $decryption < \dfrac{q}{2}$, the message is equal to 0; otherwise, it is 1.

The preceding procedure is summarized from the Oded Regev paper [5] to make it easy to follow and understand how to transpose the complexity of LWEs in reality.

Conclusion

This chapter discussed RLWE and implemented two examples of encryption schemes using the C++ programming language proposed in the works [4] and [5]. RLWE can be a space for many professional challenges and a starting approach for bringing significant contributions to this cryptographic primitive.

The chapter offered an interesting journey with LWE, including the following.

- A solid but short mathematical background of the main concepts and definitions on which RLWE is based and without which a practical implementation has many gaps to fill out

- Experimenting with the challenges brought by RLWE mathematical concepts and their transposition in practice

- The ability to implement simple examples of public-key encryption schemes based on LWE

Errors cryptography is the process of securing data against errors in transmission and storage. This process involves appropriate data formatting, encryption, and error correction methods. All these methods are used to secure data and ensure its authenticity, integrity, and accuracy. Errors cryptography is performed at three stages: transmission, storage, and processing. It uses the following principles: error detection, error correction, authentication, and data integrity. There are various types of error cryptography, such as error detection, error correction, authentication, and data integrity. Many security protocols can be used with error cryptography. Errors cryptography can secure data against errors, but it cannot secure data from being intercepted and read.

References

[1].   O. Regev, The Learning with Errors Problem, Available online: `https://cims.nyu.edu/~regev/papers/lwesurvey.pdf`. Last accessed: 11.3.2023

[2].   O. Regev, "On lattices, learning with errors, random linear codes, and cryptography", Journal of the ACM (JACM), vol. 56, no. 6, pp. 1–40, 2009.

[3].   R. Lindner and C. Peikert, "Better key sizes (and attacks) for LWE-based encryption", in Topics in Cryptology–CT-RSA 2011: The Cryptographers' Track at the RSA Conference 2011, San Francisco, CA, USA, February 14-18, 2011. Proceedings, Springer, 2011, pp. 319–339.

[4].   O. Regev, "The Learning with Errors Problem (Invited Survey)," *2010 IEEE 25th Annual Conference on Computational Complexity*, Cambridge, MA, 2010, pp. 191–204, doi: 10.1109/CCC.2010.26.

[5].   O. Regev, "Lattice-based cryptography", in Advances in Cryptology-CRYPTO 2006: 26th Annual International Cryptology Conference, Santa Barbara, California, USA, August 20-24, 2006. Proceedings 26, Springer, 2006, pp. 131–141.

[6].   C. Peikert, "Some Recent Progress in Lattice-Based Cryptography.", in TCC, 2009, p. 72.

[7].   D. Micciancio, "Cryptographic functions from worst-case complexity assumptions", in The LLL Algorithm: Survey and Applications, Springer, 2009, pp. 427–452.

[8].   NewHope – Postquantum Key Encapsulation. Available online: `https://newhopecrypto.org/`. Last accessed: 12.3.2023

[9].   J. Ding, X. Xie, and X. Lin, "A simple provably secure key exchange scheme based on the learning with errors problem", Cryptology ePrint Archive, 2012.

[10].   C. Peikert, "Lattice cryptography for the internet", in Post-Quantum Cryptography: 6th International Workshop, PQCrypto 2014, Waterloo, ON, Canada, October 1-3, 2014. Proceedings 6, Springer, 2014, pp. 197–219.

[11].   Y. Desmedt, Fiat-Shamir Identification Protocol and the Feige-Fiat-Shamir Signature Scheme. Springer, 2011.

[12].   V. Lyubashevsky, "Lattice signatures without trapdoors", in Advances in Cryptology–EUROCRYPT 2012: 31st Annual International Conference on the Theory and Applications of Cryptographic Techniques, Cambridge, UK, April 15-19, 2012. Proceedings 31, Springer, 2012, pp. 738–755.

[13].   T. Güneysu, V. Lyubashevsky, and T. Pöppelmann, "Practical lattice-based cryptography: A signature scheme for embedded systems", in Cryptographic Hardware and Embedded Systems–CHES 2012: 14th International Workshop, Leuven, Belgium, September 9-12, 2012. Proceedings 14, Springer, 2012, pp. 530–547.

[14].   Z. Brakerski and V. Vaikuntanathan, "Fully homomorphic encryption from ring-LWE and security for key dependent messages", in Advances in Cryptology–CRYPTO 2011: 31st Annual Cryptology Conference, Santa Barbara, CA, USA, August 14-18, 2011. Proceedings 31, Springer, 2011, pp. 505–524.

CHAPTER 14

Chaos-based Cryptography

In today's digital world, security is paramount to protecting your data and digital life. As technology advances, so does the need for more secure encryption methods. One such encryption technique is chaos-based cryptography, which is gaining traction as one of the most secure forms of data protection. It is based on the principles of chaos theory, which states that complex systems often produce unpredictable results. With chaos-based cryptography, generating a seemingly random sequence of numbers is possible, which is then used to encrypt a message. This random sequence is almost impossible to reverse engineer, making it extremely difficult to crack the code. Understanding chaos-based cryptography is essential for anyone who wants to keep their data secure. This chapter explores the fundamentals of chaos-based cryptography, its advantages, and how it can be used to protect data.

In chaos-based cryptography, chaos theory is applied, and its mathematical background is used to create novel and unique cryptographic algorithms. Robert Matthews initiated the first attempt to use chaos theory in cryptography in 1989 [1], which attracted considerable interest.

In contrast with regular cryptographic primitives used daily, chaos theory and its system are used efficiently by implementing chaotic maps toward confusion and diffusion. Throughout this chapter, the cryptographic algorithm is called a *chaotic system*.

What are the benefits of chaos-based cryptography? Cryptography is the process of encoding information in a way that can only be decoded by those who have a key to unlock it. The key can be a password or a special sequence of letters and numbers, often called an *algorithm*. Traditionally, cryptography has been based on one-way functions, such as rotating letters through a substitution cipher. The main drawback of these one-way functions is that they can be broken. To crack the code, someone must perform

© Marius Iulian Mihailescu and Stefania Loredana Nita 2023
M. I. Mihailescu and S. L. Nita, *Pro Cryptography and Cryptanalysis with C++23*,
https://doi.org/10.1007/978-1-4842-9450-5_14

the same one-way function to decipher the message. The more complex the one-way function, the more time and effort it takes to break the code. Chaos-based cryptography takes a different approach to encryption. The sequence the code is generated with is complex and random, making it extremely difficult to crack. The sequence is generated by applying simple mathematical functions to a specially designed formula that creates a chaotic sequence. This sequence is then used to encrypt the message. The sequence is generated through a combination of simple mathematical formulas and computer software, which makes it quicker to produce compared to complex one-way functions. It also makes it easier to share code among users, which can be helpful if your business needs to collaborate with clients or suppliers.

To understand the similitudes and the differences that lay between chaotic systems and cryptographic algorithms, Table 14-1 presents a set of correspondences introduced by L. Kocarev in [2].

How does chaos-based cryptography work? Chaos-based cryptography uses a sequence of seemingly random numbers generated by a mathematical formula to encrypt and decrypt a message. The message is fed into the formula, which then generates a sequence of numbers. The receiving party applies the same formula to the sequence of numbers to generate the original message. To crack the code, a hacker would need to use the same formula to generate the original sequence. However, this is extremely difficult to do because the sequence is generated from a complex mathematical formula that is constantly changing. This means that the formula is different every time it is used, making it almost impossible for the hacker to crack the code. To generate a sequence of numbers, the user must apply a formula to the original message. The user then applies a second formula to the first sequence of numbers to produce a new sequence of numbers. This sequence is then sent over an unbreakable communications channel. The receiving party applies the same formula to the sequence of numbers to generate the original message.

How can chaos-based cryptography be implemented? Before implementing chaos-based cryptography for your business, it is important to choose the right formula for your code. You also need to consider how you generate the sequence of random numbers. There are several formulas available for use with chaos theory-based cryptography. The choice of formula impacts the sequence of numbers generated by the code. This means you should select a formula based on the type of information you want to encrypt. If you want to protect data such as financial information or health records, select a formula that generates long sequences of numbers. This makes it harder for hackers to crack the code because it requires considerable time and effort to decode the sequence. This is especially important if you want to share the code with clients or suppliers. If you need to send a sequence of numbers over a short-range wireless device, such as Bluetooth, select a formula that generates a short sequence. This makes it easier to transmit the sequence over a short-range device, as it does not take up much data.

Table 14-1. *Similarities and Differences Between Chaotic Systems and Cryptographic Algorithms*

Chaotic System	Cryptographic Algorithm
Phase space: (sub) set of real numbers	Phase space: a finite set of integers
Iterations	Rounds
Parameters	Key
Sensitivity to a change in initial conditions and parameters	Diffusion
?	Security and Performance

The similitudes and differences in Table 14-1 are demonstrated using a shift map as an example of a chaotic system.

$$x(t+1)=ax(t)(mod\,1)$$

The phase space $x = [0, 1]$ is the unit interval, and $a > 1$ is an integer value.

From the chaos theory perspective, different functions and discrete-time systems can be used in cryptography. By analyzing them, we observe that the phase space becomes a finite set of integers, and the parameters are inter-values. The version of the shift map that uses the discrete phase space is one of the common examples:

$$p(t+1)=ap(t)(mod\,N)$$

$a > 1$, N and p are integer values, with the restrictions $p \in [0, 1, ..., N-1]$ and N being coprime to a. This representation of the shift map is invertible, which means that all the trajectories placed within a dynamical system with a finite phase space are called *periodic*. This fact introduces a new concept, namely, the period functions P_N that describe the least period of the map F, denoted F^{P_N} as its identity and P_N is minimal, as it is a function within a system of size N.

Another important metric in practical chaotic systems is the *Lyapunov exponent*, whose trivial value is 0. The reason for this is the case in which the orbit is periodic and it reiterate itself.

Figures 14-1, 14-2, and 14-3 present two concepts of block diagrams (for text encryption and image encryption) that demonstrate what an encryption scheme based on chaos theory should look like. Figures 14-1 and 14-2 show the encryption process and the decryption process, respectively, based on the logistic map. Figure 14-3 shows an example of image encryption and decryption.

A good starting point in achieving this is to use the following block diagrams as a guide from theory to practice because the models are created according to the similitudes and differences in Table 14-1.

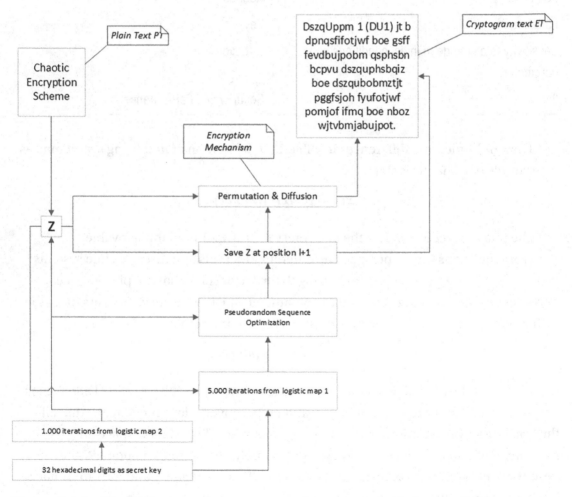

***Figure 14-1.** Block diagram for text encryption using a logistic map [14]*

Following the examples of the block diagrams, you can examine the papers listed in this chapter's "References" section to see that the encryption models and how they are built are different according to the chaotic map used. Before designing new cryptographic approaches and mechanisms based on chaos theory, it is important to understand how different chaotic maps work.

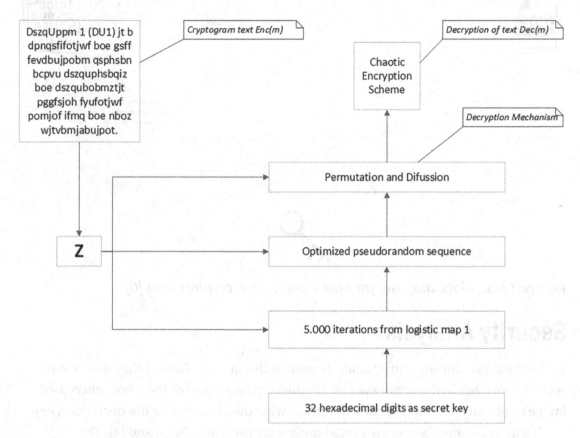

Figure 14-2. *Block diagram for text encryption using a logistic map [14]*

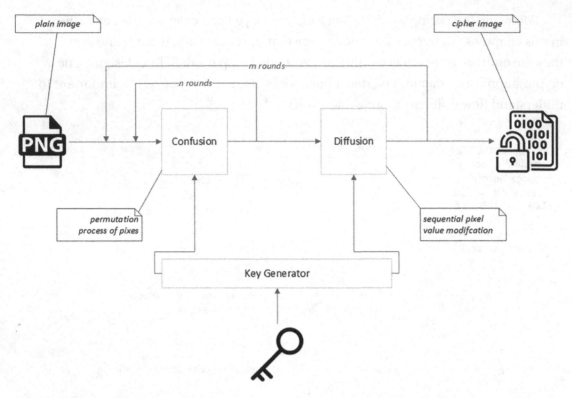

Figure 14-3. *Block diagram for image encryption cryptosystem [6]*

Security Analysis

This section presents a security analysis using techniques for finding the weakness or security breaches in the cryptosystem. We then obtain a piece or the whole encrypted image or plaintext or find the key without knowing the algorithm or the decryption key.

Examples of attacks over encrypted images are presented in [3] and [4]. The following methods, techniques, and analysis should be considered when designing a chaotic system or conducting a cryptanalytic attack.

- **Keyspace analysis** represents the number of trials for finding the decryption key and is made by trying all the possible keys from the keyspace of the encryption system. Note that the keyspace grows exponentially and simultaneously with the increment of the key's size.

- **Secret key sensitivity analysis** is important to a good image encryption system. If just a single bit is modified in the secret key, then the output image should be a completely different image (regarding encryption or decryption).

- **Statistical analysis** proves the relationship between the original image and the encrypted image.

- **Correlation coefficient analysis** is an important graphical tool that needs to be studied in the histogram, namely, the distribution of the values generated by a trajectory of a dynamic system. Among the histogram analysis, the correlation between the pixels of a plain image and the encrypted image is another important technique, as it is made between two pixels distributed vertically, horizontally, and diagonally.

- **Information entropy analysis** is based on entropy tests of the robustness of the encryption algorithm. The comparison between the entropy of the plain image and the encrypted image is very important, which shows that the entropy of the encrypted images is approximately 8-bit depth. This is useful in proving the encryption technique against the entropy attack.

- **Differential analysis** determines the sensitivity of the cryptosystem regarding any slight change in the algorithm. The sensitivity can be computed based on two criteria: NPCR (Number of Pixels Change Rate) and UACI (Unified Average Changing Intensity). When these tests are made, the high values show the small changes in the plain image that produced significant modifications in the encrypted image.

Chaotic Maps for Plaintexts and Image Encryption

This section presents chaotic maps in regard to their encryption target (text encryption or image encryption).

Many of the image encryption algorithms listed in Table 14-2 were analyzed and tested by the authors that proposed them. It is useful to validate the performance and evaluate the robustness of the encryption scheme. All the references were analyzed and chosen based on their analyses and tests.

Table 14-2. *Chaotic Map (Systems) for Image Encryption*

| Chaotic Map (System) | Metrics | | | Key | | References |
	Entropy	NPCR	UACI	Space	Sensitivity	
Lorenz	7.9973	-	-	2^{128}	High	[5]
Baker						
Lorenz	-	-	-	Large	Medium	[6]
Henon Map	7.9904	0.0015%	0.0005%	2^{128}	High	[7]
Logistic Map	7.9996	99.6231%	33.4070%	10^{45}	High	[8]
Trigonometry Maps	-	0.25%	0.19%	2^{302}	-	[9]
Arnold Cat Map	7.9981	99.62%	33.19%	2^{148}	High	[10]
Chebyshev Map	7.9902	99.609%	33.464%	2^{167}	High	[11]
Circle Map	7.9902	99.63%	33%	2^{256}	High	[12]
Arnold Map	-	0.0015%	0.004%	-	-	[13]

Rössler Attractor

The Rössler attractor represents a system formed from three nonlinear ordinary differential equations. The equations define a continuous-time dynamical system that exposes chaotic dynamics associated with the fractal properties of the attractor.

The equations of the Rössler system are as follows.

$$\{\frac{dx}{dt} = -y - z \qquad \frac{dy}{dt} = x + ay \qquad \frac{dz}{dt} = b + z(x - c)$$

When Rössler is applied in real life and practice, computing and finding the fixed points represents one of the first challenges raised. For computing the fixed points, it is sufficient that the equations are set to zero and (x, y, z) coordinates of each of the fixed points are computed by solving the resulting equations. The following general equations are for each of the fixed-point coordinates.

$$\{x = \frac{c \pm \sqrt{c^2 - 4ab}}{2} \qquad y = -\left(\frac{c \pm \sqrt{c^2 - 4ab}}{2a}\right) \qquad z = \frac{c \pm \sqrt{c^2 - 4ab}}{2a}$$

These equations are turned so that they show the current fixed points given for a set of values associated with the parameters.

$$\left(\frac{c+\sqrt{c^2-4ab}}{2}, \frac{-c-\sqrt{c^2-4ab}}{2a}, \frac{c+\sqrt{c^2-4ab}}{2a} \right)$$

$$\left(\frac{c-\sqrt{c^2-4ab}}{2}, \frac{-c+\sqrt{c^2-4ab}}{2a}, \frac{c-\sqrt{c^2-4ab}}{2a} \right)$$

These equations are used in our example in Listing 14-4, which implements a solution for generating secure random numbers using the chaos perspective of the Rössler attractor.

Complex Numbers: A Short Overview

Complex numbers represent an extension of the real numbers. The motivation behind complex numbers is the desire to solve algebraic equations that normally (using traditional real numbers) have no solution. As an example, $x^2 + 1 = 0$ has no real solution. For this situation, a symbolic solution has been created and is known as the *imaginary unit i*, which has the following property.

$$i^2 = -1$$

A complex number is represented by two components, which are known as the *real* and the *imaginary* parts. Write the following.

$$z = x + yi$$

real(z) = x denotes the real part, *imag*(z) = y denotes the imaginary part, and i represents the imaginary unit.

The arithmetic behind the complex numbers is quite straightforward and represents an extension of the arithmetic of real numbers. To understand the previous statement, we define two numbers z and w as follows.

$$z + w = (x + yi) + (u + vi) = (x + u) + (y + v)i$$

The real and imaginary components are added separately.

The next step is to multiply the numbers as follows.

$$z \cdot w = (x + yi)(u + vi) = xu + xvi + yui + yvi^2 = (xu - yv) + (xv + yu)i$$

Observe that yvi^2 represents the real product due to the property defined above $i^2 = -1$.

Listing 14-3 uses complex numbers with chaos and fractal properties to provide encryption and decryption operations.

Practical Implementation

The applications and programs that use chaotic systems have applicability for *plaintext encryption* and *image encryption*. If you look at other areas of cryptography (such as the ones discussed in this book), the research community has a significant amount of theoretical contributions. The lack of practical implementations and directions has raised multiple difficulties and challenges for researchers and professionals.

If you look at the practicability of chaos cryptography, you see few practical implementations. The following is a list of some practical approaches (referring to pseudocode algorithms) found within [15]. The work from [15] provides a very in-depth structure and good ideas and approaches on implementing different cryptosystems based on chaos theory. The ideas are provided as pseudocode. The work covers the following cryptosystem types.

- Chaos-based public-key cryptography

- Pseudorandom number generation in cryptography

- Formation of high-dimensional chaotic maps and their uses in cryptography

- Chaos-based hash functions

- Chaos-based video encryption algorithms

- Cryptanalysis of chaotic ciphers

- Hardware implementation of chaos-based ciphers

- Hardware implementation of chaos-secured optical communication systems

In [15], starting with Chapter 2, the authors propose an interesting public-key cryptosystem with a chaos approach consisting of three steps.

1. Key Generation Algorithm (Listing 14-1)

2. Encryption Algorithm (Listing 14-2)

3. Decryption Algorithm (Listing 14-3)

The scenario is a typical communication between two user entities: Alice and Bob. Next, we provide the structure of each algorithm, and at the end, we provide implementations to demonstrate the applicability.

Listing 14-1. Pseudocode: Key Generation Algorithm [15]

Start. *Alice* will need before the communication to generate the keys. For this, she will accomplish the following.

- A large integer a must be generated.

- Calculate $G_a(p)$ based on a random number selected as $p \in [-1, 1]$.

- *Alice* set her public key as $(p, G(p))$ and the private key to a.

Listing 14-2. Pseudocode: Encryption Algorithm [15]

Start. *Bob will want to encrypt a message. To achieve this, the following must be done.*

- Obtain Alice's authentic public key $(p, G_a(p))$.

- Calculate and represent the message as a number $M \in [-1, 1]$.

- Generate a large integer r.

- Calculate $G_r(p)$, $G_{r \cdot a(x)} = G_r(G_a(p))$ and $X = M \cdot G_{r \cdot s}(p)$.

- Take the ciphertext and send it as $C = (G_r(p), X)$ to Alice.

Listing 14-3. Pseudocode: Decryption Algorithm [15]

Start. *Alice wants to read the text, and to do this, he will have to recover M from the ciphertext C. To achieve this, the following steps are performed.*

- Alice has to use her private key a and calculate $G_{a \cdot t} = G_a(G_r(p))$.

- The message M is obtained by calculating $M = \dfrac{X}{G_{a.r}(p)}$.

Secure Random Number Generator Using Chaos Rössler Attractor

This section presents the implementation of a secure random number generator using a chaos Rössler attractor. The application has five files (`encryption.h`, `generation.h`, `encryption.c`, `generation.c`, and `chaos_random.cpp`). To compile and run the application, the following command needs to run in the terminal.

```
g++ -std=c++2b -o test.exe chaos_random.cpp generation.c generation.h encryption.c encryption.h
```

Next, let's examine each file and discuss the most important lines of code.

Figure 14-4 shows the execution of the program and the numbers generated for each of the keys. As you saw in the Rössler attractor section, three fixed points need to be computed to solve the equations. Each fixed point is represented by a cryptographic key (e.g., key 1, key 2, key 3).

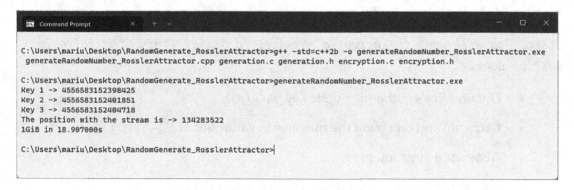

Figure 14-4. *Secure random number generator*

Listing 14-4 shows the header file (`encryption.h`) for defining the signature function for the encryption process, `encryption`. The function has three input values.

- `struct generation *g` is a struct object used for generating the mantissa, exponent, and sign for obtaining the normalization form of a real number. The definition of the struct can be found within file `generation.h` (see Listing 16-2).

340

- uint8_t *buffer is the buffer with the data used for encryption.

- size_t length is the length of the buffer.

Listing 14-4. Header file encryption.h

```
#ifndef ENCRYPTION_H
#define ENCRYPTION_H

#include "generation.h"
#include <stddef.h>

void encryption (struct generation *g, uint8_t *buffer, size_t length);

#endif
```

Listing 14-5 is the implementation of the generation.h header file, which contains definitions for the Rössler attractor (see ROSSLER(x,n)), the coordinates (A, B, and C), integral approximation (APPROXIMATION constant), removing noise constant (REMOVE_NOISE), two functions for generating the initialization on 16 and 32 bits (generation_initialization and generation 32), describing the normalization of real numbers as a union and struct type, containing for the double numbers the mantisa, exponent and sign (realbits union), and a struct (generation struct) for the generation process, which contains three variables that represent the fixed points (e.g., x, y, and z).

Listing 14-5. Header file generation.h

```
#ifndef GENERATION_H
#define GENERATION_H

#include <inttypes.h>
#include <math.h>

// the Rossler (ROL) attractor definition for plane (x,n)
#define ROSSLER(x,n) ((x = ((x << n) | (x >> (32 - n)))))

// the attractor variables (coordinates) - for this example Rossler
is chosen
#define A_Coordinate 0.5273
#define B_Coordinate 3
#define C_Coordinate 6
```

```c
// constant for integral approximation as a step size
#define APPROXIMATION 0.01

// constant used for removing the initial noise
#define REMOVE_NOISE 64

void generation_initialization(struct generation *g, uint64_t k[3]);
uint32_t generation32(struct generation *g);

// the normalization form of a real number
union realbits
{
    double d;
    struct
    {
        uint64_t mantisa: 52;
        uint64_t exponent: 11;
        uint64_t sign: 1;
    } rb;
};

struct generation
{
    union realbits x, y, z;
};

#endif
```

Listing 14-6 is the implementation function for the encryption process. Note that the encryption.c source file includes header files in Listing 14-4 and Listing 14-5. As mentioned, encryption is performed using a generation struct that contains three fixed points, a buffer used to hold the content to be encrypted, and its length. The function is self-explanatory, and its main idea is based on the position within the data stream. The number of calls plays an important role, as is using the length of the buffer and shifting to the right with 2 bits.

Listing 14-6. File encryption.c

```c
#include "encryption.h"
#include "generation.h"

#include <iostream>

using namespace std;

// performing the encryption operation
void encryption(struct generation *g, uint8_t *buffer, size_t length)
{
        uint32_t position_in_stream;
        size_t number_of_calls = length >> 2;
        size_t l_neighbor = length & 3;
        uint8_t *temporary = (uint8_t *)&position_in_stream;

        for(size_t index = 0; index < number_of_calls; ++index)
          {
                position_in_stream = generation32(g);
                buffer[(index<<2)]   ^= temporary[0];
                buffer[(index<<2)+1] ^= temporary[1];
                buffer[(index<<2)+2] ^= temporary[2];
                buffer[(index<<2)+3] ^= temporary[3];
        }

        if(l_neighbor!= 0)
        {
                position_in_stream = generation32(g);
                for(size_t index = 0; index < l_neighbor; ++index)
                    buffer[(number_of_calls<<2)+index] ^=
                    temporary[index];
        }

        std::cout<<"The position with the stream is -> "<<position_in_
        stream<<endl;
}
```

Listing 14-7 is the implementation for different operations necessary for generating the fixed points and performing the initialization process. Here, we also use the ROSSLER function defined in Listing 14-5.

Listing 14-7. File generation.c

```
#include "generation.h"

static void initialization(struct generation *gen, double initValueX,
double initValueY, double initValueZ)
{
    gen->x.d = initValueX;
    gen->y.d = initValueY;
    gen->z.d = initValueZ;
}

static void perform_iteration(struct generation *gen)
{
    gen->x.d = gen->x.d + APPROXIMATION * (-gen->y.d - gen->z.d);
    gen->y.d = gen->y.d + APPROXIMATION * (gen->x.d + A_Coordinate *
    gen->y.d);
    gen->z.d = gen->z.d + APPROXIMATION * (B_Coordinate + gen->z.d *
    (gen->x.d - C_Coordinate));
}

void generation_initialization(struct generation *gen, uint64_t
keyValue[3])
{
    initialization(gen,
                (double)keyValue[0] / 9007199254740992,
                (double)keyValue[1] / 8674747684896687,
                (double)keyValue[2] / 6758675765879568);

    for(uint8_t index = 0; index < REMOVE_NOISE - 1; ++index)
                perform_iteration(gen);
}
```

```
uint32_t generation32(struct generation *gen)
{
     uint32_t message[6];
     message[0] = (uint32_t)(gen->x.rb.mantisa >> 32);
     message[1] = (uint32_t)(gen->x.rb.mantisa);
     message[2] = (uint32_t)(gen->y.rb.mantisa >> 32);
     message[3] = (uint32_t)(gen->y.rb.mantisa);
     message[4] = (uint32_t)(gen->z.rb.mantisa >> 32);
     message[5] = (uint32_t)(gen->z.rb.mantisa);
     perform_iteration(gen);

     message[0] += message[1];
     message[2] += message[3];
     message[4] += message[5];

     for(uint8_t index = 0; index < 4; ++index)
     {
               ROSSLER(message[0],7); ROSSLER(message[3],13);
               message[5] ^= (message[4] + message[3]);
               message[1] ^= (message[2] + message[0]);
               message[2] = message[2] ^ message[0] ^ message[5];
               message[4] = message[4] ^ message[3] ^ message[1];
     }

     message[2] += message[4];
     return message[2];
}
```

Listing 14-8 is the implementation of the main program. It is necessary to specify that the path to the file that contains random numbers (similar to urandom in the Unix OS) has to be adjusted accordingly for reader confusion. The line where the path has to be modified is shown in bold as follows.

```
if((folder = open("D:/Apps C++/Chapter 14 - Chaos-based Cryptography/
ChaosSecureRandomNumberGenerator/dev/urandom", O_RDONLY)) == -1)
```

Listing 14-8. Main Program

```
#include "encryption.h"
#include "generation.h"

#include <fcntl.h>
#include <stdlib.h>
#include <stdio.h>
#include <string.h>
#include <unistd.h>
#include <windows.h>
#include <time.h>
#include <inttypes.h>
#include <iostream>

using namespace std;

const size_t MESSAGE_LENGTH = 2000000000;

uint64_t generateStringOfBytes()
{
        int folder = 0;
        ssize_t resourceFile = 0;
        uint64_t buffer = 0;

            if((folder = open("C:/Users/mariu/Desktop/RandomGenerate_
            RosslerAttractor/urandom ", O_RDONLY)) == -1)
                exit(-1);

            if((resourceFile = read(folder, &buffer, sizeof buffer)) < 0)
                exit(-1);

            buffer &= ((1ULL << 53) - 1);
        close(folder);
        return buffer;
}
```

```
int main(void)
{
        struct generation gen;
        uint64_t key[3] = {generateStringOfBytes()+rand()%3000, generate
        StringOfBytes()+rand()%5000, generateStringOfBytes()+rand()%8000};
            cout<<"Key 1 -> "<<key[0]<<endl;
            cout<<"Key 2 -> "<<key[1]<<endl;
            cout<<"Key 3 -> "<<key[2]<<endl;

        // generate 1GiB of 1s
        uint8_t *message = (uint8_t*)malloc(MESSAGE_LENGTH);
        memset(message, 1, MESSAGE_LENGTH);

        // perform encryption
        generation_initialization(&gen, key);

        clock_t s = clock();

        encryption(&gen, message, MESSAGE_LENGTH);
        clock_t e = clock();
        double spent = (double)(e - s) / CLOCKS_PER_SEC;
        printf("1GiB in %lfs\n", spent);

        free(message);
}
```

Encrypt and Decrypt Using Chaos and Fractals

This section discusses and implements a solution for encryption/decryption operations using chaos and fractals notions.

Listing 14-9 declares the main functions that deal with processing the representation of starting points and performing the projections for axes x and y.

One of the most challenging operations and tasks to achieve when using fractals and chaotic systems is to identify the path and the main root (see function identifyFirstRoot()).

The code in Listing 14-9 and 14-10 is self-explanatory and contains the necessary notes to be fully understood. Figure 14-5 shows the execution of the application.

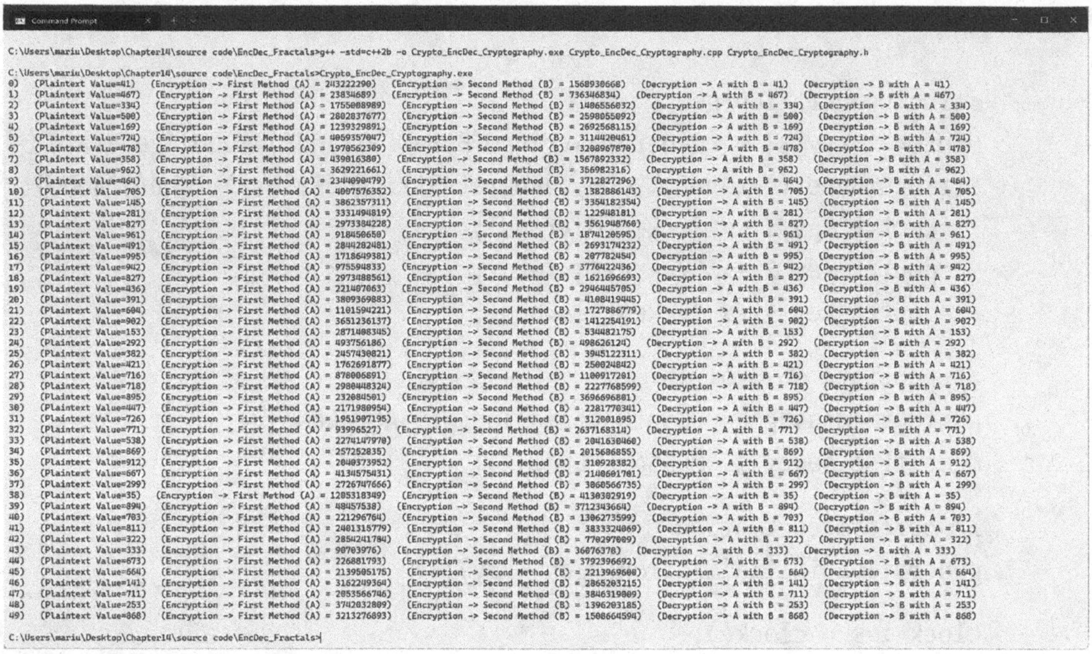

Figure 14-5. *Execution of the encryption/decryption process*

The following command must be entered in the terminal to run the program.

```
g++ -o test.exe Crypto_EncDec_Cryptography.cpp Crypto_EncDec_Cryptography.h
```

Listing 14-9. Header file Crypto_EncDec_Cryptography.h

```cpp
#ifndef CRYPTOCIPHERFRACTALS_H_
#define CRYPTOCIPHERFRACTALS_H_

#include <climits>
#include <assert.h>
#include <math.h>

class CryptoFractalCipher
{
    // point C = (x, y) - the representation in the xOy system of point C
    double c_xCoordinatePoint, c_yCoordinatePoint;

    // point Z = (x,y) - the representation in the xOy system of point Z
    double z_xCoordinatePoint, z_yCoordinatePoint; //Zx,Zy;
```

```
// get the sign of a double number
inline double getSign(double number)
{
     // in case that d is less than 0, return -1.0, making the
     number negative
     // contrary make the number positive
     if (number<0)
         return(-1.0);
     else
         return(1.0);
};

// Value 'yValue' will be projected over an integer matrix or grid.
// We have chosen this for achieving the scaling goal and
performing tests.
// The projection process is a matter of personal choice, any
other idea or
// solution can be implemented by reader.
inline unsigned int PerformProjectionFor_Y(double yValue)
{
     unsigned long q;
     const double scale=(32768.0/2.0);
     const double offset=(32768.0);

     // do the projection as a positive integerproject to
     positive integer
     q=(yValue*scale)+offset;

     //getting the LSB (least significant bit)
     q&=1;
     return q;
}

// Value 'xValue' will be projected over an integer matrix or grid.
// We have chosen this for achieving the scaling goal and
performing tests.
```

```
        // The projection process is a matter of personal choice, any
        other idea or
        // solution can be implemented by reader.
        inline unsigned int PerformProjectionFor_X(double xValue)
        {
                // used for storing the decomposition value
                double decompositionValue;

                // power value (exponent)
                int n;

                // with frexp() we will decompose the double point (xValue) as
                // argument into a normalized fraction and an integral power
                decompositionValue = frexp (xValue , &n);

                // with ldexp() we will return the result of multiplying
                'decompositionValue'
                // (the significand) with 2 and raised to the power '51'
                (exponent)
                decompositionValue = ldexp(decompositionValue,51);

                // Test if the difference between 'decompositionValue' and
                // floor(decompositionValue) is less than 0.5
                // if yes return '1', otherwise '0'.
                // With floor() we round 'decompositionValue', returning
                the largest
                // integral value that is not greater than 'decompositionValue'
                return (((decompositionValue-floor(decompositionVal
                ue))<0.5)?1:0);
        }

        inline void identifyFirstRoot()
        {
                /* Zn*Zn=Z(n+1)-c */
                z_xCoordinatePoint=z_xCoordinatePoint-c_xCoordinatePoint;
                z_yCoordinatePoint=z_yCoordinatePoint-c_yCoordinatePoint;

                // r represents the length of the vector from the origin to
                the point
```

```
// r = |z| = sqrt(x*x+y*y)
double r;

// the new point z = (x,y)
double z_xNewPointValue, z_yNewPointValue; //NewZx, NewZy
r=sqrt(z_xCoordinatePoint*z_xCoordinatePoint+z_
yCoordinatePoint*z_yCoordinatePoint);

// the below code sequence represents the implementation of the
algorithm presented in [16], from page 361 to 362.
// case 1: z>0
if (z_xCoordinatePoint>0)
{
    z_xNewPointValue=sqrt(0.5*(z_xCoordinatePoint+r));
    z_yNewPointValue=z_yCoordinatePoint/(2*z_xNewPointValue);
}

// for cases when z<0 and z=0
else
{
    // case 2: z<0
    if (z_xCoordinatePoint<0)
    {
        z_yNewPointValue=getSign(z_
        yCoordinatePoint)*sqrt(0.5*(-z_
        xCoordinatePoint+r));
        z_xNewPointValue=z_yCoordinatePoint/(2*z_
        yNewPointValue);
    }

    //case 3: z=0
    else
    {
        z_xNewPointValue=sqrt(0.5*fabs(z_
        yCoordinatePoint));
        if (z_xNewPointValue>0) z_yNewPointValue=z_
        yCoordinatePoint/(2*z_xNewPointValue);
```

```
                            else z_yNewPointValue=0;
               }
          };
          // end of the implementation

          // the values for x and y coordinates
          z_xCoordinatePoint=z_xNewPointValue;
          z_yCoordinatePoint=z_yNewPointValue;
     };

public:
     //obtains the encrypted value
     unsigned int getEncryptedMessageA(unsigned int plainValue);
     unsigned int getDecryptedMessageB(unsigned int encryptedValue);
     unsigned int getEncryptedMessageC(unsigned int stream);
     unsigned int getDecryptedMessageD(unsigned int stream);

     // gets the single bit
     unsigned int bitCodeEncryptedMessageA(unsigned int plainValue);
     unsigned int bitCodeDecryptedMessageB(unsigned int encryptedValue);
     unsigned int bitCodeEncryptedMessageC(unsigned int stream);
     unsigned int bitCodeDecryptedMessageD(unsigned int stream);

     // constructor
     CryptoFractalCipher(double cx,double cy);

     // destructor
     virtual ~CryptoFractalCipher();
};
#endif
```

Listing 14-10. Main Program

```
#include "FractalCipherCrypto.h"
#include <climits>
#include <assert.h>
#include <math.h>
#include <iostream>
```

```cpp
using namespace std;

// implementing bitCodeEncryptedMessageA from FractalCipherCrypto.h file
unsigned int CryptoFractalCipher::bitCodeEncryptedMessageA(unsigned int
bit_from_plaintext)
{
    // below we will create a cryptographic stream from the clear stream
    int crypto_bit=0;
    {
        identifyFirstRoot();

        // quadratic value
        unsigned long quadraticValue = PerformProjectionFor_X(z_
        yCoordinatePoint);

        // Do the encoding process and provide the
        // cryptographic stream from the clear stream
        // Variables used:
        //          - iV: the input value
        //          - oV: the output value
        //          - rV: the route value in the expansion of the fractal
        unsigned int iV, oV, rV;
        {
                unsigned int result1, result2, result3;
            iV=(bit_from_plaintext) & 1;

                // obtained from the iteration of the quadratic value
            result1=quadraticValue;

                // input value
            result2=iV;

                // we will copy the bits if it is set in one operand but
                // not both
            result3=result1^result2;

                // the final output value
            oV=result3;
```

```
                    // the route value that needs to be followed within the
                    expansion of the fractal
                    rV=result2;
        }
        crypto_bit=(oV);

        if ((rV) != 0)
        {
            // use the route on the second root point
            z_xCoordinatePoint=-z_xCoordinatePoint;
            z_yCoordinatePoint=-z_yCoordinatePoint;
        }
    }
    return crypto_bit;
};
unsigned int CryptoFractalCipher::bitCodeDecryptedMessageB(unsigned int
bit_from_encoding)
{
    // decode the clear value from the cryptographic stream
    int bit_from_plaintext=0;
    {
        identifyFirstRoot();

        // computing the quadratic value
        unsigned long quadraticValue = PerformProjectionFor_X(z_
        yCoordinatePoint);

        // decoding process for obtaining the clearstream from the
        cryptographic stream
        // Variables used:
        //          - iV: the input value
        //          - oV: the output value
        //          - rV: the route value in the expansion of the fractal
        unsigned int iV, oV, rV;
        {
            unsigned int result1,result2,result3;
```

```
        iV=(bit_from_encoding) & 1;

            // obtained from the iteration of the quadratic value
        result1=quadraticValue & 1;

            // input value
        result3=iV;

            // we will copy the bits if it is set in one operand but
            not both
        result2=result1^result3;

            // the output value
        oV=result2;

            // the route value that needs to be followed within the
            expansion of the fractal
        rV=result2;
    }
    bit_from_plaintext=(oV);

    if ((rV) != 0)
    {
            // use the route on the second root point
        z_xCoordinatePoint=-z_xCoordinatePoint;
        z_yCoordinatePoint=-z_yCoordinatePoint;
    }
    }
    return bit_from_plaintext;
};

unsigned int CryptoFractalCipher::bitCodeEncryptedMessageC(unsigned int
bit_from_stream)
{
    // generate the cryptographic stream from the clear stream
    int bit_from_coding=0;
    {
        identifyFirstRoot();
```

```
    unsigned long quadraticValueForY = PerformProjectionFor_X(z_
    yCoordinatePoint);
    unsigned long quadraticValueForX = PerformProjectionFor_X(z_
    xCoordinatePoint);

    // encoding process
    unsigned int iV, oV, rV;

    {   unsigned int result1, result2, result3, result4;
        iV=(bit_from_stream);

            // from the iteration of the 'y' quadratic
        result1=quadraticValueForY;

            // from the iteration of the 'x' quadratic
        result2=quadraticValueForX;

            // we will copy the bits if it is set in one operand but
            not both
        result3=iV^result1;
        result4=iV^result2;

            // the output value
        oV=result3;
        rV=result4; // branch in path to follow through IIM
    }
    bit_from_coding=(oV);

    if ((rV) != 0)
    {
            // use the route on the second root point
        z_xCoordinatePoint=-z_xCoordinatePoint;
        z_yCoordinatePoint=-z_yCoordinatePoint;
    }
}
return bit_from_coding;
};
```

```cpp
unsigned int CryptoFractalCipher::bitCodeDecryptedMessageD(unsigned int
bit_from_stream)
{
    // generate the cryptographic stream from the clear stream
    int bit_from_coding = 0;
    {
        identifyFirstRoot();

        unsigned long quadraticValueForY = PerformProjectionFor_X(z_
        yCoordinatePoint);
        unsigned long quadraticValueForX = PerformProjectionFor_X(z_
        xCoordinatePoint);

        // encoding process
        unsigned int iV, oV, rV;
        {
                unsigned int result1, result2, result3, result4;
            iV=(bit_from_stream) & 1;

                // from iterated quadratic y and x
            result1=quadraticValueForY;
            result2=quadraticValueForX;

                // we will copy the bits if it is set in one operand but
                not both
            result3=iV^result1;
            result4=result3^result2;

                // output value
            oV=result3;

                // the route value
            rV=result4;
        }
        bit_from_coding=(oV);

        if ((rV) != 0)
        {   //take branch to second root
            z_xCoordinatePoint=-z_xCoordinatePoint;
```

```
            z_yCoordinatePoint=-z_yCoordinatePoint;
        }
    }
    return bit_from_coding;
};

unsigned int CryptoFractalCipher::getEncryptedMessageA(unsigned int
clearstream)
{
    // for creating the cryptographic stream from the clear stream
    int cryptographic_stream=0;

    for (int iterationIndex=0; iterationIndex<32; (iterationIndex++))
    {
        // encoding process for obtaining cryptographic stream from
        clear stream
        unsigned int iV,oV;
        iV=(clearstream>>iterationIndex) & 1;
        oV=bitCodeEncryptedMessageA(iV);
        cryptographic_stream+=((oV)<<iterationIndex);
    }

    return cryptographic_stream;
};

unsigned int CryptoFractalCipher::getDecryptedMessageB(unsigned int
cryptstream)
{
    // for creating the clear stream from the cryptographic stream
    int clearstream=0;

    for (int iterationIndex=0; iterationIndex<32; (iterationIndex++))
    {
        // decoding process for obtaining the clear stream from the
        cryptographic stream
        unsigned int iV, oV;

        iV=(cryptstream>>iterationIndex) & 1;
```

```
        oV=bitCodeDecryptedMessageB(iV);
        clearstream+=((oV)<<iterationIndex);
    }
    return clearstream;
};

unsigned int CryptoFractalCipher::getEncryptedMessageC(unsigned int stream)
{
    // construct the cryptographic stream from clear stream
    // cv - the code value
    int cV=0;

    for (int iterationIndex=0; iterationIndex<32; (iterationIndex++))
    {
        // encoding process for generating the cryptographic stream from
        // clear stream
        unsigned int iV,oV;
        iV=(stream>>iterationIndex) & 1;
        oV=bitCodeEncryptedMessageC(iV);
        cV+=((oV)<<iterationIndex);
    }
    return cV;
};

unsigned int CryptoFractalCipher::getDecryptedMessageD(unsigned int stream)
{
    // construct the cryptographic stream from clear stream
    // cv - the code value
    int cV=0;

    for (int iterationIndex=0; iterationIndex<32; (iterationIndex++))
    {
        // encoding process for generating the cryptographic stream from
        // clear stream
        unsigned int iV, oV;
        iV=(stream>>iterationIndex) & 1;
        oV=bitCodeDecryptedMessageD(iV);
```

```
        cV+=((oV)<<iterationIndex);
    }
    return cV;
};

CryptoFractalCipher::CryptoFractalCipher(double cPoint_xValue,double
cPoint_yValue)
{
    c_xCoordinatePoint=cPoint_xValue;
    c_yCoordinatePoint=cPoint_yValue;

    z_xCoordinatePoint=z_yCoordinatePoint=0;

     // use repeating digits as for encoding process using PI value with
     the goal to find a fixed point
     for(int index=0; index<32; index++)
            getEncryptedMessageA(3141592653);
}

// destructor implementation - only if it is necessary
CryptoFractalCipher::~CryptoFractalCipher()
{
}

int main(void)
{
     // CryptoKey_rValue and CryptoKey_iValue are represented as
     // a point that is situated near the boundary of the Mandelbrot set
     // the real value of a complex number (cryptographic key)
     double CryptoKey_rValue=-0.687;

     // the imaginary unit
     double CryptoKey_iValue=-0.312;

     unsigned int Plaintext[50];
     unsigned int EncryptionA[50];
     unsigned int EncryptionB[50];
     unsigned int DecryptionOfAWithB[50];
```

```
unsigned int DecryptionOfBWithA[50];

// generate random message
for (int i=0;i<50;i++)
     Plaintext[i]=rand()%1000;

// perform message encoding using getEncryptedMessageA for A
{
     CryptoFractalCipher CFC(CryptoKey_rValue, CryptoKey_iValue);
     for (int i=0;i<50;i++)
        EncryptionA[i]=CFC.getEncryptedMessageA(Plaintext[i]);
}

// perform message encoding using getDecryptedMessageB for B
{
     CryptoFractalCipher CFC(CryptoKey_rValue, CryptoKey_iValue);
     for (int i=0;i<50;i++)
        EncryptionB[i]=CFC.getDecryptedMessageB(Plaintext[i]);
}

// perform message decoding A with B using getDecryptedMessageB for B
{
     CryptoFractalCipher CFC(CryptoKey_rValue, CryptoKey_iValue);
     for (int i=0;i<50;i++)
        DecryptionOfAWithB[i]=CFC.getDecryptedMessageB(Encryp
        tionA[i]);
}
// perform message decoding B with A using getDecryptedMessageB for A
{
     CryptoFractalCipher CFC(CryptoKey_rValue, CryptoKey_iValue);
     for (int i=0;i<50;i++)
        DecryptionOfBWithA[i]=CFC.getEncryptedMessageA(Encryp
        tionB[i]);
}
```

```
// display the output value and the results
for (int i=0;i<50;i++)
{
        cout
        <<i
        <<")    (Plaintext Value="<<Plaintext[i]
        <<")    (Encryption -> First Method (A) = "<<EncryptionA[i]
        <<")    (Encryption -> Second Method (B) = "<<EncryptionB[i]
        <<")    (Decryption -> A with B = "<<DecryptionOfAWithB[i]
        <<")    (Decryption -> B with A = "<<DecryptionOfBWithA[i]
        <<")"<<endl;
};
}
```

Conclusion

This chapter discussed a different approach to cryptography, which is chaos-based cryptography. The new cryptographic algorithms use the chaos function to generate new cryptographic primitives differently from what we have used.

In this chapter, you learned the following.

- How chaos-based cryptography primitives are built and what makes them different from normal cryptographic primitives

- How the chaos system is designed for text encryption and image encryption

How can we implement a cryptographic system based on number generators using a chaos approach and performing encryption and decryption operations with a chaos system and fractals?

Chaos-based cryptography is one of the most secure encryption methods currently available. It is based on the principles of chaos theory, which states that even simple systems can produce unpredictable results. With chaos-based cryptography, the encrypted message is fed into a mathematical formula that generates a seemingly random sequence of numbers. This sequence cannot be reproduced or replayed, which makes it almost impossible to crack. Each time the formula is used to generate a sequence, the output is different, making it impossible for hackers to crack the code.

This is because the mathematical formula is constantly changing, which makes it almost impossible for someone to identify a pattern.

Strong mathematical formulas are the backbone of chaos-based cryptography, which makes it highly secure. It is nearly impossible to crack the code as the sequence of numbers is generated by complex mathematical formulas that are constantly changing. This means that hackers can never predict the next sequence of numbers, which makes it virtually impossible to crack the code. It also makes it easier to share code, as it can be broken down into simple mathematical formulas. Chaos-based cryptography is a one-way encryption method, which means that it is almost impossible to decrypt the message once it has been encrypted. This is in stark contrast to traditional encryption methods, which can be deciphered if the correct formula is applied. This makes it the perfect method for protecting sensitive information, such as financial data or health records. It is also one of the quickest methods for generating a sequence of seemingly random numbers. Most chaos-based cryptographic systems are based on computer software, meaning they can quickly produce a sequence of random numbers. This can be helpful if you need to send encrypted data to a client or colleague quickly.

References

[1].   Robert Matthews, On the derivation of a "chaotic" encryption algorithm. Cryptologia 13, no. 1 (1989): 29–42.

[2].   L. Kocarev, "Chaos-based cryptography: a brief overview," *IEEE Circuits and Systems Magazine*, vol. 1, no. 3, pp. 6–21, 2001.

[3].   Ali Soleymani, Zulkarnain Md Ali, and Md Jan Nordin," A Survey on Principal Aspects of Secure Image Transmission", World Academy of Science, Engineering and Technology 66 2012, pp. 247–254.

[4].   D. Chattopadhyay1, M. K. Mandal1 and D. Nandi," Symmetric key chaotic image encryption using circle map", *Indian Journal of Science and Technology*, vol. 4, no. 5 (May 2011) ISSN: 0974- 6846, pp. 593–599.

[5].   Anto Steffi, Dipesh Sharma," Modified Algorithm of Encryption and Decryption of Images using Chaotic Mapping," International Journal of Science and Research (IJSR), India Online ISSN: 2319-7064, vol. 2 Issue 2, February 2013.

[6].   K. S. Sankaran and B. V. S. Krishna, "A New Chaotic Algorithm for Image Encryption and Decryption of Digital Color Images," *International Journal of Information and Education Technology*, pp. 137–141, 2011.

[7].   Somaya Al-Maadeed, Afnan Al-Ali, and Turki Abdalla, "A New Chaos-Based Image-Encryption and Compression Algorithm," Hindawi Publishing Corporation, Journal of Electrical and Computer Engineering, vol. 2012, Article ID 179693.

[8].   Hazem Mohammad Al-Najjar, Asem Mohammad AL-Najjar, "Image Encryption Algorithm Based on Logistic Map and Pixel Mapping Table."

[9].   Sodeif Ahadpour, Yaser Sadra," A Chaos-based Image Encryption Scheme using Chaotic Coupled Map Lattices.

[10].   Kamlesh Gupta1, Sanjay Silakari, "New Approach for Fast Color Image Encryption Using Chaotic Map", Journal of Information Security, 2011, 2, 139–150.

[11].   Chong Fu, Jun-jie Chen, Hao Zou, Wei-hong Meng, Yong-feng Zhan, and Ya-wen," A chaos-based digital image encryption scheme with an improved diffusion strategy", Optical Society of America, 30 January 2012/Vol. 20, No. 3/ pp 2363–2378.

[12].   D. Chattopadhyay1, M. K. Mandal1 and D. Nandi," Symmetric key chaotic image encryption using circle map", Indian Journal of Science and Technology, vol. 4 no. 5 (May 2011) pp. 593–599.

[13].   Shima Ramesh Maniyath1 and Supriya M, "An Uncompressed Image Encryption Algorithm Based on DNA Sequences," Computer Science & Information Technology (CS & IT), CCSEA 2011, CS & IT 02, pp. 258–270.

[14].   Murillo-Escobar, Miguel. (2014). A novel symmetric text encryption algorithm based on logistic map.

[15].   L. Kocarev and S. Lian, Chaos-based cryptography: theory, algorithms and applications, vol. 354. Springer Science & Business Media, 2011.

[16].   H.-O. Peitgen, H. Jürgens, and D. Saupe, Fractals for the classroom: part two: complex systems and mandelbrot set. Springer Science & Business Media, 2012.

CHAPTER 15

Big Data Cryptography

Big data is the process through which data sets of large size (in a range from a few terabytes to many zettabytes) are extracted, manipulated, and analyzed. These techniques differ from traditional techniques, as big data contain different types of data, structured or unstructured (video or audio files, images, texts, etc.).

Big data cryptography is related to data confidentiality, integrity, and authenticity, representing an important topic that needs to be treated with attention because each business has its computational model and software and hardware architecture. The cryptographic methods related to big data differ from the traditional ones because encryption systems and their related concepts are defined differently regarding the policies for access control, cloud infrastructure, and storage management and techniques.

This chapter describes a general computational model applicable in a cloud environment that enables and eases the implementation of big data analytics applications. The following presents a classification of the nodes from cloud architecture and their purpose in the big data analytics process. The types of nodes are based on the classification from [1] to [3], and the notations are extended slightly to define the following types of nodes.

- I_N represents an *input node* that handles the raw data used in the application. These types of nodes collect data from front-end users or data that are read or captured from different sensors (such as fingerprint readers, holographic signatures, and temperature sensors).

- C_N represents the *computational node* that has a significant role in the computational processes of the application. The basis of these nodes is the ingestion nodes, which are included in a computational node. In this classification, the ingestion nodes are called *consuming nodes*. Their purpose is to scan and refine the input data, meaning data preparation for the analysis process and its passing to the enrichment nodes, where the data is processed.

M. I. Mihailescu and S. L. Nita, *Pro Cryptography and Cryptanalysis with C++23*, https://doi.org/10.1007/978-1-4842-9450-5_15

- S_N represents the *storage node,* which has a significant role in applying cryptographic techniques to the data. Its purpose is to store the data involved in the computational processes applied between end users and third parties. These nodes store the input data and the output data for data analysis.

- R_N represents the *result node,* which receives the output of some processes being executed. It can make automatic decisions based on the output of the analysis process, or it can send the output to a specific client.

Figure 15-1 shows an example of cloud architecture for big data analytics that includes the elements described. The model can represent a pattern that describes a wide range of big data applications. Note the set of one or more nodes of type H, as follows H^+, where $H \in \{I_N, C_N, S_N, R_N\}$.

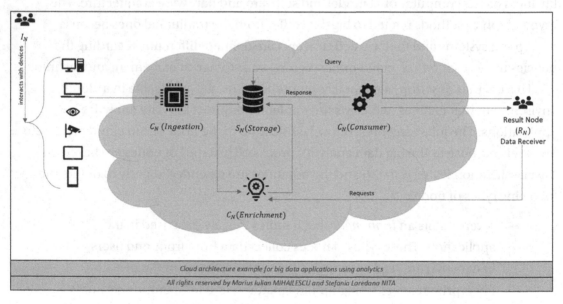

Figure 15-1. *Example of cloud architecture with big data analytics applications*

Figure 15-1 presents a general cloud model that can be applied to an application that requires data sets. In the example, node I_N initiates the process of collecting reference data sets. The input nodes send data sequences to the $C_N(Ingestion)$ node. In the ingestion node, the data sequences are used by the computation process for which they are parsed. The output data is organized in files or databases when the computational process ends. In the next step, the files and databases are sent to the storage nodes S_N (*Storage*). From time to time, the enrichment nodes C_N(*Enrichment*) perform computation over the data from the storage nodes. Mostly, these processes are performed offline and update the associated metadata according to the user's needs. In our example, R_N (*Data Receiver*) represents a user that correlates the data set with the reference data set.

Cloud computing presents many security challenges for the data that move through and between its components. To follow the path of protection techniques from cloud cryptography, you need to consider three main security goals, known as the CIA triad.

- **Confidentiality**. The data referred strictly to the input and output of the computations needs to be kept secret to be protected against untrusted parties, malicious parties, or other potential adversaries.

- **Integrity**. Any changes that are not authorized over the data must be immediately detected. Note that nefarious actors do not always cause integrity issues; software bugs or data transfer issues can also cause them. Regardless, the integrity of the data must be enforced.

- **Availability**. The data owners and the authorized data users can access the data and computational resources.

Let's focus on availability because it is one of the most important cloud characteristics but excludes cryptographic means. For this reason, confidentiality and integrity must be involved as much as possible in the cloud. Big data architecture and the way data is stored are also relevant for security and cryptographic purposes. The way in which confidentiality and integrity are achieved is dictated by how the cloud is deployed. When developing an application, it is important to establish from the beginning which participant controls which component of the cloud and the degree of trust awarded to each component and participant. Based on this, consider the following types of clouds.

- A **trusted cloud** is deployed by governmental organizations or institutions, and it is isolated completely from anything from outside (networks or adversaries). Public cloud vendors such as Microsoft have regions for US government users. The Microsoft Jedi contract with the Department of Defense covers such use and Azure cloud resources authorized for secret and top-secret use. The files of the users or clients are stored completely in a safe without being worried about corruption or stealing. However, there are situations in which some of the nodes are exposed as they may communicate with external networks. Therefore, in these situations, malware or insiders can affect these nodes.

- A **semitrusted cloud** does not specifically state if the cloud can be trusted entirely or if it cannot be trusted at all. However, a good practice is to mention the components under control and provide solutions to monitor adversarial activities at a given time.

- In an **untrusted cloud**, the nodes within the cloud or the cloud itself are not trusted at all by the data users. This scenario means no security guarantees are given, including confidentiality or integrity of the data or computations. In such situations, the cloud user should have its own solutions and protection mechanisms to ensure (a level of) confidentiality and integrity. Mainly, the untrusted cloud is associated with the public cloud model.

After these short descriptions of the cloud and big data elements, let's discuss the *cryptographic techniques* that can be applied in these environments. Cryptographic techniques are very complex to ensure the security of big data and cloud computing. It is difficult to apply them in real-life scenarios without dedicated third-party software libraries or experienced professionals.

This chapter focuses on three cryptographic techniques that can be used to achieve the security of big data applications deployed in the cloud environment.

- Homomorphic encryption (see Chapter 12)

- Verifiable computation represents the first objective of this chapter

- Secure multiparty computation (MPC)

The following are other cryptographic techniques that can be applied successfully to achieve security in cloud computing and big data.

- Functional encryption (FE)

- Identity-based encryption (IE)

- Attribute-based encryption (AE)

The next section presents a promising technique that can be applied in real environments. Many encryption schemes that fall in the FE, IE, or AE types are very difficult to use in practice because many works are based on theoretical assumptions. Most do not consider the requirements and demands of business or industry applications. Between theory and practice, it is a long path that theoreticians and practitioners must go through together and collaborate closely to find solutions for security concerns in real environments and to find and solve the existing problems and gaps.

Verifiable Computation

A *verifiable computation* or *verifiable computing* refers to machines' capability of unloading the computation quantity of some function(s) to others; for example, clients with untrusted status, while the results are being verified continuously (see Figure 15-2).

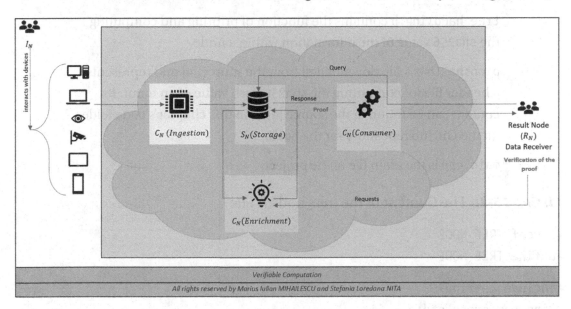

Figure 15-2. *Verifiable computation example. The cloud nodes do not have any trust level for integrity protection*

An important application of verifiable computation for real environments is Merkle trees, whose purpose is to check the integrity of the data. In big data, the Merkle tree represents a data structure used to validate the integrity of different properties for items, data, rows, sets of data, and so on. A very useful characteristic of Merkle trees is that they can be used on large amounts of data (in the context of big data). In this direction, improvements have been made by combining algorithms of verifiable computation with Merkle trees.

The example in Listings 15-1 to 15-6 presents a scenario in which a Merkle tree is self-balancing. The example is just a simulation (see Figure 15-1), and deploying the application in a real big data environment requires proper adjustments.

The code is organized in the following files.

- `tree_node.cpp` contains the implementation of the methods used with a tree node.

- `tree_node.h` contains the definitions of a tree node.

- `tree.cpp` contains the implementations of the methods used with a tree.

- `tree.h` contains the definitions of a tree.

- `tree_handling.h` contains the function of printing and computing the `sha256` value of the information within a node.

- `picosha2.h` is a file downloaded from the source [4] and represents a header file for computing the sha256 hash value of an input. Its content can be found in the source [4] or in this chapter's code folder on the GitHub repository for the book.

- `main.cpp` is the main file of the project.

Listing 15-1. The Content of the tree_node.h File

```
#ifndef TREE_NODE
#define TREE_NODE

#include <string>
using namespace std;

// define the node of the Merkle tree
struct tree_node
{
    string hash_value;      // the hash value
    tree_node *l_neighbor; // the left neighbor
    tree_node *r_neighbor; // the right neighbor
```

```
// instantiates the hash value within the node
// see the corresponding .cpp file
    tree_node(string value);
};

#endif
```

Listing 15-2. The Content of the tree_node.cpp File

```
#include "tree_node.h"
using namespace std;

// assigns the input hash value to the hash_value attribute of the tree node
tree_node::tree_node(string value)
{
    this->hash_value = value;
}
```

Listing 15-3. The Content of the tree.h File

```
#ifndef MERKLE_TREE
#define MERKLE_TREE

#include "tree_node.h"
#include "picosha2.h"
#include "tree_handling.h"
#include <vector>
#include <string>

using namespace std;

struct merkle_tree {
    tree_node* tree_root;
    merkle_tree(vector<tree_node*> vector_nodes);
    ~merkle_tree();
    void print_merkle_tree(tree_node *node, int index);
    void delete_merkle_tree(tree_node *node);
};

#endif
```

Listing 15-4. The Content of the tree.cpp File

```cpp
#include <iostream>
#include <iomanip>
#include "tree.h"

using namespace std;

merkle_tree::merkle_tree(vector<tree_node*> vector_nodes)
{
    vector<tree_node*> aux_nodes;
    while (vector_nodes.size() != 1)
    {
        print_hash_values(vector_nodes);
        for (int i = 0, n = 0; i < vector_nodes.size(); i = i + 2, n++) {
            if (i != vector_nodes.size() - 1) // check if there is a
            neighbour block
            {
                // merges the neighbor nodes and computes the hash value
                of the new node aux_nodes.push_back(new tree_node
                (compute_sha256(vector_nodes[i]->hash_value + vector_
                nodes[i + 1]->hash_value)));
                // link the new node with the left neighbor and the right
                neighbor
                aux_nodes[n]->l_neighbor = vector_nodes[i];
                aux_nodes[n]->r_neighbor = vector_nodes[i + 1];
            } else
            {
                aux_nodes.push_back(vector_nodes[i]);
            }
        }
        cout << "\n";
        vector_nodes = aux_nodes;
        aux_nodes.clear();
    }
```

```cpp
    // picks the first node as the root of the tree
    this->tree_root = vector_nodes[0];
}

merkle_tree::~merkle_tree()
{
    delete_merkle_tree(tree_root);
    cout << "The tree was deleted." << endl;
}

void merkle_tree::print_merkle_tree(tree_node *node, int index)
{
    if (node) {
        if (node->l_neighbor) {
            print_merkle_tree(node->l_neighbor, index + 4);
        }
        if (node->r_neighbor) {
            print_merkle_tree(node->r_neighbor, index + 4);
        }
        if (index) {
            cout << setw(index) << ' ';
        }
        cout << node->hash_value[0] << "\n ";
    }
}

void merkle_tree::delete_merkle_tree(tree_node *node)
{
    if (node) {
        delete_merkle_tree(node->l_neighbor);
        delete_merkle_tree(node->r_neighbor);
        node = NULL;
        delete node;
    }
}
```

Listing 15-5. The Content of the tree_handling.h File

```
#ifndef TREE_MISC
#define TREE_MISC

#include <iostream>
#include <string>
#include "tree.h"
#include "picosha2.h"

using namespace std;

// computes the hash value of the input using SHA256
inline string compute_sha256(string input_string)
{
    string hash_string = picosha2::hash256_hex_string(input_string);
    return hash_string;
}

// display the hash values from a vector of tree nodes
inline void print_hash_values(vector<tree_node*> vector_nodes)
{
    for (int i = 0; i < vector_nodes.size(); i++)
    {
        cout << vector_nodes[i]->hash_value << endl;
    }
}

#endif
```

Listing 15-6. The Content of the main.cpp File

```
#include <iostream>
#include "tree.h"

using namespace std;

int main() {
    vector<tree_node*> nodes_set;
```

```
    //create sample data
    nodes_set.push_back(new tree_node(compute_sha256("Merkle ")));
    nodes_set.push_back(new tree_node(compute_sha256("tree ")));
    nodes_set.push_back(new tree_node(compute_sha256("node ")));
    nodes_set.push_back(new tree_node(compute_sha256("example.")));
    nodes_set.push_back(new tree_node(compute_sha256("This is an example of
    merkle tree.")));

    // initialize leaves
    for (unsigned int i = 0; i < nodes_set.size(); i++) {
        nodes_set[i]->l_neighbor = NULL;
        nodes_set[i]->r_neighbor = NULL;
    }

    merkle_tree *hash_tree = new merkle_tree(nodes_set);
    std::cout << hash_tree->tree_root->hash_value << std::endl;
    hash_tree->print_merkle_tree(hash_tree->tree_root, 0);

    for (int k = 0; k < nodes_set.size(); k++) {
        delete nodes_set[k];
    }

    delete hash_tree;

    return 0;
}
```

To compile the code, the following command is used in the terminal.

```
g++ -o result.exe main.cpp tree_node.cpp tree_node.h tree.cpp tree.h
```

To run the code, type the following in the terminal.

```
result
```

The result is shown in Figure 15-3.

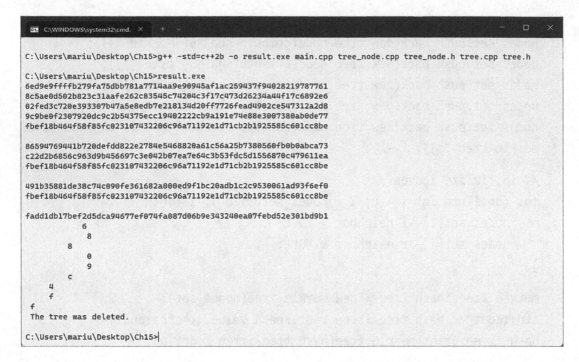

Figure 15-3. *The result of the implementation of a self-balancing Merkle tree*

Conclusion

This chapter discussed the importance of applications deployed in the big data environment and how security can be achieved through cryptographic mechanisms, such as verifiable computation. For more about cloud computing, big data, and their security, consult any of the works in this chapter's "References" section.

In this chapter, you learned the following.

- The main concepts of security from a cloud and big data environment

- How to put in practice complex cryptographic primitives and protocols, such as verifiable computation

Before implementing big data cryptography, businesses need to choose the right data set. Companies should select data sets that are large enough to provide robust protection without being overly complex. Data sets that are too small can be decrypted using traditional cryptography, making them less effective against malicious actors. Once the right data set has been selected, businesses can use it to create a secure communication channel among various parties. This communication channel can be used to share data and perform transactions, helping to protect sensitive information. Companies can also use big data cryptography to authenticate users and prove their identities without passwords. Finally, businesses can use big data cryptography to automate certain security protocols, making the process more efficient and secure. With the right data set, big data cryptography can provide businesses a wide range of advantages, helping protect their sensitive information and keep customers safe.

Using big data cryptography to secure sensitive information can be challenging since it requires expertise in various fields, including data science and cryptography. Companies can simplify implementation by partnering with an outside vendor specializing in big data cryptography. These vendors can help businesses implement big data cryptography and manage the data sets, providing more time for other business operations. Big data cryptography vendors can also provide companies many benefits, including more robust security and scalability. Companies can use big data cryptography to create unique digital signatures for every user and transaction on their network, authenticating users without passwords. This can help businesses prevent fraud while also improving scalability by reducing the need for resource-intensive authentication processes.

References

[1].   Laud P., Pankova A. (2014) Verifiable Computation in Multiparty Protocols with Honest Majority. In: Chow S.S.M., Liu J.K., Hui L.C.K., Yiu S.M. (eds) Provable Security. ProvSec 2014. Lecture Notes in Computer Science, vol. 8782. Springer, Cham.

[2].   Bogdanov D., Laur S., Talviste R. (2014) A Practical Analysis of Oblivious Sorting Algorithms for Secure Multiparty Computation. In: Bernsmed K., Fischer-Hübner S. (eds) Secure IT Systems. NordSec 2014. Lecture Notes in Computer Science, vol. 8788. Springer, Cham.

[3].   D. Bogdanov, L. Kamm, S. Laur, and P. Pruulmann-Vengerfeldt, "Secure multi-party data analysis: End user validation and practical experiments," 2014.

[4].   PicoSHA2 - a C++ SHA256 hash generator, https://github.com/okdshin/PicoSHA2

[5].   B. ÖzÇakmak, A. Özbİlen, U. YavanoǦlu, and K. Cİn, "Neural and Quantum Cryptography in Big Data: A Review," 2019 IEEE International Conference on Big Data (Big Data), Los Angeles, CA, USA, 2019, pp. 2413-2417, doi: 10.1109/BigData47090.2019.9006238.

[6].   S. Yakoubov, V. Gadepally, N. Schear, E. Shen, and A. Yerukhimovich, "A survey of cryptographic approaches to securing big-data analytics in the cloud," *2014 IEEE High-Performance Extreme Computing Conference (HPEC)*, Waltham, MA, 2014, pp. 1–6, doi: 10.1109/HPEC.2014.7040943.

[7].   Nita S.L., Mihailescu M.I. (2020) A Searchable Encryption Scheme Based on Elliptic Curves. In: Barolli L., Amato F., Moscato F., Enokido T., Takizawa M. (eds) Web, Artificial Intelligence and Network Applications. WAINA 2020. Advances in Intelligent Systems and Computing, vol. 1150. Springer, Cham.

[8].   Nita S.L., Mihailescu M.I. (2019) A Hybrid Searchable Encryption Scheme for Cloud Computing. In: Lanet JL., Toma C. (eds) Innovative Security Solutions for Information Technology and Communications. SECITC 2018. Lecture Notes in Computer Science, vol. 11359. Springer, Cham

[9].   V. C. Pau and M. I. Mihailescu, "Internet of Things and its role in biometrics technologies and eLearning applications," *2015 13th International Conference on Engineering of Modern Electric Systems (EMES)*, Oradea, 2015, pp. 1–4, doi: 10.1109/EMES.2015.7158430.

[10].   S. L. Nita and M. I. Mihailescu, "On Artificial Neural Network used in Cloud Computing Security - A Survey," *2018 10th International Conference on Electronics, Computers and Artificial Intelligence (ECAI)*, Iasi, Romania, 2018, pp. 1–6, doi: 10.1109/ECAI.2018.8679086.

[11].   Marius Iulian Mihailescu, Stefania Loredana Nita and Ciprian Racuciu, "Authentication protocol based on searchable encryption and multiparty computation with applicability for earth sciences," Scientific Bulletin of Naval Academy, vol. XXIII 2020, pp. 221–230, doi: 10.21279/1454-864X-20-I1-030.

[12].   Marius Iulian Mihailescu, Stefania Loredana Nita and Ciprian Racuciu, "Multilevel access using searchable symmetric encryption with applicability for earth sciences," Scientific Bulletin of Naval Academy, vol. XXIII 2020, pp. 221–230, doi: 10.21279/1454-864X-20-I1-030.

[13]. Stefania Loredana Nita, Marius Iulian Mihailescu and Ciprian Racuciu, "Secure Document Search in Cloud Computing using MapReduce", Scientific Bulletin of Naval Academy, vol. XXIII 2020, pp. 221–230, doi: 10.21279/1454-864X-20-I1-030.

[14]. RSA Extension for Big Data Analytics. Available online: `https://www.rsa.com/en-us/company/news/rsa-extends-big-data-analytics-to-help-organizations-identify`. Last accessed: 2.3.2023

[15]. Claudio Orlandi, "Is Multiparty Computation Any Good In Practice?" Available online: `https://www.cs.au.dk/~orlandi/icassp-draft.pdf`. Last accessed: 2.3.2023

CHAPTER 16

Cloud Computing Cryptography

Cryptography in cloud computing has gained much attention recently and is becoming one of the most important topics in cryptography and cybersecurity. It represents a key point in designing and implementing a secure cloud application. Cryptography for cloud computing involves complex encryption methods and techniques for securing the data stored and used in the cloud environment.

Cloud computing cryptography is a powerful tool that helps protect data stored in the cloud. As the amount of data stored in the cloud continues to grow, the importance of understanding cloud computing cryptography and its benefits becomes increasingly clear. Whether you're a business owner, data scientist, or simply a curious individual, learning about cloud computing cryptography is a great way to ensure your data's security and privacy. This article covers the basics of cloud computing cryptography, including what it is, why it is important, and how it can be used to protect data. You should better understand how cloud computing cryptography works and how it can benefit you.

Cloud computing cryptography is the practice of encrypting data before transmitting it to an external service, storing it in an encrypted form, and then decrypting it when retrieving it. This ensures that no one else can access your data, even people with access to the service's servers. Cloud computing cryptography ensures that your data is private, secure, and free from malicious attacks. When you use cloud computing cryptography, your data is encrypted whenever it leaves your computer. Only the intended recipient can access the data, even if they have physical or administrative access to the service's servers. This is important because cloud services often cannot guarantee the same level of security that you can achieve on your own computer. When stored in the cloud, data is often stored in multiple locations around the world. This can occasionally make it

381

M. I. Mihailescu and S. L. Nita, *Pro Cryptography and Cryptanalysis with C++23*,
https://doi.org/10.1007/978-1-4842-9450-5_16

challenging to retrieve a single piece of data. Cloud computing cryptography helps solve this problem by allowing you to retrieve the entire file and then selectively decrypt only the pieces you need.

Cloud computing cryptography offers many benefits, including data privacy and security, scalability, and cost-effectiveness. Data privacy and security are key concerns for many individuals and businesses that store data in the cloud. Using cloud computing cryptography, you can ensure that your data remains private and secure, even if the cloud service is breached. If you depend on a service's reputation to protect your data, however, you are vulnerable to even the smallest breach. Cloud computing cryptography also allows you to scale your operations quickly and easily by adding additional servers, which can help reduce the cost of scaling. You can also use hybrid cloud environments, which let you tap into private and public cloud services to meet your needs. If you have specific types of data, such as highly sensitive information that requires compliance certification, you may need to use specific types of cloud computing cryptography to meet compliance requirements.

There are three main types of cloud computing cryptography:

- **End-to-end encryption** occurs only between two devices communicating. As such, it does not involve the cloud service at all. This is useful when you want to keep your data private between two users but do not want to store it on a remote server.

- **Full-disk encryption** (FDE) encrypts all data on the drive where the operating system resides. FDE is a good choice to protect your data while it is at rest (stored on a device). It isn't recommended when your data is in motion, such as accessing it through a cloud service.

- **Cloud encryption** protects data at rest and in motion. It's the best way to protect your data in the cloud.

Cloud computing cryptography is used in many applications, including communication, data storage, and processing.

- **Communication applications**. When you use cloud communication applications, such as a cloud-based team collaboration tool, you need to ensure that all communication is encrypted to protect your data from eavesdropping.

- **Data storage applications.** When you store data remotely, you want to make sure it's encrypted to protect it from malicious attacks.

- **Processing applications**. When you use cloud computing for processing applications, such as a machine learning applications, you must protect your data from malicious attacks.

The most obvious advantage of cloud computing cryptography is that it ensures that your data is secure and private. Without encryption, your data can easily be intercepted and used maliciously. Data encryption also allows you to share data with others, even if they don't have access to your computer. This is particularly helpful in a team environment where data collaboration is key to success. Without encryption, you might need to give others your password, increasing your risk of getting hacked. Another advantage of cloud computing cryptography is that it allows data to be stored in multiple locations around the world, which helps prevent localized outages from affecting data. On the other hand, cloud computing cryptography can be challenging to set up and use, depending on your situation. If you aren't sure how to implement it, you might want to hire a data expert to help you.

Implementing cloud computing cryptography can be a complex and difficult process for inexperienced users. It is highly recommended that you enlist the help of a professional data expert if you aren't familiar with cryptography in general. Here are a few steps you can take to get started.

1. **Choose a cloud computing system.** Many different cloud computing systems are available, ranging from public providers to private cloud systems you install yourself. You need to determine which system is best for your company and then find a provider that offers a service with the features you need.

2. **Determine where you will store your data.** Depending on your system, you can choose where you store your data. If so, you must decide whether storing your data in a private or public location is better.

3. **Understand what level of security you need.** Some services offer different levels of encryption, so you'll need to determine what level of security is best for your company.

4. **Implement encryption.** This step is specific to your cloud computing system, so you'll need to consult the documentation to learn how to do this step.

There are three main types of cloud technologies that organizations adopt rapidly: infrastructure as a service (IaaS), platform as a service (PaaS), and software as a service (SaaS). The cloud brings many benefits, such as efficiency, flexibility, and scalability, which reduce overall client costs. Due to its complexity and types (public, private, or hybrid cloud), cloud computing inherits the security concerns of its components. Source [1] provides a great categorization of cloud computing security issues. The security concerns may occur on the following levels: the communication level (deals with the shared infrastructures, virtual networks their configurations), the architectural level (deals with virtualization, data storage, applications, APIs, and access control), and even contractual and legal level (it deals, for example, with service level agreements).

In addition to searchable encryption (see Chapter 11) and homomorphic encryption (see Chapter 12) to secure the cloud, the following cryptographic techniques and mechanisms are also receiving important attention from research communities and industry.

- **Structured encryption** (STE) encrypts data structures. An STE scheme uses a token based on which the data structure is queried. A special example of STE is searchable encryption. Recall that searchable encryption allows searching for a keyword through data in an encrypted format. Another example of the STE is using graph structures that can be utilized to encrypt the databases. It is a good example in the cloud context, where the applications deal with large databases for analytics and statistics.

- **Functional encryption** (FE) is a generalization of public-key encryption in which the private key owner allows an authorized user to learn a function of the encrypted ciphertext. There are more types of functional encryption: predicate encryption (PE), identity-based encryption (IBE), attribute-based encryption (ABE), hidden vector encryption (HVE), and inner product predicate.

- **Private information retrieval** (PIR) is a protocol a client uses for retrieving an element within a database without letting the rest of the database users know what element the client retrieved.

A Practical Example

For this example, imagine the following cloud scenario: an organization manages its administrative relationship with its clients using a cloud messaging platform. For example, the organization sends notifications to their clients about their products or available updates, and the clients can contact and send messages to the organization through the platform. Therefore, the cloud platform is included in the SaaS category. To ensure that the authorized receiver reads the messages, the messages should be encrypted from both sides—the organization and the clients. Both should use trusted parties for the key generation used in encryption and decryption.

To simulate this example, let's use a trusted party OpenSSL [1], which generates the public and the private keys for the RSA algorithm, keys used in our encryption technique. The source [1] provides documentation for different distributions, links to source code from the GitHub repository, examples, and more. Note that this example was created on a Windows platform. You do not download the source code for compiling yourself and then using it; instead, download directly the compiled version of the OpenSSL library that can be found at source [3] (or it can be downloaded from the GitHub repository of this book). Once the archive is downloaded, extract it, and the OpenSSL folder should be on the C:\ partition. Furthermore, open a terminal and change the current directory to the bin folder from the OpenSSL parent folder, then type **openssl** and press Enter (see Figure 16-1).

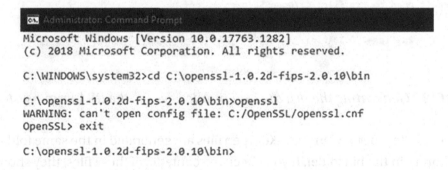

```
Administrator: Command Prompt
Microsoft Windows [Version 10.0.17763.1282]
(c) 2018 Microsoft Corporation. All rights reserved.

C:\WINDOWS\system32>cd C:\openssl-1.0.2d-fips-2.0.10\bin

C:\openssl-1.0.2d-fips-2.0.10\bin>openssl
WARNING: can't open config file: C:/OpenSSL/openssl.cnf
OpenSSL> exit

C:\openssl-1.0.2d-fips-2.0.10\bin>
```

Figure 16-1. *Checking openssl command*

The message warning shows that the OpenSSL package was used, and it is not compiled on the computer. For this section, you do not need to compile and install OpenSSL by yourself, but the complete guide for installing it can be found in the source [2].

The next step is to generate the private key for the RSA algorithm. To do this, type the following command in the terminal and check Figure 16-2.

```
C:\openssl-1.0.2d-fips-2.0.10\bin>openssl genrsa -out privateKey.pem 2048
```

The preceding command says that the `openssl` library generates the RSA private key (`genrsa`) in the output file `privateKey.pem`, which has a length of 2048 bits.

Then, to generate the public key, type the following command in the terminal and check Figure 16-2.

```
C:\openssl-1.0.2d-fips-2.0.10\bin>openssl rsa -in privateKey.pem -pubout >
publicKey.pem
```

The preceding command says that the `openssl` library is used to compute the public key of the cryptosystem saved in the output file `publicKey.pem`, based on the input file (private key) `privateKey.pem`.

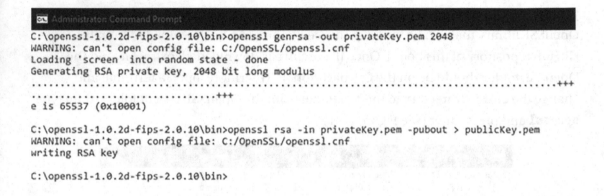

Figure 16-2. *Generating the private and public keys for the RSA cryptosystem*

The `publicKey.pem` and `privateKey.pem` files are generated in the same folder as the `openssl` library in the bin folder. If you check the contents of these files, they should look like what's in Figures 16-3a and 16-3b.

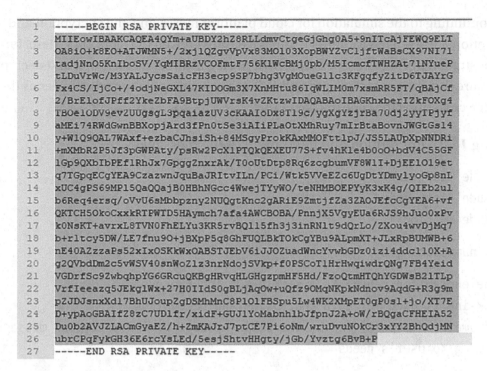

Figure 16-3a. *The private key*

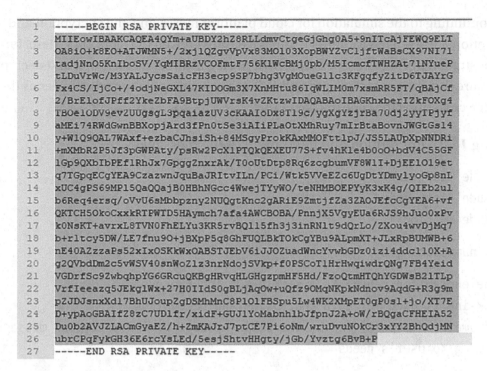

Figure 16-3b. *The public key*

Figures 16-3a and 16-3b show the difference between the keys' lengths. Furthermore, to use them in a C++ program, read them from the .pem files. First, you need to remove the extra messages from the files that are not part of the keys, namely, the first and last lines of the files. Make sure that no additional space characters are left at the end of the keys to avoid altering them.

Continuing to the simulation for cloud platform messaging, the encryption and decryption are given in Listing 16-1, and the output is given in Figure 16-4. Here, for demonstration purposes, use a simple XOR-ing algorithm for encryption and decryption. Make sure that the publicKey.pem and privateKey.pem are in the same folder as the .cpp file containing the code in Listing 16-1.

Listing 16-1. Encryption and decryption of the messages

```cpp
#include <iostream>
#include <fstream>
#include <string>

using namespace std;

// the encryption scheme is a simple XOR-ing process
// XOR-ing is used for both encryption and decryption
// parameter "message" can be the plain message or the encrypted message,
according to user's needs

string xor_string(string message, string key)
{
    string out_message(message);
    unsigned int key_len(key.length()), message_len(message.
    length()), pos(0);

    for(unsigned int index = 0; index < message_len; index++)
    {
        out_message[index] = message[index] ^ key[pos];
        if(++pos == key_len){ pos = 0; }
    }
    return out_message;
}

int main()
{
    // read the message to be encrypted from the console

    string plain_text;

    cout<<"Enter the message: ";
```

```
    getline (cin, plain_text);

    // the public key is read from the .pem corresponding file
    string row1;
    string public_key = "";
    ifstream public_key_file ("publicKey.pem");

    if (public_key_file.is_open())
    {
        while (getline (public_key_file, row1) )
        {
            public_key += row1;
        }
        public_key_file.close();
    }

    // to check that the public key is read correctly, it is displayed on
    the console
    cout<<"Public key:"<<endl<<public_key<<endl<<endl;

    // the private key is read from the.pem corresponding file
    string row2;
    string private_key = "";
    ifstream private_key_file ("privateKey.pem");
    if (private_key_file.is_open())
    {
        while (getline (private_key_file, row2) )
        {
            private_key += row2;
        }
        private_key_file.close();
    }

 // to check that the public key is read correctly, it is deposited on
the console
    cout<<"Private key:"<<endl<<private_key<<endl<<endl;
```

```
// the encryption of the plain message is stored into encrypted_message
string encrypted_text = xor_string(plain_text, public_key);

cout << endl << "The encryption of the message is: " << endl <<
encrypted_text << endl;

// to decrypt the message, the receiver should proceed with some steps
// 1. the receiver should xor his/her private key with his/her
public key
string xor_keys = xor_string(public_key, private_key);

// 2. the receiver should xor the encrypted text with the result
from step 1
string xor_result = xor_string(encrypted_text, xor_keys);

// 3. The decryption is made by xor-ing the result from the previous
step with the private key
string decrypted_message = xor_string(xor_result, private_key);

cout << endl << "The decryption of the message is:  << endl <<
decrypted_message << endl;

return 0;
}
```

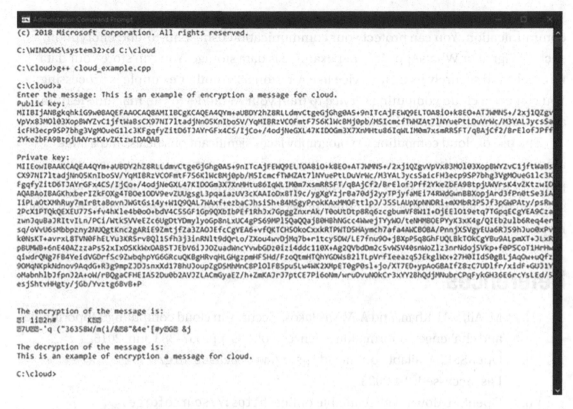

Figure 16-4. *The output of Listing 16-1*

In Figure 16-4, the private and public keys do not contain the extra messages initially included in the .pem files.

Conclusion

This chapter has mentioned the most important cryptographic primitives that can be cloud environments. You learned about cloud computing security issues and the advanced concepts and cryptographic primitives that can be applied to prevent these issues.

There are many useful resources related to cloud computing cryptography online. If you're interested in learning more about cryptography, the National Institute of Standards and Technology (NIST) has a great resource to get you started. To learn more about cloud computing cryptography, you can start with Amazon Web Services (AWS) and Google Cloud Platform, two of the most popular cloud computing providers.

Cloud computing cryptography is used in many ways. One example is communication. You can protect your communication using end-to-end encryption, such as Signal or WhatsApp. Another example is data storage. You can store your data remotely and securely using a service like Amazon S3. Another example is processing. You can use a cloud computing service to train your AI model to run machine learning algorithms, such as TensorFlow.

The use of cloud computing Cryptography faces significant obstacles, and a large amount of current literature contains multiple theoretical frameworks with no actual practical directions. Except for the standard security policies made available by cloud solution providers, however, this context provides professionals and researchers with strong research directions and the opportunity to develop new ideas for enhancing cloud security.

References

[1].   M. Ali, S. U. Khan, and A. V. Vasilakos, 'Security in cloud computing: Opportunities and challenges', Information Sciences, vol. 305, pp. 357–383, Jun. 2015.

[2].   OpenSSL, Available online: `https://www.openssl.org/`.
        Last accessed: 2.4.2023

[3].   OpenSSL download, Available online: `https://sourceforge.net/projects/openssl/files/openssl-1.0.2d-fips-2.0.10/openssl-1.0.2dfips-2.0.10.zip/download`. Last accessed: 2.4.2023

[4].   R. Chatterjee, S. Roy, and U. Scholar, "Cryptography in Cloud Computing: A Basic Approach to Ensure Security in Cloud", Jul. 2017.

[5].   A. N. Jaber and M. F. B. Zolkipli, "Use of cryptography in cloud computing", in *2013 IEEE International Conference on Control System, Computing and Engineering*, Nov. 2013, pp. 179–184.

[6].   J.P. Kaur, and R. Kaur, "Security issues and use of cryptography in cloud computing", in International Journal of Advanced Research in Computer Science and Software Engineering, 4(7), 2014.

[7].   M. Chase and S. Kamara, "Structured Encryption and Controlled Disclosure", in Advances in Cryptology - ASIACRYPT 2010, M. Abe, Ed., in Lecture Notes in Computer Science. Berlin, Heidelberg: Springer, 2010, pp. 577–594.

[8].   M. Brenner, J. Wiebelitz, G. von Voigt, and M. Smith, "Secret program execution in the cloud applying homomorphic encryption", in 5th IEEE International Conference on Digital Ecosystems and Technologies (IEEE DEST 2011), May 2011, pp. 114–119.

PART III

Pro Cryptanalysis

CHAPTER 17

Starting with Cryptanalysis

Cryptanalysis is concerned with discovering weaknesses in security systems and cryptographic algorithms. The ultimate objective is to discover the true nature of the cryptographic keys or encrypted messages and their nature.

Cryptanalysis is the practice of analyzing and deciphering secret codes and ciphers. Cryptanalysis can be used to gain insight into the security of a system's encryption. It can also retrieve data from encrypted systems, such as bank accounts and online messages. If you have ever wanted to learn more about cryptanalysis, this step-by-step guide is the perfect place to start. Here, you'll get an overview of what cryptanalysis is, what you need to get started, and the resources available to help you understand the basics of this fascinating discipline. Whether you're just curious or want to become an expert in cryptanalysis, this guide will help you get started.

Cryptanalysis can be defined as an activity from two sides: one side is represented by authorized persons, and research and academic institutions represent the second side.

From a legal perspective, *cryptanalysis* is the process that should be conducted by authorized persons, such as professionals (ethical hackers, information security officers, etc.). Any cryptanalysis activity outside the legal framework is known as *hacking,* which covers personal and nonpersonal interests.

From the research/academia side, *cryptanalysis* is the study of methods for obtaining the meaning of encrypted information without access to the secret key. Many different techniques are used in cryptanalysis, including frequency analysis, differential cryptanalysis, and linear cryptanalysis. To begin with cryptanalysis, it is important to have a strong understanding of the mathematical foundations of cryptography, including number theory and abstract algebra. Additionally, having experience with programming and the ability to write code to implement and test cryptanalysis techniques is helpful.

© Marius Iulian Mihailescu and Stefania Loredana Nita 2023
M. I. Mihailescu and S. L. Nita, *Pro Cryptography and Cryptanalysis with C++23*,
https://doi.org/10.1007/978-1-4842-9450-5_17

Some resources for learning about cryptanalysis include books such as *Introduction to Cryptography* by Johannes Buchmann [15] and *Cryptanalysis of Number Theoretic Ciphers* by Samuel S. Wagstaff Jr. [16].

There are many online tutorials and courses available that cover the basics of cryptanalysis. It is also important to keep up with the current research in the field, as new advances and techniques are constantly being developed. Attending conferences and joining online communities of cryptanalysts can be a great way to stay informed and connect with other researchers in the field.

This chapter covers the most important methods and techniques for conducting general and in-depth cryptanalysis. It discusses the necessary baggage of knowledge and tools, such as software tools, methods, cryptanalysis types and algorithms, and penetration-testing platforms.

Conducting cryptanalysis can be a tricky and difficult task to achieve, and many aspects must be taken into consideration before doing it. The situation becomes much easier if you conduct cryptanalysis as a legal entity. If a nonlegal entity conducts cryptanalysis, then you are dealing with a more complex process, and hacking methods are involved, methods covered later in our discussion. Both ways are needed to get our hands dirty. The process of cryptanalysis is time-consuming, and many obstacles and obstructions could occur due to many reasons, such as system complexity, the size of the cryptographic key, hardware platform, or access permissions.

While it's true that cryptanalysis requires a certain degree of skill and practice, this doesn't mean that you need to be a computer scientist to start a career in cryptanalysis. Anyone can learn the basics of cryptanalysis with the right resources and guidance. First and foremost, you'll need a basic understanding of mathematics and computer science. Cryptanalysis is, after all, largely based on algorithms and mathematical concepts. You also need a computer that meets the basic requirements for code-breaking. Ideally, your computer should meet or exceed the minimum system requirements for the code-breaking software you use. To increase productivity during your code-breaking sessions, you may want to invest in some accessories, such as a code-breaking wrist pad or a code-breaking pen.

Cryptanalysis is more exciting and challenging than cryptography. The knowledge that a cryptanalyst needs is very wide and complex. It covers several complex fields divided into three main categories: *informatics (computer science), computer engineering,* and *mathematics.* Let's specify the important disciplines for each of the categories as follows.

- Informatics (computer science)
    - Computer networks
    - Programming languages
    - Databases
    - Operating systems
- Computer engineering and hardware
    - Field-programmable gateway array (FPGA)
    - Programming languages (e.g., VHDL)
    - Development platforms (Xilinx, etc.)
- Mathematics
    - Number theory
    - Algebra
    - Combinatorics
    - Information theory
    - Probability theory
    - Statistical analysis
    - Elliptic curve mathematics
    - Discrete mathematics
    - Calculus, lattices
    - Real analysis
    - Complex analysis
    - Fourier analysis

Part III: Structure

The purpose of the third part of this book is to provide the tools for implementing and providing the methods, algorithms, and implementations of attacks and how to design and implement a cryptanalysis strategy.

The third part of the structure is as follows.

- Chapter 18 introduces a classification of cryptanalysis and techniques used in association with the field of cryptanalysis. The theory of algorithm complexity, statistical-informational analysis, encoding in the absence of perturbation, cryptanalysis of classic ciphers, and cryptanalysis of block ciphers are discussed.

- Chapter 19 discusses linear and differential cryptanalysis. Their importance is vital when cryptanalysis is performed.

- Chapter 20 covers the integral cryptanalytic attack, which can be applied only for block ciphers based on substitution-permutation networks.

- Chapter 21 presents some examples of brute-force and overflow techniques.

- Chapter 22 covers the most important techniques used in text characterization. It discusses the chi-squared statistic; monogram, bigram, and trigram frequency counts; quadgram statistics as a fitness measure; and more.

- Chapter 23 covers some case studies for implementing cryptanalysis methods.

Cryptanalysis Terms

This section introduces a list of cryptanalysis keywords and frequently used terms. Before proceeding further, it is very important to get used to the terms listed in Table 17-1. It helps to have a clear image of the process and who interacts with what.

Table 17-1. *Cryptanalysis Terms*

Keyword/Term	Definition
Black hat hacker	A *black hat hacker* represents someone with bad intentions and breaks a computer system or network. He intends to exploit any security vulnerabilities for financial gain, steal and destroy confidential and private data; shut down systems and websites; corrupt network communication, and so on.
Gray hat hacker	A *gray hat hacker* (aka *cracker*) exploits the weak security points of a computer system or software product to bring those weaknesses to the owner's attention. Compared with a *black hat hacker,* a gray hat hacker acts without malicious intent. The *general goal* of a gray hat is to provide solutions and improve computer systems and network security.
White hat hacker/ethical hacker	A *white hat hacker* is an authorized or certified hacker working for or employed by a government or organization to perform penetration tests and identify loopholes within their systems.
Green hat hacker	A *gray hat hacker* is an amateur person and different from *script kiddies.* Their purpose consists in striving to become full-blown hackers.
Script kiddies	*Script kiddies* are the most dangerous hackers. A *script kiddie* is a person without too many skills who is using some scripts or download tools that other hackers provide. Their goal is to attack network infrastructures and computer systems. They are looking to impress their community or friends.
Blue hat hacker	A *blue hat hacker* is similar to a script kiddie. They are quite beginners in the field of hacking. If someone dares to mock a script kiddie, a blue hat hacker gets revenge. Blue hat hackers get revenge on those who address any challenges to them or challenge them.
Red hat hacker	Also known as eagle-eye hackers, their goal is to stop black hat hackers. The operation mode is different. They are ruthless when they are dealing with malware actions that are coming from black hat hackers. The attacks performed by red hat hackers are very aggressive.
Hacktivist	They are known as online activists. A hacktivist represents a hacker who is part of a group of anonymous hackers who can gain unauthorized access to files stored within government computers and networks, which are served further to social or political parties and groups.

(continued)

Table 17-1. (*continued*)

Keyword/Term	Definition
Malicious insider/ whistleblower	Such a person may be an employee of a company or government institution aware of the illegal actions occurring within the institution. This could lead to personal gain by blackmailing the institution.
State or nation sponsored hackers	This type of hacker is assigned by a government to provide information security services and gain access to confidential information from different countries. For example, consider Stuxnet, the malicious computer worm from 2010, designed and engineered to bring down the Iranian nuclear program. Another example is the US Eighth Air Force, which in 2009 became US Cyber Command.

A Bit of Cryptanalysis History

To have a comprehensive history of cryptanalysis, very challenging and exciting research must be done. This section covers some aspects and moments in time that influenced cryptanalysis as a separate field and how it evolved over different periods of history.

The *history of cryptanalysis* starts with Al-Kindi (801–873), the father of Arabic philosophy. He discovered and developed a method based on the variations in the occurrence frequency of letters. This method helped him to analyze and exploit different ways to break ciphers (e.g., frequency analysis). The work of Al-Kindi was influenced by Al-Khalil's (717–786) work. Al-Khalil wrote the *Book of Cryptographic Messages,* and the work contained permutations and combinations for all possible Arabic words (both types of words, with and without vowels).

One of the best ways to learn the history of cryptanalysis and cryptography is to start and divide the subject into periods of time. It is very important to examine cryptanalysis history with respect to cryptography. The following is a short classification of the cryptanalysis history and focus on the most important achievements of each of the periods.

- **600 B.C.** The Spartans invent scytales to send secret messages during their fights. The device was composed of a leather strap and a wooden stem. To decrypt the message, the wooden stem needed to be a specific size, the size used when the message was encrypted. The message cannot be decrypted if the receiver or malicious person does not have the same wooden stem size.

- **60 B.F.** Julius Caesar sets the basis for the first substitution cipher, which encodes the message using shifting techniques for the characters using three spots: A becomes D, B becomes E, and so on. An implementation of this cipher can be seen in Chapter 2.

- **1474** Cicco Simonetta writes a manual for deciphering encryptions for Latin and Italian text.

- **1523** Blaise de Vigenère introduces his encryption cipher, the Vigenère cipher.

- **1553** Giovan Battista Bellaso sets the basis for the first cipher that uses an encryption key. The encryption key was characterized as a word that was commonly agreed upon by the sender and receiver.

- **1854** Charles Wheatstone creates the Playfair cipher, which encrypts a specific set of letters instead of encrypting letter by letter. This raises the cipher's complexity and, in conclusion, becomes harder to crack.

- **1917** Edward Hebern sets the basis for the first electromechanical machine in which the rotor from the machine is used for an encryption operation. The encryption key is stored within a rotating disc. It has a table used for substitution that is modified with every character that is typed.

- **1918** Arthur Scherbius creates the Enigma machine. The prototype was for commercial purposes. Compared with the Edward Hebern machine, where one rotor is used, the Enigma machine uses several rotors. German Military Intelligence immediately adopts his invention for encoding their transmissions.

- **1932** Marian Rejewski studies the Enigma machine and determined how it operates. Starting in 1939, French and British Intelligence Services, using the information provided by Poland, allowed cryptographers such as Alan Turing to crack the key, which was changing daily. It was crucial to the Allies' victory in World War II.

- **1945** Claude E. Shannon publishes his work entitled *A Mathematical Theory of Cryptography*. This is the point where classic cryptography ended, and modern cryptography appeared.

- **1970** IBM creates a block cipher to protect customer data.

- **1973** The United States adopts the block cipher and sets a national standard called the Data Encryption Standard.

- **1975** Public key cryptography is introduced.

- **1976** The Diffie-Hellamn key exchange is introduced.

- **1982** Richard Feynman introduces a theoretical model of a quantum computer.

- **1997** DES is cracked.

- **1994** Peter Shor introduces an algorithm for quantum computers dedicated to integer factorization.

- **1998** Quantum computing is introduced.

- **2000** Advanced Encryption Standard (AES) officially replaces DES. AES wins an open public competition.

- **2016** IBM launches the IBM Q Experience with a five-qubit quantum processor.

- **2017** Microsoft introduces Q# (Q Sharp), a domain-specific programming language for implementing quantum algorithms and cryptography applications.

This list can continue and be improved, but it includes the main events of history that contribute to the appearance of cryptanalysis, such as concepts, models, and frameworks.

Understanding Cryptanalysis Techniques

To understand the different techniques used in cryptanalysis, it is important to look at the essential elements of cryptography. These include the algorithm, the key, and the ciphertext. Before you can begin analyzing the encrypted information, you must first understand how each component works and how it is used. Algorithm: The algorithm is the mathematical formula used for encryption. The algorithm is normally kept secret, so understanding it is one of the biggest challenges in cryptanalysis.

The *key* is the piece of information used to decrypt the ciphertext. The key may be kept secret or shared openly, depending on the encryption method.

The *ciphertext* is the encrypted message that you want to decrypt. The ciphertext is often represented as a string of numbers or letters.

Cryptanalysis is the process of breaking a cipher or encryption system to access the information it is protecting. Several techniques can be used in cryptanalysis.

- **Brute-force** involves trying every possible key or combination of characters until the correct one is found. A brute-force attack is a cyberattack in which an attacker systematically attempts to guess a website or system's login credentials (e.g., username and password). The attacker uses a script or program to automatically generate and test potential combinations of characters until the correct credentials are found. Brute-force attacks can be used to gain unauthorized access to a wide range of systems, including email accounts, social media accounts, and online banking accounts. They can also be used to crack encryption and decrypt sensitive data.

- **Frequency analysis** involves analyzing the frequency of letters, words, or patterns in the ciphertext to determine the plaintext. Frequency analysis is a method of analyzing and deciphering encrypted messages by determining the frequency of letters or groups of letters in the encoded message. This can be used to identify patterns and reveal clues about the underlying plaintext message, which can then be used to break the encryption. It is one of the oldest and most basic cryptanalysis methods and is often used with other techniques to analyze and decrypt messages.

- **Differential cryptanalysis** involves analyzing the differences between plaintext and ciphertext to determine the key. It is a method used to analyze and evaluate cryptographic systems. The method uses pairs of plaintext and corresponding ciphertext to determine the characteristics of a cryptographic algorithm. By comparing the differences between the plaintext and the ciphertext, researchers can infer information about the key used to encrypt the data and potentially discover weaknesses in the algorithm. Differential cryptanalysis is often used to analyze symmetric-key algorithms, such as the Data Encryption Standard. It breaks cryptographic systems based on the differences between plaintext and ciphertext pairs. It involves studying the differences between pairs of plaintexts and their corresponding ciphertexts and using this information to recover the key or the plaintext.

- **Linear cryptanalysis** is a method of analyzing and breaking cryptographic systems based on linear operations. It involves studying the linear relations between the plaintext, ciphertext, and secret key in a cryptographic system and using this information to recover the key or the plaintext.

Linear and differential cryptanalysis both involve analyzing the linear approximations of the encryption function to determine the key. Both linear and differential cryptanalysis are types of cryptanalytic attacks used to study the inherent weaknesses in a particular cryptographic algorithm or system. They can be used to find the secret key or plaintext.

- **Side-channel attacks** involve analyzing information leaked through a system's physical implementation, such as power consumption or electromagnetic radiation. A side-channel attack is a type of security exploit that relies on information gained from implementing a computer system rather than weaknesses in the system's design or software. These attacks can take many forms, but they all involve extracting secret information, such as cryptographic keys, by analyzing power consumption, electromagnetic emissions, or timing data. This can be done through power, electromagnetic, and timing analyses. These attacks can be difficult to detect and prevent, as they do not rely on exploiting a vulnerability in the system itself but rather on the physical characteristics of the implementation.

- **Social engineering** involves tricking or manipulating people to reveal passwords or other secret information. Social engineering uses psychological manipulation to influence individuals or groups to divulge confidential information or act against their best interests. This can include tactics such as phishing scams, pretexting, baiting, and quid pro quo. Social engineering aims to trick people into giving away sensitive information or access to systems and networks, often to commit fraud or other malicious activities.

- **Algebraic attacks** involve using algebraic properties of the encryption scheme to simplify the problem of finding the key. In general, algebraic attacks refer to a class of methods for breaking cryptographic systems based on solvable mathematical problems using algebraic methods. These attacks often break symmetric-key encryption algorithms, such as those based on RSA or elliptic-curve cryptography (ECC) systems. Examples of algebraic attacks include the algebraic attack on RSA and Coppersmith's attack on elliptic-curve cryptography. These attacks exploit weaknesses in the mathematical structure of the encryption system, such as low-degree polynomials, to recover the private key used for encryption.

Analyzing Cryptographic Algorithms

The first step in cryptanalysis is to analyze the algorithm used in the encryption. During this process, you want to look at several aspects of the algorithm, such as the speed of the algorithm, the algorithm's complexity, and algorithm strength. After you have analyzed the algorithm, you can move on to the next step. You need to create a mathematical model for the algorithm. You'll need to break down the algorithm and find its weak points. While this may sound easy, it can be challenging, especially for complex algorithms.

Cryptographic algorithms can be analyzed in terms of their strengths and weaknesses and suitability for different applications. Strength analysis evaluates the algorithm's resistance to brute-force, cryptanalysis, and side-channel attacks. Weakness analysis includes evaluating the algorithm's susceptibility to attacks such as replay, man-in-the-middle, and chosen-plaintext attacks. Suitability analysis includes evaluating the algorithm's performance and efficiency in terms of computational resources, such as memory and processing power, and the application's specific requirements, such as key size and block size. It is important to note that no cryptographic algorithm can be considered completely secure. Regularly reviewing and updating cryptographic systems is important to ensure they meet the latest security standards.

Cracking Cryptographic Systems

After you have analyzed the algorithm and created a mathematical model for the algorithm, you can move on to the next basic cryptanalysis technique—cracking the cryptographic system. To crack the cryptographic system, you'll first have to find a weakness in the algorithm or encryption method. Once you have identified a weakness, you can use the mathematical model you created earlier to identify a solution. You can then apply the solution to the cryptographic system and retrieve the original data. To find a weakness in the cryptographic system, you must first understand the system's operation. Next, you must look for weaknesses in the cryptographic system. Weaknesses can be found in everything from the encryption method to the key used in the system.

Understanding Cryptographic Systems

Now that you've learned how to crack cryptographic systems, it's time to learn how to understand them. Understanding cryptographic systems requires learning about different types and how they work. There are many different types of cryptographic systems. These types are based on the encryption method used in their system. The most common types of cryptographic systems include the following.

- **Symmetric cryptographic systems** use a single secret key for both encryption and decryption.

- **Asymmetric cryptographic systems** use two keys: a public key and a private key. The public and private keys are mathematically linked, but the public key can be used to decrypt the private key.

Understanding Cryptographic Keys

Now that you understand how cryptographic systems work, it's time to move on to understanding cryptographic keys. Understanding cryptographic keys means learning how cryptographic keys are used in different cryptographic systems. There are several types of cryptographic keys, including private and public keys. Private keys are used in asymmetric cryptographic systems and can be used to decrypt messages encrypted with the public key. Public keys are used in asymmetric cryptographic systems to encrypt messages decrypted with the private key.

Understanding Cryptographic Weaknesses

Now that you understand how to analyze cryptographic systems and keys, it's time to learn how to understand cryptographic weaknesses. Understanding cryptographic weaknesses requires learning about common issues with cryptographic systems and how to avoid them.

There are several common issues with cryptographic systems. These issues include the following.

- **Key reuse** occurs when the same key is used for multiple cryptographic systems. This is a major issue because it makes it easier for attackers to decipher the cryptographic system.

- **Using a short key** is another common cryptographic weakness. Short keys are usually used in symmetric cryptographic systems and are easier to crack than longer keys.

Analyzing Cryptographic Keys

Now that you understand how to analyze cryptographic weaknesses, it's time to learn how to analyze cryptographic keys. You can start by analyzing the length of the key. This can help you identify the type of cryptographic system used. Next, you can analyze the algorithm used for the key. After that, you can analyze the cryptographic key's distribution method. From there, you can examine the key's entropy level and soundness.

Cryptographic keys encrypt and decrypt data to secure it from unauthorized access. There are two main types of keys: symmetric and asymmetric. Symmetric keys use the same key for encryption and decryption, while asymmetric keys use a public key for encryption and a private key for decryption. When analyzing cryptographic keys, it is important to consider their strength, which is determined by the length of the key. The longer the key is, the more secure it is. It is also important to ensure that the keys are generated, stored securely, and regularly updated. It is also important to ensure that the encryption and decryption processes are implemented correctly and resistant to known cryptographic attacks. This can be done by regularly reviewing and testing the cryptographic implementation and staying up-to-date on current cryptographic research. Overall, analyzing cryptographic keys involves assessing the strength of the keys, ensuring secure key generation and storage, and regularly reviewing and testing the encryption and decryption implementation to ensure resistance to known attacks.

Penetration Tools and Frameworks

This section covers several penetration tools and frameworks that can be used successfully in penetration testing, a process that a certified professional conducts.

The tools are divided into two categories: Linux hacking distributions and penetration tools/frameworks.

- Linux hacking distributions

    - **Kali Linux** is the most advanced platform for penetration testing. It has support for different devices and hardware platforms.

    - **BackBox** is a Linux distribution for penetration testing and also includes security assessment.

    - **Parrot Security OS** is new in this sphere. Its target is the cloud environment, which provides online anonymity and a strong encryption system.

    - **BlackArch** specializes in penetration testing platforms and security research. It is built on top of Arch Linux.

    - **Bugtraq** is an impressive platform with forensic and penetration tools.

    - **DEFT** (**D**igital **E**vidence & **F**orensics **T**oolkit) **Linux** is a very important distribution for computer forensics, with the possibility of running it as a live system.

    - **Samurai Web Testing Framework** is a powerful collection of tools that can be used in penetration testing on the web. Notably, it is a virtual machine file supported by VirtualBox and VMWare.

    - **Pentoo Linux** is a distribution intended for security and penetration testing. It is available live and is based on Gentoo.

    - **CAINE** (**C**omputer **A**ided **In**vestigative **E**nvironment) is a powerful distribution with a serious set of system forensics modules and analysis in its own tools.

- **Network Security Toolkit** is a favorite distribution tool and live ISO built on Fedora. It contains a very important set of open source network security tools. It provides a professional web user interface for network and system administration, monitoring tools, and analysis.

- **Fedora Security Spin** is a professional distro for security audits and tests. Various professionals use it in industry and academia.

- **ArchStrike**, also known as ArchAssault, is a distro built on Arch Linux for professionals in the field of security and penetration testers.

- **Cyborg Hawk** contains more than 750 tools for security professionals and performing penetration tests.

- **Matriux** is promising and can be used for penetration tests, ethical hacking, forensic investigations, vulnerability analysis, and more.

- **Weakerth4n is** not well known in hacking or cryptanalysis, but it is an interesting approach for penetration tests and is built using Debian (Squeeze).

- Penetration tools/frameworks (Windows and Linux platforms)

  - **Wireshark** is a well-known packet sniffer. It provides a powerful set of tools for network package and protocol analysis.

  - **Metasploit** is one of the most important frameworks for penetration testing, framework development, and executing exploits.

  - **Nmap** (Network **m**apper) is a powerful network discovery and security auditing tool for security professionals. Its goal is to exploit its targets. For each port you scan, you can see which operating system is installed, what services are running, and what firewall is installed and used.

Conclusion

This chapter discussed cryptanalysis in general and covered the foundation of cryptanalysis, its tools, and working methods. You learned about the following.

- Cryptanalysis

- The main events during history and how the appearance of different ciphers and algorithms influenced the cryptanalysis discipline

- Common terms and how to make the difference between different types of hackers

- Hacking and penetration platform distributions

- The most important frameworks and penetration tools that can be used independently, according to the user flavor/OS platform

References

[1].   Cohen, F (1990). A short history of cryptography. Retrieved May 4, 2009, from Available online: `http://www.all.net/books/ip/Chap2-1.html`. New World Encyclopedia (2007). Last accessed: 28.3.2023

[2].   Cryptography. Retrieved May 4, 2009, Available online: `http://www.newworldencyclopedia.org/entry/Cryptography`. Last accessed 28.3.2023

[3].   M. Pawlan, "Cryptography: the ancient art of secret messages", 1998. Retrieved May 4, 2009, Available online: `http://www.pawlan.com/Monica/crypto/`. Last accessed: 28.3.2023

[4].   J. Rubin, "Vigenere Cipher", 2008. Retrieved May 4, 2009, Available online: `http://www.juliantrubin.com/encyclopedia/mathematics/vigenere_cipher.html`. Last accessed: 28.3.2023

[5].   K. Taylor, "Number theory 1", 2002. Retrieved May 4, 2009, Available online: `http://math.usask.ca/encryption/lessons/lesson00/page1.html`. Last accessed: 28.3.2023

[6].   M. E. Whitman and H. J. Mattord, *Principles of Information Security*. Cengage Learning, 2021.

[7].   S. Singh, *The Code Book: The Secret History of Codes and Code-Breaking*, HarperCollins, 2010.

[8].   A. Ibraham, "Al-Kindi: The origins of cryptology: The Arab contributions," Crypto logia, vol. 16, no 2 (April 1992) pp. 97–126. Available online: `https://www.history.mcs.st-andrews.ac.uk/history/Mathematicians/Al-Kindi.html`. Last accessed: 28.3.2023

[9].   Philosophers: Yaqub Ibn Ishaq al-Kindi Kennedy-Day, K. al-Kindi, Abu Yusuf Ya'qub ibn Ishaq (d.c. 866–73), Available online: `https://www.muslimphilosophy.com/ip/kin.html`. Last accessed: 28.3.2023

[10]. S. H. Nasr and O. Leaman, History of Islamic Philosophy. Routledge, pp. 421–434, 2001.

[11]. Al-Faruqi, R. Ismail R. and L. L. al-Faruqi, Lois Lamya. *Cultural Atlas of Islam.* Macmillan Publishing Company. pp. 305–306, 1986.

[12]. Encyclopaedia Britannica, Inc. Encyclopaedia Britannica. Chicago: William Benton. pp. 352, 1969.

[13]. Buchmann, Johannes A. *Introduction to Cryptography.* Springer US, 2001.

[14]. Wagstaff, Samuel S. *Cryptanalysis of Number Theoretic Ciphers.* CRC Press/ Chapman & Hall, 2003.

CHAPTER 18

Cryptanalysis Attacks and Techniques

This chapter covers the most important and useful cryptanalytic and cryptanalysis standards, validation methods, classification, and operations of cryptanalysis attacks.

The cryptanalysis discipline is very wide, and writing about it requires hundreds and thousands of pages. The following sections go through all the elements necessary for practitioners to use in their daily activities.

Standards

It is very important to understand the importance of standards when conducting cryptanalysis attacks for business purposes only to test the security within an organization.

The following are the main institutes and organizations that provide high standards for cryptography and cryptanalysis methods, frameworks, and algorithms.

- **IEFT Public-Key Infrastructure (X.509)** is the organization that deals with standardizing protocols used on the Internet, which are based on public key systems.

- The **National Institute of Standards and Technologies (NIST)** deals with the elaboration of standards FIPS for the US government.

- The **American National Standards Institute (ANSI)** administers the standards from the private sector.

- **Internet Engineering Task Force (IEFT)** is an international community of networks, operators, and traders of services and researchers that deals with the evolution of Internet architecture.

© Marius Iulian Mihailescu and Stefania Loredana Nita 2023
M. I. Mihailescu and S. L. Nita, *Pro Cryptography and Cryptanalysis with C++23*,
https://doi.org/10.1007/978-1-4842-9450-5_18

- The **Institute of Electrical and Electronical Engineering (IEEE)** elaborates on theories and advanced techniques from different fields, such as electronics, computer sciences, and informatics.

- The **International Organization for Standardization (ISO)** represents a nongovernmental organization with more than 100 countries. Its main purpose is to promote the development of standardization to facilitate the international exchange of services.

FIPS 140-2, FIPS 140-3, and ISO 15408

ISO 15408 represents the evaluation of IT security and is used in the international community as a reference system. The standard defines a set of rules and requirements from the IT field to validate the product's security and cryptographic systems.

FIPS 140-2/140-3 represents a set of guidelines that must be followed to fulfill a specific set of technical requirements exposed on four levels.

You must consider both standards when developing a specification or criteria for a certain application or cryptographic module.

The products that are developed with respect to these standards need to be tested to obtain validation and to confirm that the criteria were followed and respected properly.

Validation of Cryptographic Systems

If the business requires cryptanalysis and cryptography operations to be implemented within the software and communication systems, then cryptographic and cryptanalysis services are needed. Certification organizations authorize these services, including functionalities such as digital signature generation and verification, encryption and decryption, key generation, key distribution, and key exchange.

Validation of cryptographic systems is the process of testing and evaluating the security and functionality of a cryptographic system to ensure that it meets the required security standards and specifications. This process typically includes a combination of theoretical analysis, testing, and implementation reviews to assess the strength and robustness of the system. Validation ensures that the system is secure against known and potential attacks and functions correctly in the intended environment. Some examples of validation techniques include penetration testing, formal verification, and side-channel analysis.

The model shown in Figure 18-1 depicts a general model for testing the security based on cryptographic and cryptanalysis modules.

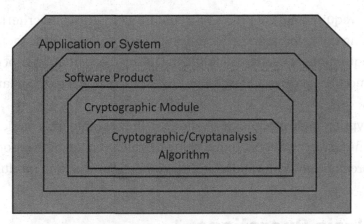

Figure 18-1.   *Verification and testing framework*

A proper testing and verification process requires only two steps—the *cryptographic/ cryptanalysis algorithm* and the *cryptographic module*. For example, if you are developing a cryptographic product or a desktop or web software application, it is necessary for the company/institute/developer to perform the tests and to send them to CMVP[1] (Cryptographic Module Validation Program) to be tested with respect to FIPS 140-2[2] and FIPS 140-3[3].

A *cryptographic module* represents a combination of specialized software and hardware processes. The main advantages of using validated cryptographic and cryptanalysis modules are as follows.

- The modules should satisfy the requirements.

- Making sure that the authorized and technical personnel are informed and instructed within a stand that is commonly agreed upon and that it was tested.

- Ensuring that the final user (end user) is aware that the cryptographic module was verified and tested in accordance with some well-defined security requirements.

---

[1] CMVP, https://csrc.nist.gov/projects/cryptographic-module-validation-program
[2] FIPS 140-2, https://csrc.nist.gov/publications/detail/fips/140/2/final
[3] FIPS 140-3, https://csrc.nist.gov/publications/detail/fips/140/3/final

- A high level of reliability for security needs to be fulfilled to develop similar and specific applications.

The security requirements of FIPS 140-2 contain 11 metrics and criteria for designing and implementing the cryptographic module. For each cryptographic module validated, the following requirements need to be fulfilled. During the validation process, the cryptographic modules receive a mark from 1 to 4, proportional to the guaranteed security level.

Once the cryptographic modules are validated, they contain information such as the name of the manufacturer, address, name of the module, version of the module, type of module (software or hardware), validation date, validation level, and module description.

Cryptanalysis Operations

Designing a cryptographic system must be done using the following simple principles.

- The opponent should not be underestimated.

- A cryptanalyst can evaluate the security of a cryptographic system.

- Before the evaluation of the cryptographic system is performed, the knowledge of the adversary is taken into consideration.

- The secret of the cryptographic system must rely on the key.

- In the process of cryptographic system evaluation, all the elements within the system, such as key distribution and cryptographic content, must be considered.

According to the father of information theory, Claude Elwood Shannon,[4] the following criteria must be considered when performing cryptosystem evaluation.

- One of the winnings of the cryptanalyst is gained once a message is decrypted with success

- The key length and complexity

- The level of complexity of performing an encryption-decryption process

---

[4] Claude Elwood Shannon, https://www.itsoc.org/about/shannon

- The size of the encrypted text in accordance with the text size

- The error propagation method

The basic operations for having a solution for each cryptogram are as follows.

- Finding and determining the language used

- Determining the cryptographic system

- Reconstructing a specific key for a cryptographic system or partial or complete reconstructing for a stream cryptographic system

- Reconstruction of such a system or establishing complete plaintext

Classification of Cryptanalytics Attacks

This section covers the types of attacks on cipher algorithms, cryptographic keys, authentication protocols, protocols and systems, and hardware attacks.

Cryptanalytic attacks can be broadly classified into two categories.

- **Ciphertext-only attacks** involve only the ciphertext and no information about the plaintext or the key used. Examples include frequency analysis, differential cryptanalysis, and linear cryptanalysis.

- **Known-plaintext attacks** involve both the ciphertext and a known plaintext-ciphertext pair. Examples include the chosen-plaintext attack and the related-key attack.

Another way to classify cryptanalytic attacks is based on the amount of computational resources required to carry out the attack.

- **Brute-force attacks** involve trying all possible keys until the correct one is found.

- **Statistical attacks** involve analyzing patterns in the ciphertext to try to determine the key.

- **Side-channel attacks** involve analyzing information leaked during the encryption process, such as power consumption or electromagnetic radiation, to extract information about the key.

Attacks on Cipher Algorithms

Table 18-1. *Attacks on Ciphering Algorithms*

Types of Attacks on Ciphering Algorithms	
Attack Title	**Attack Description**
Known-plaintext attack	The cryptanalyst has an encrypted text, and his correspondent has the plaintext. The goal is to separate the encryption key from the information.
Chosen text attack	The cryptanalyst can indicate the plaintext, which is encrypted. By using this type of attack, the cryptanalyst tries to separate the information of the text from the encryption key, having the possibility to obtain the encryption algorithm or the key through specific methods.
Cipher-cipher text attack	The cryptanalyst holds a plaintext and his correspondent the same text, which is encrypted with two or more different keys.
Divide et Impera attack	The cryptanalyst may realize a series of correlations between different inputs and outputs of the algorithm to separate different inputs in the algorithm, which makes him break the problem into two or more problems that are easy to solve.
Linear syndrome attack	The cryptanalysis method consists of designing and creating a linear equation system specific for the pseudorandom generator and verifying the equation system with the encrypted text, obtaining the plaintext with a high probability.
Consistency linear attack	The cryptanalytic method consists of elaborating a linear equation system specific to the pseudorandom generator starting from an equivalent cryptographic key and verifying the system by the pseudorandom generator with the probability of 1, obtaining in this way the plaintext with a high probability.
Stochastic attack	Also known as a *forecasting attack*, this attack is possible if the generator's output is autocorrelated, the cryptanalyst managing to obtain the output of the pseudorandom generator and the encrypted text as input data. In this way, the clear text is obtained.
Informational linear attack	Also known as a *linear complexity attack*, this attack is possible if there is any chance to equalize the generator with a Fibonacci algorithm. It is possible if the linear complexity is equivalent to the generator is low. With this attack, it is possible to build a similar algorithm and cryptographic key.
Virus attack	This attack is possible if the encryption algorithm is implemented on a vulnerable, unprotected PC.

Attacks on Cryptographic Keys

The most frequent attacks that occur on cryptographic keys are listed in Table 18-2.

Table 18-2. *Attacks on Cryptographic Keys*

	Attacks on Keys
Type	**Description**
Brute-force attack	The attack consists of the exhaustive verification of the keys and passwords, and it is possible if: the encryption key size is small and the encryption key space is small.
Intelligent brute-force attack	The level of key randomness of the encryption key is small (the entropy is small) and allows finding the password, similar to the words from the utilized language.
Backtracking attack	The attack is based on implementing the backtracking type method, which consists of conditions for continuing the search in the desired direction.
Greedy attack	The attack provides the optimal local key, different from the optimal global key.
Dictionary attack	The attack consists of searching for passwords or keys using a dictionary.
Hybrid dictionary attack	This attack is made by modifying the words from the dictionary and initializing the brute-force attack with the help of the words from the dictionary.
Virus attack	This attack is possible if the keys are stored on an unprotected PC.
Password hash attack/ cryptographic key	This attack occurs if the password hash is short or wrong elaborated.
Substitution attack	The original key is substituted by a third party and replaced in the entire network. It can be done with the help of viruses.
Storing encryption key	If this is done incorrectly (together with the encryption data) in plaintext without any physical protection measures or cryptographic software or hardware, it can lead to an attack on the encrypted message.

(continued)

Table 18-2. (*continued*)

Attacks on Keys	
Type	**Description**
Storing old encryption keys	This attack leads to the compromise of the old documents that are encrypted.
Key compromise	Only the documents assigned with that key are compromised if the symmetric key is compromised. If the public key is compromised, which can be found stored on different servers, the attacker can be substituted with the legal owner of the data having a bad and negative impact on the network.
Master keys	Represents different phases in the cryptographic system.
Key lifetime	It is an essential component that excludes the possibility of a successful attack being undetected.

Attacks on Authentication Protocols

The authentication protocols are exposed to different types of attacks. Table 18-3 covers the most important ones, which are frequently used. It is very important to consider that an authentication protocol of a system is very important and vital. Once corrupted, vital information can be exposed, and attackers can gain many personal, financial, and other benefits.

Table 18-3. *Attacks on Authentication Protocols*

Attacks on Authentication Protocols	
Type	**Description**
Attack on the public key	The attack takes place on the signature within the protocol. This is available only for systems with public keys.
Attack on the symmetric algorithm	The attack takes place on the signature within the authentication protocol. This is available only if a symmetric key is used.
Passive attack	The attacker intercepts and monitors the communication on the channel without intervention.
Attack using third person	A third party actively intercepts the communication of two partners within a communication channel.
Fail-stop signature	It is a cryptographic protocol in which the sender can bring evidence of whether his signature was forged.

Authentication protocols are methods used to verify the identity of a user before they are allowed access to a service. Authentication is the process of determining whether a user attempting to access a system is who they claim to be. Authentication protocols can be implemented on both wired and wireless networks and control access to the network and any resources connected to it. Authentication protocols protect against unauthorized access to systems and networks by verifying the user's identity. Each protocol has its own specific way of doing this, but some commonalities exist. The first step is always to ask the user to provide some sort of identifier. This could be a code generated by a token, a passphrase, or a biometric identifier such as a fingerprint or an eye scan. The authentication protocol then examines this identifier to see if it corresponds to the user.

With the ever-growing presence of the Internet and its services, it is essential to understand the various types of attacks on authentication protocols and how to protect your data. Authentication protocols are used to verify the identity of a user before access to a service is granted. However, these protocols are vulnerable to various types of attacks, such as man-in-the-middle attacks, brute-force attacks, and replay attacks. Understanding the different types of attacks and how to prevent them is essential for any individual or organization wanting to protect their data from unauthorized access. With proper knowledge and implementation of security measures, organizations can protect their data from cybercriminals and malicious actors.

The following summarizes several types of attacks on authentication protocols.

- A **password-guessing attack** is a man-in-the-middle attack in which an attacker tries to log into a system using different passwords until they find the correct one. This is done either manually or with automated software. Sometimes this attack is made by recording authentication sessions, trying to log in with a random password, and then replaying the recording to the real server.

- A **brute-force attack** occurs when an attacker tries to enter a system by trying passwords or passphrases until they find the correct one. They do this by trying different combinations of letters, digits, or symbols until they find a code that works. With a network protocol, an attacker could use a software program to log into a system using a large number of passwords until they find the correct one. Brute-force attacks are difficult to protect against. The best way is to set a strong password and try to avoid reusing the same password across multiple systems.

- A **replay attack** occurs when an attacker obtains hold of a valid authentication session and replays it to access a system. This is possible because authentication protocols typically use a single-use session identifier. There are a few ways to protect against replay attacks. One way is to use a Public Key Infrastructure (or PKI) with digital signatures. With PKI, the server and client generate a pair of keys—one public and one private. The server publishes its public key and marks it as "private" so it cannot be accessed. The client looks up the server's public key and uses it to encrypt a message.

- A **man-in-the-middle attack** occurs when an attacker puts themselves between two communicating parties and pretends to be each of them. To do this, the attacker must first obtain control of a network connection and then place themselves between the two parties. When a user tries to log into an account using an authentication protocol, the attacker would first need to obtain control of the network connection between the user and the authentication server. They would then have to forward the user's authentication request to the authentication server and send their own authentication request to the server. When the authentication server responds to the attacker, the attacker forwards the response to the user. Because the attacker is in the middle of the two parties, they can see both sides of the conversation.

Conclusion

Authentication protocols are designed to verify the identity of a user before they are allowed access to a network or system. However, they are vulnerable to different types of attacks, such as man-in-the-middle attacks, brute-force attacks, and replay attacks. It is important to understand the different types of attacks on authentication protocols and how to protect against them. The best ways to protect against these attacks are to use strong passwords, establish two-factor authentication, implement proper encryption, and monitor user activity.

The chapter covered the most important and useful cryptanalytic and cryptanalysis guidelines and methods. After reading, you should now be capable of managing the standards to test and verify the implementation of cryptographic and cryptanalytic algorithms and methods. In summary, you learned about the following.

- Cryptanalysis attack classification

- Cryptanalysis operations

- Standards FIPS 140-2 and FIPS 140-3

- Standard 15408

- Validation of cryptographic systems

References

[1].   A. Atanasiu, *Matematici in criptografie*. Universul Stiintific, 2015. [Romanian Language]

[2].   A. Atanasiu, *Securitatea Informatiei, vol. 1 (Criptografie)*, InfoData, 2007. [Romanian Language]

[3].   A. Atanasiu, *Securitatea Informatiei, vol. 2 (Protocoale de securitate)*, InfoData, 2009. [Romanian Language]

[4].   S. J. Knapskog, "Formal specification and verification of secure communication protocols", in Advances in Cryptology — AUSCRYPT '90, J. Seberry and J. Pieprzyk, Eds., in Lecture Notes in Computer Science. Berlin, Heidelberg: Springer, 1990, pp. 58–73.

[5].   K. Koyama, "Direct demonstration of the power to break public-key cryptosystems", in Advances in Cryptology — AUSCRYPT '90, J. Seberry and J. Pieprzyk, Eds., in Lecture Notes in Computer Science. Berlin, Heidelberg: Springer, 1990, pp. 14–21.

[6].   P. J. Lee, "Secure user access control for public networks", in Advances in Cryptology — AUSCRYPT '90, J. Seberry and J. Pieprzyk, Eds., in Lecture Notes in Computer Science. Berlin, Heidelberg: Springer, 1990, pp. 45–57.

[7].   R. Lidl and W. B. Müller, "A note on strong Fibonacci pseudoprimes", in Advances in Cryptology — AUSCRYPT '90, J. Seberry and J. Pieprzyk, Eds., in Lecture Notes in Computer Science. Berlin, Heidelberg: Springer, 1990, pp. 311–317. doi: 10.1007/BFb0030371.

[8].   A. J. Menezes and S. A. Vanstone, "Elliptic curve cryptosystems and their implementation", J. Cryptology, vol. 6, no. 4, pp. 209–224, Sep. 1993, doi: 10.1007/BF00203817.

[9].   M. J. Mihaljevic and J. Dj. Golic, 'A fast iterative algorithm for a shift register initial state reconstruction given the noisy output sequence', in Advances in Cryptology — AUSCRYPT '90, J. Seberry and J. Pieprzyk, Eds., in Lecture Notes in Computer Science. Berlin, Heidelberg: Springer, 1990, pp. 165–175.

CHAPTER 19

Differential and Linear Cryptanalysis

This chapter covers two important cryptanalysis types: *linear* and *differential*. To understand how to merge theoretical and practical concepts, basic concepts and advanced techniques on how professionals implement them are discussed first.

Despite some of the differential and linear mechanisms being outdated, there is plenty of room to find new challenges that could be exploited to obtain new results. The research literature about linear and differential cryptanalysis provides many theoretical approaches and mechanisms. But only a few theories could be applied in practice, developing professional solutions for differential and linear cryptanalysis attacks.

The difference between theoretical and applied cryptanalysis is significantly large and has its own differences. The results published in the last 12 years, such as algorithms, methods, and game theory aspects, led researchers and professionals on different paths. Most of them were whimsical, chimeras (complex mathematical systems without real applicability), fancy algorithms, and others being applicable with success in practice.

Conducting research in cryptanalysis and increasing its potential value for being applied in practice and for different scenarios requires time, experience, and continuous cross-collaboration between theoreticians and practitioners, without isolation between these two types of categories.

Carrying out cryptanalysis work and increasing its potential value to be implemented in practice for various scenarios involves time, expertise, and ongoing cross-collaboration between theoreticians and practitioners without separating these two groups. Their importance is crucial in the field of cryptanalysis, providing the necessary tools and mechanisms to construct cryptanalysis attack schemes for block and stream ciphers.

Differential Cryptanalysis

E. Biham and A. Shamir implemented differential cryptanalysis in the early 1990s. Usually, differential cryptanalysis is designed for block ciphers, but it can also be used for stream ciphers or hash functions. Differential cryptanalysis checks whether the cryptogram traces some locations from the key with a probability greater than others. The checking process can be carried out with any order with grade 1. The test represents a complicated approximation of order 2 of a test cycle.

Differential cryptanalysis exposes the weak points of the cryptography algorithm. The following example of differential cryptanalysis is illustrated for *stream cryptography algorithms*. The pseudocode of the algorithm is as follows.

INPUT: the key is chosen as $K = (k_1, ..., k_n)$ with $k_i \in \{0, 1\}$

OUTPUT: the weak points of the cryptography
          algorithm together with the resistance decision for
          differential cryptanalysis.

1. $\alpha \leftarrow$ rejection rate value

2. choose n sets of keys with perturbation property sets, starting from key K.

$$for\ i = 1\ to\ n\ do\ K^{(i)} = \left(\delta_{1i} \oplus k_1, \ldots, \delta_{ni} \oplus k_n \right):$$

$$\delta_{1i} = \begin{cases} 1, & if\ j \neq i, \\ 0, & if\ j = i. \end{cases}$$

    for i,j=1,...,n. Here, the ith key is obtained from the base key by changing the bit from the ith position.

3. *Constructing the cryptograms.* The first step is to build $n + 1$ cryptograms using the basic key, perturbed keys and clear text M. We denote the obtained cryptograms with $C^{(i)}$, $i = 1, ..., n + 1$. As plaintext M, we can choose for text 0 – everywhere.

4. *Constructing the correlation matrix.* Here, we build the matrix $(n + 1) \times (n + 1)$ for the correlation values C:

$$c_{ij} = corellation \left(cryptogram\ i, cryptogram\ j \right),$$

corelation c_{ij} denotes the value of the statistical test applied to the sequence ($cryptogram\ i \oplus cryptogram\ j$). The matrix C is represented as a symmetrical matrix having 1 on the main diagonal.

5. *The computational process for the significant value.* It counts the values of significant correlation that are situated above the main diagonal. A value is called *significant* if

$$c_{i,j} \notin \left[u_{\frac{\alpha}{2}} ; u_{1-\frac{\alpha}{2}} \right].$$

Consider T the number of significant values that represents the number of rejects of the correlation test.

6. *Decision and result interpretation.* If

$$\frac{T - \alpha \cdot \dfrac{n(n+1)}{2}}{\sqrt{\alpha(1-\alpha) \cdot \dfrac{n(n+1)}{2}}} \notin \left[u_{\frac{\alpha}{2}} ; u_{1-\frac{\alpha}{2}} \right],$$

once computed, we can decide the nonresistance to differential cryptanalysis ($u_{\frac{\alpha}{2}}$ and $u_{1-\frac{\alpha}{2}}$ represents the quantiles of the normal distribution of order $\dfrac{\alpha}{2}$ and $1-\dfrac{\alpha}{2}$ and fixes the (i,j) elements with $n \geq i > j \geq 1$, for which c_{ij} is significant. These elements represent weak points for the algorithms. Otherwise, we cannot mention anything about the resistance to this type of attack.

In this section, a very simple cipher that shifts the plain message with the secret key and then inverts it to obtain the encrypted message is presented. Then, differential cryptanalysis is applied to break the cipher. The code is presented in Listing 19-1. The output is shown in Figure 19-1.

Listing 19-1. Simple Differential Attack

```
#include <iostream>
#include <cstdlib>
#include <ctime>

using namespace std;
```

```c
//helper function that inverts the input value
unsigned char invert(unsigned char value) {
    return ~value;
}

//helper function that shifts the input value to left
unsigned char shift_left(unsigned char value) {
    return ((value << 1) & 0x0F) | ((value >> 3) & 0x01);
}

//simple encryption function that shifts the message to left then
inverts it
unsigned char cipher(unsigned char message, unsigned char key) {
    return shift_left(invert(message ^ key));
}

int main() {
    //declare two plain messages and the secret key
    unsigned char message1 = 0x02;
    unsigned char message2 = 0x03;
    unsigned char key = 0x06;

    //compute the corresponding encrypted messages
    unsigned char encrypted_message1 = cipher(message1, key);
    unsigned char encrypted_message2 = cipher(message2, key);

    int pairs_no = 10000;
    int total_ok_pairs = 0; //total number of pairs that satisfy the
    condition

    //threshold for success of probability
    double threshold = 0;

    //cryptanalysis attack
    for (int k = 0; k < 16; k++) {
        unsigned char computed_key = k;
        int different_pairs = 0;
        int ok_pairs = 0;
```

```
//compute the number of differential pairs that satisfy the condition
for (int j = 0; j < pairs_no; j++) {
    //randomly generate two plain messages
    unsigned char aux_message1 = rand() % 16;
    unsigned char aux_message2 = aux_message1 ^ message1;

    //compute the corresponding ciphertexts using the computed key
    unsigned char aux_encrypted_message1 = cipher(aux_message1,
    computed_key);
    unsigned char aux_encrypted_message2 = cipher(aux_message2,
    computed_key);

    //check if the pairs satisfy the condition
    if ((aux_encrypted_message1 ^ aux_encrypted_message2) ==
    (encrypted_message1 ^ encrypted_message2)) {
        ok_pairs++;
    }

    different_pairs++;
}

//compute the probability of correctly guessing the computed key
double probability = (double)ok_pairs / different_pairs;

if (probability > threshold) {
    total_ok_pairs++;
    cout << "Computed key: " << hex << (int)computed_key << ",
    probability of success: " << probability << endl;
}
}

//verify if the computed key is the same as the correct key
if (total_ok_pairs > 0) {
    cout << "Correct key: " << hex << (int)key << " found." << endl;
} else {
    cout << "Correct key not found." << endl;
}

return 0;
}
```

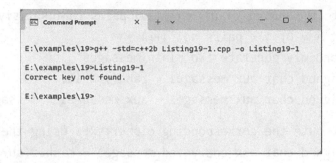

Figure 19-1. *The output for differential attack*

This example produces a pair of plain messages that differ by a single bit and use a fixed key to compute the corresponding encrypted messages. A differential cryptanalysis attack is conducted by guessing each potential key value and counting the number of differential pairings satisfying the condition (aux_encrypted_message1 ^ aux_encrypted_message2) == (encrypted_message1 ^ encrypted_message2), where aux_message1 and aux_message2 are random plain message values.

This method is continued for a large number of random plain message pair iterations and calculates the likelihood of success for each key guess. If the success probability of a key estimate exceeds a specific threshold (in this example, 0.10), it's considered a possible candidate for the actual key. Finally, let's determine if the estimated key matches the actual key.

Linear Cryptanalysis

Linear cryptanalysis was developed as a theoretical framework for the Data Encryption System (DES) and implemented in 1993. Linear cryptanalysis is commonly used inside block ciphers and is a good starting point for designing and executing complex attacks.

Linear cryptanalysis is a linear relationship between the key, the plaintext structure, and the ciphertext structure. The plaintext is structured and represented as characters or bits. It is required to have the structure as a chain of operations characterized by exclusive-or, as the following describes.

$$A_{i_1} \oplus A_{i_2} \ldots \oplus A_{i_u} \oplus B_{j_1} \oplus B_{j_2} \oplus \ldots \oplus B_{j_v} = Key_{k_1} \oplus Key_{k_2} \oplus \ldots Key_{k_w}$$

$\oplus$ represents the XOR operation as a binary operation, A_i represents the bit from the ith position of the input structure $A = [A_1, A_2, ...]$, B_j represents the bit from the jth position of the output structure $B = [B_1, B_2, ...]$ and Key_k represents the kth bit of the key $Key = [Key_1, Key_2, ...]$.

Performing Linear Cryptanalysis

Usually, in the most important cases, performing linear cryptanalysis starts from the idea that we acknowledge the encryption algorithm except the private key. As the following describes, executing linear cryptanalysis against a block cipher is represented as a framework.

- The first step is based on identifying the linear approximation for nonlinear components. The goal is to characterize the encryption algorithm (e.g., S-boxes).

- Computing a combination of linear approximations of substitution boxes, including the operations executed against the encryption algorithm. Professionals should focus on linear approximation because it represents a special function that contains and deals with the clear text and cipher text bits and those from the private key.

- Computing and designing the linear approximation should be a guideline for the cryptographic keys used for the first time. The guideline proves its power and helps professionals save important computational resources for all the possible values of the cryptographic keys. Using multiple linear approximations, you have a very powerful process of computation to eliminate the key numbers necessary for trying.

In this section, a very simple cipher is presented that XORes the plain message with the secret key to obtain the encrypted message. Then, linear cryptanalysis is applied to break the cipher [10]. The code is presented in Listing 19-2. The output is shown in Figure 19-2.

Listing 19-2. Simple Linear Cryptanalysis Example

```cpp
#include <iostream>
#include <bitset>
#include <random>

using namespace std;

// a very simple cipher that XORes the message with the key
bitset<4> cipher(bitset<4> message, bitset<4> key) {
    bitset<4> encrypted_message = message ^ key;
    return encrypted_message;
}

int main() {
    //set the parameters to generate random messages and keys
    random_device rand_value;
    default_random_engine generate(rand_value());
    uniform_int_distribution<int> distance(0, 15); //generates random
    numbers between 0 and 15

    bitset<16> messages; //stores messages
    bitset<16> encrypted_messages; //stores encrypted messages

    //generate randomly 16 messages, the keys, each of them on 4-bit then
    compute the corresponding encrypted messages
    for (int i = 0; i < 16; i++) {
        bitset<4> message(distance(generate));
        bitset<4> private_key(distance(generate));
        bitset<4> encrypted_message = cipher(message, private_key);

        messages[i] = message.to_ulong();
        encrypted_messages[i] = encrypted_message.to_ulong();
    }

    //applying linear cryptanalysis to compute the key
    ////first, the compued key and the maximum bias are set to 0
    bitset<4> key_compute(0);
    int maximum_bias = 0;
```

```cpp
//all possible key are computed
//for each key the bias value is computed using linear approximation
for (int k = 0; k < 16; k++) {
    bitset<4> local_key(k);
    int local_bias = 0;

    //compute the bias value for each pair of message -
    encrypted message
    for (int i = 0; i < 16; i++) {
        bitset<4> aux_message(messages[i]);
        bitset<4> aux_encrypted_message(encrypted_messages[i]);

        bitset<4> aux1(aux_message ^ local_key); // XOR the message
        with the local key
        bitset<4> aux2(aux_encrypted_message ^ local_key); // XOR the
        encrypted message with the local key

        //compute the linear approximation
        //update bias value
        if ((aux1.count() + aux2.count()) % 2 == 0) {
            local_bias++; //the bias value is increased if the linear
            approximation occurs
        } else {
            local_bias--; //the bias value is decreased if the linear
            approximation does not occur
        }

        //verify if the computed key is the same as local (real) key
        if (key_compute == local_key) {
            cout << "The key was correctly computed: " << key_compute
            << " / ";
        } else {
            cout << "The key was not correctly computed: " << key_
            compute << " / ";
        }

        cout << "The correct key: " << local_key << endl;
    }
```

```
        if (abs(local_bias) > abs(maximum_bias)) {
            maximum_bias = local_bias;
            key_compute = local_key;
        }
    }

    // Output the key guess and maximum bias
    cout << "Computed key: " << key_compute.to_ulong() << endl;
    cout << "Bias value: " << maximum_bias << endl;

    return 0;
}
```

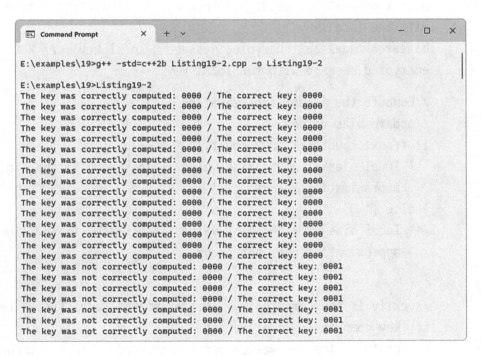

Figure 19-2. *The output for linear cryptanalysis*

This code creates 16 random plain messages and keys and then uses a simple cipher function to encrypt each message with a random key to produce the appropriate encrypted message. The cipher is then exposed to a linear cryptanalysis attack by testing all possible keys and computing the bias of each key using the linear approximation. Eventually, the highest-biased key is chosen as the correct guessed key.

Conclusion

The chapter has discussed differential and linear cryptanalysis attacks and how these kinds of attacks can be designed and implemented in real practice. It introduced the theoretical background elements and main foundations that must be known before designing such cryptanalysis attacks.

You learned the following.

- How to identify theoretically the main components on which a cryptanalyst should focus

- How vulnerable those components are and how they can be exploited

- How to implement linear and differential cryptanalysis attacks

References

[1].   J. Daemen, L. Knudsen, and V. Rijmen, "The block cipher Square", in Fast Software Encryption, E. Biham, Ed., in Lecture Notes in Computer Science. Berlin, Heidelberg: Springer, 1997, pp. 149–165.

[2].   H. Heys, "A Tutorial on Linear and Differential Cryptanalysis," *Cryptologia*, vol. XXVI, no. 3, pp. 189–221, 2002.

[3].   M. Matsui, "Linear Cryptanalysis Method for DES Cipher", Advances in Cryptology - EUROCRYPT '93, Springer-Verlag, pp. 386–397, 1994.

[4].   E. Biham, "On Matsui's linear cryptanalysis", in Advances in Cryptology — EUROCRYPT'94, A. De Santis, Ed., in Lecture Notes in Computer Science. Berlin, Heidelberg: Springer, 1995, pp. 341–355.

[5].   A. Biryukov, C. De Cannière, and M. Quisquater, "On Multiple Linear Approximations", in Advances in Cryptology - CRYPTO 2004, M. Franklin, Ed., in Lecture Notes in Computer Science. Berlin, Heidelberg: Springer, 2004, pp. 1–22.

[6].   L. Keliher, H. Meijer, and S. Tavares, "New Method for Upper Bounding the Maximum Average Linear Hull Probability for SPNs", in Advances in Cryptology — EUROCRYPT 2001, B. Pfitzmann, Ed., in Lecture Notes in Computer Science. Berlin, Heidelberg: Springer, 2001, pp. 420–436.

[7].   L. R. Knudsen and J. E. Mathiassen, "A Chosen-Plaintext Linear Attack on DES", in Fast Software Encryption, G. Goos, J. Hartmanis, J. van Leeuwen, and B. Schneier, Eds., in Lecture Notes in Computer Science. Berlin, Heidelberg: Springer, 2001, pp. 262–272.

[8].   M. Matsui and A. Yamagishi, "A New Method for Known Plaintext Attack of FEAL Cipher", in Advances in Cryptology — EUROCRYPT' 92, R. A. Rueppel, Ed., in Lecture Notes in Computer Science. Berlin, Heidelberg: Springer, 1993, pp. 81–91.

[9].   M. Matsui, "The First Experimental Cryptanalysis of the Data Encryption Standard", in Advances in Cryptology — CRYPTO '94, Y. G. Desmedt, Ed., in Lecture Notes in Computer Science. Berlin, Heidelberg: Springer, 1994, pp. 1–11.

[10].   N. Ferguson, B. Schneier, and T. Kohno, *Cryptography Engineering: Design Principles and Practical Applications*. John Wiley & Sons, 2011.

CHAPTER 20

Integral Cryptanalysis

Integral cryptanalysis is a technique designed for block ciphers constructed on substitution-permutation networks. Since an integral cryptanalysis attack can be launched against a Square block cipher [1], it is also known as a Square attack and was designed by Lars Knudsen.

An exposed point of the block ciphers is the network of substitution-permutation. When the networks can be discovered (intuitively), the exploitation of the vulnerabilities of the block cipher has a high negative impact on the entire cryptosystem. Another exposed point of the block ciphers is the key itself and the table involved in the permutation of the key. The system can be broken when a false key is similar (or identical) to the correct one.

The next section presents the formal basis regarding block ciphers, which can be implemented, and the elements that are required to focus on initiating an integral cryptanalysis attack, for example, building Feistel networks and generating permutation tables for cryptographic keys. Once there is a clear understanding of these two phases, it is very clear how integral cryptanalysis must be conducted.

Basic Notions

For implementing and designing the integral cryptanalytic attack, it is very important to have the formal elements before implementing it. Moving further, let's look at the following concepts as the main starting point for designing and implementing such an attack for education purposes.

Consider $(G, +)$ as a finite abelian group with the order k. The following product group $G^n = G \times \ldots \times G$ is the group with elements with the structure $v = (v_1, \ldots, v_n)$, where $v_i \in G$. The addition within G^n is defined as component-wise; therefore, $u + v = w$ holds for $u, v, w \in G^n$ when $u_i + v_i = w_i$ for all i.

© Marius Iulian Mihailescu and Stefania Loredana Nita 2023
M. I. Mihailescu and S. L. Nita, *Pro Cryptography and Cryptanalysis with C++23*,
https://doi.org/10.1007/978-1-4842-9450-5_20

Let's denote with B the set with multiple vectors and define the integral over B. This integral represents the sum of all vectors S. The integral is defined as $\int S = \sum_{v \in B} v$, and the addition operation is defined in terms of the group operation for G^n.

When the integral cryptanalytic is designed, an important thing that should be known is the number of words in the plain text and the encrypted text. In the example from this chapter, this number is denoted with n. Another important number that should be known is the number of clear texts and encrypted texts, denoted with m. In general, $m = k$ (i.e., $k = |G|$), the vectors $v \in B$ denote the plain text and the encrypted text, and $G = GF(2^B)$ or $G = Z/kZ$.

Going further to the attack, it is because one of the involved entities predicts the values placed in the integrals after a particular number of rounds of encryption. Keeping this in mind, three cases can be distinguished: (1) when the words have the same length (e.g., i), (2) when the words have different lengths, and (3) the sum of a particular value that is predicted in advance.

Furthermore, consider $B \subseteq G^n$ as described and a fixed index i. The following three cases can be distinguished.

- $v_i = c$, for all $v \in B$

- $\{v_i : v \in B\} = G$

- $\sum_{v \in B} v_i = c'$

$c, c' \in G$ are some values known and fixed in advance.

The next example is a common situation in which $m = k$, the number of vectors from B, is the same as the number of elements in the considered group. From Lagrange's theorem, it results that if all words, a general word placed at the ith position, have the same length, then it is intuitive that the ith word from the integral has the value of the neutral element from G.

The following two theorems are necessary and represent a must for any practical developer that wants to translate into practice integral cryptanalysis.

Theorem 20-1 [1, Theorem 1, p. 114]

Let's consider $(G, +)$ a *finite abelian additive group*. The subgroup of elements of order 1 or 2 is denoted as $L = \{g \in G : g + g = 0\}$. Let's consider writing $s(G)$ as the sum $\sum_{g \in G} g$ of all the elements found within G. Next, consider $s(G) = \sum_{h \in H} H$. Moreover, it is very important to understand the following analogy $s(G) \in H$: $s(G) + s(G) = 0$.

According to Theorem 1, for $G = GF(2^B)$ there is the value $s(G) = 0$ and for Z/mZ there is the value $s(Z/mZ) = m/2$ when m is an even value, or it is 0. The following theorem represents the multiplicative case for written groups (see Theorem 20-2).

Theorem 20-2 [1, Theorem 2, p. 114]

Let's consider $(G, *)$ a *finite abelian multiplicative group*. The subgroup of elements of order 1 or 2 is denoted as $H = \{g \in G : g * g = 1\}$. Consider writing $p(G)$ as being the product $\prod_{g \in G} g$ of all the elements of G. Next, consider $p(G) = \prod_{h \in H} h$. Moreover, it is very important to understand the following analogy $p(G) \in H$, or $p(G) * p(G) = 1$.

As an example, if $G = (Z/pZ)^*$ where p is prime, $p(G)$ is -1, $p(G) = -1$. This is proven using Wilson's theorem.

Practical Approach

This section presents a very simple cipher that shifts the plain message with the secret key and then inverts it to obtain the encrypted message. Then, integral cryptanalysis is applied to break the cipher [2]. The code is presented in Listing 20-1. The output is shown in Figure 20-1.

Listing 20-1. The Main Program

```
#include <iostream>

using namespace std;

//helper function that inverts the input value
unsigned char invert(unsigned char value) {
    return ~value;
}

//helper function that shifts the input value to left
unsigned char shift_left(unsigned char value) {
    return ((value << 1) & 0x0F) | ((value >> 3) & 0x01);
}
```

```
//simple encryption function that shifts the message to left then
inverts it
unsigned char cipher(unsigned char message, unsigned char key) {
    return shift_left(invert(message ^ key));
}

int main() {
    //declare the plain message and the secret key
    unsigned char message = 0x02;
    unsigned char key = 0x06;

    //compute the corresponding encrypted message
    unsigned char encrypted_message = cipher(message, key);

    int pairs_no = 10000;
    int total_ok_pairs = 0; //total number of pairs that satisfy the
    condition

    //threshold for success of probability
    double threshold = 0;

    //integral analysis attack
    for (int k = 0; k < 16; k++) {
        unsigned char computed_key = k;
        int ok_pairs = 0;

        //compute the number of pairs that satisfy the condition
        for (int i = 0; i < 16; i++) {
            for (int j = 0; j < 16; j++) {
                //compute the corresponding encrypted messages using the
                computed key
                unsigned char aux_encrypted_message1 = cipher(i,
                computed_key);
                unsigned char aux_encrypted_message2 = cipher(j,
                computed_key);

                //check if the condition is met
                if ((aux_encrypted_message1 ^ aux_encrypted_message2) ==
                encrypted_message) {
```

```
            ok_pairs++;
        }
    }
}

//compute the probability of correctly guessing the computed key
double probability = (double)ok_pairs / (16 * 16);

if (probability > threshold) {
    total_ok_pairs++;
    cout << "Computed key: " << hex << (int)computed_key << ",
     probability of success: " << probability << endl;
}
}

//verify if the computed key is the same as the correct key
if (total_ok_pairs > 0) {
    cout << "Correct key: " << hex << (int)key << " found." << endl;
} else {
    cout << "Correct key not found." << endl;
}

return 0;
}
```

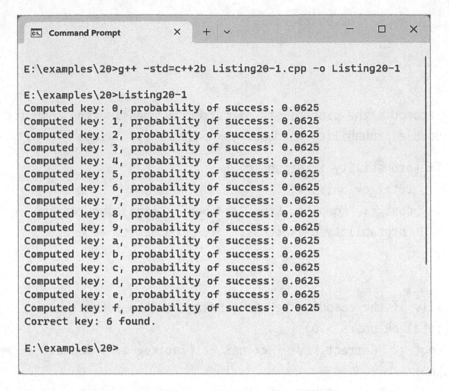

Figure 20-1. *Integral cryptanalysis attack*

This code executes an integral cryptanalysis attack by counting the number of plain message pairs satisfying the requirement (aux_encrypted_message1 ^ aux_encrypted_message2) == encrypted_message) for each potential key guess. This is accomplished by repeatedly traversing all potential plain message-encrypted message pairings, computing their associated ciphertexts using the computed key, and determining if they meet the criteria. Then, compute the success probability for each computed. Finally, determine if there is at least one key guess with a substantial success probability (e.g., more than 0.1) and output it if there is.

Conclusion

This chapter covered integral cryptanalysis and how such attacks can be designed and implemented. The chapter developed a block cipher cryptosystem with vulnerable points to illustrate how to use the integral cryptanalysis attack in practice.

You learned how to do the following.

- Design and implement a simple integral cryptanalysis attack

- Understand the vulnerable points of this kind of attack and generate permutation tables to permutate the key

- Use permutation tables and how to work with them over the keys

References

[1].   J. Daemen, L. Knudsen, and V. Rijmen, "The block cipher Square", in Fast Software Encryption, E. Biham, Ed., in Lecture Notes in Computer Science. Berlin, Heidelberg: Springer, 1997, pp. 149–165.

[2].   Ferguson, N., Schneier, B., and Kohno, T. (2011). *Cryptography Engineering: Design Principles and Practical Applications*. John Wiley & Sons.

CHAPTER 21

Brute-Force and Buffer Overflow Attacks

This chapter covers two of the most significant attacks against C++ programs and applications: buffer overflow and brute-force attacks.

Some attackers use software, hardware, or applications to carry out brute-force or buffer overflow attacks. Their techniques are designed to exploit various word combinations for confirmation forms. Attackers have been known to try to corrupt web applications by, for instance, scanning for session IDs. The attacker's objectives include data theft, infecting target computers with malware, and requesting assistance in exchange for a predetermined sum of money. Some attackers choose to physically carry out brute-force attacks. The majority of brute-force and buffer overflow attacks are currently carried out by bots. A bot is a software program meant to perform automated activities or communicate with humans through text or speech, frequently imitating human behavior. Bots may be found in a variety of applications, including social media, messaging platforms, and online games, and perform various functions, including customer service, amusement, and data collection.

It is advised to consider the following suggestions to safeguard the company and organization from these attacks.

- Online data and information from untrusted sources should not be used.

- Use as many characters as you can.

- Use a variety of letter, number, and special character combinations; (e.g., symbol).

- Do not use common pattern letters (e.g., qwerty).

- Create unique passwords for every user account.

- Change passwords often (e.g., every two months).

- Use and create lengthy, secure passwords. Use password generators (such as key generation from KeyPass) if you have no inspiration for passwords.

- Put multifactor authentication into work [1].

- If biometrics are an option, use them [2].

Brute-Force Attack

A brute-force attack is one in which the attacker submits several passwords or passphrases to guess the right one. The attacker checks each password or passphrase individually until the right one is discovered. Additionally, the attacker has a chance of determining the key. The key is usually derived from the password using a function. An exhaustive key search is the name given to this procedure.

The following are among the wide range of brute-force attacks.

- **Attacks that use rainbow tables.** A rainbow table represents a predetermined and precalculated table. The objective is to reverse the cryptographic hashing process.

- **Attacks that use reversing brute-force attacks.** A common password or a specific group of passwords is used in the assault against numerous usernames.

- **Credential attacks.** A variety of websites are being attacked utilizing sets of username-password combinations.

- **Hybrid brute-force attacks.** The attack determines what password type can be used to succeed before moving on to a general procedure for testing various types.

Further examples of these types of attacks show how they can be used and deployed in real-life scenarios (algorithms).

- **Brute-force attack on Caesar cipher.** The example is based on the Caesar cipher (see Figure 21-1 and Listing 21-1). Due to the cipher's simplicity, it is the first example of a brute-force attack.

- **String generation for brute-force attacks.** The scenario shown in Figure 21-2 and Listing 21-2 demonstrates how simple string creation can be carried out to produce complex lists and dictionaries that can be used during brute-force attacks.

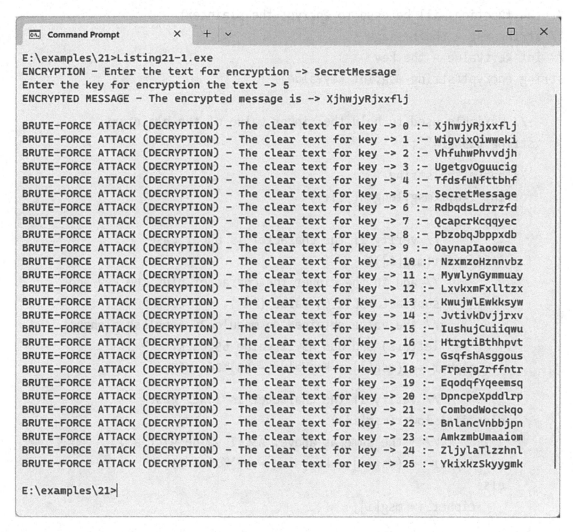

```
E:\examples\21>Listing21-1.exe
ENCRYPTION - Enter the text for encryption -> SecretMessage
Enter the key for encryption the text -> 5
ENCRYPTED MESSAGE - The encrypted message is -> XjhwjyRjxxflj

BRUTE-FORCE ATTACK (DECRYPTION) - The clear text for key -> 0 :- XjhwjyRjxxflj
BRUTE-FORCE ATTACK (DECRYPTION) - The clear text for key -> 1 :- WigvixQiwweki
BRUTE-FORCE ATTACK (DECRYPTION) - The clear text for key -> 2 :- VhfuhwPhvvdjh
BRUTE-FORCE ATTACK (DECRYPTION) - The clear text for key -> 3 :- UgetgvOguucig
BRUTE-FORCE ATTACK (DECRYPTION) - The clear text for key -> 4 :- TfdsfuNfttbhf
BRUTE-FORCE ATTACK (DECRYPTION) - The clear text for key -> 5 :- SecretMessage
BRUTE-FORCE ATTACK (DECRYPTION) - The clear text for key -> 6 :- RdbqdsLdrrzfd
BRUTE-FORCE ATTACK (DECRYPTION) - The clear text for key -> 7 :- QcapcrKcqqyec
BRUTE-FORCE ATTACK (DECRYPTION) - The clear text for key -> 8 :- PbzobqJbppxdb
BRUTE-FORCE ATTACK (DECRYPTION) - The clear text for key -> 9 :- OaynapIaoowca
BRUTE-FORCE ATTACK (DECRYPTION) - The clear text for key -> 10 :- NzxmzoHznnvbz
BRUTE-FORCE ATTACK (DECRYPTION) - The clear text for key -> 11 :- MywlynGymmuay
BRUTE-FORCE ATTACK (DECRYPTION) - The clear text for key -> 12 :- LxvkxmFxlltzx
BRUTE-FORCE ATTACK (DECRYPTION) - The clear text for key -> 13 :- KwujwlEwkksyw
BRUTE-FORCE ATTACK (DECRYPTION) - The clear text for key -> 14 :- JvtivkDvjjrxv
BRUTE-FORCE ATTACK (DECRYPTION) - The clear text for key -> 15 :- IushujCuiiqwu
BRUTE-FORCE ATTACK (DECRYPTION) - The clear text for key -> 16 :- HtrgtiBthhpvt
BRUTE-FORCE ATTACK (DECRYPTION) - The clear text for key -> 17 :- GsqfshAsggous
BRUTE-FORCE ATTACK (DECRYPTION) - The clear text for key -> 18 :- FrpergZrffntr
BRUTE-FORCE ATTACK (DECRYPTION) - The clear text for key -> 19 :- EqodqfYqeemsq
BRUTE-FORCE ATTACK (DECRYPTION) - The clear text for key -> 20 :- DpncpeXpddlrp
BRUTE-FORCE ATTACK (DECRYPTION) - The clear text for key -> 21 :- CombodWocckqo
BRUTE-FORCE ATTACK (DECRYPTION) - The clear text for key -> 22 :- BnlancVnbbjpn
BRUTE-FORCE ATTACK (DECRYPTION) - The clear text for key -> 23 :- AmkzmbUmaaiom
BRUTE-FORCE ATTACK (DECRYPTION) - The clear text for key -> 24 :- ZljylaTlzzhnl
BRUTE-FORCE ATTACK (DECRYPTION) - The clear text for key -> 25 :- YkixkzSkyygmk

E:\examples\21>
```

Figure 21-1. *Running the brute-force attack*

Listing 21-1. Brute-Force Attack Using Caesar Cipher

```cpp
#include<iostream>

using namespace std;

// the function will be used to encrypt the plaintext
// string msg - the message
// int keytValue - the key
string encrypt(string msg,int keyValue)
{
    // variable used to hold the cipher value of the plaintext
    string cipher="";

    // parse the string
    for(int i=0;i<msg.length();i++)
    {
            // verify if the character is upper case
        if(isupper(msg[i]))
                // add to the cipher the character plus the key and
                subtract ASCII 65 value ('A').
                // the value obtained do modulo 26 (english alphabet
                letters) and add ASCII value 65 back.
            cipher += (msg[i] + keyValue - 65)%26 + 65;

                // verify if the character is lower case
        else if(islower(msg[i]))
                //** the same as above. ASCII value 97 ('a')
            cipher += (msg[i] + keyValue - 97)%26 + 97;
        else
            cipher += msg[i];
    }
    return cipher;
}

// The decryption will be done using the brute force attack by
// checking all possible keys
// string encMessage - the encrypted message
```

```cpp
void decrypt(string encMessage)
{
    // the variable for storing the plaintext
    string plaintext;

    // we will try for each key and we will do the decryption
    for(int keyTry=0;keyTry<26;keyTry++)
    {
        plaintext = "";
                // parse accordingly based on the message length
        for(int i=0;i<encMessage.length();i++)
        {
                // check if the character is upper case
            if(isupper(encMessage[i]))
            {
                if((encMessage[i] - keyTry - 65)<0)
                    plaintext += 91 + (encMessage[i] - keyTry - 65);
                else
                    plaintext += (encMessage[i] - keyTry - 65)%26 + 65;
            }
                // check if the character is lower case
            else if(islower(encMessage[i]))
            {
                if((encMessage[i] - keyTry - 97) < 0)
                    plaintext += 123 + (encMessage[i] - keyTry - 97);
                else
                    plaintext += (encMessage[i] - keyTry - 97)%26 + 97;
            }
            else
                plaintext += encMessage[i];
        }
        cout << "BRUTE-FORCE ATTACK (DECRYPTION) - The clear text for key
        -> " << keyTry << " :- " << plaintext << endl;
    }
}
```

```cpp
int main()
{
    int encKey;
    string cleartext;
    cout << "ENCRYPTION - Enter the text for encryption -> ";
    getline(cin,cleartext);

    cout << "Enter the key for encryption the text -> ";
    cin >> encKey;

    string encryptedMessage = encrypt(cleartext,encKey);
    cout << "ENCRYPTED MESSAGE - The encrypted message is -> " <<
    encryptedMessage << endl << endl;

    //** brute force attack
    decrypt(encryptedMessage);
}
```

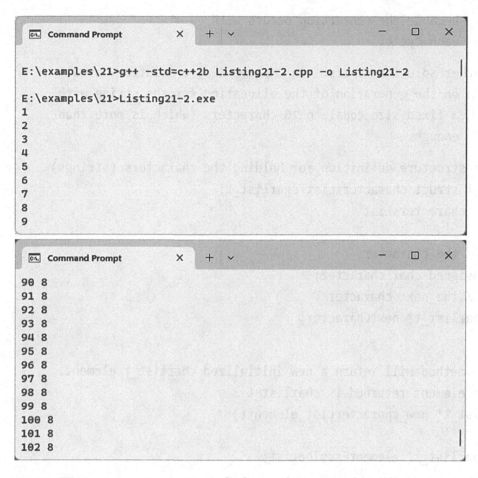

Figure 21-2. *Basic string generation of a brute-force attack—different states of generating strings*

Listing 21-2. Basic String Generation Source Code

```
#include <string.h>
#include <stdio.h>
#include <stdlib.h>

// We are using a linked list data structure.
// The reason is to avoid some of the restrictions
//      based on the generation of the string length.
// Our list has to be converted to string in
//      such way that it can be used. The current conversion
//      might be slightly slower compared with other methods
```

```
//       because the conversion occurs with
//       each cycle.

// Another solution consists in implementing a solution based
//       on the generation of the allocation for the string with
//       a fixed size equal to 20 characters (which is more than
//       enough.

// the structure definition for holding the characters (strings)
typedef struct charactersList charlist_t;
struct charactersList
{
    // the character
  unsigned char character;
    // the next character
  charlist_t* nextCharacter;
};

// The method will return a new initialized charlist_t element.
// The element returned is charlist_t
charlist_t* new_characterList_element()
{
    charlist_t* elementFromTheList;

    if ((elementFromTheList = (charlist_t*)
    malloc(sizeof(charlist_t))) != 0)
    {
        elementFromTheList->character = 0;
        elementFromTheList->nextCharacter = NULL;
    }
    else
    {
        perror("The allocation using malloc() has failed.");
    }

    return elementFromTheList;
}
```

```c
// allocation free memory by the characters list
// listOfCharacters - represents a pointer for the first element within
the list
void freeAllocation_CharactersList(charlist_t* listOfCharacters)
{
    charlist_t* currentCharacter = listOfCharacters;
    charlist_t* nextCharacter;

    while (currentCharacter != NULL)
    {
        nextCharacter = currentCharacter->nextCharacter;
        free(currentCharacter);
        currentCharacter = nextCharacter;
    }
}

// the function display the current list of characters
// the function will iterate through the whole list and it will print all
the characters
void showCharactersList(charlist_t* list)
{
    charlist_t* nextCharacter = list;
    while (nextCharacter != NULL)
    {
        printf("%d ", nextCharacter->character);
        nextCharacter = nextCharacter->nextCharacter;
    }
    printf("\n");
}

// the function will return the next sequence of characters.
// the characters are treated as numbers 0-255
// the function proceeds by incrementation of the character from the first
position
```

```
void nextCharactersSequence(charlist_t* listOfCharacters)
{
    listOfCharacters->character++;
    if (listOfCharacters->character == 0)
    {
        if (listOfCharacters->nextCharacter == NULL)
        {
            listOfCharacters->nextCharacter = new_characterList_element();
        }
        else
        {
            nextCharactersSequence(listOfCharacters->nextCharacter);
        }
    }
}

int main()
{
    charlist_t* sequenceOfCharacters;
    sequenceOfCharacters = new_characterList_element();

    // this while will work for all possible combinations
    // this has to be stopped manually
    while (1)
    {
        nextCharactersSequence(sequenceOfCharacters);
        showCharactersList(sequenceOfCharacters);
    }

    freeAllocation_CharactersList(sequenceOfCharacters);
}
```

Buffer Overflow Attack

A *buffer* is a short-term space that is used to store data. An additional data overflow occurs when the programs or system processes add more data.

In a buffer overflow attack, the extra data being held can contain particular instructions intended to carry out instructions placed by malicious users or hackers. For instance, the data overflow may cause a function or process to be called that would delete files or divulge users' personal information.

The attacker uses a buffer overflow to take advantage of running software and wait for user input. Buffer overflows are available in two types: heap-based and stack-based. It is extremely challenging to launch and carry out attacks that rely on flooding the memory area set out for the program and its execution in a heap-based system. In a stack-based system, the memory stack—the area used to hold user input data—is where applications and programs are exploited.

The danger of such scenarios for C++ applications is demonstrated in Figure 21-3 and Listing 21-3. The example doesn't implement any harmful code injection but demonstrates a primary buffer overflow procedure. Modern compilers offer options for overflow checking during the compilation or linking process. But at runtime, it is quite challenging to check the situation without having a protection mechanism, such as the handling process of the exceptions. This is a comparison between modern compilers and old compilers.

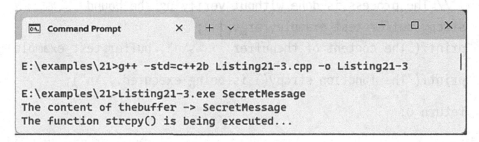

Figure 21-3. *Buffer overflow execution*

Listing 21-3. Implementation of Buffer Overflow Example

```
#include <stdio.h>
#include <string.h>
#include <stdlib.h>
#define _CRT_SECURE_NO_WARNINGS

int main(int argc, char *argv[])
{
```

```
    // We allocate a buffer of 5 bytes that also includes the
    termination, NULL.
    // The allocation should be done as 8 bytes which is two
    double words.
    // For the overflowing process, we will need more than 8 bytes.

    // if the user provides more than 8 characters for the input,
    // an access violation and fault segmentation
char buffer_test_example[5];
    // execution of the program
if (argc < 2)
{
        printf("Function strcpy() will not be executed...\n");
        printf("The syntax: %s <characters>\n", argv[0]);
        exit(0);
}

    // Take the input from the user and copy it to the buffer.
    // The process is done without verifying the bound
strcpy(buffer_test_example, argv[1]);
printf("The content of thebuffer -> %s\n", buffer_test_example);

printf("The function strcpy() is being executed...\n");

return 0;
}
```

Conclusion

This chapter focused on brute-force attacks and buffer overflow attacks. You learned about the following.

- How to recognize buffer overflow and brute-force attacks

- The fundamental ideas that go into creating such attacks

- The drawbacks of heap-based vs. stack-based buffer overflows

References

[1].   M. I. Mihailescu and S. L. Nita, "Three-Factor Authentication Scheme Based on Searchable Encryption and Biometric Fingerprint", in 2020 13th International Conference on Communications (COMM), IEEE, 2020, pp. 139–144.

[2].   M.I. Mihailescu, S. L. Nita and V. C. Pau, "Applied cryptography in designing e-learning platforms", in 16th International Scientific Conference "eLearning and Software for Education" Bucharest, Apr. 2020, vol. 2, pp. 179–189.

CHAPTER 22

Text Characterization

The chi-squared statistic and pattern searching are crucial metrics for cipher and plaintext analysis examined in this chapter (monograms, bigrams, and trigrams). Text characterization as a technique is crucial in the cryptanalysis toolbox when working with both traditional and contemporary encryption.

Chi-Squared Statistic

The chi-squared statistic is an essential metric that calculates the degree of similarity between two probability distributions. When the chi-squared statistic yields a result of 0, it indicates that the two distributions are similar, while a greater value indicates that they are significantly different.

The following formula gives the chi-squared statistic.

$$\chi^2(C,E) = \sum_{i=A}^{i=Z} \frac{(C_i - E_i)^2}{E_i}$$

Listing 22-1 presents an example of computation for the chi-squared distribution.

Listing 22-1. Chi-Squared Distribution Source Code

```cpp
#include <iostream>
#include <random>

int main()
{
  const int number_of_experiments=10000;
  const int number_of_stars_distribution=100;    // maximum number of stars
                                                  to distribute
```

```
std::default_random_engine theGenerator;
std::chi_squared_distribution<double> theDistribution(6.0);

int p[10]={};

for (int i=0; i<number_of_experiments; ++i)
{
  double no = theDistribution(theGenerator);
  if ((no>=0.0)&&(no<10.0)) ++p[int(no)];
}

std::cout << "chi_squared_distribution (6.0):" << std::endl;

for (int i=0; i<10; ++i) {
  std::cout << i << "-" << (i+1) << ": ";
  std::cout << std::string(p[i]*number_of_stars_distribution/number_of_
  experiments,'*') << std::endl;
}

return 0;
}
```

The output is listed in Figure 22-1.

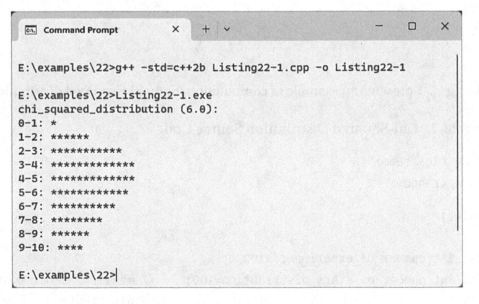

Figure 22-1. *The output of the chi-squared distribution sample*

How can we use the example of the chi-squared distribution for cryptanalysis and cryptography?

The first thing to do is determine how frequently each character appears in the ciphertext. The second step is to compare the two frequency distributions that are related to one another with the frequency distribution of the language used for encryption (for example, English). Thus, there is a chance to identify the shift applied during encryption. This method is conventional and easy to follow, and it may be applied to ciphers such as the Caesar cipher. This occurs when the frequency of English characters and the frequency of the ciphertext line up. (We know the probabilities of the occurrences for English characters.)

Let's consider the following ciphertext obtained by applying the Caesar cipher. It has 46 characters (see Figure 22-2 for letter frequency).

ZHOFRPHWRDSUHVVWKLVLVHQFUBSWHGZLWKFDHVDUFLSKHU

An important thing to note is that the chi-squared statistic relies on counts rather than probabilities. In Figure 22-1, the expectation is that the letter E occurs 12.7 times within 100 characters; therefore, its chance of occurrence is 0.127.

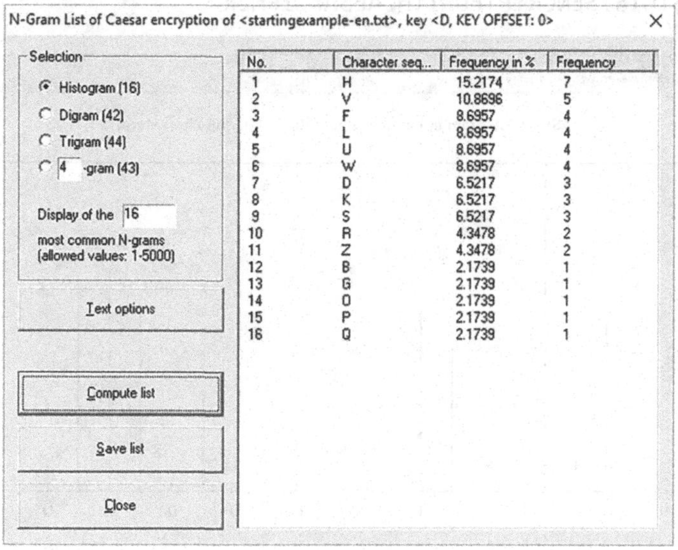

Figure 22-2. *Letter frequency for encrypted text*

The length of the ciphertext must be multiplied by the probability of the letter to determine the expected count. The ciphertext in Figure 22-2 consists of 46 characters in total. Following the example of the letter E, we expect the letter E to occur $46 \times 0.127 = 5.842$ times.

You must employ each of the 25 possible keys, utilizing both the letter and the position of the letter inside the alphabet, to decipher the encrypted text from the example. For this reason, whether the count begins at 0 or 1 is crucial. For each key, the chi-squared must be calculated. The procedure is to compare the letter count to what you would anticipate the counts to be if the text were written in English.

When counting each letter in our ciphertext and calculating the chi-squared statistic, you discover that the letter H appears seven times. If English is used, it should be $46 \times 0.082 = 3.772$ times. You can compute the following using the output.

$$\frac{(7-3.772)^2}{3.772} = \frac{3.228^2}{3.772} = \frac{10.420}{3.772} = 2.762$$

This process is also performed for the remaining letters, adding up all the probabilities (see Figure 22-3).

The decrypted text from this example is the following.

WELCOMETOAPRESSTHISISENCRYPTEDWITHCAESARCIPHER

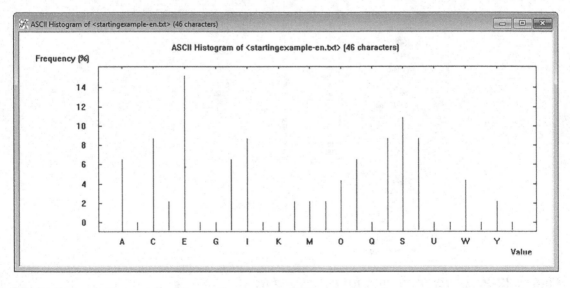

Figure 22-3. *Encryption letter frequency (%)[1]*

Cryptanalysis Using Monogram, Bigram, and Trigram Frequency Counts

To break the cipher, frequency analysis is one of the finest methods for determining the appearance frequency of ciphertext characters. Bigrams (or digraphs), a method for measuring the occurrences of pairs of characters within the text, can be measured and counted using an analysis based on patterns.

This section concentrates on text characterization using ciphers based on bigrams and trigrams, for example, the Playfair cipher. We also perform trigram frequency analysis, which counts the frequency of three-letter tuples.

Counting Monograms

Counting monograms is one of the best techniques for the Caesar cipher, the Polybius square, and other substitution ciphers. Because the English language has a distinct frequency distribution, the approach performs extremely well. This implies that it is also not concealed by substitution ciphers. The distribution pattern resembles that seen in Figure 22-4.

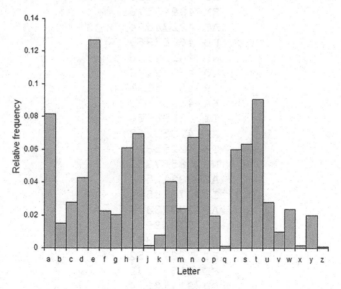

Figure 22-4. *Letter frequency for the English language*

Counting Bigrams

The concept behind counting bigrams is the same as that behind counting monograms. Bigrams count the frequency of pairwise occurrences rather than single-character occurrences.

A few of the common frequent bigrams used during the cryptanalysis process are included in Figure 22-5. We implemented a solution that deals with counting the occurrences of bigrams in Listing 22-2. The results of the example for counting the bigrams are shown in Figure 22-6. The `bigram.txt` file, which has the content from Figure 22-5, is used in the source code in Listing 22-2.

```
TH  11699784·
HE  10068926:
IN  87674002
ER  77134382
AN  69775179
RE  60923600
ES  57070453
ON  56915252
ST  54018399
NT  50701084
EN  48991276
AT  48274564
ED  46647960
ND  46194306
TO  46115188
OR  45725191
EA  43329810
TI  42888666
AR  42353262
TE  42295813
NG  38567365
AL  38211584
IT  37938534
AS  37773878
IS  37349981
HA  35971841
ET  32872552
SE  31532272
OU  31112284
OF  30540904
```

Figure 22-5. *Bigrams*

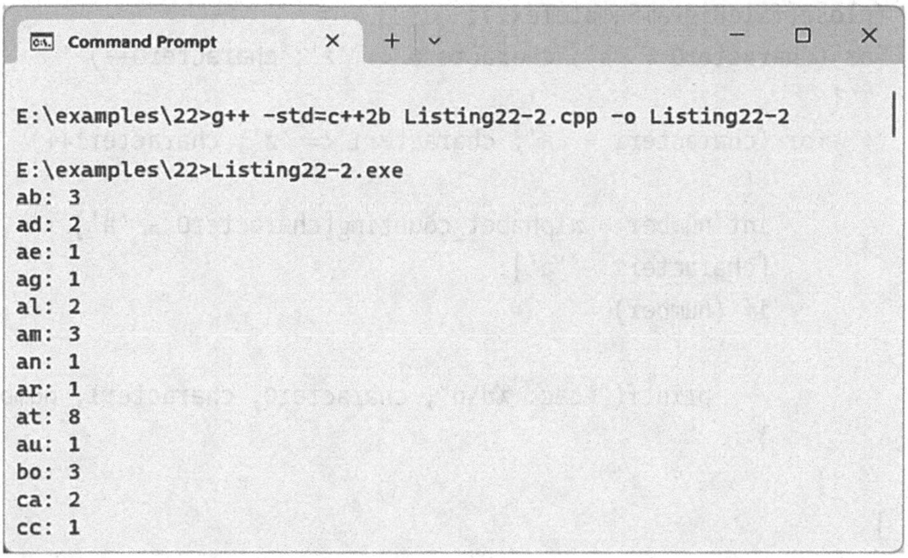
Command Prompt
E:\examples\22>g++ -std=c++2b Listing22-2.cpp -o Listing22-2
E:\examples\22>Listing22-2.exe
ab: 3
ad: 2
ae: 1
ag: 1
al: 2
am: 3
an: 1
ar: 1
at: 8
au: 1
bo: 3
ca: 2
cc: 1

Figure 22-6. *Counting bigrams*

Listing 22-2. Computing Bigrams

```
#include <stdio.h>
#define _CRT_SECURE_NO_WARNINGS

int main(void)
{
    int alphabet_counting['z' - 'a' + 1]['z' - 'a' + 1] = {{ 0 }};
    int character0 = EOF, character1;
    FILE *fileBigramSampleText = fopen("bigram.txt", "r");

    if (fileBigramSampleText != NULL)
      {
        while ((character1 = getc(fileBigramSampleText)) != EOF)
           {
            if (character1 >= 'a' && character1 <= 'z' && character0 >= 'a'
            && character0 <= 'z')
                {
                alphabet_counting[character0 - 'a'][character1 - 'a']++;
            }
            character0 = character1;
        }
```

```
        fclose(fileBigramSampleText);
        for (character0 = 'a'; character0 <= 'z'; character0++)
          {
            for (character1 = 'a'; character1 <= 'z'; character1++)
              {
                int number = alphabet_counting[character0 - 'a']
                [character1 - 'a'];
                if (number)
                    {
                        printf("%c%c: %d\n", character0, character1, number);
                    }
              }
          }
    }
    return 0;
}
```

Listing 22-3 and Figure 22-7 present a more general version, which handles character tuples with 8 bits.

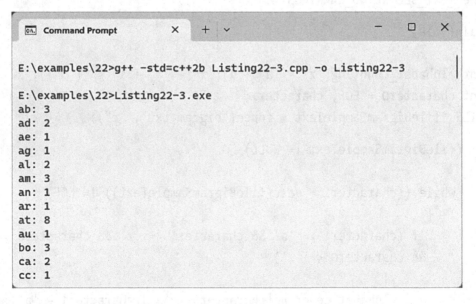

Figure 22-7. *Output for character pair with 8-bit*

Listing 22-3. General Version for Working with 8-Bit Character Pairs

```c
#include <stdio.h>
#include <string.h>
#define _CRT_SECURE_NO_WARNINGS

int main(void)
{
    // the last five bytes corresponds to ISO/IEC 8859-9
    const char alphabet[] = "abcdefghijklmnopqrstuvwxyz\xFD\xFxE7\xF6\xFC";
    const int length_of_alphabet = (sizeof(alphabet) - 1);
    int count[length_of_alphabet][length_of_alphabet];
    char *position0 = NULL;
    int character1;
    FILE *fileTextForCountingBigrams = fopen("bigram.txt", "r");

    memset(count, 0, sizeof(count));

    if (fileTextForCountingBigrams != NULL)
      {
        while ((character1 = getc(fileTextForCountingBigrams)) != EOF)
          {
            char *p1 = (char*)memchr(alphabet, character1, length_of_
            alphabet);
            if (p1 != NULL && position0 != NULL)
                {
                   count[position0 - alphabet][p1 - alphabet]++;
                }
            position0 = p1;
          }
        fclose(fileTextForCountingBigrams);
        for (size_t i = 0; i < length_of_alphabet; i++)
          {
            for (size_t j = 0; j < length_of_alphabet; j++)
                {
                   int n = count[i][j];
                   if (n > 0)
```

```
            {
                printf("%c%c: %d\n", alphabet[i], alphabet[j], n);
            }
        }
    }
    }
    return 0;
}
```

Counting Trigrams

The distinction between counting trigrams and bigrams is that trigrams are counted as triple characters.

Figure 22-8 includes a few of the most frequent bigrams seen throughout the cryptanalysis process. Furthermore, we implemented a method for identifying and tracking trigram occurrences in texts in Listing 22-4 (see Figure 22-9). The solution differs from the ones in Listings 22-2 and 22-3.

```
THE 77534223
AND 30997177
ING 30679488
ENT 17902107
ION 17769261
HER 15277018
FOR 14686159
THA 14222073
NTH 14115952
INT 13656197
ERE 13287155
TIO 13285065
TER 12769843
EST 11956466
ERS 11823017
ATI 11227573
HAT 10900482
ATE 10712298
ALL 10501105
ETH 10304110
HES 10189449
VER 10156140
HIS 10051039
OFT 9434246
ITH 9142241
FTH 9036651
STH 9024058
OTH 8869058
RES 8835871
ONT 8757161
DTH 8745845
ARE 8741156
REA 8700830
EAR 8697937
WAS 8640940
```

Figure 22-8. *Trigrams*

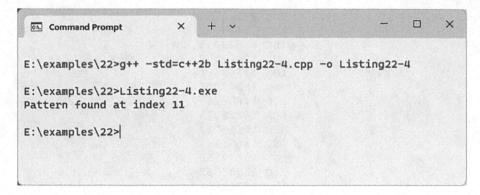

Figure 22-9. Displaying a sample of a trigram

Listing 22-4. Counting Trigrams

```cpp
#include <iostream>
using namespace std;

void printTrigramOccurance(string fullText, string trigramPattern)
{
    int occurance = fullText.find(trigramPattern);
    while (occurance!= string::npos)
    {
        cout << "Pattern found at index " << occurance << endl;
        occurance = fullText.find(trigramPattern, occurance + 1);
    }
}
int main()
{
    string fullText = "Welcome to Apress.";
    string trigramPattern = "Apr";
    printTrigramOccurance(fullText, trigramPattern);
}
```

Conclusion

The chapter discussed text characterization and demonstrated how crucial it is to the cryptanalysis procedure. When decrypting substitution ciphertexts, you can use chi-squared statistics and work with monograms, diagrams, and trigrams. In conclusion, you learned about the following.

- Text characterization

- Utilizing trigrams, diagrams, and monograms

- Use of the chi-squared statistic

- Implementations of monograms, diagrams, and trigrams

References

[1].   Singh, Simon (2000). *The Code Book: The Science of Secrecy from Ancient Egypt to Quantum Cryptography*. ISBN 0-385-49532-3.

[2].   Helen F. Gaines (1989). *Cryptanalysis: A Study of Ciphers and Their Solution*.

CHAPTER 23

Implementation and Practical Approach of Cryptanalysis Methods

As you have seen so far, cryptanalysis is a powerful tool that can be used to secure data from malicious users. It can also detect weaknesses in existing security measures and identify potential threats. As cyber threats become more advanced and sophisticated, it is increasingly important for individuals and organizations to keep up with the latest developments in cryptanalysis. Organizations can ensure their networks and data remain safe from attackers by implementing the best methods for maximum security. This chapter provides a practical approach to cryptanalysis, including an overview of the techniques available and how to best utilize them. It also discusses the importance of staying up-to-date with the latest developments in the field and strategies for implementing the latest techniques. With the right approach and implementation of the best methods, organizations can gain confidence in their security measures and ensure their data remains safe.

The current chapter is based on a general discussion that brings to attention a methodology for cryptanalysis methods and how those methods can be applied quickly and efficiently. The proposed methodology is dedicated to classic and actual (modern) cryptography/cryptanalysis algorithms and methods. Quantum cryptography is not included at this moment.

There are several different techniques available for cryptanalysis. Each approach has its own strengths and weaknesses, and each can be applied in different scenarios. These techniques can be combined to create a comprehensive strategy for maximizing security. This approach can be applied to many scenarios, including online payment systems and data transmission. This can be used to analyze an existing code, crack an

© Marius Iulian Mihailescu and Stefania Loredana Nita 2023
M. I. Mihailescu and S. L. Nita, *Pro Cryptography and Cryptanalysis with C++23*,
https://doi.org/10.1007/978-1-4842-9450-5_23

existing code, or create a new code that is more secure. While many of these techniques are complex and challenging to implement, they can provide an effective approach to cryptanalysis.

- A **brute-force attack** attempts to break an encrypted code using every possible combination of characters until the correct sequence is found. It is often used against weak encryption methods, such as single-word passwords. Although it can be effective, a brute-force attack is often time-consuming and does not guarantee a successful outcome. Brute-force attacks can be automated to speed up the process, which can be challenging and resource-intensive. Brute-force attacks can be mitigated by using a more advanced code or increasing the rate at which incorrect guesses are accepted.

- **Substitution ciphers** can be decoded using a letter-frequency or word-frequency chart. By analyzing these charts and comparing them to the original message, it is possible to identify potential letter replacements. This method can be applied to both single-substitution and multiple-substitution ciphers.

- **One-time pads** are used to create secure communications and prevent eavesdropping. However, if the pad is not used correctly, it can be vulnerable to attack.

The methodology proposed (see Figure 23-1) is designed to help the cryptanalyst to be aware of where he is situated during the cryptanalysis process. This methodology allows the cryptanalyst to use the map presented in Figure 23-1 to choose the proper tool or method for his work.

Proceeding with the implementation of the cryptanalysis methods can be a very laborious task for achieving the desired results if we don't hold proper information about the cryptographic method. The following presents a short process for cryptanalysts to identify the necessary elements for conducting the cryptanalysis process. The cryptanalysis process consists of four general steps.

- Step 1 is based on identifying what type of cryptanalysis should be conducted.

- Step 2 consists in gathering everything that we know about cryptography algorithms.

- Step 3 is dedicated to building a proper attack model.

- Step 4 consists in choosing the proper tools.

Step 1

This step deals with what kind of cryptanalysis should be performed. The cryptanalyst decides within the business environment what role he plays—a legal and authorized cryptanalyst, an ethical hacker, or a malicious cracker. As soon as he decides on his role, he moves to step 2.

Step 2

If the cryptanalyst is legitimate, he must know two things before getting started: the *cryptography algorithm* and the *cryptographic key*. Based on the experience of some of the cryptanalysts, this is not a requirement, but in some cases, it is very useful to know. As soon as the cryptanalyst is aware of the cryptography algorithm and cryptographic key, he can easily start the cryptanalysis process by applying the proper methods and testing the security of the business applications.

Step 3

This step is based on setting up the attack model or the attack type. Attack models or attack types point out a quantitative variable used to indicate how much information a cryptanalyst can access when he performs cracking methods on the encrypted message. The following are the most significant attacks.

- Ciphertext-only attack

- Known-plaintext attack

- Chosen-plaintext attack

- Chosen-ciphertext attack

  - Adaptive chosen-ciphertext attack

  - Indifferent chosen-ciphertext attack

Step 4

After the attack model has been picked or another model has been created and adapted properly to the case and requirements, let's move to the next step, which is based on choosing the software tools. Choosing the software tools from the ones that already exist or creating your own tools can be time-consuming but, in practice, have massive contributions. The following lists some tools that can be used in the cryptanalysis process, according to what is being "tested."

- Penetration tools: Kali Linux, Parrot Security, BackBox

- Forensics: DEFT, CAINE, BlackArch, Matriux

- Databases: sqlmap (standalone version), Metasploit framework (standalone version), VulDB

- Web and network: Wireshark, Nmap, Nessus, Burp Suite, Nikto, and OpenVas

- Other tools: CryptTool (useful and amazing tool)

These tools represent a selection of very used in practice and can produce desired results (see Figure 23-1).

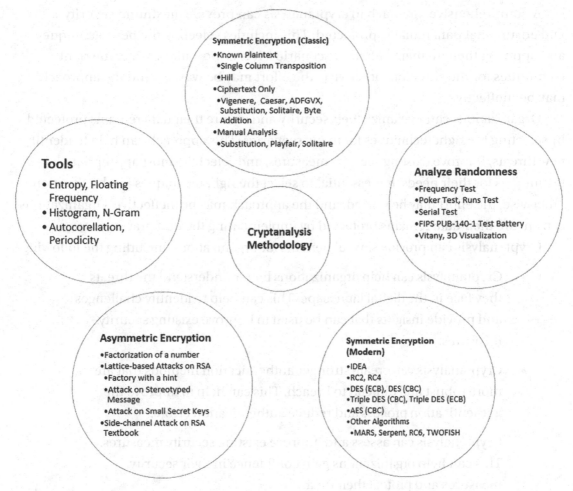

Symmetric Encryption (Classic)
- Known Plaintext
  - Single Column Transposition
  - Hill
- Ciphertext Only
  - Vigenere, Caesar, ADFGVX, Substitution, Solitaire, Byte Addition
- Manual Analysis
- Substitution, Playfair, Solitaire

Tools
- Entropy, Floating Frequency
- Histogram, N-Gram
- Autocorellation, Periodicity

Cryptanalysis Methodology

Analyze Randomness
- Frequency Test
- Poker Test, Runs Test
- Serial Test
- FIPS PUB-140-1 Test Battery
- Vitany, 3D Visualization

Asymmetric Encryption
- Factorization of a number
- Lattice-based Attacks on RSA
- Factory with a hint
- Attack on Stereotyped Message
- Attack on Small Secret Keys
- Side-channel Attack on RSA Textbook

Symmetric Encryption (Modern)
- IDEA
- RC2, RC4
- DES (ECB), DES (CBC)
- Triple DES (CBC), Triple DES (ECB)
- AES (CBC)
- Other Algorithms
  - MARS, Serpent, RC6, TWOFISH

Figure 23-1. *The cryptanalysis methodology*

Cryptanalysis has existed for many years, and many different techniques are available. While these approaches are effective in certain scenarios, they are often difficult to implement and require a great deal of time and effort. As cyber threats become more sophisticated, staying up-to-date with the latest developments in cryptanalysis is important. This can help organizations identify new threats, improve security measures, and select the most appropriate techniques. Selecting the right techniques for the situation; otherwise, the effort may be wasted, and the approach may be ineffective. By staying up-to-date with the latest developments in the field, organizations can identify new threats, improve existing security measures, and select the most appropriate techniques for their needs. This approach can help to ensure data remains protected.

A comprehensive approach to cryptanalysis can provide maximum security and ensure that data remains protected. This includes selecting the best techniques and applying them to many different scenarios. It is important to select the right techniques for the situation; otherwise, the effort may be wasted, and the approach may be ineffective.

Organizations can maximize their security and ensure their data remains protected by selecting the right techniques for many scenarios. This approach can help to identify new threats, improve existing security measures, and select the most appropriate techniques for their needs. It is essential to select the right techniques for the situation; otherwise, the effort may be wasted, and the approach may be ineffective. Organizations can ensure their data remains protected by implementing the best practices;

Cryptanalysis can provide several benefits for organizations, including the following.

- Cryptanalysis can help organizations better understand the threats they face in the digital landscape. This can help to identify challenges and provide insights that can be used to improve existing security measures.

- Cryptanalysis can create stronger authentication methods that are more robust and difficult to breach. This can help to improve the authentication process and reduce authentication errors.

- Cryptanalysis can assess and improve existing security measures. This can help organizations gain confidence in their security measures and protect their data.

Ciphertext-Only Attack (COA)

A *ciphertext-only attack* represents the weakest attack. A cryptanalyst can easily use it because he just encoded the message.

The attacker/cryptanalyst has access to a set of ciphertexts. The attack is successful if the corresponding plaintexts are deduced with the key.

In this type of attack (see Figure 23-2), the attacker/cryptanalyst can observe the ciphertext. Everything the cryptanalyst sees is represented by scrambled and nonsense characters that create the output based on the encryption process.

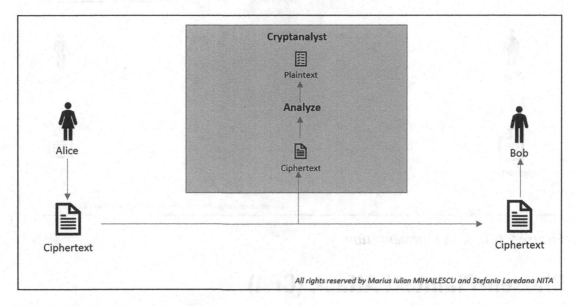

Figure 23-2. *COA representation*

Known-Plaintext Attack (KPA)

The *known-plaintext attack* (see Figure 23-3) helps the cryptanalyst to generate the ciphertext because he is aware of the ciphertext.

The cryptanalyst follows a simple procedure by selecting the plaintext, but he observes the pair compounded from the plaintext and ciphertext. The chance of success is better compared with COA. Simple ciphers are quite vulnerable to this attack.

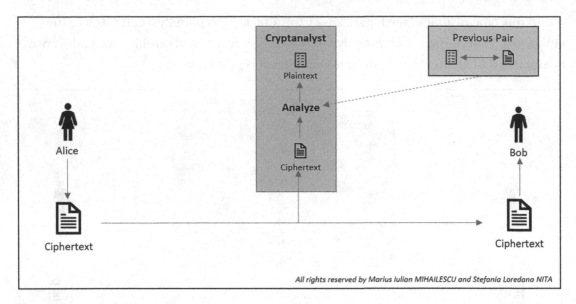

Figure 23-3. *KPA representation*

Chosen-Plaintext Attack (CPA)

In a *chosen-plaintext attack*, a cryptanalyst may select the plaintext that has been sent encrypted using an encryption algorithm, and he can observe how the ciphertext is generated. This can be observed as an active model in which cryptanalysts have the chance to select the plaintext and realize the encryption.

Cryptanalysts can observe vital details about ciphertext based on selecting and picking any plaintext. This gives them a strong advantage in understanding how the algorithm works inside and the chance to get into the secret key possession.

A professional cryptanalyst has a strong database that contains known plaintexts, ciphertexts, and possible keys. Listing 23-1 and Figure 23-5 provide an example of generating possible keys automatically. It is a simple example illustrating how possible keys can be generated. They can be used with the pairs for determining the cipher text input (see Figure 23-4).

Cryptanalysis can help organizations to better understand the threats they face in the digital landscape. This can help to identify challenges and provide insights that can be used to improve existing security measures. Cryptanalysis can be used to create stronger authentication methods that are more robust

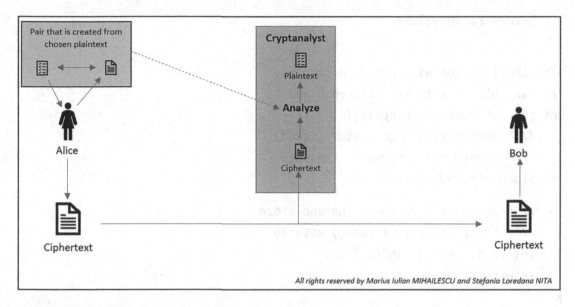

Figure 23-4. *CPA representation*

Listing 23-1. Automatic Generation of Random Keys

```
#include <stdio.h>
#include <time.h>
#include <iostream>

using namespace std;

//** generate an integer that is situated between 1 to 4
int generateInteger()   {
    //** pseudo-random generator (srand).
    //** time(NULL) represents the seed
    srand(time(NULL));

    //** generate a random value and store
    //** the remainder of rand() to 5
    int randomValue = rand() % 5;

    //** if the value is equal with 0, move to the
    //** next value of i and return that value
    if (randomValue == 0)
        randomValue++;
```

481

```
    return randomValue;
}

//** the function will generate randomly
//** an integer situated between 0 and 25
int generateRandomlyInteger(){
    //** pseudo-random generator (srand).
    //** time(NULL) represents the seed
    srand(time(NULL));

    //** generate a random value and store
    //** the remainder of rand() with 26
    int random_key = rand() % 26;
    return random_key;
}

//** based on the length provided, the function
//** will generate a cryptographic key
void generate_crypto_key(int length){
    //** create a string variable for cryptography
    //** key and initialize it with NULL
    string crypto_key = "";

    //** variable used for cryptography key generation
    string alphabet_lower_case = "abcdefghijklmnopqrstuvwxyz";
    string alphabet_upper_case = "ABCDEFGHIJKLMNOPQRSTUVWXYZ";
    string special_symbols = "!@#$%&";
    string digits_and_numbers = "0123456789";

    //** local variables and their initializations
    int key_seed;
    int lowerCase_Alphabet_Count = 0;
    int upperCase_Alphabet_Count = 0;
    int digits_And_numbers_count = 0;
    int special_symbols_count = 0;

    //** the variable count will save the length
    //** of the cryptography key.
```

```
//** initially we will set it to zero
int countingLengthCryptoKey = 0;
while (countingLengthCryptoKey < length) {
//** generateInteger() function will return a number that
//** is situated between 1 and 4.
//** The number that is generated will be used in
//** assignation with one of the strings that has been
//** defined above (for example: alphabet_lower_case,
//** alphabet_upper_case, special_symbols, and
//** digits_and_numbers).
//** This being said, the following correspondence will
//** be applied: (1) for alphabet_lower_case, (2) for
//** alphabet_upper_case, (3) for special_symbols, and
//** (4) digits_and_numbers
int string_type = generateInteger();

//** For the first character of the cryptography key we
//** will put a rule in such way that it should be a
//** letter, in such way that the string that will be
//** selected will be an lower case alphabet or an upper
//** case alphabet. The IF condition is quite vital as
//** the switch is based on it and the value that
//** string_type variable will have.
  if (countingLengthCryptoKey == 0) {
      string_type = string_type % 3;
      if (string_type == 0)
         string_type++; }

   switch (string_type) {
     case 1:
            //** based on the IF condition, it is
            //** necessary to check the minimum
            //** requirements of the lower case alphabet
            //** characters if they have been accomplished
            //** and fulfilled. If we are dealing with the
            //** situation in which the requirement has
```

```
        //** not been achieved we will situate ourself
        //** in the break phase.
        if ((lowerCase_Alphabet_Count == 2)
                    && (digits_And_numbers_count == 0
                     || upperCase_Alphabet_Count == 0
                     || upperCase_Alphabet_Count == 1
                     || special_symbols_count == 0))
            break;

        key_seed = generateRandomlyInteger();
        crypto_key = crypto_key +
                    alphabet_lower_case[key_seed];
        lowerCase_Alphabet_Count++;
        countingLengthCryptoKey++;
        break;

case 2:
        //** based on the IF condition, it is
        //** necessary to check the minimum
        //** requirements of the upper case alphabet
        //** characters if they have been accomplished
        //** and fulfilled. If we are dealing with the
        //** situation in which the requirement has
        //** not been achieved we will situate ourself
        //** in the break phase.
        if ((upperCase_Alphabet_Count == 2)
                    && (digits_And_numbers_count == 0
                     || lowerCase_Alphabet_Count == 0
                     || lowerCase_Alphabet_Count == 1
                     || special_symbols_count == 0))
            break;
        key_seed = generateRandomlyInteger();
        crypto_key = crypto_key +
                    alphabet_upper_case[key_seed];
        upperCase_Alphabet_Count++;
        countingLengthCryptoKey++;
        break;
```

```
case 3:
        //** based on the IF condition, it is
        //** necessary to check the minimum
        //** requirements of the numbers if they have
        //** been accomplished and fulfilled. If we
        //** are dealing with the situation in which
        //** the requirement has not been achieved we
        //** will situate ourself in the break phase.
        if ((digits_And_numbers_count == 1)
                && (lowerCase_Alphabet_Count == 0
                || lowerCase_Alphabet_Count == 1
                || upperCase_Alphabet_Count == 1
                || upperCase_Alphabet_Count == 0
                || special_symbols_count == 0))
            break;
        key_seed = generateRandomlyInteger();
        key_seed = key_seed % 10;
        crypto_key = crypto_key +
                digits_and_numbers[key_seed];
        digits_And_numbers_count++;
        countingLengthCryptoKey++;
        break;

case 4:
        //** based on the IF condition, it is
        //** necessary to check the minimum
        //** requirements of the special characters if
        //** they have been accomplished and
        //** fulfilled. If we are dealing with the
        //** situation in which the requirement has
        //** not been achieved we will situate ourself
        //** in the break phase.
        if ((special_symbols_count == 1)
                && (lowerCase_Alphabet_Count == 0
                || lowerCase_Alphabet_Count == 1
                || upperCase_Alphabet_Count == 0
```

```cpp
                        || upperCase_Alphabet_Count == 1
                        || digits_And_numbers_count == 0))
                    break;

                key_seed = generateRandomlyInteger();
                key_seed = key_seed % 6;
                crypto_key = crypto_key +
                                special_symbols[key_seed];
                special_symbols_count++;
                countingLengthCryptoKey++;
                break;
        }
    }
    cout << "\n----------------------------\n";
    cout << "       Cryptography Key          \n";
    cout << "----------------------------\n\n";
    cout << " " << crypto_key;
    cout << "\n\nPress any key to continue... \n";
    getchar();
}

int main() {
    int option;
    int desired_length;

    //** designing the menu
    do {
        cout << "\n-------------------------------------\n";
        cout << "  Random Cryptography Key Generator    \n";
        cout << "-------------------------------------\n\n";
        cout << "     1 --> Generate a Cryptography Key"
            << "\n";
        cout << "     2 --> Quit the program"
            << "\n\n";
        cout << "Enter 1 for Generating Cryptograpy Key or 2
                            to quit the program  : ";
        cin >> option;
```

```cpp
switch (option) {
case 1:
    cout << "Set the length to :   ";
    cin >> desired_length;
    //** if the length entered is less than 7, an
    //** error will be shown
    if (desired_length < 7) {
        cout << "\nError Mode : The Cryptography Key
                    Length hould be at least 7\n";
        cout << "Press a key and try again \n";
        getchar();   }
    //** The desired length should bot be bigger than
    //** 100, otherwise an error will be shown
    else if (desired_length > 100)      {
        cout << "\nError Mode : The maximum length of
                the cryptography key should be 100\n";
        cout << "Press a key and try again \n";
        getchar(); }
    //** in ohter cases, call generate_crypto_key()
    //** function to generate a cryptography key
    else
        generate_crypto_key(desired_length);
    break;
default:
    //** in case if an invalid option is entered, show
    //** to the user an error message
    if (option != 2) {
        printf("\nOups! You have entered a choice that
                                    doesn't exist\n");
        printf("Enter ( 1 ) to generate cryptography
                key and ( 2 ) to quit the program.\n");
        cout << "Enter a key and try again \n";
        getchar();}
    break; }
```

```
    } while (option != 2);
    return 0;
}
```

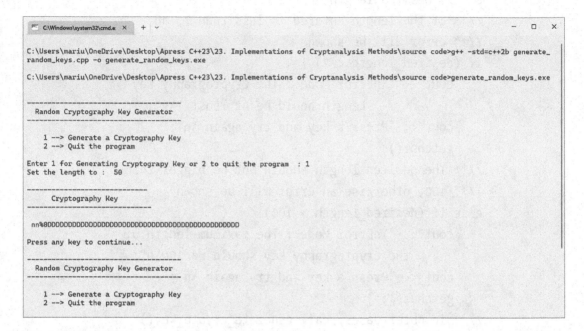

Figure 23-5. *The keys and possible passwords generated (three characters were used for a shorter process)*

Chosen-Ciphertext Attack (CCA)

In a *chosen-ciphertext attack*, a cryptanalyst can perform encryption and decryption of the information. Within this attack (see Figure 23-6), the cryptanalyst can pick the plaintext, encrypt it, observe how the ciphertext is generated, and reverse the process.

In this attack, the cryptanalyst's mission is not finding only the plaintext but identifying the algorithm and secret key used for the encryption process.

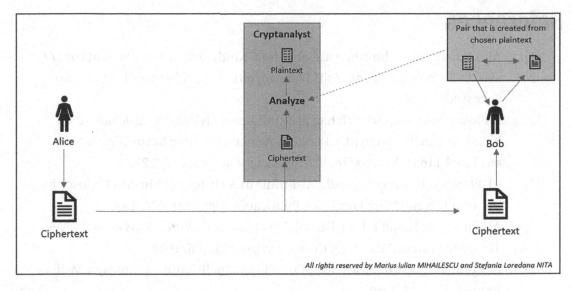

Figure 23-6. *CCA representation*

Conclusion

This chapter discussed implementing a cryptanalysis method and defining a process for cryptanalysts. You learned about the following.

- Attack models

- How to follow a straightforward methodology in the cryptanalysis process

- How to simulate and generate a database with keys and possible passwords

Cryptanalysis can provide several benefits for organizations, including the following.

- It can help improve security measures and strengthen authentication methods while reducing vulnerabilities and risks.

- It can help organizations better understand the threats they face in the digital landscape.

References

[1].   Abu Yusuf Yaqub ibn Ishaq al-Sabbah Al-Kindi. Available online: `https://www.trincoll.edu/depts/phil/philo/phils/muslim/kindi.html`. Last accessed: 5.4.2023

[2].   Philosophers: Yaqub Ibn Ishaq al-Kindi Kennedy-Day, K. al-Kindi, Abu Yusuf Ya'qub ibn Ishaq (d. c.866–73). Available online: `https://www.muslimphilosophy.com/ip/kin.html`. Last accessed: 5.4.2023

[3].   Al-Ehwany, F. Ahmad Fouad, "Al-Kindi" in A History of Muslim Philosophy Volume 1. New Delhi: Low Price Publications. pp. 421-434, 1961.

[4].   Al-Faruqi, R. Ismail L.L. al-Faruqi, Lois Lamya, *Cultural Atlas of Islam New York*, Macmillan Publishing Company. pp. 305-306, 1986.

[5].   Encyclopaedia Britannica, Inc., Encyclopaedia Britannica. Chicago: William Benton. pp. 352, 1969.

Index

A

Abstract algebra, 395
Access control methods, 8
add_plain_inplace() methods, 302
Advanced encryption standard
    (AES), 14, 402
Amazon Web Services (AWS), 391
American National Standards Institute
    (ANSI), 413
ArchStrike, 409
Asymmetric cryptographic systems, 406
Asymmetric-key algorithms, 6
Asymmetric-key encryption algorithm, 14
Asymmetric keys, 407
Attribute-based encryption (ABE), 368, 384

B

Bhulbhulaya number system, 107
Big data, 365
Big data cryptography
    business operations, 377
    CIA triad, 367
    cloud architecture, 366
    cloud computing, 376
    cloud types, 367
    communication channel, 377
    methods, 365
    notations, 365
    techniques, 368
    verifiable computation, 369–376
Big integers, 126

Bjarne Stroustrup, 146
Boost Multiprecision library, 143
Bootstrappable encryption schemes, 286
Boson scattering, 285
Botan, 192, 203
Bots, 445
Brute-force attack, 421, 474
    Caesar cipher, 448, 449
    definition, 446
    examples, 446
    key search, 446
    string generation source code, 451–454
Buffer overflow attack, 455, 456

C

C++23
    headers, 146, 151
    WG21, 146
Caesar cipher, 195
C/C++ libraries
    CT, 193–202
    hash function, 172
    implementations, 171, 172
CERT coding standards, 154
    automated detection processes, 162
    exceptions, 160
    identifiers, 159
    noncompliant code examples/
        compliant solutions, 159
    risk assessment, 160, 161
    software developers, 158